Rethinking America's Highways

Rethinking America's Highways

*A 21st-Century Vision
for Better Infrastructure*

ROBERT W. POOLE JR.

THE UNIVERSITY OF CHICAGO PRESS   CHICAGO AND LONDON

The University of Chicago Press, Chicago 60637
The University of Chicago Press, Ltd., London
© 2018 by The University of Chicago
Published 2018
Paperback edition 2020
Printed in the United States of America

29 28 27 26 25 24 23 22 21 20   1 2 3 4 5

ISBN-13: 978-0-226-55757-1 (cloth)
ISBN-13: 978-0-226-75930-2 (paper)
ISBN-13: 978-0-226-55760-1 (e-book)
DOI: https://doi.org/10.7208/chicago/9780226557601.001.0001

Library of Congress Cataloging-in-Publication Data

Names: Poole, Robert W., 1944– author.
Title: Rethinking America's highways : a 21st-century vision for better infrastructure /
    Robert W. Poole Jr.
Description: Chicago ; London : The University of Chicago Press, 2018. |
    Includes bibliographical references and index.
Identifiers: LCCN 2017051766 | ISBN 9780226557571 (cloth : alk. paper) |
    ISBN 9780226557601 (e-book)
Subjects: LCSH: Roads—United States—Finance. | Transportation—Privatization. |
    Transportation and state—United States. | Transportation and state—
    United States—History—20th century.
Classification: LCC HE336.E3 P66 2018 | DDC 388.1/220973—dc23
LC record available at https://lccn.loc.gov/2017051766

Contents

Tables and Figures

Preface

The idea for this book did not just spring into my head one day. It evolved over several decades of public policy work, which began with research into competitive contracting for municipal public services in the 1970s. In the course of that work I learned that a considerable number of 20th-century North American toll bridges had been privately financed, though hardly any had survived as private bridges past the Great Depression.

In those years I was president and CEO of the fledgling Reason Foundation, so my policy research efforts were necessarily part-time. My turn towards serious research on highways was stimulated when Reason relocated from bucolic Santa Barbara to massive Los Angeles in 1986, and for the first time I confronted the daily grind of commuting on traffic-choked freeways. A decade earlier, a friend who was an engineer at Caltrans had told me that the long-distance toll roads in France had been privately financed and were operated as businesses. I idly wondered whether there might be some way to have private companies finance and build second decks on LA's freeways, on the basis of toll revenue.

By attending the annual conferences of the Transportation Research Board, I'd become aware of considerable academic work on "road pricing," including the idea that a higher price during rush hours would give some people an incentive to shift the time of their travel to nonpeak times, and encourage others to carpool or use public transit, but also give those who really needed to be somewhere on time a less congested or even a noncongested route. But putting toll booths on already congested freeways was obviously impractical.

In 1987, the Amtech Corporation unveiled its Toll-Tag, the first practical toll transponder. I went to Dallas to see it in action on the Dallas North Toll Road, where it was being installed to allow cars to roll through toll lanes at five miles per hour instead of having to stop and pay cash. The transponder would debit the customer's prepaid account, eliminating the need for cash. When I asked the Amtech people whether they could read a toll-tag at highway speeds, they confirmed that their testing showed that it was feasible.

In 1988 I put three ideas together in my first policy paper on future highways. The Reason Foundation study, "Private Tollways: Resolving Gridlock in Southern California," combined private finance, high-speed transponder tolling, and variable pricing, to be applied to new lanes added to congested freeways. In effect, I'd invented what we now call express toll lanes.

Because California was then in a highway funding crunch, the idea came to the attention of Caltrans and the governor's office, and the result was 1989 legislation for a pilot program to test these ideas. I served on a Caltrans advisory committee to oversee implementation of the new law, and the first project developed was the 91 Express Lanes on State Route 91, a very congested freeway in Orange County. It became the prototype for all that followed.

In subsequent decades I became active in two standing committees of the Transportation Research Board: the Congestion Pricing Committee and later the Managed Lanes Committee. Over the years, I wrote papers to present at the annual meeting, and some of them made the cut to be published in the TRB's peer-reviewed journal, *Transportation Research Record*.

During the 1990s I commissioned a number of outside researchers to write Reason policy studies on various aspects of tolling, pricing, highway design innovations, and highway finance. I also wrote a number of such papers myself. One of those policy studies introduced the term "high-occupancy toll (HOT) lanes" to the transportation world—basically proposing that poorly performing high-occupancy vehicle (HOV) lanes be converted to express toll lanes that also offered free or reduced-rate passage to car pools. The Federal Highway Administration soon adopted the term, and their Value Pricing Pilot Program sponsored workshops in metro areas across the country where there was interest in HOT lanes and other forms of pricing. I was a speaker at many of those workshops.

My transportation career took a major step forward in 2001, when I stepped down as founding CEO of the Reason Foundation and became its full-time director of transportation policy instead. This opened the door to far more serious research, speaking, serving on advisory bodies, and so on. Early in this period, I coauthored (with Ken Orski) a Reason policy paper that took the next step in express toll lanes: entire networks of such lanes, overlaid on congested freeway systems. At that time, most of the existing priced lanes were HOT lanes, so we named the concept HOT networks. This idea also took hold, and networks of this kind are now in the long-range transportation plans of about a dozen very large US metro areas.

Here and there in my new full-time transportation career, I accepted consulting assignments on my own time, mostly with public agencies. Over a period of about a decade, I consulted with the Florida DOT on developing the state's first express-toll-lanes project, on I-95 in Miami, and then on the conceptual plan for their emerging network of express toll lanes in southeastern Florida. I served for a year on a special study committee on the role of private participation in toll projects in Texas. I advised then Governor Mitch Daniels on the privatization of the Indiana Toll Road, and testified before the Indiana legislature on that subject. And I defended the idea against congressional criticism in a contentious hearing of the House Transportation and Infrastructure Committee. I also served as a member of an expert review panel on the feasibility of a major express-toll-lanes project in the Seattle metro area, and presented the panel's findings to a legislative committee; much of that project has now been built on I-405, and is open to traffic.

Along the way, I have despaired at the dysfunctional nature of our 20th-century highway model. Although recently a handful of transportation officials have started to refer to the highway system as a utility, endless battles over whether or not to increase gas taxes bear little or no relationship to the way in which people's electricity, water, cable, and smartphone bills provide reliable revenue streams to ensure high levels of service from these utilities. Whether run by governments or by investor-owned companies, these utilities all charge their customers based on the services they use, and the resulting revenue streams pay for the capital and operating costs of the systems, including needed expansions.

If we want a capable and well-maintained 21st-century highway system, I finally concluded, it needs to be transformed into some kind of network utility, operated along principles similar to those of the other utilities that we depend on. While this would certainly be a major change from the status quo, I think the idea has such merit that it should be seriously pursued.

In this book I present my case for this transformation, explaining how we got to where we are, assembling the evidence for how and why things could be better, and sketching how such a major change could come about.

CHAPTER ONE

Our Troubled Highway System

We sit in daily traffic congestion, frustrated at seemingly endless delays. We watch or read stories of major bridges collapsing. Many highways are rough and potholed, making for unpleasant drives and increased vehicle repairs. In the world's wealthiest country, why do these problems exist? And what can be done to fix them?

We Americans tend to take our road and highway system for granted. We rely on it more than any other mode for personal transportation; 89 percent of all passenger miles of surface travel in 2009, including passenger cars and buses, took place on paved roadways.[1] The Census Bureau's American Community Survey found that 88.6 percent of our commuting trips are made on streets and highways (85.8 percent by car, 2.8 percent by bus).[2] And to a far greater extent than most of us realize, we also rely on highways for the goods that fill our stores. Some 80 percent of all freight, by value, moves on trucks (for which highways provide the infrastructure).[3]

Yet more and more Americans are becoming aware that our highways are beset with serious problems. Anyone who commutes by car in a large metro area confronts chronic traffic congestion on a daily basis. The most recent analysis by the Texas A&M Transportation Institute (TTI) finds that congestion continues to extract a high cost from commuters in America's major urban areas in particular. Conservatively valuing the amount of wasted time and fuel of motorists stuck in congestion, TTI put the annual direct cost of congestion in the New York metro area at $14.7 billion, with Los Angeles close behind at $13.3 billion per year. Over all 471 US urban areas, the estimated direct cost was found to be $160 billion per year.[4] And that figure does not include estimates of the lost productivity in urban areas suffering from congestion. Some studies put that indirect cost equal to or greater than the direct cost of wasted time and fuel, so that the total economic cost of congestion likely exceeds $300 billion per year.[5]

A second major problem is the extent of disrepair of US highways and bridges. While the common political trope that US highways and bridges are "crumbling" is an exaggeration, disrepair is a serious problem. Nationwide, the average condition of highway pavement and bridges has improved modestly over the past two decades, but there is still a huge backlog of bridges—21 percent—that are either structurally deficient or functionally obsolete for current and projected traffic. And while most Interstate highways are in "good" condition, according to the Federal Highway Administration (FHWA), only 61 percent of other rural highways are rated "good," and only 40 percent of urban-area arterials and boulevards are in good condition.[6] The extent of disrepair varies enormously from state to state, which suggests that some states have done far better than others at allocating resources to proper ongoing maintenance and repair.

One contributing factor to both poor highway performance (congestion) and the extent of disrepair is a growing funding shortfall. Highways and bridges are funded largely by federal and state user taxes on gasoline and diesel fuel, while local streets and roads are funded by local taxes, especially property taxes. For most of the 20th century, this system of dedicated revenues from highway users functioned pretty well, ensuring that funding grew generally in step with the growth in highway travel. But that system no longer keeps pace with highway needs. The latest federal assessment of highway capital investment found that federal and state governments spent a total of $105.2 billion (including federal stimulus funds) in the most recent year measured. That should be more than enough to keep pavement and bridge conditions and traffic congestion from getting any worse, since the Federal Highway Administration's model estimates that only $89.9 billion per year would be sufficient to maintain status-quo conditions. But if we want to improve highway conditions and performance (i.e., achieve lower congestion and better pavements), the same model estimates that it would take $142.5 billion per year to implement all highway improvement projects whose benefits are greater than their costs.[7]

What has happened to the 20th-century fuel-tax funding system? It is breaking down for four principal reasons. First, federal policy imposes ever stricter fuel economy mandates for new vehicles. By 2025, the average new passenger vehicle must achieve 54.5 miles per gallon, about double the fuel efficiency of cars produced in the first decade of this century. Enabling vehicles to go twice as far on a gallon of gas will benefit the environment by reducing tailpipe emissions, but it will be devastating for highway funding. That's because the tax is levied on gallons consumed, not on miles driven. Other things being equal, in the years after 2025, new personal vehicles will generate only half as much fuel tax revenue as typical vehicles do today for the same number of miles driven.

A second problem is that fuel tax rates are not indexed to inflation, except for state gas taxes in a handful of states. But most of what fuel-tax revenues are spent on—adding lanes, rebuilding worn-out highways and bridges, or performing maintenance—goes up in cost year by year, and construction costs often go up faster than do consumer prices. Thus, the real, inflation-adjusted value of fuel tax proceeds declines year by year. The most recent increase in the *federal* gas tax (to 18.4 cents per gallon) took effect in 1993. To have the same buying power in 2017, that rate would have to be 31.5 cents per gallon.

The third problem is that it has become difficult, politically, for elected officials to *increase* the rates at which gasoline and diesel fuel are taxed. Even though these are called user taxes, they are no longer spent exclusively to benefit highway users—and are increasingly seen simply as "taxes." Thus, any increase is considered as a "tax increase" and therefore as politically radioactive. This problem is greater at the federal level, where there seems to have been a considerable loss of trust in the 20th-century model that was used to build the Interstate highway system: uniform federal user taxes on gasoline and diesel, dedicated to the federal Highway Trust Fund and redistributed to states by formula. While the federal fuel tax rates have not been increased since 1993, 38 of the 50 states have enacted one or more fuel tax rate increases during that same time.[8]

The fourth reason is the small but growing market share for vehicles that are powered by something other than gasoline or diesel. All these alternative fuel vehicles make the same use of our highways and streets as those powered by gasoline and diesel, but under current laws in nearly all states they pay nothing for the upkeep and modernization of those roads. The most successful alternative is the hybrid vehicle (like the Toyota Prius), which uses an electric motor supplemented by a traditional internal combustion engine. Future alternatives include all-electric vehicles (such as the growing line of Tesla vehicles), natural gas vehicles, and possibly hydrogen fuel-cell vehicles.

For all of these reasons, there is a growing consensus among transportation researchers, as well as a number of state transportation departments, that America must begin a transition from charging for road use *per gallon* of fuel to charging, in some manner yet to be determined, *per mile* driven. A growing number of states have pilot programs under way to test various methods and technologies, but we are a long way from arriving at a consensus on how and when to make such a transition.

Another problem with today's highway system is an apparent decline in the productivity of highway investments. A number of academic studies have attempted to measure the return on highway investment, much as businesses do in analyzing proposed capital investments to see if they are likely to bring in more in revenues than what they cost. Since highways are not businesses and, except for toll roads, do not directly generate revenues for the road provider, these academic studies instead estimate the benefit to the economy from better highways. These studies generally report high returns on the highway investments of the 1950s and 1960s, when major new toll roads (e.g., the Ohio Turnpike, Florida's Turnpike, etc.) and the Interstate highway system were being built; lower returns in the 1970s and 1980s; and still lower returns in the 1990s and 2000s.[9]

Of course, such studies can only analyze the highway investments that were actually made in each time period. During the same decades in which the academic studies found lower rates of return, urban freeways reached new highs each year in congestion cost—yet very little capital investment was made in those expressways to better balance supply (capacity) with demand. In addition, the way state legislators and state departments of transportation (DOTs) divide up each year's available highway money puts a premium not on funding the highest-return projects first, but rather on spreading the money around to every member's district. A single megaproject that would yield major benefits in reduced congestion could easily consume most of the state's highway capital budget for several years—but that spending and the associated construction jobs would all be in just one member's district, something that is hardly politically feasible. So the conclusion of the academic studies reflects poorly on the highway capital investments that are actually being made. But that does not demonstrate that we have run out of productive investment opportunities in the highway system, as the FHWA's modeling indicates.

Another serious problem is that what used to be purely highway user monies have increasingly been diverted to nonhighway uses, at both state and federal levels of government. At the federal level, the dedicated tax on gasoline and diesel was enacted in 1956 along with creation of the federal Highway Trust Fund. This mirrored the practice in numerous states, since they began collecting fuel taxes in 1919, of dedicating highway user tax revenues to highway uses. Once the majority of the Interstate system was built, Congress began thinking up other things that Highway Trust Fund monies could be spent on. Initially, this "diversion" was minor, but in 1982 the Reagan administration supported a major change: the creation of a transit account within the Highway Trust Fund. Initially, the transit account was to receive one cent out of the five-cent increase in the federal fuel tax rate. But over time, Congress regularly expanded nonhighway uses until by 2010 fully 23 percent of Highway Trust Fund monies could go for nonhighway purposes: urban transit, bike paths, sidewalks, recreational trails, historical preservation, and even transportation museums.[10]

There are organized interest groups favoring each and every one of those uses. And opinion poll results show that many people favor more spending on those uses, especially when not asked about how they should be paid for. But it is not at all clear that a typical voter concerned about traffic congestion and potholes understands that the more uses that are authorized for Trust Fund monies, the less money remains available for the highways and bridges that he or she depends on. On the contrary, it is quite plausible that the gradual conversion of the Highway Trust Fund into an all-purpose transportation public works program has contributed to the voting public's distrust of the program and resulting opposition to increasing federal fuel tax rates. Such a voter can assess a proposed federal fuel tax increase as follows: "If I urge my Congress member to support that increase, and it passes, the only thing I can be sure of is that my cost of driving will go up. I have little or no confidence that the increase will lead to any meaningful improvement in the transportation systems that I use and depend on."

An Appreciation of the 20th-Century Model

Despite the litany of problems besetting the US highway system today, we should not lose sight of the tremendous accomplishments of the 20th-century highway model.

Paved highways were unknown in the 19th century, prior to the development of motor vehicles. Early in the 20th century, a "good roads movement" emerged to advocate the creation of paved highways around the country, similar to the paved streets that were becoming common in cities. Two early proponents for paved highways were bicyclists and farmers. Bicyclists wanted smooth, durable pavements outside the cities, while farmers sought paved "farm-to-market" roads. They were subsequently joined by various components of the auto industry: vehicle makers, tire makers, and fuel providers.

From the outset, funding was the biggest obstacle to achieving paved highways. Several early multistate highway efforts were coordinated by coalitions of private groups: the east-west Lincoln Highway and the north-south Dixie Highway are the best-known examples. These projects ignored the large history of 19th-century (pre-auto) toll roads (discussed in chapter 3). Instead, their funding model unrealistically relied on land donations for right-of-way and fund-raising for paving. The limitations of that model soon led to its displacement. The idea of taxing motor fuel and using the proceeds exclusively for highways was first implemented in Oregon in 1919. This funding method was seen by many advocates as second-best to tolling, but the administrative and collection costs of tolling were seen as too high to be viable, and the toll revenues, in those early days of motor vehicles, were expected to be too low to finance paved highways. The fuel tax / highway fund model caught on rapidly, and by 1930 all 48 states had such mechanisms in place.[11]

Between 1919 and America's entrance into World War II in 1941, miles of paved highway grew substantially. States laid out and built extensive networks of intercity and farm-to-market roads, on a pay-as-you-go basis (highway construction and maintenance were paid for on a cash basis out of annual fuel tax revenues). Congress created the Bureau of Public Roads in 1918. That agency, the predecessor of today's Federal Highway Administration, made modest grants to states to help pay for a system of paved US highways, consistently numbered from US 1 on the East Coast to US 101 on the West Coast, complemented by such important east-west highways as the iconic US (Route) 66. When the US Office of Public Road Inquiries, a predecessor of the Bureau of Public Roads, made its first census of rural roads in 1904, out of 2.2 million miles, only 257,000 (11.7 percent) were paved in some manner. By 1921, total rural mileage had increased to 2.9 million, but still only a modest 367,000 miles (12.6 percent) were paved.[12] Ten years, later the miles of paved roads had more than doubled to 830,000, and by the eve of World War II in 1941, the total had reached 1.38 million miles paved out of a total of just over 3 million miles, which meant that 45 percent of all rural roads were paved by then.

While the new paved highways were state-owned and state-maintained, their routes were laid out in cooperation with the Bureau of Public Roads to facilitate interstate commerce. In 1932, Congress authorized a one-cent-per-gallon federal gasoline tax as a budget deficit-reduction measure. There was no connection between that tax on motor fuel and the modest federal highway assistance grants, which came out of the general fund. That federal gas tax was increased to 1.5 cents per gallon in 1940 and to two cents per gallon in 1951, but there was still no linkage to federal highway spending.[13]

In the years shortly before and the decade after World War II, the next major development was the superhighway, of which the Pennsylvania Turnpike was the first. In contrast to existing state and US highways, the superhighway was *limited-access*: a vehicle could enter or exit only at designated on-ramps and off-ramps, typically spaced many miles apart. There were two or more lanes in each direction, to make it easier for faster vehicles to pass slower ones. There was separation between the lanes going one direction from those going in the other direction, for increased safety. There were no traffic lights, and the roads were designed for faster travel than on existing highways; they had broader curves, shallower grades, and complete separation from other roads or railroads.

The cost of building a superhighway was significantly more than that of building ordinary highways, but the service a superhighway could offer was clearly superior. So Pennsylvania reintroduced tolling as the funding source, offering motorists much better service in exchange for a toll payment. Instead of using each year's toll revenue to build a few dozen more miles, the Pennsylvania Turnpike Commission issued revenue bonds based on projected toll revenue. This is how electric utilities and railroads pay for major capital projects. Doing this is called *financing* a project, as opposed to *funding* it out of each year's revenues, as is done by state transportation agencies using fuel tax monies.

The first section of the Pennsylvania Turnpike opened in 1940, and its full length was not completed until shortly after the war. Once the war was over, the evident success of the Pennsylvania superhighway led to similar projects in Connecticut, Florida, Indiana, Illinois, Kansas, Kentucky, Maine, Massachusetts, New Hampshire, New Jersey, New York, Ohio, and Oklahoma—all launched prior to the 1956 act of Congress authorizing the Interstate Highway program. With the exception of the Florida Turnpike, all or major portions of the superhighways were incorporated into the new Interstate system, and allowed to retain their tolling, on which their initial financing and ongoing expansion and maintenance were based.

The cost to build the Interstate system was estimated by the Federal Highway Administration as $128.9 billion in 1991,[14] but that figure was not adjusted for inflation between 1956 and 1991. In a 1996 report, Wendell Cox estimated that the total cost to completion was $329 billion, which equates to a cost in 2017 dollars of $519.5 billion.[15]

The system proved far more popular than most people expected, stimulating both personal travel and the growth of commercial trucking. One much-cited indication of the use of Interstate highways is the fact that these highways (including their urban expressway components) today handle 25 percent of all vehicle miles of travel in America using just 2.5 percent of all the roadway lane-miles, according to federal highway statistics. Among the outgrowths of Americans' increased personal travel was the development of national chains of hotels and motels ("motor hotels") and of both fast-food and sit-down restaurant chains.

Commercial trucking grew at a rapid rate, from 3.2 billion tons in 1955 to 10.6 billion tons in 2005, according to the American Trucking Associations. The ability of trucks to go wherever there are paved roads led to a revolution in freight logistics, especially when the trucks were coupled with the development of standardized intermodal shipping containers. As railroads got regulatory approval to shut down money-losing branch lines, the growing trucking industry moved in to replace them. Major retail chains established regional distribution centers to which long-distance trucks brought containerized freight from manufacturers and seaports, which was unpacked and reloaded on short-haul and medium-haul delivery trucks to specific retail outlets within a geographic area. A similar logistics revolution emerged to serve manufacturers, with distribution centers for parts and components ready for delivery on short notice to assembly plants, in a just-in-time manner. This logistics revolution produced steady, long-term reductions in overall freight shipping costs and the emergence of a new industry: third-party logistics companies.

Yet another benefit of the 20th-century model was that it led to a mostly user-funded highway system. Much confusion exists on this point, reflecting numerous academic debates involving different ways to calculate things. Broadly speaking, state and federal highways, as opposed to local streets and roads, have generally been funded mostly or entirely by federal and state fuel taxes (plus tolls). Local streets and roads, for which vehicle owners still pay fuel taxes on every gallon purchased, are paid for mostly out of local revenues such as property taxes. That is consistent with the view that access to one's property via a paved road network increases the property's value as compared with that of one accessible only via a dirt road or a trail.

Those who allege that "highways are subsidized" make misleading comparisons. They go to federal highway statistics tables that include *all* roads, including local streets, and total up federal, state, and local government funding for all those categories of roadway. They then compare that annual total with the amount of money that federal and state governments raise from highway user taxes. The fairly large difference, they say, shows that general taxpayers heavily subsidize highways. But since it is well known that local streets and roads are not paid for out of fuel tax revenues, that conclusion is preordained. By contrast, if the comparison is limited to highways—the type of road that is supposed to be funded by highway user taxes—most studies find that users pay 80 to 100 percent of highway costs via those dedicated taxes.[16]

Another misleading use of figures is to define the amount the federal government spends on each mode of transportation as a "federal subsidy," and then to lament that the feds "subsidize" highways far more than they do urban transit or Amtrak, since the total amount spent on highways is much larger than federal spending on Amtrak or transit. A careful analysis from the US Department of Transportation's Bureau of Transportation Statistics (December 2004) compared federal highway spending with federal highway user tax revenue over the previous 10 years.[17] On this basis, the federal revenues generated from highway users slightly *exceeded* federal spending on highways, demonstrating that at the federal level, at least, there were no highway "subsidies" during the previous decade.[18] By contrast, of course, since Amtrak user revenues (fares) covered only a fraction of that entity's annual budget, all the federal dollars appropriated by Congress and spent on Amtrak constitute a subsidy, and the same is true for federal transit spending.

That picture has changed since the Great Recession (which occurred following the 2008 financial markets crisis), as unemployment and higher fuel prices led to decreases in vehicle miles of travel and hence in federal fuel tax revenue. In order to prevent a reduction in federal highway and transit assistance to states, Congress has each year since 2008 transferred money from the federal general fund into the Highway Trust Fund. Thus, it is only in very recent years that one could accurately say that federal (general fund) subsidies to highways exist. The change from self-funded to partly subsidized highways is another reason to look for a better approach. In coming years, with the explosion in federal entitlement spending, the federal general fund will be under increasing pressure, and will not likely be available to subsidize the Highway Trust Fund.

Is It Time for a New Paradigm?

America's 20th-century highway model, or paradigm, of user taxes on fuel, deposited in state or federal trust funds and used primarily to pay for highways, worked pretty well. It led to the development of a network of paved state and US highways, and later to the development of most of the Interstate Highway System. But, as we have seen earlier in this chapter, the 20th-century paradigm is breaking down in a number of ways:

- America has a problem of chronic traffic congestion, mostly in urban areas, whose full cost probably exceeds $300 billion per year.
- While our highways are not "crumbling," there is a large backlog of bridges and highways in poor condition, which reduces the benefits Americans derive from the highway system.
- There is well-documented evidence that, overall, we are not investing enough in highway system *improvements*, because the funds to do so simply aren't available, given the choices made by legislative bodies.
- Another reason for the funding shortage is the nonsustainability of per-gallon fuel taxes, given trends and policies prevalent in the 21st century.
- The investments now being made in the highway system are less effective in increasing economic productivity, which suggests there is a problem in setting investment priorities.
- Nearly 25 percent of what motorists and truckers pay in highway user taxes is diverted to other transportation and nontransportation uses.

It seems clear that we need a better model—a new paradigm—for highways in America. The purpose of this book is to suggest such a new paradigm, one aimed at overcoming all the now evident shortcomings of the system that worked pretty well under the different conditions of the 20th century but is increasingly unsuited to 21st-century realities. Given the major changes we can expect in this century—increased traffic due to large-scale use of autonomous vehicles, shared-ride services like Uber, ubiquitous all-electronic tolling, and a shift from charging per gallon to charging per mile—a more flexible and entrepreneurial highway system is even more important.

The key to this new paradigm is the idea of network utilities. A network utility is a system that delivers a vital service to numerous users via a large set of links and nodes (the network). There are many such network utilities:

electricity, natural gas, water supply, pipelines, telephones, and other forms of telecommunications. In the United States, the majority of network utilities consist of investor-owned companies, but government-run utilities and user cooperatives also exist, mostly in water supply and portions of the electricity market. Regardless of ownership, these network utilities all follow similar methods of operation and funding:

- They charge customers directly for the services they provide, typically via monthly utility bills.
- They price their services based largely on how much a business, household, or individual uses of the various services offered.
- When it comes to deciding on major capital investments to add capacity or improve service delivery, they typically finance such projects over time, rather than paying for them out of annual cash flow, as most highway projects are funded today.
- Project decisions are generally based on return-on-investment criteria, similar to how nonutility businesses decide on capital investments.
- Since their revenue depends on satisfied customers, they pay serious attention to proper maintenance, to ensure the network remains in good condition.
- When customers pay their utility bills, they know that the money goes directly to the utility to pay its operating, maintenance, and capital costs.

When it comes to highways, America has made a category mistake. In the mistaken belief that highways are the kind of thing that only government can provide, we created a 20th-century system based on government provision. And in the belief, which was partly true prior to electronic tolling, that charging direct user fees would be costly and inconvenient, we adopted a second-best approach of user taxes on fuel. The consequences of this category mistake are increasingly evident, as was discussed earlier in this chapter.

Table 1 provides a quick overview comparison of the 20th-century US highway system and the typical network utility model. We will explore these differences in subsequent chapters of this book. The remainder of the book is organized as follows. Chapter 2 provides a preview of what a difference something like the new paradigm can make, using recent examples of private-sector projects that are adding market-priced express lanes to congested freeways. Chapter 3 tells the story of how we got the 20th-century highway paradigm, despite the prevalence of investor-owned toll roads in the pre-automobile era. In chapter 4 we explore a precursor

TABLE 1. **Network utilities vs. US highway system**

	Network utility	Current US highway system
Structure	Interconnected network, multiple providers	Interconnected network, multiple providers
Ownership	Mix of investor-owned companies, government companies, and user co-ops	Mostly state DOTs, some toll agencies
Revenue source	Direct user charges, paid to the utility	Indirect user taxes, paid to the government
Investment criteria	Return on investment, adding value for customers	Political process, gaining political benefits
Pricing	Partly demand-based, to optimize use of the network	Virtually no pricing, except toll roads
Response to congestion	Raise prices to generate more revenue, add capacity	Discourage use by rationing, diverting customers to alternatives
Rationale for maintenance	Risk of decreased business, decline in asset value	Risk of insufficient legislative appropriations
Response to new technology	Managerial	Political

of the proposed new paradigm as it has evolved in other countries since World War II—first in Europe and later in Australia, Asia, and Latin America. Chapter 5 recounts the introduction of this new paradigm in the United States on a small scale in the early years of the 21st century. Chapter 6 explores the benefits that large-scale application of the new paradigm could bring, compared with continuation of the 20th-century highway model. In chapter 7 we review arguments raised against the new paradigm by American critics on both the right and the left. Chapter 8 then presents a more fleshed-out explanation of how a US highway industry could work, drawing on lessons from overseas as well as from other forms of US network utilities. Chapter 9 applies the utility model to long-distance highways, while chapter 10 does the same for urban expressways. Chapter 11 addresses several concerns about whether we will still need a large highway sector in coming decades. The final chapter provides a summary and conclusions.

CHAPTER TWO

How the Private Sector Is Reinventing America's Freeways

Introduction: Urban America's Congestion Problem

The idea that the private sector might actually transform America's highways may sound fanciful on first hearing. To illustrate the kinds of changes that might come about if the highway utility concept gains acceptance, this chapter (an earlier version of which appeared in *Reason* magazine),[1] is intended as a kind of preview of the rest of this book. It recounts how toll concession companies, working with innovative state DOTs, have implemented a customer-friendly approach to providing relief from traffic congestion in some of America's most congested metro areas.

If you work anywhere in America except New York City, chances are you commute to work every day by car. That means you battle congestion twice a day, every weekday. It's not your imagination that congestion is much worse than it used to be. The average urban commuter, in metro areas of all sizes, wastes 42 hours a year in rush-hour congestion today, compared with just 18 hours in 1982. The Texas A&M Transportation Institute (TTI) has been measuring the direct cost of traffic congestion (wasted time and fuel) since 1982. In current dollars, they estimate that the *annual* cost has increased from $42 billion in 1982 to $160 billion in 2014, the latest year for which complete data are available.[2]

Those figures are the average for all 471 US urban areas. But if you live and work in one of the 15 largest metro areas, you experience far worse congestion. In Los Angeles, the average commuter wastes 80 hours a year stuck in traffic (compared with 50 hours in 1982). In Dallas–Fort Worth, it's 53 hours a year wasted now (vs. 36 in 1982). And in the Washington, DC, area, it's a whopping 82 hours a year now, compared with 36 in 1982.

TABLE 2. **Growth of traffic congestion in 15 major metro areas, 1982–2014**

Metro area	Yearly delay per auto commuter (in hours)		Yearly congestion cost per auto commuter (in dollars)	
	1982	2014	1982	2014
Washington, DC	36	82	$1,016	$1,834
Los Angeles / Long Beach	50	80	$1,627	$1,711
San Francisco / Oakland	50	78	$1,766	$1,675
New York / Newark	32	74	$1,209	$1,739
San Jose	19	67	$520	$1,422
Boston	31	64	$1,163	$1,388
Seattle	32	63	$825	$1,491
Chicago	31	61	$1,199	$1,445
Houston	42	61	$1,129	$1,490
Riverside / San Bernardino	19	59	$438	$1,316
Dallas / Fort Worth	36	53	$791	$1,185
Atlanta	22	52	$458	$1,130
Detroit	33	52	$1,425	$1,183
Miami	26	52	$706	$1,164
Portland, OR	20	52	$523	$1,273
15-**metro average**	32	63	$986	$1,430
471-**metro average**	18	42	$400	$960

Source: Texas A&M Transportation Institute, http://tamu.edu

Table 2 provides comparison numbers for 15 of the most congested large urban areas.

Congestion does far more harm than simply wasting time and fuel. By reducing the area you can traverse in a typical 30-minute drive, congestion shrinks your "opportunity circle" of jobs, entertainment, housing, and even dating. My Reason Foundation colleagues Ted Balaker and Sam Staley discussed these impacts in their 2006 book, *The Road More Traveled*.[3] Economists find that reduced opportunity circles due to congestion inhibit the best matches between skilled workers and employer needs, reducing the economic productivity of congested urban areas. The chief economist at the US Department of Transportation has estimated that the true economic cost of congestion is at least *double* the $160 billion annual figure noted above.[4]

Why does congestion keep getting worse, and what can be done about it? While there is no single answer to either question, one of the principal reasons for ever-worse congestion is that the demand for road space, especially on urban freeways, greatly exceeds the supply. That's because after the initial burst of freeway building in the 1960s and '70s, additions to freeways slowed way down while population and economic growth continued. Some have described the result as like trying to fit ten pounds of potatoes into a five-pound sack.

A review of 30 years of congestion data compiled by the Texas A&M Transportation Institute for America's 15 most congested metro areas is enlightening. Over the 30 years from 1982 to 2011, daily traffic on the freeway systems in those areas increased by 166 percent. But their freeway capacity (measured in lane-miles) grew by an average of less than half as much (72 percent). In most cases this means that freeways today are attempting to handle far more traffic than they were designed for. It also explains why "rush hour" today runs about three hours in the morning and another three or more hours in the evening in major metro areas.

SIDEBAR 1 **A Note on Congestion Data**

Even though the congestion data assembled and analyzed by the Texas A&M—Transportation Institute (TTI) are widely used and accepted by state DOTs and metropolitan planning organizations (MPOs), those data have their critics. Some criticisms come from advocates of "smart growth" who want transportation policy to discourage automobile use and encourage walking, bicycling, and use of public transit. Those critics question assumptions such as the value of time used in computing congestion cost estimates, and the difference in travel time that congestion produces. TTI has responded in detail to those critiques, which in my view are primarily ideological, though often framed as methodological.[1]

But some transportation researchers raise more fundamental points. The most important of these criticisms is that measurement techniques have improved considerably over the decades, especially now that nearly everyone commutes with a smartphone that permits researchers at companies like INRIX to measure actual traffic speed. But can today's refined congestion measurements be accurately compared to those of the 1980s, as TTI routinely does, and as is done in table 2? TTI's answer to this is that when it began using data from INRIX, which first appeared in its *2010 Urban Mobility Report*, it compared INRIX data from 2007, 2008, and 2009 with TTI's own estimated data for those years, and was thereby able to develop adjustment factors for its data for those prior years. Congestion data for

1. Tim Lomax, "Congestion Measurement in the Urban Mobility Scorecard," Texas A&M Transportation Institute, October 2016, http://tti.tamu.edu/documents/TTI-2016–14.pdf.

years prior to 2007 were subsequently adjusted to make them comparable to the INRIX-derived data reported since then.

One critic of TTI's comparison of current congestion data with data from 1982 opined that a yearly delay of only 18 hours per auto commuter in 1982 was not credible. But that figure is the average delay across 471 metro areas; as table 2 makes clear, the average 1982 delay for the 15 large and very large urban areas in that table was 32 hours, which has essentially doubled to 63 hours as of 2014.

TTI's detailed explanation of the methodology used for all the measures in its Urban Mobility Scorecard is online, updated periodically, at http://mobility.tamu .edu/ums/methodology.

"We Can't Build Our Way out of Congestion"

Given the enormous cost of congestion, and its relentless increase over the past 30 years, why haven't more metro areas at least attempted to keep pace with the growth in traffic? There are two principal reasons. First, it has become far more costly to widen freeways and build new ones, as urban areas have filled in with expensive development. That "cost" is both political and economic. Unlike in the early days of freeway building, you just can't bulldoze neighborhoods wherever a new freeway would make transportation sense, and anything you do build must go through costly and time-consuming environmental reviews.

But the other reason is the widely held idea that it's futile to add roadway capacity in hopes of solving congestion. If you build more, critics say, the new lanes will simply fill up with more cars within a few years, and you'll be back where you started. No one would make this argument about schools or water supply, nor should it be applied unthinkingly to highways, where it is at best a half-truth. Some research does show that if you add a small amount of capacity in a place like Los Angeles, where roadway supply and demand are massively out of whack, the latent demand for faster travel during rush hours will generally fill up the new capacity in short order. On the other hand, the long-term data from TTI demonstrate clearly that if a metro area can keep growing capacity in step with demand, it will have far less congestion than places that don't follow this policy.

A few metro areas, like Atlanta and Houston, have more than doubled their freeway capacity over the past three decades. But others, like Los Angeles, San Francisco, and New York, have added only 23 to 43 percent more capacity. The TTI *Urban Mobility Report 2012* provides a graph (exhibit 13) that shows a strong correlation between increased capacity and smaller increases in congestion. The 17 metro areas that expanded freeway capacity the most now had 2012 congestion only about 60 percent worse than in 1982, whereas the 56 metro areas whose gap between demand and capacity was the greatest ended up with congestion about 200 percent worse than in 1982.

Yet the idea that "we can't build our way out of congestion" is widely believed—by transportation planners, by editorial writers and other pundits, by chambers of commerce, and by a great many politicians. As a result, the long-range transportation plans of most large metro areas these days are premised on attempts to "get people out of their cars." Adding any significant amount of roadway capacity generally gets low priority, while major emphasis (and planned spending) focuses on expanding mass transit, and on encouraging "active transportation" (biking and walking) by expanding sidewalks and creating bikeway networks, and so on. And in many of the largest metro areas over the past two decades, just about the only expansions of freeway capacity to make it through the approval process have been additions of carpool lanes. The planners' rationale here is that if people are going to stick with driving, at least encourage them to share rides by giving them preferential lanes for high-occupancy vehicles (HOVs) only. But despite the addition of numerous HOV lanes over the past three decades, the fraction of commuters car-pooling to work declined from 19.7 percent of all commuter trips in 1980 to just 9.7 percent in 2010.[5]

A New Dimension: Congestion Pricing

During the 1980s, a small band of transportation researchers became convinced that the missing ingredient in bringing freeway demand into sync with capacity was *market pricing*. This work was pioneered in the United States by the subsequent Nobel Prize–winning economist William Vickrey. But road pricing, later to become known as congestion pricing, had languished due to the lack of a workable means of charging variable prices. That lack was just then in the process of being remedied by the development of the first "toll-tag" transponder, by a company called Amtech, in the late 1980s. A device about the size of a deck of playing cards, the transponder contained a chip encoding a driver's toll account number, and an antenna that could receive an interrogation signal from a roadside or overhead gantry and send back the account number—and do this at highway speed. So the transponder would make it feasible not merely to automate toll collection but also to charge different prices at different times.

Also in the 1980s, US transportation researchers became aware that for several decades, high-quality toll roads had been financed, built, and operated by investor-owned companies in France, Italy, and Spain (as we will explore in more detail in chapter 4). The government would grant a company a long-term franchise, like those used for investor-owned electric utilities in the United States. Based on the franchise, called a "concession," they could raise the capital to build the toll road, repaying their investors over the years from ongoing toll revenues. A Reason Foundation policy paper in 1988 proposed that the private sector be invited to finance, develop, and operate market-priced congestion-relief lanes, to be added to the congested freeways of Southern California.[6]

As is discussed in more detail in chapter 5, that paper came to the attention of state officials, and in 1989 they secured passage of legislation to permit four pilot projects based on that idea.[7] The first to be developed was the 91 Express Lanes, four new variably priced lanes in the wide median on 10 miles of the highly congested SR 91 freeway in Orange County. The lanes opened in December 1995, built for just $130 million (partly because there was no cost to acquire right-of-way).[8] Though derided by skeptics, the express lanes proved hugely popular with commuters willing to pay for the never-before-available option of bypassing congestion to get to or from work, to the airport, to important meetings, to pick up kids from day care, and so on. And the demand for improved mobility was high enough that the express lanes fully covered their cost of construction, financed via long-term bank loans, as well as all operating and maintenance costs including policing and property taxes.[9]

That landmark project demonstrated four very important things. First, the long-term toll-concession model from Europe is transferable to the United States. Second, many people are willing to pay for faster and more reliable rush-hour trips in highly congested freeway corridors. Third, transponder technology is a practical way of implementing congestion pricing. And fourth, variable, demand-based pricing is effective in keeping priced lanes flowing freely at the speed limit, even during the busiest rush-hour periods. The 91 express lanes have remained uncongested and free-flowing at all hours for more than two decades, and have inspired many other congestion-relief toll projects.

Challenging the HOV Lane Model

Initially, the success of the 91 express lanes did not stimulate a lot of private-sector investment in other congestion-relief-lane projects. But it did spark a wave of state transportation agency conversions of HOV lanes to something else the Reason Foundation invented: high-occupancy toll (HOT) lanes—today often called express toll lanes or managed lanes.[10] By the early 1990s, research had found that HOV lanes make sense in only very limited cases.[11] Most such lanes—being limited to buses, van pools, and car pools—were seriously underutilized, even during rush hours. Commuters stuck in congestion in the regular lanes fumed at the "empty-lane syndrome" usually evident in adjacent HOV lanes. By contrast, in a limited number of cases in very congested metro areas, some HOV lanes were jammed, to the point where they became nearly as congested as regular lanes. The remedy was supposed to be to increase the required occupancy from two people to three—but that proved very difficult politically, so it was hardly ever done. Thus, most HOV lanes were and are either too empty or too full; this became known as the Goldilocks problem.

Nearly all HOV lanes were built with federal money, and it was illegal to convert them to regular lanes despite their unpopularity with many motorists. (The only known case of such conversion took place for two HOV facilities in New Jersey, whose members of Congress slipped a provision authorizing it into an unrelated bill.)[12] So why not make lemonade out of these lemons, Reason Foundation's study proposed, by selling the excess capacity in underutilized HOV lanes to willing buyers? Over the next 20 years, several dozen HOV lanes were converted to HOT lanes in metro areas ranging from San Diego to Minneapolis to Miami, with each conversion adding to the evidence that commuters welcome the choice between congested free lanes and uncongested pay lanes.

This evidence was not lost on those interested in investor-owned, toll-financed projects in the United States, modeled after the 91 express lanes. The second major project of this nature was proposed to the Virginia DOT in 2002. It was to add express toll lanes to the congestion-choked Capital

Beltway in the northern Virginia suburbs of Washington, DC. The Beltway was known to many locals as "the world's largest parking lot" during morning and evening peak periods. Motorists desperately wanted relief, but the only plan the Virginia DOT had to offer was a $3 billion project to add two HOV lanes in each direction on the most congested 14-mile portion of the Beltway (the southwest quadrant). There were only two problems with this plan. It faced enormous opposition because it required the "taking" (by condemnation) of more than 300 homes and businesses in order to widen the Beltway. And VDOT didn't have anything close to $3 billion available.

The Private Sector Thinks outside the Box

Fortunately, the Virginia legislature in 1995 had enacted the Public-Private Transportation Act, which authorized public-private partnerships such as long-term toll concessions.[13] Like California's 1989 pilot-program law, it allowed the private sector to make unsolicited proposals rather than only respond to requests for proposals to do projects that VDOT already knew it wanted to pursue. So in 2002, with VDOT's $3 billion proposal going nowhere, one of America's leading engineering and construction firms, Fluor, made a proposal to fix the congestion problem on the Beltway. Rather than building tax-funded HOV lanes, Fluor proposed toll-financed HOT lanes. And rather than massively widening the Beltway, Fluor offered a value-engineered approach that would still add two lanes in each direction, but with condemnation of only six properties, rather than 300, mostly to accommodate rebuilt bridges and on- and off-ramps. The cost was estimated at $1 billion, one-third the cost of VDOT's plan, to be financed on the basis of toll revenues.[14] This was a much bigger deal than the 91 express lanes.

VDOT responded cautiously but positively to the proposal, and began what ended up being five years of discussions and negotiations about all the "design exceptions" Fluor wanted in order to reduce the cost and the footprint of the project (see sidebar 2). Meanwhile, Fluor set about pitching the project to dozens of business and community groups in the Virginia suburbs. Gary Groat, who was then Fluor's project development director, explained that federal rules (which must be followed, since the Beltway is the Interstate highway I-495) forbid a state DOT from "taking sides" on a proposed highway project while it is in the environmental evaluation phase. But no such restriction applies to the private-sector proponent. So Groat organized presentation after presentation, explaining HOT lanes and congestion pricing, the much lower cost of the project, and the proposed financing, based on toll revenue, that would make it possible to build the project in the near term, unlike VDOT's unaffordable HOV lanes. But most of all, Groat stressed the huge reductions in land condemnation in the HOT lanes plan. Over several years, these presentations turned what had been huge opposition to the HOV lanes plan into large-scale support for the HOT lanes alternative.

As negotiations with VDOT got to the detailed stage, the agency required many changes that would increase the project's cost; in addition, construction costs had gone up a lot during five years of review and negotiation. With the cost now approaching $1.9 billion, it became apparent to Fluor that toll revenues alone would no longer suffice to pay for the project. This led to two key changes. First, Fluor teamed up with Australian toll road developer-operator Transurban as both an investor and as the planned operator of the lanes. Second, the deal became a public-private partnership in which VDOT would contribute $409 million to cover most of its changes while Fluor and Transurban would finance the remaining $1.5 billion on the basis of toll revenues. The deal was finalized in 2007, and the "financial close" took place in December of that year. It's noteworthy that investors were willing to commit to the project during the early months of the credit markets crunch that led to the Great Recession. That's one indication of how robust the case for congestion-relief toll lanes appears to be.

Construction began in spring 2008 and the project opened to traffic on schedule in autumn 2012. Relief from rush-hour gridlock was finally available for hard-pressed Beltway commuters. And the reality of the Beltway HOT lanes stimulated serious research and planning for a possible network of market-priced toll lanes in the DC metro area. Fluor and Transurban gained approval and completed a second link in this network, by converting the existing reversible two-lane HOV facility on I-95 approaching DC from the south to HOT lanes.[15] The busiest northern section now has three reversible lanes instead of two, and they are open to anyone willing to pay the variable toll.

Commuters in the DC metro area have been wasting 82 hours a year stuck in congestion, at a per-commuter cost (in time and fuel) in excess of nearly $1,800 per year. The overall DC metro-area congestion cost in 2014 was $4.6 billion, nearly twice as high as the $2.5 billion cost in 1982. So it's a promising sign that the Metropolitan Washington Council of Governments is refining plans for a region-wide network of congestion-priced lanes that could become an official part of the region's long-range transportation plan in the near future.

Dallas and Fort Worth Test the New Paradigm

Although policymakers in Texas have been more favorable to adding highway capacity than their counterparts in much of the rest of the country have been, Texas has grown so much over the last 30 years that its limited highway fuel-tax funds have simply not kept pace. Consequently, the Dallas-/Fort Worth metro area ranks seventh in the nation in congestion cost, at $4.2 billion per year, with 70 percent of rush-hour traffic taking place in congested conditions. In the early 2000s the Texas legislature passed a sweeping transportation public-private partnership act, aiming to tap into toll-based private capital to add needed capacity, especially to urban freeways.[16]

The congestion champion in Dallas had long been the LBJ Freeway, I-635. It constitutes the northern and eastern portion of an inner beltway (or "loop," in local parlance) around Dallas. When the LBJ was last expanded, years ago, the project was controversial due to the high-value properties along much of the corridor. Texas DOT made a commitment at that point that this would be the last widening of the freeway's footprint. But with continued growth in the whole metro area, the LBJ once again ran out of capacity, experiencing massive congestion.

Because of its commitment not to expand the freeway's footprint, TxDOT's plan to add HOT lanes to some or all of the LBJ envisioned that the new tolled lanes—up to three in each direction—would have to be built as tunnels beneath the existing freeway. When the agency issued its request for proposals, however, it took the open-minded approach of allowing the companies that were bidding to propose alternatives. Of the two finalists, one went with the tunnels idea, at an estimated cost of $3.3 billion. But the winning bid, from Cintra/Meridiam, proposed an alternative that would cost only $2.6 billion. Via creative engineering, they proposed building most of the new toll lanes depressed below the level of the main freeway lanes, with the latter overhanging the toll lanes. While in some ways more complicated to build, this approach produced significantly more roadway per dollar.

As with the Beltway project in northern Virginia, what TxDOT required—including full reconstruction of the existing lanes and maintenance of the whole project for 52 years—was more costly than the projected toll revenues could finance. So, up-front, TxDOT offered up to $700 million of state highway funds. But the winning bidder requested only $496 million, so TxDOT got the project it wanted while saving over $200 million for other needed projects. And since Cintra/Meridiam had to finance only $2.1 billion, what they need to recover in toll revenues is significantly less than what would have been required with a tunnels approach to the project.

This project was financed in the aftermath of the credit markets crunch, in June 2010.[17] The tax-exempt private activity bonds received an investment-grade rating. Cintra, Meridiam, and the local fire and police pension fund together invested $665 million in private equity—an indication of their confidence in the robustness of the projected toll revenues over the 52-year concession period. Phase 1 opened in December 2013, phase 2 in July 2014, and the balance opened three months ahead of schedule, on September 10, 2015.

Only six months earlier, the same Cintra/Meridiam team had reached financial close on a slightly less ambitious toll-lanes project on the other side of the Metroplex: the $2.1 billion North Tarrant Express in Fort Worth.[18] It doubles the capacity of a 13-mile stretch of I-820 and SH 121/183 on the city's northeast side, providing access from there to the huge Dallas–Fort Worth (DFW) Airport. On I-820, the four new toll lanes fit into the median, between the existing regular lanes. But on SH 183, some of the new lanes are elevated, due to much less available right of way.

SIDEBAR 2 **Adding Lanes Where It "Couldn't Be Done"**

The Capital Beltway's Value Engineering

When Fluor's engineers looked carefully at Virginia DOT's unaffordable $3 billion plan to add HOV lanes to the Capital Beltway, they zeroed in on how to reduce the 300-odd land condemnations that VDOT said were necessary to do the widening. It turns out that a huge fraction of that cost came from replacing all the interchanges and bridges crossing over the route. It was "necessary" in order to use what highway engineers call the "desirable" cross section for the expressway: lane widths, shoulder widths, a concrete barrier between the regular and new lanes, and so on. By going instead with the "minimum" cross-section, Fluor figured it could get by with only modifications of the bridges and interchanges, saving well over a billion dollars and eliminating nearly all the property takes. Further savings came from less comprehensive improvements to all the interchange ramps. Nevertheless, the final negotiated cost was well above Fluor's initial $1 billion proposal. Fluor's Gary Groat explained that the increases were primarily due to VDOT requirements that increased the project's scope, such as adding direct access ramps at the Dulles Toll Road, replacing all existing noise walls, and adding direct HOV to HOT ramps at the Springfield Interchange.[1]

"Six Lanes on Six Feet" in Tampa

When the Tampa Hillsborough Expressway Authority (THEA) needed to add lanes to their Selmon Expressway toll road, they, too, had a right-of-way problem. There was not enough room in the 40-foot median to add the needed lanes, and widening the corridor would have meant years of effort to acquire land alongside by either voluntary purchase or land condemnation. The innovative solution designed for them by the Figg Bridge Company elevated the new lanes above the median, using precast segments produced off-site and trucked to the expressway at night to be hoisted into place. And since traffic on this commuter route is highly directional—westbound in the morning peak and eastbound in the afternoon—THEA planned the new elevated lanes as reversible express lanes. The pillars supporting the three reversible lanes take up only six feet of space in the median. Since the three lanes provide the equivalent of six bidirectional lanes, the project has become known as providing "six lanes on six feet" of right-of-way.[2]

France's Tunnel beneath Versailles

For more than three decades, the outer ring road around Paris, the A86, —had a six-mile missing link. Transportation planners' maps showed the route cutting right through historic Versailles, and that generated massive resistance, leading to a stalemate. The French investor-owned toll road operator Cofiroute came to the

1. Email from Gary Groat to Robert Poole, August 29, 2011.
2. Peter Samuel, "Tampa EL Going Great: Underlines Case for All Electronic Toll Collection," Tollroadsnews.com, June 7, 2007.

rescue with an unsolicited proposal in 1988: Let us build the missing link as a deep-bore tunnel beneath Versailles and pay for its $2 billion cost by charging tolls. Despite the practicality of the idea, it took many years to overcome political and other obstacles, but the project was finally completed by the end of 2008 and opened the following spring after all of its systems were tested.[3] When the tunnel was opened to traffic, it eliminated that notorious gap in the ring road and spared Versailles a large amount of unwanted through traffic. To minimize construction costs, Cofiroute came up with a double-deck design, requiring a single tunnel bore 38 feet in diameter. To make that possible, French authorities agreed that only auto-size vehicles and not trucks would be allowed to use the tunnel.

Will a Tunnel Finally Close an LA Freeway Missing Link?

The situation that led to the A86 tunnel had a directly parallel situation in Los Angeles. For nearly 40 years the I-710 freeway has had a five-mile missing link through the pleasant bedroom community of South Pasadena. Decades ago, the state DOT (Caltrans) staked out the route and bought up the homes that would have to be demolished to allow the building of a link, but litigation and political opposition stymied the project again and again. Could this gap instead be closed by a deeply bored toll tunnel? A few transportation planners in both the public and the private sectors (including the late Joe Jacobs, founder of Jacobs Engineering), were enthusiastic, but the idea didn't gain a critical mass of support. In 2015, however, with money tight and congestion worsening, the toll tunnel beneath South Pasadena became the top-priority highway project for the Los Angeles County Metropolitan Transportation Authority, and was being considered as one of that agency's first major public-private partnership projects.

3. Peter Samuel, "French Low Ceiling Tunnelways of Duplex A86 Comfortable to Drive, 'Not Claustrophobic,'" Tollroadsnews.com, December 24, 2008.

Congestion Relief: Coming Soon to a Metro Area Near You?

While these are still early days in using private capital and congestion pricing to give commuters meaningful congestion relief, the success of HOV to HOT conversions and the demonstrated ability of private firms to raise large sums based on projected toll revenues have stimulated activity in many of the nation's most congested metro areas. Whereas in the 1990s about the only politically acceptable form of adding freeway capacity was to build HOV lanes, it is now becoming politically acceptable to add capacity with HOT or express toll lanes. Here is a sampling of projects in other major urban areas as of 2016.

Atlanta. After several years of detailed study, the Georgia DOT in December 2009 adopted a $16 billion plan to add express toll lanes to nearly all the metro area's freeways. The first project, converting HOV lanes to HOT lanes on a 15-mile stretch of I-85, opened to traffic in late 2011. Two much larger projects are under way, adding new express toll lanes to I-75 and I-575 in the metro area's northwest area and adding similar lanes on I-75 south of the I-285 ring road (known locally as the Perimeter).

Miami. The Florida DOT added one lane of capacity each way and converted the existing HOV lanes to provide two HOT lanes each way on I-95 in Miami. The variably priced express toll lanes have brought major congestion relief, as well as faster and more reliable express bus service. FDOT used a public-private partnership to rebuild I-595 in Fort Lauderdale, adding three reversible express toll lanes to this congested east-west commuter route. A two-county network of express toll lanes is underway with new express toll lanes under construction on I-75 in Broward County (Fort Lauderdale) and on the Palmetto Expressway in Miami-Dade County. In addition, the Florida Turnpike is adding express toll lanes to its Homestead Extension in southern Miami-Dade County.

Houston. The local toll agency financed the addition of two HOT lanes each way as part of the complete reconstruction of the Katy Freeway (I-10), which opened to traffic in 2008. Houston Metro then converted its HOV lanes on five other freeways to HOT lanes. And a public-private partnership model is being used for major portions of a new outer beltway, the Grand Parkway.

Phoenix. The Arizona legislature passed public-private partnership legislation for transportation in 2009, and the Arizona DOT and the metropolitan planning organization for greater Phoenix are developing plans for HOT lanes in the region, most of which are expected to be privately financed and developed.

Los Angeles. The longtime congestion capital of America until recently had only one express-toll-lanes project, the landmark 10-mile 91 express lanes in Orange County. But in 2012 and 2013, Los Angeles county converted the HOV lanes on both the Harbor and San Bernardino Freeways to HOT lanes. The metropolitan planning agency completed a major study of a region-wide network of such lanes, and express toll lane projects are in the planning or development stages in Los Angeles, Orange, Riverside, and San Bernardino counties. In addition, current plans call for using public-private partnerships to add several missing links to the region's freeway system, including the planned 63-mile High Desert Corridor in northern Los Angeles county.

San Francisco. Although no PPP proposals have yet surfaced, the Bay Area has opened several HOT lanes in the East Bay and in Silicon Valley. Its metropolitan planning organization was one of the first in the nation to include a region-wide network of HOT lanes in its long-term transportation plan, which is underway, based largely on converting its extensive network of HOV lanes to HOT lanes.

Seattle. The Washington state DOT reintroduced toll financing in the Puget Sound region for the second span of the Tacoma Narrows Bridge, which opened in 2007. Two other major projects—a toll tunnel to replace the structurally unsound Alaskan Way Viaduct, and a new toll bridge to replace the SR 520 floating bridge—add to the use of tolling and toll finance in the metro area. After the modest success of the conversion of the SR 167 HOV lanes to HOT, a much larger project is adding express toll lanes to about 40 miles of I-405 just east of Seattle—an area that includes Renton, Bellevue, and Redmond, home of Microsoft.

Of the 15 most congested metro areas, whose 2014 congestion cost totaled $78.9 billion (out of the national total of $160 billion), the only ones thus far not introducing express toll lanes for congestion relief are New York; Philadelphia; Boston; Detroit; and Portland, Oregon.

Where Might This All Lead?

These privately financed projects provide a preview of a possible paradigm shift for US highways. The ultimate end result might be that investor-owned limited-access highways (today's freeways and Interstates) become a new category of investor-owned utility, analogous to America's largely investor-owned electricity, natural gas, and telecommunications sectors, and the partially investor-owned water utility sector. We will explore this idea in some detail in chapter 8.

One of the pioneers of this concept was Steve Lockwood, who was a senior policy official at the Federal Highway Administration during the

George H. W. Bush administration. Lockwood helped build the case for loosening federal restrictions on tolling and pricing in the 1991 reauthorization of the federal highway and transit program. In a series of talks over a period of several years, he made the analogy between highways and other network utilities, and even suggested that in the 21st century state DOTs might evolve into public/private "transcorps" that would operate as businesses, more like state turnpike agencies than like typical DOTs.[19] The concept of investor-owned highways was independently fleshed out by the former World Bank transport economist Gabriel Roth in his 1996 book *Roads in a Market Economy*,[20] and further explored in the collection he edited, *Street Smart*.[21]

Despite the 19th-century history of privately franchised toll roads, most people have trouble seeing highways as businesses. If they've been exposed to economics, they think of "roads" as classic examples of "public goods," which must be provided by government because there's no way to exclude those who won't pay for them. While doing that might be more costly, and perhaps privacy-invading, for city streets and boulevards, it is not a problem for limited-access highways, where access can only occur at limited points, and where charging for use is easy thanks to 21st-century electronic tolling, which is eliminating tollbooths altogether. Just as electric utilities can charge variable rates to encourage customers to not use power-hungry appliances during periods of peak demand, so can expressway companies charge more during rush hour to encourage nonessential trips to shift off-peak.

Looked at from the perspective of ever-worsening congestion, America's urban freeways constitute a serious case of government failure. They do not give their "customers" the kinds of reliable mobility they want, and their method of charging, via flat-rate fuel taxes, undercharges urban users (especially during rush hours) and generally overcharges rural highway users, whose roads cost far less to build (due to fewer lanes, cheap land, etc.) and maintain.[22] Yet without market pricing, we don't know how much urban expressway capacity people would be willing to pay for.

The private sector appears to be capable of taking on the challenge of reinventing America's freeways. In recent years, several hundred global-infrastructure investment funds have been created—by investment banks, by fund managers, and by pension funds. As of 2016, *Infrastructure Investor* reported that the 50 largest of these funds had raised $250 billion over the previous five years.[23] It also estimated that all such funds had raised well over $300 billion over that period. That money is intended as equity investment, perhaps 25 percent of a project's cost, with the other 75 percent financed by debt (like the mortgage on a house, covering the balance remaining after a down payment). Thus, if these funds invest their $300 billion as equity in infrastructure projects, that would make possible $1.2 trillion worth of projects.

Another factor that could help bring about a paradigm shift is the increasing obsolescence of the fuel tax as America's primary highway funding source. The rising price of oil motivated both business and government to seek alternatives to gasoline and diesel-powered vehicles. Federal Corporate Average Fuel Economy (CAFE) regulations have already reduced the yield of per-gallon fuel taxes, as people today can drive twice as far on a gallon of gas as they did 25 years ago. Average fuel economy is mandated to double again by 2025, producing gaping shortfalls in highway-dedicated revenue unless legislators are willing to double the current federal and state fuel-tax rates.

Thus, we will likely have to shift to a more direct means of paying for highway use—and some form of per-mile electronic toll charge is probably the best way forward. As the reality of this change sinks in, people may be able to appreciate the concept of paying a monthly highway bill, just as they pay their monthly electricity, gas, and water bills.

Chronic freeway congestion ought to be intolerable to Americans. It's a crude form of rationing, by time instead of money, like Soviet bread lines. And the idea that everyone should be equally miserable, stuck in congestion, is similarly offensive—like mandating that nobody purchase coffee at Starbucks, because Folgers instant is good enough for everyone. HOT lanes and toll concessions have given us a glimpse at a better future. We will explore this possible future in more detail in subsequent chapters.

CHAPTER THREE

Where America's 20th-Century Highway Model Came From

The Origins of Highways

E ver since wheeled carts, chariots, and wagons were invented, there has been a need for roadways. As early as 2000 BC the Minoan empire built a 30-mile paved road in Crete. In 500 BC, the Persian emperor Darius the Great built a large road system that included the Royal Road, nearly 1,700 miles in length. The famous Roman roads linked all major parts of the Roman Empire. Most were constructed of crushed stone topped with gravel, but the major ones had a top layer of paving stones.

During the Middle Ages the Roman roads deteriorated, and there was little serious European road building until the dawning of the Industrial Revolution in England and northern Europe. The first major highway in Britain was built between 1725 and 1737 to better connect England and Scotland, using the Roman crushed-stone-and gravel method.[1] But the first toll bridges in Europe go back much further. King Henry II granted Saint Mary Colechurch in London the right to collect tolls to recover the cost of building the Old London Bridge across the Thames River.[2] Peter Samuel of *TollRoadsNews.com* reports that there were many such concessions in England and on the continent during the Middle Ages.

Most significant roads in 18th-century Britain were toll roads. Parliament enacted a Turnpike Act in 1707 to facilitate improvements to the road between London and Chester. It authorized creation of a turnpike trust that would use a combination of (1) funding from each parish through which the road passed and (2) tolls charged to users. This became the general pattern for highway improvement, applied first to the radial roads centered on London and later to roads connecting those radials.[3] From

150 trusts in 1750 the numbers grew rapidly to more than 700 by 1800, and peaked at 1,116 trusts by 1837, responsible for 22,000 miles of highway in England and Wales. These turnpike trusts were basically local nonprofit corporations granted their authority by Parliament.

The 18th-century turnpikes were mostly gravel, and of rather poor quality. Early in the 19th century, the civil engineer Thomas Telford developed more durable paving, with a deep foundation of heavy stones and a surface of gravel. In addition, his roads sloped downward from the center on both sides, to facilitate drainage.[4] Another noted pioneer of paved roads was John McAdam, a Scottish civil engineer and contemporary of Telford. Though his roads dispensed with Telford's heavy stones, substituting an eight-inch layer of broken stone topped by two inches of gravel, they proved to be more durable than Telford's, and "macadam" roads were the primary kind built for British turnpikes in the 19th century.[5] Subsequent road builders added various kinds of binders to the surface layer, to reduce dust and produce a smoother surface.

Early US Toll Roads and Bridges

The first US toll bridge was built in 1785 across the Charles River in Massachusetts, connecting Boston with Charlestown. Following the British model, the legislature granted a charter to a special-purpose entity called the Charles River Bridge Company. In exchange for building and maintaining the bridge, the company could charge tolls for 40 years, after which it would turn the bridge over to the state government. The bridge was so successful that it repaid its investors long before the 40 years were up. In so doing, it inspired a toll bridge boom in the Northeast, leading to 59 bridge companies by 1800.[6]

The British turnpike model was also embraced by the fledgling United States. In 1792 Pennsylvania granted a charter for a toll road to connect Philadelphia to Lancaster, 78 miles to the west. As chronicled by economic historian Daniel Klein, between 1792 and 1845, some 1,562 private toll road companies were incorporated in the Northeast and Midwest, with New York, Pennsylvania, and Ohio having several hundred apiece.[7] Most were 15 to 40 miles in length, and were generally surfaced in gravel.

Unlike the British turnpike trusts, the US toll road companies were intended as for-profit ventures, and were financed largely by private stock subscriptions. Much of the investment came from citizens of communities along the route who would benefit from the improved access provided by the toll road. Few of these toll roads ended up being profitable, however. First, some were built in anticipation of settlement, resulting in lower use, and hence lower revenue, than expected. Moreover, state governments imposed restrictions such as limits on toll rates, toll exemptions for local residents, and restraints on companies' ability to restrict people's ability to go around toll booths.

The toll roads boom in the Midwest and Northeast was curtailed in the 1830s and 1840s by two competing transportation modes: canals and railroads. Canals, often state-subsidized, offered a lower-cost way to ship large volumes of freight, though many uneconomic canals were also produced due to state subsidies. Railroads offered faster passenger travel than wagons or coaches on gravel roads. Between 1826 and 1845, notes Klein, turnpike mileage dropped considerably.

But the competition also stimulated attempts to provide better road surfaces. The first improvement, as in Britain, was macadam, which offered a harder surface than gravel. The first "macadamized" US highway linked Hagerstown and Boonsboro, Maryland, as part of the road between Baltimore and Wheeling, West Virginia. The second was the Valley Turnpike between Harrisonburg and Winchester, Virginia. Built and operated by the Valley Turnpike Company under a charter granted in 1838, it was a 68-mile macadam highway. It later merged with another macadam toll road betweenHarrisonburg and Staunton, making it America's longest paved turnpike at 93 miles. It remained a toll road until 1918, when the state bought it and turned it into US 11.

A second attempt at a better road surface was the "plank road," surfaced with wooden planks. Klein reports that more than a thousand such toll roads were built in the late 1840s and 1850s, mostly as relatively short feeder roads to connect with railroad and canal stations. Although the planks were expected to last eight years or so before needing replacement, they lasted only half that long, ruining the economics of plank road companies. Most of these companies went bankrupt, though others replaced their planks with gravel—or, in a few cases, macadam.

The West was settled much later than the East, but a similar pattern of private turnpikes emerged there as well. California authorized private toll roads in 1853, leaving control of toll rates to counties. Under this general enabling act, 222 turnpike companies were incorporated. In addition, another 102 toll road companies received special charters via individual acts of legislation by 1870. However, as in the East, more companies were chartered than turnpikes were built. Klein and Yin found that out of a total of 414 that were authorized, only 159 were actually built and operated.[8] The last few incorporations took place around the turn of the 20th century, and another 200 or so turnpikes were constructed in Colorado and Nevada.

The Minimal Early Federal Role in Highways

From the very first, the role of the federal government in highways was a subject of controversy. Early presidents looked to the powers enumerated in the Constitution to decide what the federal government was permitted to do. So early advocates of a strong federal role in "internal improvements" such as highways based their cases on either the provision calling for post roads (to facilitate mail delivery by the Post Office) or the more nebulous General Welfare Clause.

The original draft of the Constitution called only for establishing post offices, but it was amended (by a vote of six states to five) to add "and post roads."[9] For the most part, the post roads provision in the 19th century was used only to *designate* certain state or local roadways as post roads. In his message to Congress in 1806, President Thomas Jefferson supported the idea of federal funding for internal improvements, but argued that an amendment to the Constitution would be necessary for this purpose. But Jefferson was not entirely consistent on the federal role. Several years earlier he had assented to the Homestead Act of 1802, to open up the Northwest Territory. Of the proceeds from federal land sales to settlers, five cents of every dollar received was allocated for transportation improvements (roads and canals) to facilitate settlement in the territory.[10] That marked the first federal aid for highways. Jefferson, also in 1806, signed the Cumberland Road Act to lay out the route for what came to be called the National Road into the Northwest Territory.

Jefferson was followed as president in 1808 by his friend James Madison, one of the drafters of the Constitution. On his next-to-last day in office, Madison vetoed the so-called Bonus Bill as unconstitutional, in part due to its intent to spend federal funds on roads and canals, based on the General Welfare Clause.[11] Madison's successor, James Monroe, likewise vetoed the Cumberland Road Bill, which would have authorized states to charge tolls on their portions of the emerging National Road. Monroe deemed the bill an unconstitutional extension of power that could not be conveyed to any state without amending the Constitution.

Continuing the pattern, in 1830 President Andrew Jackson vetoed a bill intended to help fund the Maysville Turnpike in Kentucky by authorizing the federal government to buy stock in the state-authorized turnpike company. Joseph Wood argues that this veto "brought most discussion of direct federal involvement in internal improvements to a close" for the rest of the 19th century.[12]

The National Road was laid out to open up the Northwest Territories from Cumberland, Maryland, to Vandalia, Illinois. The initial section, from Cumberland to Wheeling, Virginia (now West Virginia), was completed in 1821 at a cost of $13,000 per mile, more than twice the initial estimate of $6,000.[13] By contrast, the privately funded Lancaster Turnpike in Pennsylvania cost only $7,500 per mile.[14] Groundbreaking for the western portion of the National Road took place in 1825. In 1831 Congress began transferring completed portions of the roads to the states through which they ran, and by the time of transferring the last-completed section to Indiana in 1849, the total cost had exceeded $1.1 million (about $32 million in 2015 dollars).[15] By that time, most states had converted their sections to toll roads to be able to afford some degree of maintenance. But the National Road's generally poor condition, along with competition from the fast-developing railroads, drastically reduced traffic on it by 1850. And despite the addition of tolls, the road never came close to paying for itself.

Politics intruded from the very beginning of the National Road. Jefferson's treasury secretary, Albert Gallatin, used his influence to shift the route of the initial section through his home town, Uniontown, Pennsylvania, assuring Jefferson that this would yield important votes in the next election.[16] A number of other route choices were similarly driven by political considerations, which helps to explain the large cost overruns. And as noted previously, maintenance was generally very poor. As early as 1820, Postmaster General R. J. Meigs "found the road almost impassable and the mail, therefore, almost undeliverable."[17] By contrast, the numerous investor-funded turnpikes were better maintained, on average.

Increased Governmental Involvement in the Early 20th Century

Agitation for paved highways actually predates the advent of the automobile. The good roads movement had its origins with the growing bicyclist community, which organized the League of American Wheelmen (LAW) in 1880. While most urban roads were paved at that time, most rural roads were not. America was still very rural at the time, and rural roads mostly served farmers, for whose horse-drawn wagons the unpaved roads were acceptable. Farmers considered the LAW as "pampered interlopers who wanted other people to foot the bill for their recreation."[18] After 1890, LAW began to emphasize the benefits that paved roads would bring to farmers, such as more efficient transport of their crops to market and increases in the value of their properties due to better highway access. The Civil War veteran General Roy Stone became LAW's chief spokesman. In 1892 he helped found the National League of Good Roads as a broad-based advocacy group with its own magazine, *Good Roads*.

One of the league's first successes occurred in 1893, when Congress gave the Department of Agriculture funds to study and disseminate information on paved rural roadways. The agency created the Office of Road Inquiry in October of that year, with Stone hired to lead it. ORI's efforts received a boost when the Post Office in 1896 began to experiment with "rural free delivery" of mail. By 1899 there were 383 such RFD routes. ORI and the Post Office shared an interest in getting more paved rural roads. ORI was succeeded by a larger Office of Public Road Inquiries in 1899. OPRI carried out a national road census in 1904, finding that, out of more than two million miles of rural road, only 154,000 had any kind of pavement.[19]

The big challenge facing the good roads movement was to figure out how to pay for paved highways. Federal funding was seen as out of the question, given the 19th-century constitutional battles. So their early efforts focused on state governments. New Jersey's legislature authorized $75,000 to assist county road projects in 1891, and in 1893 Massachusetts created the first state highway agency, the Massachusetts Highway Commission, to oversee the state's highway aid fund. Between 1894 and 1903 it disbursed $6.75 million in such funding.[20] A growing number of states followed suit after the turn of the century, and in 1905 the Office of Public Road Inquiries became the Office of Public Roads, one of whose main duties was to provide technical advice to states on highway funding.

During those early-20th-century years, a private-sector approach to highway development emerged. Several organizations were formed to promote the building of specific long-distance highways. The best known were the Dixie Highway, from the Midwest to Florida; the Lincoln Highway, from New York to San Francisco; and the Bankhead Highway, from Washington, DC, to San Diego. The associations in each case consisted of business leaders, many with ties to the emerging automobile industry, plus officials of local and state governments along the proposed routes. A prime mover in the first two groups was Carl Fisher, founder of the Indianapolis 500. In 1913 the Lincoln Highway Association selected a route consisting largely of existing roads, many not paved, including some that later became US 30 from Philadelphia to Aurora, Illinois. They identified gaps and sought state and local funding to fill them in, and spent much of their effort installing signage to keep people from getting lost. The Lincoln Highway Association (LHA) continued until 1928, by which time many but not all segments of the route had been paved, and governments were increasingly involved in highway funding and development.[21]

The Dixie Highway Association was launched in 1914, inspired by the launch of the LHA the year before. In 1915 it decided to pursue two routes: one from Chicago to the west coast of Florida, and the other from Detroit to the east coast of Florida. Its composition and funding were similar to that of the LHA, and its routes were laid out and built in various segments from 1915 through 1927, at which point the DHA was disbanded.[22] Portions of the route in southeastern Florida still bear the name Dixie Highway.

The Bankhead Highway was championed by Senator John H. Bankhead (D-AL). It ran from Washington, DC, to San Diego, avoiding mountains and winter driving conditions to become "the nation's first all-weather, coast-to-coast highway." Though Bankhead championed the project in Congress, the driving force in the Bankhead Highway Association was John Asa Rountree, who also headed the US Good Roads Association. The route was finalized in 1920 and most of the road had been completed by 1931.[23]

While the highway associations were pursuing their projects, the Post Office and its allies in Congress pushed for more paved rural roads, so that parcels as well as letters could be delivered in rural areas. In 1912 a House parcel-post bill called for the federal government to pay rent to states for postal use of designated post roads in the states, but the Senate did not concur with that proposal. The final bill set up a joint committee to study the issue. When the Joint Committee on Federal Aid in the Construction of Post Roads released its 323-page report in 1915, it presented nine different possible ways to allocate federal funds for this purpose. That report provided the basis for the Federal Aid Road Act of 1916, the first ongoing program of federal aid to states for highways.[24] It provided aid to states on a 50/50 basis as long as the state had a state highway agency in place. In 1918 the highway function within the Department of Agriculture was reorganized as the Bureau of Public Roads.

But federal aid for post roads was quite limited. With the rapid growth of motor vehicles and the continued demands of the good roads movement for more paved highways, state governments came under increasing pressure to act. By 1917, all 48 states had enacted some kind of road aid law, and by 1924 all states had defined a system of state highways.[25] But where was the funding to come from? As noted, the 1916 Federal Aid Road Act required states to match federal funds on a 50/50 basis. State matching funds initially came from recently established annual registration fees for motor vehicles. But this soon proved grossly inadequate to what was seen as the demand to build and maintain paved highways.

Two Oregon legislators, both elected on a good roads platform, came up with the idea of a tax on motor fuels to be used for highway construction and maintenance. The point of collection would be at the wholesaler rather than the gas station, to keep collection costs low. Introduced in 1918, their gas tax bill was passed in 1919, and rapidly became the model that other states followed. By the end of 1919 Colorado, New Mexico, and North Dakota had followed suit. By 1924 a motor fuels tax had been enacted in 44 states and the District of Columbia, and the remaining four states enacted theirs by 1929.[26] The relatively young American Association of State Highway Officials had worked hard to achieve this result. And as highway development increased, states faced little resistance to increasing the rate per gallon—typically from the initial one or two cents to three or four cents by the 1930s. Those increases were practically invisible, because the cost of gasoline was declining, thanks to economies of scale and new methods of refining.

When the Great Depression arrived, most federal tax revenue sources decreased considerably. The Treasury Department pointed out to Congress that, by contrast, state fuel tax receipts had hardly declined at all—and suggested a federal tax on gasoline. Stakeholder groups, such as the American Automobile Association and the American Petroleum Association, opposed the idea of a federal gasoline tax, arguing that this revenue source should be left to the states for highways. Despite these groups' opposition, the Revenue Act of 1932 imposed a federal gas tax of one cent per gallon, as a one-year deficit-reduction measure. But as the Depression continued beyond 1932, so did the federal deficit-reduction gas tax. This temporary tax was renewed every year of the Great Depression.[27]

The Depression hit state budgets hard, too. Even though all but five states had set up dedicated highway funds into which their gas tax money was deposited, hard-pressed states began diverting money from gas tax receipts to help with their general funds. A review of state budget records found that the five states without dedicated highway funds were by far the largest diverters.[28] Total state diversions of gas tax revenues climbed from 2.81 percent of the total in 1930 to 18.9 percent in 1936.[29] Congress reacted negatively, based on widespread sentiment that states were reneging on the original deal by spending the state portion of highway user tax money on nonhighway purposes. In 1934 Congress enacted the Hayden-Cartwright Act, requiring the Bureau of Public Roads to withhold post roads money on the basis of the extent of a state's gas-tax diversion, and the Highway Act of 1938 provided for the redistribution of those withheld funds to the remaining states.[30] The National Highway Users Conference began urging states to pass constitutional amendments forbidding diversion from highway funds, and by 1941, 11 states had done so—a total which resumed growing after World War II, with 27 states having adopted such amendments by 1962.[31]

But Congress itself turned out to be the champion diverter of all, since it had never established any linkage between the one-cent federal gas tax and the annual post road grants. When the "temporary" tax was raised to 1.5 cents a gallon and made permanent in 1941, highway groups protested, since the proceeds did not go to highways—but to no avail. After the war, Congress again increased the tax rate, to two cents per gallon, this time to help pay for the Korean War. Comparing the amount raised over the years by the federal gas tax with the amount spent on post-road grants, Philip Burch found that nearly 60 percent had been diverted to nonhighway uses prior to 1956.[32]

Early-20th-Century Toll Roads and Bridges

Almost forgotten by transportation historians, the private toll road idea from the 19th century was revived early in the automobile era. William K. ("Willie") Vanderbilt, grandson of the railroad magnate Commodore Cornelius Vanderbilt, was an early auto enthusiast and race car driver. After a number of arrests for speeding on public roads, he decided to finance and build a toll road specifically for use by high-speed automobiles. In 1906 he incorporated the Long Island Motor Parkway Corporation for this purpose. Its board of directors included Henry Ford, August Belmont, John Jacob Astor, and other wealthy business leaders. They sold $2.5 million worth of bonds to finance what ultimately became the $6 million ($145 million in 2015 dollars) Long Island Motor Parkway. When completed in 1911, the road extended 48 miles, from Flushing in Queens across Nassau County, to the Islip area in Suffolk County. With two 11-foot concrete lanes and 64 reinforced concrete overpasses, it was America's first limited-access, cars-only highway. There were 12 "toll lodges" along the route, each housing a toll collector expected to be on duty 24 hours a day, seven days a week.[33]

Vanderbilt's Parkway never recovered its full costs, and was eventually put out of business by Robert Moses's parallel nontolled Grand Central and Northern State Parkways, which opened in 1933. By 1938 Vanderbilt's company gave up, ceding the Parkway to the governments of the three counties it traversed. But its ideas lived on in the various limited-access parkways built by Robert Moses in the 1930s, most of which were tolled: the Bronx River Parkway, the Hutchinson River Parkway, the Saw Mill River Parkway, and so on.[34] It also inspired the first toll roads in adjacent Connecticut—the Merritt Parkway and the Wilbur Cross Parkway. These were all government projects, but they were funded largely or entirely by tolls.

The private toll road principle lived on in America's toll bridges, both 19th-century ones that survived well into the 20th century, and new ones financed and built in the first half of the 20th century. According to a report produced for the 75th anniversary meeting of the International Bridge, Tunnel & Turnpike Association (which began as the American Toll Bridge Association in 1922), as of 1932 the United States had 322 toll bridges, of which nearly two-thirds were privately owned.[35]

The largest and best-known of these toll bridges is the Ambassador Bridge, linking Detroit with Windsor, Ontario. Because it would link two countries, the bridge required approval of both the Canadian and the US governments. The civil engineer Charles Fowler organized two companies, one in each country, and obtained permission from Congress for the bridge in the 1920s, but he was unable to raise the needed funds. The banker Joseph Bower came to the rescue, buying up Fowler's companies and their franchise. He commissioned the design of what would then be the world's longest suspension bridge, and raised the capital to construct it. He also overcame political opposition from the mayor of Detroit, winning a referendum there by an eight-to-one margin. Construction began in May 1927 and was completed by November 1929, at a cost of $23.5 million ($322 million in 2015 dollars)[36]. Though it has changed hands several times since 1929, the bridge survived the Depression via a refinancing and remains investor-owned today.

Far less well known is the private-sector origin of most of the toll bridges in the San Francisco Bay Area. While the best-known ones—the Golden Gate Bridge and the San Francisco–Oakland Bay Bridge—were government toll projects, the other major toll bridges in the Bay Area originated as private franchises like the Ambassador Bridge. The American Toll Bridge Company in 1923 received a 25-year franchise from Contra Costa County and completed the Antioch Bridge in 1925. Under a similar franchise, it completed the Carquinez Bridge in 1927. Likewise, the Dumbarton Bridge Company negotiated a franchise with Alameda and San Mateo Counties to build the Dumbarton Bridge across the lower portion of the Bay in 1924, and opened that bridge in 1927.And the San Francisco Bay Toll Bridge Company received a 50-year franchise from San Mateo County in 1927 and opened the 7.1-mile-long San Mateo Bridge in 1929. The two government toll bridges were financed and built in the 1930s, with the San Francisco–Oakland Bay Bridge opening in 1936 and the Golden Gate Bridge in 1937.[37]

All six of these bridges suffered declines in traffic and revenue due to the Depression, but the Bay Bridge and the Golden Gate opened closer to its end and were therefore less affected. Their financing costs were also lower, with the Bay Bridge getting low-cost financing from the New Deal's Reconstruction Finance Corporation, and the Golden Gate being able to issue tax-exempt toll revenue bonds, rather than the taxable bonds issued by the toll bridge companies. In addition, the California legislature voted in 1933 to relieve the Bay Bridge of having to cover operating and maintenance costs out of toll revenues, allocating state highway fund (gas tax) monies to cover those costs. The four private toll bridges all went into receivership by 1940. Unlike the Ambassador Bridge, they were unable to work out refinancing plans and were eventually acquired by the state, with the Dumbarton and San Mateo transfers not taking place until the early 1950s; their shares traded on the Pacific Coast Exchange until then.[38]

A similar fate befell many of the other 200-odd private toll bridges during the Depression. The Reconstruction Finance Corporation provided low-cost loans to public-sector toll bridges, but not to investor-owned ones. Relatively new government toll agencies offered buyouts to struggling bridge owners during those years. The New York State Bridge Commission bought four private toll bridges over the Hudson River; the Delaware River Joint Toll Bridge Commission acquired at least six private toll bridges; and the city of Dallas bought the toll bridge on the Trinity River in order to eliminate the tolls.[39] By 1940, the Public Roads Administration (the former Bureau of Public Roads, now part of the Federal Works Agency) reported that the number of US toll bridges had declined to 241, of which 142 were still investor-owned. But nearly all the bridges had been bought out by toll agencies or state and local governments by the mid-1950s.[40]

During the 1920s and 1930s, populist antitoll sentiment arose in some states. In Louisiana a group of investors had won a franchise to build a five-mile-long toll bridge across Lake Ponchartrain. A preexisting state law had called for a nontolled bridge, but there were no funds available to build it. Anticipating that he would soon run for governor, Huey Long campaigned against it, telling the promoters, "Go build that bridge, and before you finish it, I will be elected governor and you will have free bridges right alongside it."[41] Long ran for governor in 1928, and was elected shortly after the toll bridge opened. Though he did not serve a full term as governor, being elected to the US Senate during his first term, he brought about the construction of two nontolled bridges along US 90, east of the toll bridge. With much of its traffic diverted, the toll bridge went into receivership and was sold to the state in 1938 for $940,000.

Government Toll Authorities

The idea of a public-sector "authority" to finance, build, and operate toll facilities arose around the turn of the 20th century in New York. One antecedent was the fiasco over building the Brooklyn Bridge. In 1866 the New York state legislature passed a bill authorizing construction of a toll bridge over the East River, between Brooklyn and Manhattan. In 1867 the New York Bridge Company was incorporated, and it obtained the franchise to develop the project as a private toll bridge. The noted New York City political operator William "Boss" Tweed and his Tammany Hall colleagues were deeply involved with the company, and a highly publicized scandal led to Tweed's arrest in 1871 on charges of bribery, fraud, and grand larceny. As a result, the legislature revoked the company's franchise, and the project proceeded as a public-sector toll bridge, finally opening in 1883. The initial toll was 10 cents for a horse and wagon, 5 cents for a horse and rider, and 1 cent for a pedestrian. New York City rescinded tolls in 1911, paying off the bonds out of general city revenues.[42]

The corruption associated with the original private toll model for the Brooklyn Bridge served to discredit this model in many people's eyes, especially in New York City, the financial and media capital of the country. The Progressive Era, beginning around the turn of the century, fostered the idea of replacing political influence with scientific management by technical experts—and to the Progressive reformers this meant a much larger role for government. This perspective was reflected in the trend of states setting up highway departments, frequently led by engineers. And for major, more costly highways and bridges, it also led to the idea of government toll authorities intended to operate much like business enterprises, but serving only the public good rather than seeking profits.

The idea had originated in Europe, with some public authorities dating back as far as the reign of Queen Elizabeth I. By the early 20th century, the example best known to US Progressives was the Port of London Authority. It became the model for the Port of New York Authority, set up via an interstate compact between New York and New Jersey, and later renamed the Port Authority of New York and New Jersey (PANYNJ). It was created in 1921, it issued its first bonds in 1926, and (according to Robert Moses' biographer Robert A. Caro), it did "not become financially successful until 1931, when after five years of near fiscal disaster, it would persuade the two states to let it take over the highly successful Holland Tunnel, which had been constructed by an independent commission."[43] In the early 1930s the Port Authority persuaded the bond community to accept a new method of toll finance. Instead of each bond issue being backed by the toll revenues from a specific project, it would issue bonds based on the toll revenues from its *portfolio* of projects, new and old, as the agency expanded and did new projects, some of which might be much harder to finance on a stand-alone basis. The first project financed in this manner was the new Lincoln Tunnel.

Robert Moses, the legendary public-sector developer of New York parkways, bridges, tunnels, and much else, adopted this model after initially having created single-project authorities for several bridges and parkways. For his later projects, he persuaded the legislature to modify the law that had set up his Triborough Bridge Authority, expanding the scope of its authority and essentially enabling it to become permanent, rather than being limited to the life of its bonds. That meant the toll revenues on all its projects would be pledged to meet the debt service (bond payment) needs of all its projects, so that the tolls would continue indefinitely. While solving the problem of funding weaker projects (via cross-subsidies from stronger ones), it also created incentives to fund boondoggle projects whose transportation benefits were less than their costs.

The New Turnpike Era

The public authority model was seen as financially successful, and it became the dominant way in which 20th-century US toll roads were developed. The prototype for what became known as the turnpike era was the Pennsylvania Turnpike. Following the limited-access model pioneered by Vanderbilt's Long Island Motor Parkway—superior pavement, banked curves for high speed, overpasses or underpasses at all intersecting roadways, and so on—it added an additional feature for safety: a median separating the eastbound and westbound lanes, to minimize the chances of head-on collisions. The cost of such a superhighway was far beyond that of normal highways of the 1930s, so it made sense to finance the project based on toll revenues. And the superior performance offered to motorists created a value proposition that justified paying more than ordinary gas taxes to use it. This proposition was borne out by the huge popularity of the turnpike when its first 160 miles opened in 1940. Using the turnpike, drivers could get from Harrisburg to Pittsburgh in just two and a half hours, compared with about six hours on the two-lane US 30.[44] After World War II, the turnpike was extended west to the Ohio border and east to Valley Forge, and then to the New Jersey border.

Many other states followed suit, with the Maine and New Hampshire Turnpikes opening in 1947; the Massachusetts Turnpike and New Jersey Turnpike in 1951; the Oklahoma Turnpike in 1953; the Garden State Parkway (in New Jersey), New York State Thruway, Ohio Turnpike, and Illinois Tollway in 1954; the Connecticut Turnpike in 1955; the Indiana Toll Road and Kansas Turnpike in 1956; the Florida Turnpike and West Virginia Turnpike in 1957; and the Delaware Turnpike and Kennedy Memorial Highway (in Maryland) in 1963.[45] All these turnpikes, except for Florida's, were grandfathered into the Interstate Highway System authorized by Congress in 1956, and were allowed to continue their tolling despite the 1956 legislation's ban on tolls for all new Interstates begun thereafter and paid for via fuel taxes.

The faster-growing urban areas—especially in the Southeast and West—needed more expressway capacity than could be funded via fuel taxes, so the 1960s witnessed the beginning of a second wave of public-authority toll roads in Atlanta; Dallas–Fort Worth; Denver; Houston; Miami; Orlando; Orange County, California; Richmond; Tampa; and the northern Virginia suburbs of Washington, DC.

The Interstate Highway System

From the earliest days of the United States, some had called for the federal government to master-plan and fund a set of highways linking the states together. Indeed, in 1808 Treasury Secretary Albert Gallatin produced such a plan in response to a Senate request. His report proposed that the federal government fund the construction of highways linking key Atlantic coast cities such as Boston, New York, Philadelphia, and Washington) to Western cities such as Detroit, Saint Louis, and New Orleans. When Congress some years later enacted a bill to charter a special-purpose bank to finance Gallatin's roads, President Madison vetoed it.[46]

Thereafter, as noted previously in this chapter, the federal role was far more modest, helping the states to fund post roads well into the early decades of the 20th century. The Depression, and especially the New Deal, stimulated proposals for the federal government to fund public works in order to create more employment. Advocates of an expanded federal highway role took great interest in the fledgling German autobahn superhighway system, begun under Adolf Hitler in 1933. Pennsylvania's Rep. J. Buell Snyder in 1938 proposed a superhighway plan: it called for three major east-west routes and five or six north-south routes, to be financed by toll revenue bonds.[47] Officials at the Bureau of Public Roads (BPR) were asked to study the issue. Their report, *Toll Roads and Free Roads*, contended both that tolled superhighways would not provide enough capacity to address growing traffic needs, and would not generate enough toll revenue to pay off their bonds—a somewhat contradictory pair of conclusions. Indeed, both contentions were called into question several years later by the stunning success of the Pennsylvania Turnpike. Nevertheless, though rejecting toll finance, BPR drafted a plan for 26,000 miles of federal superhighways. The idea was popularized by the General Motors "Futurama" exhibit at the 1939–40 New York World's Fair, with its model of 12-lane high-speed superhighways.

In 1941 President Roosevelt appointed a National Interregional Highway Committee, chaired by BPR leaders, to further develop the federal superhighways concept. Its 1944 report inspired the Federal-Aid Highway Act of 1944, which added a proposed 40,000-mile superhighway system to the existing set of highways eligible to receive federal aid. But the question of how to fund the system was left unaddressed.[48] With the huge increase in postwar automobile traffic, Congress began debating how to pay for the planned superhighways. Despite hearings on the subject in 1948, 1950, and 1952, no agreement on funding was reached. It was during this time that many states in the Northeast and Midwest emulated the Pennsylvania Turnpike model, planning and financing tolled superhighways on their own. But low early turnpike traffic in thinly populated Oklahoma and West Virginia suggested that the toll-finance model might not work nationwide in the America of the early 1950s.

When Dwight Eisenhower became president early in 1953, he asked his senior advisors to revisit the toll-finance approach, despite the antitoll mindset at BPR. They concluded that an overall toll-based interstate highway system could be feasible if revenues from high-traffic states could be used to help support the bonds of the corridors in lower-traffic states. They also advised that the system not include costly urban expressways, but rather should provide bypasses around urban areas—a position that FDR had also held. In 1954 Eisenhower appointed a committee to review the options and recommend the best way forward. In January 1955 the Clay Committee, chaired by Gen. Lucius Clay, recommended a $25 billion interstate superhighway system paid for by toll revenue bonds.[49]

Congress rejected the Clay proposal, due to antitoll concerns of some members, but especially due to the antidebt position of the powerful Sen. Harry F. Byrd (D-VA), chairman of the Senate Finance Committee. That led to proposals in both the House and the Senate for an increased federal motor fuels tax to pay for a new Interstate Highway System. There was strong opposition from the oil industry, the tire industry, and the trucking industry, and neither bill was enacted in 1955. Several factors led to success in 1956. First, BPR had quickly come up with plans to add 5,000 miles of urban Interstate to the overall plan, which led to support from previously uninterested members of Congress from urban constituencies. Second, both the oil industry and the trucking industry changed their positions after rethinking the benefits that a national superhighway network could bring them. Another important change was an amendment by the House requiring that all revenue from the new federal fuel taxes go into a highway trust fund and be used only for the Interstate program. The Federal Aid Highway Act of 1956 was passed, and was signed by President Eisenhower on June 29, 1956.

Over the next 40 years, state highway departments built nearly all of the originally planned rural and most of the urban Interstates. In contrast to the 1956 bill's $25 billion cost estimate, the total cost was estimated by the transportation scholar Jonathan Gifford as $418 billion in 2001 dollars.[50]

In 1956 dollars that would be $64 billion, which is 2.5 times the original estimate. Gifford also noted that, with its major role for the federal government in planning and funding, despite state ownership and operation of the highways themselves, the Interstate system was a great exception to the normal pattern: "most U.S. infrastructure systems developed from the bottom up," even though the federal government did play some role—for example, by providing land grants to the developers of the first transcontinental railroad, and by granting AT&T a monopoly over most telephone service for the majority of the 20th century. Gifford concluded that "the sense of normalcy [of a dominant federal role] to which the transportation community has become accustomed for the past half-century is ending."[51]

Along the way, what had begun as a federal program solely to fund the building of the Interstate Highway System turned into a tool by which the federal government extended its remit into every detail of surface transportation. After the first decade of Interstate construction, it became evident that the program would cost a lot more than expected, and would take far more time than the initially estimated 15 years to be completed. Accordingly, the three-cent-per-gallon gas tax was increased to four cents in 1959, and the program began a long process of being periodically "reauthorized" for additional periods of years. (The fuel taxes would have expired at the end of each such period unless Congress reauthorized them.)

As the Interstates neared completion, state highway departments broadened their scope to become departments of transportation, or DOTs. By this time, they had become accustomed to getting large fractions of their budgets as federal highway aid, so the idea of the trust fund and the federal fuel taxes as something temporary gradually faded away. The Highway Trust Fund also took over what had once been grants for building post roads, meaning that all federal fuel taxes—plus assorted other small transportation excise taxes, such as those on tires—went into the trust fund and could be used for any number of federal-aid highway programs. Thus, what had been a temporary program focused on a specific, time-limited objective gradually evolved into an all-purpose federal-aid highway program. But the principle that highway user taxes would be spent solely to benefit highway users was maintained.

That pure users-pay / users-benefit principle was breached in 1970, when a new law, PL 91-605, allowed federal highway monies to be used for bus lanes, bus facilities, and park-and-ride lots. Many urban interests and transit advocates wanted to open up the Highway Trust Fund much further, since they were dissatisfied with the extent of funding available from the Urban Mass Transportation Administration (UMTA), created by 1964 legislation to provide federal grants to local transit agencies. UMTA was originally located within the Department of Housing and Urban Development (HUD), but was shifted to the Department of Transportation when the latter agency was created in 1967. Several years later, in 1973, Congress went further in this direction, enacting PL 93-87, which (1) allowed Highway Trust Fund monies to be used for capital expenditures for buses and rail transit facilities, and (2) permitted a state to petition the US Department of Transportation for permission to withdraw a planned urban Interstate project and build a public transit system instead, using federal general fund monies up to the amount that the Interstate segment would have cost.

President Jimmy Carter proposed consolidation of the highway and transit programs, merging the Federal Highway Administration (FHWA) and UMTA, as part of the 1978 highway bill. But that bill ended up making only minor program changes. And that status quo prevailed until the early years of the administration of President Ronald Reagan. Secretary of Transportation Drew Lewis had been persuaded of a need for increased federal highway investment, but had difficulty convincing Reagan to support the corresponding federal fuel tax increase. To build transit groups' support for the measure, "he [Lewis] promised to create a mass transit account in the Highway Trust Fund that would receive 20 percent of the revenue from a five cent per gallon tax hike (the 'transit penny'). This convinced many big city Democrats and liberals to support the measure, despite their concern over the effects of the tax on the poor."[52] After first promising to veto the bill, Reagan changed his mind after the 1982 elections, and signed the bill after it finally passed, in January 1983. The federal gas tax more than doubled, from four cents to nine cents per gallon.

That bill, the Surface Transportation Assistance Act of 1982 (PL 97-424), established a Mass Transit Account within the Highway Trust Fund, to receive "one-ninth of the amounts appropriated to the Highway Trust Fund" from all federal motor fuels taxes from then on. As Jeff Davis's history of the Trust Fund notes, the changes from 1973 through 1982 "represented a shift away from the 'benefit taxation' model . . . whereby user fees are levied on system users in proportions that are as close as feasible to the direct benefit that the users get out of the system." He adds that, "although the votes brought to the table by the transit lobby were the key to getting the biggest-ever increase in the 'user fee' on drivers and truckers, the addition of mass transit to the Trust Fund made the gas and diesel taxes resemble true 'user fees' much less."[53] The gas tax was increased again, to 14.1 cents per gallon in 1990.

Since the 1982 legislation, every subsequent reauthorization of the federal program has led to further departure from the users-pay / users-benefit principle. The most sweeping change occurred with the enactment of the Intermodal Surface Transportation Efficiency Act (ISTEA) in 1991. It created two new programs within the Highway Trust Fund, both of which were to be "flexible" in that states and metro areas could switch funds from highway to nonhighway uses. The Surface Transportation Program (STP), funded at $23.9 billion over six years, allowed highway funds to be spent not merely on transit projects, but on bike paths, sidewalks, recreational trails, landscaping, and historic preservation—all under the rubric of "transportation enhancements." The Congestion Mitigation and Air Quality Program (CMAQ), funded at $6 billion, funded a wide variety of projects intended in some manner to reduce emissions and/or reduce congestion. To help pay for these new programs, the gas tax was increased again, to 18.4 cents per gallon. ISTEA also imposed extensive new transportation planning requirements on metropolitan planning organizations (MPOs). As the political scientist James Dunn notes, "The increased complexity of planning infrastructure investments reflects so many goals (air quality, promoting public transit, historic preservation, wetlands protection, environmental justice) that moving cars can get lost in the shuffle."[54]

Subsequent reauthorization measures—TEA-21 in 1998 and SAFETEA-LU in 2005—further expanded the extent of "flexibility" and increased both the number of specific transportation programs and the complexity of transportation planning requirements.

All of this illustrates the loss of national purpose and focus in the federal transportation program as it now exists. When legislation in 1956 expanded the federal government's role in transportation to create the Interstate system, the Interstates were clearly a national project with national benefits in fostering interstate commerce. They continue to provide national benefits for both goods movement and personal travel, for recreation and for business. Other major highways that connect one state to another also have national benefits. Urban Interstates and other principal urban arterials offer a combination of local and national benefits.

Traffic calming in Tampa and Boise or bike paths in Buffalo and Phoenix do not provide national benefits. Paying for them with highway user fees also diminishes the users-pay / users-benefit principle, and increasingly transforms fuel taxes from user fees to transportation taxes paid by one group to benefit other groups. While the evolution of the federal highway program into a kind of all-purpose transportation-related public works program is understandable on a political level, this transformation has very likely undermined voter support for increasing federal fuel tax rates, since those taxes are no longer as credible as "user fees" as they once were.

In this chapter we have seen that tolling and the private provision of highways have a long history, with failures as well as successes. We have also seen how US policy moved away from those concepts in the 20th century, to give us the highway institutions that were characterized in chapter 1 as an increasingly flawed system. In chapter 4 we will review how a number of other advanced countries rediscovered toll finance and private-sector involvement in major highways during the second half of the 20th century.

CHAPTER FOUR

The Rediscovery of Toll Road Companies Overseas

How Other Countries' Highway Systems Differ from Ours

M ost Americans take our system of highway funding and management for granted, assuming that other countries use more or less the same system. In fact, the United States is virtually the only country that, however imperfectly, dedicates motor fuel taxes to highways. To be sure, all developed countries charge taxes on gasoline and diesel—indeed, in Europe those taxes are four to eight times higher than US fuel tax rates.[1] But other countries' fuel taxes are not "user taxes"—they are general revenue sources for the government. And to the extent that those governments have evolved a political philosophy that cars are less desirable than mass transit and passenger trains, they have increased motor fuel taxes to very high levels in order to discourage driving and to subsidize other alternatives.

Without a dedicated funding source for highways, what determines how much those governments spend on their highways? In a word, politics. Every year when parliaments convene, highways are just one of numerous items competing for however much money the government decides is available to be allocated—for schools, medical care, parks, pensions, and so on. Demand by people for better highways has little to do with these political decisions, except when a transportation crisis occurs. The German government collects 1.8 times as much in fuel taxes as it spends on all forms of surface transportation combined; the UK government collects nearly *three times* as much in fuel taxes as it spends on surface transportation infrastructure.[2]

Besides politicized funding, the situation for European highway users is worse than America's in another way. Most governments in Europe are far more centralized than in the United States. We saw in chapter 3 that all major US highways, including the Interstates, are owned and operated by state governments or by their agencies, (such as turnpike authorities). In most of Europe, with exceptions discussed below, highways are owned by national governments. In the United States, competition among states means that a state that chronically neglects its highways will be less attractive as a place to live and do business than a state with good highways. In many European countries, bad highway policy may apply to nearly all highways—although within the European Union, countries do compete with one another for residents and businesses.

That dismal situation does have some notable exceptions. The need to compete with other countries in Europe stimulated the development of tolled superhighways in several countries, mostly after World War II, when the continent's infrastructure needed major reconstruction. And these countries' rediscovery of the private turnpike idea proved so successful that it was picked up in Australia, Asia, and Latin America by the end of the 20th century. How and why this happened is the subject of this chapter.

Europe's Motorways

The Superhighway Pioneers: Italy and Germany

The story begins in Italy, which pioneered the idea of tolled motorways in the 1920s. The first such road, developed as an investor-owned utility, received authorization from the national government in 1921, and the first link between Milan and Varese opened in 1924. By the end of the 1930s, more than 250 miles of two-lane and four-lane *autostrade* were in operation. It took some years after World War II ended before Italy's economy had recovered enough to support expansion of the system. A government holding company that had been created during the Depression, IRI (Institute for Industrial Reconstruction), took the lead in expanding the *autostrade* system. In 1950, IRI created a wholly state-owned company, Autostrade Concessions and Construction, for this purpose. Autostrade negotiated an agreement with a company called ANAS to build and operate the Autostrade del Sole (the limited-access A-1, from Milan to Naples), which was completed in 1964. Many other toll roads followed, creating a tolled motorway system that today encompasses more than 4,000 miles, most of it four-lane or six-lane. Unlike the practice in the United States, where Interstate highways were built through the middle of cities, the Italian *autostrade* system built bypasses around—not through—major cities, including Bologna, Catania, Milan, Rome, and Turin.[3]

In 1982 the company that evolved from ANAS and Autostrade Concessions was incorporated as the Autostrade Group, which as of then operated 52 percent of Italy's tolled motorways. The other postwar additions were developed by investor-owned companies operating under long-term franchises called toll concessions. IRI was the majority shareholder of Autostrade Group, with a small number of private shareholders owning the rest. After a moratorium on building *autostrade* between 1978 and 1991, expansion of the system resumed in the 1990s and 2000s, with major routes being widened and some existing routes extended further into southern Italy. In 1999 the Autostrade Group was privatized via a public share offering. With its status changed to that of an investor-owned company, Autostrade Group signed long-term concession agreements with the government for its existing toll roads, putting it on the same footing as the other toll road operators. In 2007 Autostrade was renamed Atlantia.[4]

The only other country to develop superhighways prior to World War II was Nazi Germany. Its famed system of autobahns, originally called *Reichsautobahnen*, was wholly a government project aimed both at individual travelers (as was the government-developed Volkswagen, or people's car) and at reindustrialization and military transport. By 1942 the system extended to some 1,300 miles, at which point further development stopped due to the war. The autobahns, like the Pennsylvania Turnpike that they inspired, were the first true superhighways, with two or more travel lanes each way separated by a wide median, limited entry and exit points, and grade separations at all intersecting roads. In keeping with the system's nature as a top-down government project, there were no private-sector operators like in Italy, and no tolls. The national government used tax money to pay for the whole system.

West Germany continued this model as the country was rebuilt following the war, making selective additions to the autobahn network, and retaining the top-down national government ownership and operation, along with tax funding. When Germany was reunified following the fall of the Berlin Wall in 1989, the national government spent billions upgrading the autobahn system in the former East Germany, in many cases adding far more capacity than would be needed for a long time.

France Evolves to Modern Toll Concessions

The French tolled motorway system is one of the world's largest. It evolved over several decades, beginning in the mid-1950s. Due to burgeoning traffic as the economy recovered from the war, the government decided to supplement the extensive national system of two-lane highways with a network of four-lane superhighways called *autoroutes*. Because government resources were limited, in 1955 a new law was enacted allowing toll-financed autoroutes as an exception to the general rule that highways should be free. The toll-financed autoroutes were to be developed only by mixed-economy companies, called Societes d'Economie Mixte (SEMs), with a majority of the ownership being governmental. By the end of the 1950s, two such SEMs had been created and awarded concessions for two short autoroutes.[5]

Initial progress on building the network was slow, so in 1960 a more aggressive plan for a 2,175-mile network was approved, and three additional SEMs were created. Toll finance became the general rule, rather than an exception. The initial main routes linked Paris to Lyon and Marseilles in the south and to Lille in the north, and also included east-west routes from Paris to Caen and from Marseille to Nice. During the 1960s the French Highway Directorate actually built and operated the new autoroutes for the SEMs, while the SEMs themselves focused mostly on tolling and debt-service payments. But under this system, only 700 miles of roads had been completed by the end of the 1960s.

The incoming government of Georges Pompidou made three key changes to accelerate progress on the network. It permitted wholly private companies to bid for concessions to develop and operate new autoroutes. It also enabled the SEMs to play a much larger role, designing, building and operating their autoroutes, not just being financiers and toll collectors. The third change was a new master plan that called for adding another 1,865 miles of roadway during the 1970s. Four investor-owned companies won competitions for new autoroutes in the early 1970s, and the newly empowered SEMs also got new routes.

But the oil price shocks in 1974 dealt a serious blow to the autoroutes. Construction costs more than doubled between 1971 and 1978, and interest rates increased as well. Traffic that had been growing rapidly leveled off. Together, much higher costs and stagnant toll revenue led to serious financial problems for SEMs and private concessionaires, even as the expansion goals were met. By 1980 there were more than 3,100 miles of autoroute in operation, 2,300 miles of which were toll concessions.[6]

The new Socialist government of Francois Mitterand that took office in 1981 made further changes in government policy. The Communist minister in charge of highways, Charles Fiterman, sought to take over the

private concession companies and abolish all tolls. The latter was financially impossible, since the government would have had to pay off all the
bonds and had no resources to do so. Fiterman was persuaded that one of
the concession companies, Cofiroute, was viable despite higher construction costs and lower-than-expected toll revenues, but he nationalized the
other three, converting two to SEMs and requiring an existing SEM to ab-
sorb the third. Fiterman also tried to make toll rates uniform nationwide,
but due to some autoroutes having much higher debt service costs due to
more costly construction, he settled for reducing the disparity between
the highest and lowest rates per mile from three to one down to two to
one. He also created a new government agency, Autoroutes de France, to
engage in cross-subsidies among SEMs (partly to counter the impact of
his attempt at toll harmonization). Despite its faults, this system stabilized
the finances of the SEMs and Cofiroute, making possible a further expansion of the network under a 1990 master plan aiming at a 5,900-mile network. By 1997, the total in operation had grown to 5,550 miles, of which
4,030 miles were toll concessions.[7]

Major changes took place in the last years of the 20th century and the
first decade of the 21st. Instead of just relying on the existing SEMs and Cofiroute, the government decided once again to open the market for new toll
projects to the private sector. The impetus for this change was a plan from
the Haute-de Seine regional government for a hugely ambitious 30-mile
underground road and rail project just west of Paris, called Maille Urba-
ine Souterraine Express (MUSE)[8]. With the cost estimated at $4.7 billion,
funding it was far beyond the government's means, even with toll revenues.
The private sector was invited to submit bids, and a 50-year concession was
awarded to Bouygues/SGE in 1993. But the project was dependent on a
subsidy from the national government, which the Communist transport
minister refused to give, so the project was never developed.

A smaller but still risky project to close the missing link in the A86 ring
road around Paris with a 6.2-mile, $2 billion toll-financed tunnel ended
up winning approval. The original surface route had been planned to cut
through the middle of historic Versailles, and was understandably fought
bitterly for many years. Cofiroute made an unsolicited proposal to the
French government in 1988 to finance, develop, and operate the project
as a toll concession without government subsidy. Its innovative design reduced the diameter of the tunnel, and hence its cost, by limiting its use to
auto-size vehicles, on two decks: one northbound, the other southbound.
Because France had no formal concession law at that point, the original
agreement was overturned in the courts in 1998, after construction had

begun in 1996. A new competition was held and Cofiroute won, negotiating a new 70-year concession agreement. Construction resumed in 2000, and the tunnel opened to traffic in June 2009 (northern section) and January 2011 (southern section).[9]

By 2000, soliciting competitive bids from concession companies for new toll roads had become the new standard, with the proviso that the government was prepared to put in some degree of funding for projects it deemed desirable but were not fully toll-financeable. The first two concessions awarded under this new approach were the 78-miles A28 tolled autoroute in northern France ($265 million) and the 1.55-mile Millau Viaduct, conveying the A75 over the Tarn Valley in southeastern France ($265 million). The beautiful cable-stayed viaduct is the world's highest bridge, with the deck 800 feet above the valley floor. Developed under a 75-year concession agreement, it opened to traffic in 2004.[10] Since then, many other toll concessions have been awarded.

Another major change was the privatization of the SEMs early in the 21st century. In 2001, Finance Minister Laurent Fabius announced plans to sell many state-owned enterprises, including the SEMS, using the proceeds to reduce the national debt. The first sale was a part-interest in the largest SEM, Autoroutes du Sud de la France (ASF). The initial share sale in 2002 transferred 49.7 percent of the ownership to investors. This was followed by a public share offering of 30 percent of the second largest SEM, Societe des Autoroutes Paris-Rhin-Rhone (SAPRR) in 2004, raising $1.8 billion. Another share sale led to Vinci acquiring 23 percent of Societe des Autoroutes du Nord et de l'Est de la France (SANEF). Finally, in 2005 the government sold all of its remaining interest in the SEMs. Through a competitive bidding process, the remaining shares generated $17.8 billion for the government, converting ASF, SAPRR, and SANEF into investor-owned concession companies. Vinci became the majority owner of ASF, with Eiffage and Macquarie winning the majority of APRR, and a consortium headed by Spain's Abertis winning the majority of SANEF.[11]

Thus, by 2005 all of France's toll motorway network—nearly 5,000 miles—had become the responsibility of investor-owned companies.

Spain and Portugal

Both Spain and Portugal followed France's lead, somewhat later in time. And both also went through changes of government that led to support for and opposition to both tolling and concessions.

Spain's first law authorizing toll highways was enacted in 1953, but only one small concession (for a tunnel near Madrid) was approved during that decade. As the economy grew, congestion became a problem on Spain's national network of two-lane highways. Finally in 1967, the government adopted a national motorway plan calling for the construction of 2,980 miles of tolled *autopistas* by 1985.[12] Between 1967 and 1972, five companies were granted concessions, with the initial routes focused on Barcelona and the Mediterranean coast to Valencia and Alicante, as well as radial routes to and from Madrid, Bilbao, and Seville. These projects worked well, so the government in 1972 formalized the terms and structure of toll concessions and the next year increased the size of the planned network to 4,100 miles. Seven more concessions were awarded from 1973 to 1975. During this period the government provided no cash subsidies, but did provide loan guarantees and protection from exchange-rate risk on foreign loans taken out by the concessionaires.

The oil crisis of the mid-1970s led to financial problems for the concession companies similar to those experienced in France. The socialist government elected in 1982 brought a radical change in direction for highway policy. The new highway plan for 1984–91 called for building the rest of the motorway network as nontolled *autovias*, rather than tolled *autopistas*. But the government could not afford to build them to superhighway standards, so they opted to upgrade many of the two-lane highways, avoiding the need for all-new right-of-way and accepting their sharper curves, shorter ramps, and some at-grade intersections. The plan called for a total of 3,500 miles, of which 2,000 miles would be lower-standard, nontolled autovias and the other 1,500 miles would be tolled autopistas. The government also nationalized three of the concession companies that were in the deepest financial distress.

Toll concessions made a comeback, due to subsequent changes in government policy. First, although the national government was responsible for all intercity highways, regional and city governments were responsible for urban-area highways. By the late 1980s, the regional government in Catalonia decided to use toll concessions to develop tolled expressways for the Barcelona metro area. Between 1987 and 1990 it granted three such concessions, two of which developed a major tunnel beneath the mountains separating Barcelona from its western suburbs. By 1984, Spain's national government was concerned about the autovia program being behind schedule, especially with the impending 1992 Olympics in Barcelona and World's Fair in Seville. This led to a 1988 highway plan that increased the network to 3,800 miles to be completed by 1991, with newer autovias developed to the same design standards as the tolled autopistas. The considerably higher cost of this expanded program led the national government back to toll finance and concessions.[13]

Accordingly, toll concessions expanded considerably in the late 1990s and early 2000s. Major Spanish concession companies, short of new business during the autovia era, had expanded overseas, particularly in Latin America. By the time Spain turned back to concessions, major concessionaires such as Cintra, ACS, Acciona, and FCC were larger and financially stronger as a result of their non-Spanish projects.[14] In 2000 the government awarded toll concessions to build and operate four tolled expressways to relieve congestion on the radial autovias linking Madrid with its suburbs: the R-2, R-3, R-4, and R-5. Another tolled expressway followed in 2003, linking Madrid to its new Barajas International Airport. In 2004, the development ministry Fomento awarded four toll concessions for new intercity autopistas that cost $2.5 billion to construct.

Because the cost of expanding the nontolled autovia system was becoming unaffordable, both the national government and the regional governments implemented a new way to finance these projects. The idea was to use a type of concession, originated in the United Kingdom, under which the private company would still finance, build, operate, and maintain the highway but the government would pay a "shadow toll" for each trip made on the highway. This would spread the government's cost over several decades, rather than having it occur all upfront. The stream of shadow toll revenue was assumed to be certain enough for the winning company to obtain financing, similar to what was done in normal toll concessions backed by actual tolls paid by motorway users. Some very large projects were financed in this way by regional governments including Catalonia, Galicia, Madrid, and Valencia. One of the largest national projects was $5 billion worth of shadow toll projects to upgrade (to full expressway standards), operate, and maintain more than 700 miles of autovias built in the 1980s, under 19-year concessions.

Another major development was the privatization of Empresa Nacional de Autopistas (ENA), the state-owned toll agency that owned and operated 293 miles of autopistas. ENA had been created in 1984 to bail out and finish construction of concession projects that had fallen victim to the financial crisis resulting from the oil shocks of the 1970s. Nearly all the major Spanish toll companies bid, as did some foreign institutions, and the winner was Sacyr, paying $1.8 billion. As in France and Italy, the

privatization of the state-owned toll operator led to negotiating concessions of various lengths, ranging from 34 to 75 years, for the individual toll
roads in its portfolio.[15]

Portugal followed Spain's lead about a decade later, but this time the
initiative came from the private sector. A group of investors, construction
companies, and banks incorporated a toll concession company in 1972
called Brisa Auto-estradas de Portugal. Its goal was to finance, build, and
operate a 245-mile network of tolled motorways under concessions from
the national government. When some of the participating banks were nationalized in 1975, that made the government the majority owner of Brisa,
thus making it a mixed enterprise like France's SEMs (ironically, its largest
private shareholder at that point was a subsidiary of the French construction giant Eiffage). The next year, Brisa's fledgling toll roads were hit by the
oil crisis, putting the company into financial distress.

In 1985, with the network partially in operation, the government enacted a program of economic reform which included an effort to make
Brisa economically viable. Accordingly, the government temporarily
(from 1985 to 1991) took responsibility for debt service, as well as financing the unbuilt 40 percent of the network. As the network expanded, traffic and therefore toll revenue increased, and by 1997 the company had
reimbursed the government for all funds advanced to finish building the
network, and had begun developing plans to return to the private sector.
In November of that year, the government sold 35 percent of Brisa to
investors, with another 35 percent sold in 1998 and 13 percent more sold
in 1999, leaving the government only as a minority (17-percent) owner.[16]

As part of the economic development program following its entry into
the European Union in 1986, Portugal's government decided to open the
toll concession market to other companies. It held a major competition
for a concession to finance, build, and operate a new 10.5-mile toll bridge
across the Tagus River near Lisbon. The resulting Vasco de Gama Bridge
cost €1 million (about $1.3 billion at that time), and was one of the larg-
est toll concessions in Europe. Two new toll motorway concessions were
awarded in 1997, and another five in 1999 and 2000.

Another part of the program featured an expansion of the motorway
network to corridors with lower traffic potential than those in Brisa's original network. Portugal adopted Spain's model of shadow toll concessions
for this purpose. Some €3 billion worth of shadow toll projects—referred
to as SCUTs, meaning "without passing costs on to the users"—were
awarded competitively in 1999 and 2000.

The Great Recession of 2008–10 hit the real-toll and shadow-toll systems hard in both Spain and Portugal. Unprecedented levels of unemployment led to large reductions in traffic and hence toll revenue for the toll concession projects, while the severe budget problems of the national and regional governments made it difficult for them to provide the promised shadow toll payments, even though these were now lower than projected because of lower traffic levels. Even worse from the government's standpoint, some of Portugal's SCUTs had been financed not on the basis of shadow tolls based on actual traffic counts, but on the basis of "availability payments." In those cases, the government's payments depended solely on the extent to which all the lanes of the highway were in operation and were maintained in good condition. Hence, unlike in the case of shadow tolls, where the reduced traffic reduced the government's payment obligations, with availability payments those obligations were unchanged. In 2010, Portugal's Court of Auditors rejected nearly all the availability-payment concessions awarded since 2008 as unsustainable.[17] In 2011, one condition of a €78 billion financial bailout from the European Union and the International Monetary Fund was to halt all concession deal-making until completion of an external review of the liabilities involved. And in 2012, the government imposed a 30-percent cut in availability payments to those companies.[18] We will return to these problems in chapter 6, discussing the lessons learned from other countries' experience with highway concessions.

Australia's Urban Tollways

With most of its population living in a handful of coastal metro areas (Sydney, Melbourne, Brisbane, Perth, etc.), most expressway-type highways in Australia have been within, rather than between, those metro areas. And unlike in most of Europe, where highways are planned at the national level, in Australia the individual states are responsible for most highways, as they are in the United States. There are no fully grade-separated, limited-access divided highways between the major cities, though portions of routes such as Melbourne to Sydney do have those characteristics. Thus, the mostly urban pattern of motorway development in Australia differs considerably from that of Europe.

The most extensive urban motorway system is in the largest metro area, Sydney. The state government of New South Wales (NSW) developed four short freeways in and near downtown Sydney during the 1950s, but the policy focus changed in the 1960s and '70s to a combination of mass transit and traffic-signal coordination on arterial roadways. These policies failed to cope with rising traffic congestion, especially as Sydney rapidly suburbanized during those decades. The idea of tolled motorways evolved out of a project in the 1980s to relieve congestion on the iconic Harbor Bridge by adding a parallel tunnel. Since that bridge had been financed by tolls, the same method seemed the logical way to finance the new 1.7-mile tunnel. What was new was the idea that the private sector would build and operate it, under a version of the long-term concession model. The winning bidder was a 50/50 joint venture of Australia's Transfield and Japan's Kumagai Gumi. The NSW government did the financing, so the concessionaire was responsible for design, construction, operation (including toll collection), and for maintenance for a period of 30 years from the time construction finished in 1992.[19]

The revival of urban expressways began in the late 1980s while the Harbor Tunnel was under construction. The initial plan was to build radial routes to link the burgeoning suburbs to downtown Sydney, and the first project to gain approval (in 1988) was the M2 (Hills Motorway) to the northern suburbs. This time, the government opted for a true toll concession, in which the developer-operator took on traffic and revenue risk, in addition to risks in construction and operation, and invested equity in addition to issuing toll revenue bonds. The success of this first toll concession led to other radial motorways based on the same concession model: the M4 Western Motorway, the M5 Toll Road to the southwest, and later the M1 Eastern Distributor, linking downtown to the Sydney International Airport, mostly via tunnel. In the 2000s, several more motorways were added: the M7 Orbital Motorway, running north-south in the western suburbs and connecting to several of the radials, and two toll tunnels: the A$750 million Cross-City and the A$1.1 billion Lane Cove.[20] These two tunnels were the only failures among the NSW toll concessions; both went bankrupt within a few years of opening due to greatly overoptimistic traffic and revenue forecasts. Consistent with the risk-transfer provisions of the concession agreements, there were no government bailouts; only investors took the losses, and new operators bought up the concessions at less than half the construction costs, refinancing the tunnels on the basis of more realistic traffic and revenue projections.[21]

The NSW government's confidence in the toll concession model was demonstrated by its continued use in recent years. In 2010, the government negotiated for the M2 concessionaire to widen that motorway at its own expense, in exchange for an extension of the duration of its concession. A similar agreement was reached in 2011 for widening of the M5. And in 2013, a major new 20-mile, A$17 billion motorway in the western suburbs, the WestConnex, was approved as a toll concession, with both NSW and the national government providing a portion of the capital, given the very high costs of this project.

Melbourne, Australia's second largest city, has followed a somewhat similar path, though it started later. Like Sydney, it had a few freeways dating from the 1960s, but in this case they were radial routes from the suburbs that stopped well short of downtown. The first toll concession project, the 14-mile Melbourne CityLink, was a way to link them up, permitting through trips from one suburban area to another. Due to the built-up nature of downtown Melbourne, significant portions of CityLink were built either elevated or as tunnels. The lack of room for toll plazas led to CityLink being Australia's first all-electronic toll road. Proposed in 1992, it was approved in 1994, and the winning bidder for the 34-year toll concession was Australian company Transurban. The A$1.8 billion project was opened to traffic in 1999 and has been quite successful.[22]

On the basis of that initial success, the Victoria government embarked on a larger project, ConnectEast, a 24-mile north-south toll road through Melbourne's eastern suburbs. Two consortia competed for the concession in autumn 2003, and the winning bidder was the team of Macquarie Bank and two construction companies owned by Leighton Holdings. The A$2.5 billion project opened to traffic in 2008, five months ahead of schedule. Unfortunately for the concessionaire, although traffic was respectable, it was below projections and the project was not profitable. In 2011 the owner ConnectEast Group accepted a A$2.4 billion offer from Horizon Roads.[23]

The disappointing results from ConnectEast led to the decision by Partnerships Victoria, the state's public-private partnership agency, to adopt a different concession model for the next motorway project, Peninsula Link. This 17-mile expressway to the southeast of Melbourne was procured on a design-build-finance-operate concession, in which the concessionaire is compensated not by toll revenue or shadow tolls but by availability payments from the government over the 25-year term. There are no tolls on this expressway, whose cost was A$759 million. The financing was closed (completed) in early 2010, and Peninsula Link opened to traffic in 2013.[24]

A fourth Melbourne expressway concession—the A$6.8 billion 11-mile East-West Link, including a major tunnel—was awarded to a consortium in autumn 2014. But an election shortly thereafter led to a new government, which opposed building the project. After months of negotiation, a termination agreement was reached in which the Victoria government agreed to pay A$339 million to cover the consortium's bidding, design, and preconstruction costs.[25]

The story of expressway concessions in Brisbane is not as positive as the results in Sydney and Melbourne. The Queensland state government initially developed several of its expressways as state-owned tollways: the Gateway, Gateway Extension, and Logan motorways. After noting the success of toll concessions in Sydney and the similar success of CityLink in Melbourne, state transportation planners decided to think big. Their first two toll concession projects were both major urban toll tunnels in Brisbane.

The North-South Bypass Tunnel (later called CLEM 7) was a A$3 billion project, awarded in 2006 after a competition to RiverCity Motorway, a consortium led by Leighton Contractors, as a 49-year toll concession. Of the total length of 4.2 miles, 2.9 miles were twin tunnels. In addition to the usual debt plus equity financing, the consortium also issued shares to individual investors on the stock market. CLEM 7 opened to traffic in 2010, but after just 11 months it was forced into receivership, wiping out the equity of shareholders, both individual and corporate. The cause was drastically overestimated traffic and revenue. A buyer was found in 2013, paying just A$618 million for the project.[26]

Brisbane's second project was the A$4.8 billion Airport Link toll road, awarded to BrisConnections, a consortium of the Australian firm Macquarie and construction subsidiaries of Leighton in 2008. Although only four miles long, it was nearly all twin tunnels. As with the CLEM 7 project, the consortium raised part of the finances by an initial public offering of shares to the public, raising A$1.2 billion from them. After opening to traffic in 2012, it suffered the same fate as CLEM 7, with traffic and toll revenue far below projections. It suspended trading on the stock exchange in November 2012, and filed for bankruptcy in February 2013.[27] It was later acquired by Transurban for A$1.9 billion.

These spectacular bankruptcies, including that of Lane Cove in Sydney, led to five lawsuits lodged by various parties against the companies that had provided overly optimistic traffic and revenue forecasts. Among the points raised in these suits were misleading and defective conduct and negligent misstatement. The noted former traffic and revenue forecaster Robert Bain served as an expert witness in some of these cases, and has dubbed them examples of "advocacy forecasting," raising questions of professional ethics.[28] Based on his years in the forecasting profession, Bain has written a guidebook on the subject, explaining not only limitations in current forecasting models but also ways in which traffic and revenue forecasts can be inflated, if pressures to do that exist.[29]

In both the Brisbane cases, investors lost their equity, and debt providers had to reduce the value of what they were owed. When Brisbane sought bidders for a third tunnel project in 2010, it opted for a different model: a toll project funded by availability payments. The winning bidder for the A$1.5 billion Northern Link Toll Road was a consortium led by Spain's Acciona. The concession is for just 10 years, during which the company will build and operate the tunnel.[30]

Having not done well with risky "greenfield" projects—brand-new toll roads and tunnels—the Queensland government changed course on involving the private sector. State-owned Queensland Motorways Ltd., operator of the legacy Gateway Motorway, the Go-Between Bridge, the Logan Motorway, and CLEM 7, was acquired by the state-owned Queensland Investment Corporation in 2013, and that entity put these highway assets on the market as a 40-year concession. In 2014 the winning bidder was selected: a consortium of Transurban, Australian Super (a pension fund), and Tawreed Investments (a sovereign wealth fund). Financial close was reached in July 2014 for this A$7.1 billion acquisition.[31]

Asia Adapts the Model

Japan's equivalent of the US Interstate highway system was developed by government toll agencies. In 2005 these agencies were privatized, with the largest, the Japan Highway Public Corporation, broken up into East, Central, and West Highway Companies and the three urban toll authorities converted to commercial companies. Since many of the toll roads had been developed for political reasons rather than sound economic reasons, altogether they had accumulated $395 billion in debt, far more than their toll revenues could support. The debt was taken over by a newly created government holding company, Japan Expressway Holding & Debt Repayment Agency (JEHDRO), which holds title to all the toll roads and bridges. The new toll companies now must pay rent to the government holding company, which hopes to retire the debt over a period of 50 years or so.[32]

Toll roads and concessions came to China via Hong Kong. Prior to its handover to China in 1999, Hong Kong had developed its major bridges and tunnels as toll-financed concession projects. As the Shenzhen economic zone adjacent to Hong Kong developed into an economic powerhouse, the need for better highway infrastructure became apparent. Hong Kong business leader Gordon Wu, a graduate of Princeton University who had marveled at the New Jersey Turnpike while a student there, was the prime mover in bringing about China's first toll concession highway, the 76-mile Guangzhou-Shenzhen Superhighway, which opened in 1994.

China had previously announced plans for a National Trunk Highway System of more than 40,000 miles, and as time went on, many portions of it were developed via toll financing. Often these projects were sponsored by companies owned by provincial governments, and were carried out under concession-type arrangements, but over time some of the companies were privatized, either via public share offerings or by acquisition of majority ownership by overseas companies. Macquarie's International Infrastructure Fund, for example, in 2007 bought 90 percent of South China Highway Development Ltd., the developer and operator of a 19-mile tolled expressway in Guangzhou, under a 27-year concession agreement.[33] A report from China's National Audit Office in 2008 estimated the total length of tolled highways in the country by that point at 82,700 miles, with the large majority sponsored by local and provincial governments.[34] By 2010 a number of Chinese toll road companies had been listed on the Shanghai and Hong Kong stock exchanges, and China Infrastructure Investment Corporation was listed on the NASDAQ.

A number of China's toll concession projects qualify as megaprojects. The world's largest ocean crossing is the $2 billion, six-lane Hangzhou Bay Bridge, which first opened in 2008. Another is the $1.9 billion Changjiang Tunnel-Bridge Expressway, which links Shanghai's Pudong area to Chongming Island; it includes a cable-stayed bridge and twin 50.5-foot-diameter tunnels nearly six miles long. Another such project is the 5.5-mile Jiazhou Bay Tunnel, which opened in 2011. An even bigger megaproject is the $10 billion, 31-mile Hong Kong-Zuhai-Macao Bridge across the Pearl River Delta, scheduled for completion in 2017.

Japan and China are not the only Asian adopters of the toll concession model. A number of tolled expressways have been developed in India, Indonesia, Malaysia, and South Korea, using variants of toll concessions. Despite its huge size, India only began a serious national highway program in 2006, aiming to expand about 8,000 miles of two-lane intercity highways to four or six lanes. Ambitious goals to use toll concessions for major portions of this network have been announced several times, beginning in 2008. But the credit markets crunch in 2008–10 slowed things down considerably. In 2011, India's transport minister announced a revised $41 billion private-sector highway investment goal over the next four years, but only a fraction of that has materialized.

Two of the major concession projects in South Korea are the $1.6 billion, 7.6-mile Incheon Bridge, opened in 2009, and the $1.8 billion Busan-Geoje fixed-link bridge-tunnel project, opened in 2010.[35] Malaysia's most impressive project is the SMART Tunnel in Kuala Lumpur, the world's first dual-use tunnel. It combines a six-mile stormwater tunnel with a two-mile double-deck roadway within a single 37-foot-diameter tunnel. Usually there is no water in the tunnel, but when flooding is expected, it is closed to vehicles.[36]

Latin America Embraces Toll Concessions

Mexico was the first country in Latin America to adopt the toll concession model, in the 1990s. But its program was poorly structured, awarding most concessions based on the shortest proposed length of the concession term. The result was that toll rates were set so high that few autos or trucks used the new toll roads, and most went bankrupt and were taken over by the government by early in the 2000s. By 2005 the government had resumed awarding concessions for new toll roads on a more realistic model, and in 2007 it began auctioning off the toll roads it had previously nationalized. To make toll concessions more appealing to investors, in 2009 it extended the maximum concession term to 50 years, allowed state-owned banks to provide credit for such projects, and permitted pension funds to invest in such projects.[37]

South America's largest country, Brazil, also has the continent's largest toll concession program. As early as 2007, the national government alone had more than 5,000 miles of toll-concession highways in operation, mostly upgrades of former two-lane highways into four-lane limited-access tollways. That same year, state governments began offering toll concessions to upgrade state highways on a similar basis. After a pause during the 2008–9 credit-markets crunch, both state and federal toll-road concessions resumed at the end of that decade. And in 2015, the recession-plagued government announced a new $64 billion concessions program, including $21 billion worth of toll-highway projects.

Another major player in South America is free-market-oriented Chile, a long, narrow country that has used toll concessions to upgrade much of the Pan American Highway over its length. Its other showcase for concessions is the 93-miles urban expressway system of Santiago, its capital city. The system has developed over a number of years via toll concessions won by four different consortia, with most of the corridors in operation by 2006. Common tolling standards permit full interoperability, so a motorist in the metro area needs only one vehicle-mounted transponder and one toll account, no matter which expressways he or she uses. Chile's concessions law was modified in 2008, after which new concessions were awarded for several additions to the Santiago network as well as several new intercity toll roads.[38] In 2014 the government announced plans for a new concessions agency and an expanded program, with $22 billion needed over the next five years in the transport sector.[39]

In the 1990s, Argentina was an early adopter of toll concessions at both the national and the provincial level. But, as part of an interventionist plan to recover from a major bond default in the early 2000s, the government froze toll rates until 2009, leading to bankruptcies of some of the concession companies. Nevertheless, in 2009 the province of Buenos Aires was able to find a willing bidder to develop remaining portions of a 930-mile toll road and to take over concessions that were expiring. The total value of that project was estimated at $1.9 billion.

Colombia and Peru are relative latecomers to toll concessions, but both have ambitious projects underway. In Peru, one set of concessions covers major upgrades to its section of the Pan American Highway (Ruta del Sol). The other major project is a 1,550-mile highway system linking Peru's three main coastal ports with Brazil's Amazon region. And Colombia's National Institute of Concessions is underway on a program to double the route-miles of toll road in the country, aimed at adding 3,100 miles via concessions. The program includes both intercity and urban tollways, including Colombia's portion of the Pan American Highway.

The United Kingdom, Germany, and Canada Take a Different Route

Despite Britain's long history of turnpikes and toll bridges, toll concessions have not caught on there. The same is true of Canada and autobahned Germany. All three have enlisted the private sector to upgrade and maintain various highways, using availability-payment concessions rather than toll concessions.

The United Kingdom once had a dedicated highway fund, created in 1909 and based on motor vehicle taxes, a decade before Oregon's pioneering gasoline tax. Within a few years, surpluses began to accumulate in the UK Road Fund, and Financial Secretary John Walker Hills began arguing in 1923 that the surpluses should be transferred to the general fund. His argument won over the new chancellor of the exchequer, Winston Churchill, who began doing so in 1926. Parliament formally abolished the dedicated revenue stream in 1936.[40]

Faced with a serious infrastructure investment shortfall in the 1980s, Margaret Thatcher's administration authorized several UK toll bridge concessions, such as the Dartford Crossing, a four-lane, cable-stayed bridge over the Thames River, to relieve congestion in the existing Dartford Tunnels. Only one toll concession highway project, the M6Toll (the Birmingham Northern Relief Road), was authorized in 1989, the year before Thatcher stepped down. Construction was delayed by legal challenges until 2000, and the road opened in 2003. Traffic and revenue were still far below projections at the end of 10 years, leading concessionaire Macquarie to cede ownership to the project's 27 lenders. They opened bidding for the concession in the autumn of 2016.

The subsequent Conservative government of John Major wanted private-sector involvement in highways as well as other infrastructure, but it did not favor tolls. Under its Private Finance Initiative (PFI), the government offered concessions for companies to finance, build or refurbish, operate, and maintain buildings, highways, and other infrastructure in exchange for a stream of payments from the government over the full term of the concession. For highways the payments were to be shadow tolls, as in Spain and Portugal, based on traffic counts. The first eight projects, with 30-year concessions, were offered in 1994 to upgrade and maintain eight highways.[41] The subsequent Labour government, not keen to reward growth in driving, changed the model for subsequent concessions to availability payments. The largest of these projects, announced in 2005, was to widen and maintain half of the M25 ring road around London. The winning bidder, in 2008, was a Balfour Beatty/Skanska consortium. The $8 billion project was awarded as a 30-year concession.

Canada has followed a similar path. Apart from a handful of toll bridges and one major toll highway—Toronto's 407ETR, the world's first all-electronic toll road—Canadian provinces have used availability payment concessions for most large highway projects since the turn of the 21st century. Among the projects being undertaken in accordance with this model are the ring road around Calgary, the Sea-to-Sky highway and Golden Ears Bridge projects in British Columbia, the Disraeli Bridge in Winnipeg, and Montreal's A25 highway. Montreal's $2.2 billion Champlain

Bridge will be one of the largest availability payment concessions in North America.

Germany in recent years has used tolls very selectively, mostly via a nationwide program that charges heavy trucks a more proportionate share of highway costs. Its only toll concessions were for two toll bridge projects, neither of which proved to be financially viable. Instead, the government has brought in the private sector to widen and maintain various stretches of the autobahn via shadow-toll concessions, which it calls A-model highway projects. Six of these 30-year concessions were awarded between 2007 and 2011, with an explicit shift in the most recent of them to availability payments instead of shadow tolls. A second wave of A-model concessions was announced at the end of 2013, encompassing seven more autobahn widenings.

Generally lacking dedicated highway user revenues, German highways and bridges are increasingly in bad shape. A 2015 report by the *Christian Science Monitor* referred to "Germany's chronic underinvestment" in transportation infrastructure, citing German headlines about "crumbling bridges, lengthy detours, [and] snarled traffic on an aging autobahn." It cited figures from the German Institute for Economic Research (DIW) in Berlin that found 46 percent of bridges, 41 percent of streets, and 20 percent of highways in need of repair. The lack of investment seems to be tied to the German practice of funding transportation infrastructure out of general tax revenues rather than user fees. Hence, such investment "has been constrained by [Germany's] drive to balance its budget."[42] The television network CNBC did a follow-up report in 2016, finding that Germany's infrastructure "has been slowly deteriorating from a lack of investment over the past few decades."[43]

Conclusions

A wide array of countries, beginning with France and Italy in the 1960s, have brought private finance, development, operation, and maintenance into the highway sector, to an extent that dwarfs the very small start down this road taken by the United States in recent years (as we will see in chapter 5). The French, Italian, Portuguese, and Spanish counterparts of our Interstate highway system were all developed and operated by what are now for-profit businesses, operating under long-term concession agreements. The toll concession model has also been the primary vehicle for major urban and intercity motorways in Australia, China, other Asian countries, and the major countries in Latin America.

The reasons for this extensive use of tolling and private-sector investment and management vary from country to country, but one key factor has been the lack of a dedicated funding source for highways, such as our more-or-less dedicated federal and state fuel taxes. The types of projects done via concessions also vary, from developing intercity superhighways from scratch in much of Europe, to upgrading two-lane highways into modern motorways in Latin America, and to developing modern urban expressways in Australia's largest cities as well as in several major cities in Latin America.

The concessions tend to be long-term, with few shorter than 30 years and some exceeding 70 years, depending on the size and riskiness of the projects. The financial bases of the concessions are of two basic types. In traditional toll concessions, the government delegates tolling authority to the concessionaire, which thereby takes on the risk that traffic and revenue may not be enough to cover all costs. But in shadow-toll and availability-payment concessions, the funding comes from government, not from highway users, thus shifting the payment responsibility and the traffic and revenue risk to the government. The relationship between the government and the concessionaire varies considerably, depending on the type of concession and the provisions of the concession law in each country. We will explore these differences, and their implications, in chapter 6.

CHAPTER FIVE

Toll Concessions Return to America

During the mid-1980s, privatization of government functions was in the air. In Britain, Margaret Thatcher's government had been divesting state-owned enterprises such as British Airways, the British Airports Authority, British Gas, the state-owned electricity and water industries, and much more. In the United States, the Reagan administration sold off the nationalized Conrail freight railroad, long-term leased Dulles and National Airports, and appointed the President's Commission on Privatization to look at other federal entities that could be divested or contracted out. At the state level there was a new level of interest in urban toll roads, with new projects underway by public-sector toll agencies in Denver; Houston; Orange County, California; and the northern Virginia suburbs of Washington, DC. In this time of ferment and innovation, pioneers stepped forward to reintroduce to the United States the toll concession concept, under which investor-backed companies would enter the toll roads market. One project was in Virginia and the other in California. These initial projects laid the groundwork for state-enabling legislation to permit such projects in more than half the states by 2010.

The Toll Concession Pioneers and Their Landmark Projects

Ralph Stanley and the Toll Road Corporation of Virginia

Ralph Stanley was part of the Reagan administration's cadre of change agents. When he was appointed head of the Urban Mass Transportation Administration in 1983, the 32-year-old Princeton graduate was the youngest administrator of any federal agency. He moved aggressively to shake it up, creating an Office of Private Sector Initiatives and holding annual conferences on the private sector and public transit.

In 1986 the Municipal Development Corporation (MDC) was launched in New York City to assist state and local governments with various forms of privatization, from competitive contracting for service delivery to development and operation of new infrastructure such as wastewater treatment plants and toll roads. One of MDC's first proposals was to privately finance and develop a 14-mile westward extension of the relatively new state-run Dulles Toll Road in northern Virginia. The extension would connect Dulles Airport with Leesburg.

Ralph Stanley left UMTA in 1987 to become vice chairman of MDC, relocating to New York. One of his first projects was a small private toll bridge across the Red River, linking Fargo, North Dakota, with Moorhead, Minnesota. The project was a joint venture of MDC and a local firm, the Bridge Company, organized several years earlier to get the bridge built. The Bridge Company had already obtained tax-exempt bond financing via the city of Moorhead, but local lawsuits against the project were holding up construction. MDC purchased a half-interest in the Bridge Company in September 1987, providing additional capital as well as a short-term loan to jump-start construction. With the lawsuits settled, construction took only eight months, and the bridge opened in June 1988. It took first place in the streets/highways/bridges category in *American City & County*'s fifth annual Awards of Merit competition. Stanley subsequently did extensive research on deficient bridges, aiming to launch a company (or a division of MDC) called the Bridge Corps, to finance and develop the replacement of worn-out bridges.

As an appointee on the President's Commission on Privatization in 1987, Stanley began spending more time in Washington again, and he pursued MDC's interest in the Dulles Toll Road Extension project. He found that 20th-century Virginia law had no provisions for private-sector toll roads, and that a 1950s law banned charging tolls for profit, so he began to lobby for enabling legislation. The most straightforward approach seemed to be to add investor-owned toll roads to the set of utilities regulated by the State Corporation Commission. The idea found favor with Democratic Governor Gerald Baliles, and the result was the Virginia Highway Corporation Act, enacted in 1988.[1]

With the law in place, Stanley set up the Toll Road Corporation of Virginia and began the task of getting permission to develop and operate the Dulles extension project. Initially, the Virginia Department of Transportation (VDOT) was not favorable, seeing the extension as its future turf. Stanley managed to persuade the Commonwealth Transportation Board anyway, which issued a permit in July 1988 for TRCV to do the project rather than VDOT. But Stanley's hard work was only beginning. In addition to creating the detailed financing plan required by the Corporations Commission, he had to assemble a team that could finance, build, and operate the project. He also had to explain the project to citizens, landowners, and environmental groups to build support and counteract any serious opposition.

His initial team included the construction firm Kiewit, the investment bank Goldman Sachs, the consulting engineering firm Parsons Brinckerhoff, and the traffic forecaster Vollmer Associates. Since the enabling legislation did not grant land condemnation power to TRCV, Stanley had to persuade the mostly rural landowners to donate right-of-way on the basis of expected land-value increases from the much-improved access the tollway would provide. He recruited Magalen Bryant, a wealthy landowner and conservationist, as one of his key backers, and made a point of adjusting the right-of-way to avoid wetlands and other sensitive land uses.

These efforts took years longer than anyone expected, but by 1992 the environmental permits were in hand, 49 of the 50 needed parcels of land had been obtained, and VDOT and the Corporations Commission were on board. But the financing proved to be very difficult to arrange, eventually resulting in the ouster of Stanley and his team and in TRCV being restructured as a partnership called Toll Road Investment Partnership 2 (TRIP 2). Most of the project team of engineering and financial firms changed, too, with a new financing deal put together by early 1993. Groundbreaking finally took place in September 1993, with the toll road renamed the Dulles Greenway. TRIP 2 consisted of Mrs. Bryant's family investment firm Lochnau Ltd., the Italian toll road owner-operator Autostrade International, and the general contractor Brown & Root, which together provided $68 million in equity. The institutional investors included Cigna, John Hancock, and Prudential Power, and provided $258 million of long-term toll revenue bonds.[2]

The difficult path to that groundbreaking and subsequent construction is documented in detail by Bill Reinhardt in a case study published in *Public Works Financing*:

> That the Dulles extension got funded and put under construction as a taxable, privately sponsored startup toll road is viewed by many as a minor miracle. From the land assembly, to the environmental permitting, to the comprehensive agreement with the state on the design, construction, and operational details, to the toll and rate of return regulation, to the coordination among the

five jurisdictions that had veto power over land use—any one [of which] could have stopped the deal before it got to the financing stage.

That they didn't is a testament to the unity of purpose of the public and private sponsors behind Dulles. Successive governors and local political leaders have been strong supporters of the off-budget financing offered by the private developers. State transportation needs far outstrip available funds. Surplus revenues from the existing Dulles toll road from the airport to the Capital Beltway are tied up in Richmond. And rural Loudoun County is being strangled by congestion as traffic grows each year.[3]

The good news is that, once begun, the Dulles Greenway construction was finished six months ahead of schedule, in September 1995. We will look into the toll road's subsequent performance later in this chapter.

Ralph Stanley moved on in 1993, becoming a senior executive at a new joint venture called United Infrastructure Corporation (UIC), created by Bechtel and Kiewit to pursue private toll road projects nationwide.

Carl Williams, Bob Best, and the Caltrans Private Toll Road Pilot Program

Similar late-1980s discussions of privatization and toll roads took place in California, which, like Virginia, had struggled with population growth and inadequate highway funding. The subject came to the attention of the transportation community when articles appeared in local media about the toll concession motorways in France and Italy. Several major design and engineering companies communicated their interest in such projects to the author.

There was also growing interest in road pricing as a way to reduce traffic congestion. Charging a higher price during rush hours would lead some motorists to shift nonessential trips to other times of day, and motivate others to car-pool or use public transit for their commutes. A system of this kind had been implemented in Singapore in 1975 and had significantly reduced congestion. But it did not charge variable prices; in order to use the expressways during peak periods, motorists had to purchase and display stickers on their windshields (daily, weekly, or monthly). Singapore stationed numerous watchers on overpasses to spot vehicles without stickers, for enforcement purposes—a costly and not very accurate system. What was needed for variable pricing was some way to do electronic road pricing.

Transportation agencies in several states, including California, had been working to develop systems for automatic vehicle identification (AVI)—basically a unique identification number that could be read electronically as a vehicle passed a radio-frequency antenna. The first such system was developed for the trucking industry in the 1980s, to automate truck weigh stations on highways so that preapproved trucks would not have to stop. This became the heavy-vehicle electronic license plate (HELP) program, now operational in 31 states under the name PrePass.[4] Caltrans also tested a prototype AVI system for toll collection on the Coronado Bay Bridge in San Diego.

But the first commercially successful AVI system was the "toll tag" developed and marketed by the Amtech Corporation. In December 1987, Amtech signed a contract to equip the Dallas North Tollway with its system for electronic toll collection at all of its toll plazas. For the lanes so equipped, there would be no need for toll collectors and no need for the car to stop. All drivers who mounted a small electronic toll tag on their windshield could go through special toll lanes at low speed but without stopping, "paying" their toll electronically. But while the Dallas North Tollway was using the system simply to reduce costs and increase throughput at its toll booths, the larger potential lay in using it to implement variable pricing: charging variable tolls at highway speeds without any toll booths at all.

Three key ideas were brought together in a Reason Foundation policy paper called "Private Tollways: Resolving Gridlock in Southern California."[5] It called for adding express lanes to congested freeways based on three key ideas:

- private-sector finance, development, and operation on the European toll concession model,
- congestion pricing with variable tolling, and
- highway-speed electronic toll collection using the new toll-tag technology.

The Reason Foundation paper was released in May 1988, but it generated no immediate interest. The California transportation community's attention was focused on a statewide transportation bond issue on the June ballot. When the ballot measure was defeated, an op-ed piece in the *Los Angeles Times* summarized the private alternative.[6] The next day both the governor's office and the Caltrans director's office requested copies of the policy paper.

After reading the paper and engaging in several long discussions with its author, Caltrans Assistant Director Carl Williams proposed putting together a workshop called "Private Sector and Urban Congestion." With participants from a number of companies that had been exploring the private-concession idea (the Parsons Corporation, De Leuw Cather, Cushman Realty, and the French company Spie Batignoles), the workshop took place in Pasadena on August 5. The discussion was sufficiently positive that Williams decided to seek enabling legislation, with the support of his boss, Caltrans Director Bob Best.

The bill they drafted, AB 680, was introduced by Republican Assemblyman Bob Baker, and was generally supported by Republican legislators. Democrats instead wanted a phased-in gas tax increase. The eventual compromise was a package of bills to be voted on together, including the private tollway bill and the gas tax increase, with the latter subject to voter approval. The package was enacted on June 30, 1989. AB 680 authorized four toll-financed projects, of which at least one had to be in northern California. Winning bidders would each be granted a 35-year concession. There would be no state or federal funding whatever. Beyond that, the legislation left the details up to Caltrans.

Best put Carl Williams in charge of implementing the new legislation, and Williams later became director of the new Office of Privatization. One of his first actions was to create a Privatization Advisory Steering Committee to develop the implementation process. It included three private-sector members (including the author) along with eight Caltrans people (mostly directors of its urban districts). Best and Williams decided that the process should be wide open and global. Instead of selecting projects and then inviting private firms to bid, the solicitation would be open-ended: "Have the private sector market projects to us," Best explained at the initial Steering Committee meeting.[7]

The committee created a several-step process. The first step, in October, was to publicize the new program via advertisements in the *Wall Street Journal*, key overseas publications, and transportation media. Next step was a request for qualifications for toll revenue transportation projects, inviting companies to form consortia and demonstrate their qualifications to finance, design, build, and operate toll-financed projects, issued in November. By the deadline date in January 1990, 13 teams had submitted qualifications, 10 of which were deemed fully qualified. Next we debated and developed evaluation criteria for the proposals the qualified firms would be invited to submit. The formal request for proposals was sent out in March, with proposals due August 1, 1990.

Eight consortia submitted proposals for seven projects; two had selected the same project, SR 125 in San Diego County. Using the evaluation criteria from our committee, a Caltrans selection committee scored the proposals and selected the four highest-scoring ones as the winners, subject to successful negotiation of concession agreements. Three proposals were for new urban-area toll roads, filling in missing links in long-range freeway development plans, and the fourth was for express toll lanes, along the lines of the Reason Foundation paper,[8] to be added to SR 91, a congested freeway in Orange County. The winners were announced on September 14, 1990. The total proposed investment in the four projects was $2.5 billion.[9]

Negotiating the concession agreements was complicated, since neither Caltrans nor the US members of the winning consortia had any experience with this type of project. But all four agreements were completed by January 1991. Since both Caltrans and the private sector were leery of subjecting these new projects to the regulatory control of the California Public Utility Commission, the AB 680 legislation allowed European-type regulation via terms and conditions built into the concession agreement. In addition, utility-type price regulation would not work for projects with variable tolls whose purpose was not only to pay for the project, but to ensure free-flowing traffic. With advice from financial consultant Price Waterhouse, Caltrans decided not to regulate the prices charged, but to put a cap on the investors' overall rate of return on their debt and equity. Specific rate-of-return ceilings were negotiated for each project, and in any future year in which toll revenues led to a return in excess of the agreed-upon rate-of-return ceiling, the excess revenues would be given to Caltrans and used for the state highway fund.

After the four concession agreements had been signed in 1991, a powerful state senator, Bill Lockyer, who would later become state treasurer, introduced a bill that would rescind the contracts; it failed to gain traction. The Caltrans engineers' union, Professional Engineers in California Government (PECG), filed suit arguing that the concession agreements were unconstitutional, but that suit was dismissed by the state Appeals Court in 1993.

Only two of the four projects ended up being implemented. Extensive local and environmental opposition doomed the proposed Mid-State Tollway in the eastern part of the San Francisco Bay Area. And the proposed Santa Ana Viaduct Express in Orange County (essentially an 11-mile tollway built above the concrete channel of the Santa Ana River) fell victim to a combination of excessive cost and local opposition. The first project to be built was the express toll lanes in Orange County, dubbed the 91

Express Lanes. The project opened to traffic in December 1995, and these express lanes have delivered uncongested rush-hour trips every year since then. But the South Bay Expressway (SR 125) in San Diego County faced a much greater challenge. It took more than a decade of litigation with environmental groups and others before the project finally cleared environmental review in 2003. It was then financed and built, opening to traffic at last in 2007.[10]

The Difficult Next Wave

Despite the delays in working out the details of the Dulles Greenway in Virginia, and the difficulties encountered by three of the four winning projects in California, the fact that some of the best companies in the business—both overseas and domestic—were willing and able to finance and develop new toll-financed projects had a powerful impact on financially stressed state DOTs, governors, and legislators.

Three individual projects moved forward in 1990—in Illinois, Puerto Rico, and Texas. In Illinois a consortium was formed to pursue a project that had been studied for several years: a proposed $2.2 billion, 400-mile toll road between Chicago and Kansas City, aimed especially at attracting heavy trucks via higher weight limits and higher speed limits.[11] That project eventually died, due to unclear financial feasibility as well as the lack of enabling legislation in Illinois. A Texas landowner launched a feasibility study of a 21-mile toll road across his land, aimed at giving trucks from the border crossing at Laredo a faster and more direct expressway route to I-35. The resulting Camino Columbia toll road was subsequently built and opened to traffic in 2000, but it went bankrupt in 2003, with the investors taking the loss.[12] The only success from this trio of proposals was a new toll bridge providing a direct connection between downtown San Juan, Puerto Rico, and its airport. The bridge was financed in 1992, built, and put into operation via a 35-year toll concession agreement with the Spanish company Abertis.[13]

State private toll road enabling acts were introduced and debated in a number of states. Arizona enacted a four-project pilot program law in 1991, largely inspired by the California and Virginia enabling acts. Florida passed a general enabling act that same year, while legislatures in both Illinois and Minnesota debated but did not pass toll concession legislation that year. In 1993 Minnesota and Washington State enacted enabling legislation, and bills to do likewise were debated in Georgia and Massachusetts. In 1995 new toll road measures were enacted in Delaware, Missouri, Oregon, and South Carolina.

Private toll road proposals were sought and received under the new enabling legislation in Arizona in 1992,[14] in Washington State in 1994,[15] and in Minnesota in 1995.[16] In all three cases, by 1996 local opposition to tolling and unease about private firms making profits from roads had torpedoed even the projects that looked most viable. The Washington state DOT, for example, selected six projects and negotiated preliminary concession deals. All but one were killed by local opposition. The only survivor was the new Tacoma Narrows Bridge, which United Infrastructure had proposed as a toll concession, but which ended up being procured as a design-build toll bridge, financed by tax-exempt state general obligation bonds.[17] None of the selected projects survived in Arizona and Minnesota.

Several projects had been proposed in Florida, but none got as far as being selected or negotiated, largely because of the serious risk created by the enabling law's requirement that any such negotiated deal would then have to be approved by a vote of the legislature (meaning that the project could be canceled after the winning company had spent many months and millions of dollars on analysis and negotiations). Still, state legislatures continued enacting private toll road enabling measures, with 14 in place by 1997.[18]

Virginia's legislature approved a new approach in its 1995 Public Private Transportation Act (PPTA).[19] It exempted new toll projects from utility-type rate regulation, as had been used for the Dulles Greenway, replacing it with California-type regulatory provisions written into the long-term concession agreement. It also allowed a mix of public-sector and private funding, with the projects conceived not as "private toll roads" but as "public-private partnerships"—called public-private transportation projects in Virginia, but public-private partnerships everywhere else, and generally abbreviated as P3s. The PPTA also permitted P3s to be organized as nonprofit, tax-exempt corporations, to make it possible to use tax-exempt revenue bonds, which carry a lower interest rate than the taxable bonds used by the Dulles Greenway and California private-toll-road projects.

The response to Virginia's PPTA was very positive. After the political failures of the proposed "private toll road" projects in Arizona, Minnesota, and Washington state, there was considerable appeal in repositioning the concept as P3s. First, this meant stronger public and political support, and hence a lower risk of political rejection. Second, using some state highway funding would reduce the amount the private sector had to finance and repay out of toll revenues, thereby increasing the number of highway and bridge projects that could be procured in this manner. Third, lowering the cost of debt financing by allowing use of tax-exempt revenue bonds), would enhance the projects' financial feasibility. Virginia began receiving unsolicited proposals under the new law, and its P3 approach gradually became the model that other states adopted, replacing what had come to be seen as naive initial "private toll roads" legislation.

The nonprofit corporation approach was embraced by two projects for new toll roads, one in Greenville, South Carolina, and the other in Richmond, Virginia. Though proposed by transportation officials, both projects were championed by highway developers, who could see the value in getting projects built much sooner via toll financing than by waiting for the state DOT to come up with enough gas-tax funding to pay for the project with cash. They urged the creation of local nonprofit corporations under IRS Revenue Ruling 63-20. The nonprofit, with a board consisting of prominent local citizens, would serve as a "tax-exempt shell" to issue the bonds.[20] Once built, the toll road would be turned over to the state DOT to operate and manage during the 30-year life of the bonds. The developer's role would end once the ribbon was cut and the road was opened to traffic.

The Southern Connector in Greenville was approved by the South Carolina DOT in 1996 and financed in 1997. It was completed and opened to traffic in 2001. Alas, the traffic was only a fraction of what had been projected, and the Connector had difficulty in paying the debt service on its bonds. After exhausting its reserve funds, it declared bankruptcy in 2010, leaving its bondholders in the lurch.[21]

In Richmond, the Pocahontas Parkway was approved in 1997, also financed via a 63-20 nonprofit corporation, and it had its groundbreaking in 1999. It opened in 2002, but its performance was similar to that of the Greenville project—traffic well below forecast, and hence great difficulty in meeting its debt-service commitments. In addition, its cost was far higher than its traffic could support, due to the political requirement that it include a costly high-level bridge across the James River, in anticipation of a planned port just upriver that never materialized. The parkway was nearly bankrupt by 2006, at which point VDOT sought to rescue it by leasing the toll road to Transurban for 99 years; that company refinanced it on a longer-term basis.[22] But that was not enough to make the toll revenue cover the costs. Transurban ceded the project to its lenders in 2013, writing off its equity investment. After several subsequent changes of ownership among financial firms, a 2016 auction selected the Spanish concession company Globalvia as the new operator.[23]

Analysis of these two projects pointed to a fundamental incentive problem. As nonprofit toll roads, they had no equity investor-owners. Therefore, nobody other than the bondholders had a long-term stake in their economic viability. The board members of the nonprofit corporation were not toll road or financial experts; they were well-meaning citizens who apparently took at face value the optimistic traffic and revenue forecasts that had been presented to them. The developers, having no real interest beyond the construction phase, would make money no matter how flawed the traffic and revenue projections turned out to be.[24] Noted P3 legal expert Karen Hedlund pointed out at the time that a 63-20 corporation "lacks any independent financial commitment to the project since it is a nonprofit corporation and cannot earn an equity return on any investment. . . . How then can this entity be relied on to act in the long-term interest of the private parties (including the developer/sponsor, contractors, and bondholders) as well as the government unit?"[25]

Even Virginia's original toll concession, the Dulles Greenway, experienced difficult early years after opening to traffic in September 1995. Its first-year traffic had been forecast as 34,000 trips a day, but was running at only 11,000 a day at the six-month mark. A sharp decrease in the toll rate—from $1.75 down to $1 at that point—increased daily volume to 27,000, but this still produced only about half the projected revenue. By the end of its first year, when the first debt-service payments were due to be made to the lenders, TRIP 2 disclosed that it did not have sufficient funds after paying operating and maintenance costs. Negotiations with the lenders proceeded for two years under a "standstill agreement" during which no payments were made, with a refinancing agreement finally reached by the end of 1998, issuing new bonds at then-available lower interest rates and resuming debt-service payments.[26]

Why did the project encounter such early difficulties? First, by the time the Greenway opened in late 1995, the local real estate market had entered a severe downturn, yet the projected traffic and revenue numbers were based on continued rapid development in what had been rural Loudoun county—development that has since occurred. Second, Dulles Airport's growth in that time period was lower than predicted. Third, the Virginia DOT found the money to widen and improve nearby Route 7 and Route 28—

something that the traffic and revenue forecasters had assumed (but not guaranteed) would not happen. And fourth, the original $1.75 toll was nearly twice the rate per mile being charged on the original Dulles Toll Road, and that deterred use, as illustrated by the large increase in volume after the Greenway toll was reduced to $1. The toll rates were gradually increased in the years thereafter.

These difficulties, along with grass-roots and environmental opposition to most of the new "private toll roads" proposed in Arizona, California, Minnesota, and Washington state, flashed caution signs to potential financiers and developers as the century neared its end. As noted above, Camino Columbia, the private toll road in Texas, survived only three years after its October 2000 opening, with lenders foreclosing in December 2003. Truck traffic was only a fraction of what had been forecast, mainly due to the city of Laredo opening a new bridge closer to existing customs facilities. Primary creditor John Hancock bid the winning $12 million for the $85 million project at the bankruptcy auction in January 2004, but sold it five months later to thevTexas DOT for $20 million. The highway remains in service as a state-owned toll road. Rather than losing any money, taxpayers got a great bargain—a usable new highway at about a quarter of its cost to develop.[27]

Foreign Investors Launch a Second Toll-Concession Wave

With all the difficulties experienced by would-be private toll road developers in the 1990s, one would have been hard pressed to predict the renaissance that took place during the first decade of the 21st century. Despite the gun-shyness of most US highway developers in the early 2000s, overseas toll road developer-operators and global financial institutions launched the second wave of US toll concessions.

As we saw in chapter 4, by that point in time the state-owned toll motorway companies in France, Italy, Portugal, and Spain had all been privatized: the state had sold these companies to investors, conveying to them long-term concessions to operate, maintain, and improve their existing toll roads, along with the right to charge tolls consistent with the provisions of the concession agreements. This was not very controversial in Europe because (1) these motorways had been tolled from the outset, and (2) much other infrastructure in Europe was being privatized, including airports, railroads, seaports, and electric, gas, and water utilities.

But when the idea of leasing existing toll roads surfaced in America, it initially struck many people as bizarre. Back in 1991, privatization-friendly Governor William Weld had proposed selling the Massachusetts Turnpike. Three firms submitted unsolicited proposals, and Goldman Sachs offered to do a financial feasibility study, but political opposition squelched further consideration of the proposal.[28] In 1993 a boutique investment bank headed by a former director of the Illinois Tollway proposed that the city of Chicago sell its historically money-losing Chicago Skyway to investors— and state legislator Jeffrey Schoenberg, a Democrat, introduced legislation for that purpose.[29]

Nothing much was heard of the Skyway idea until a decade later, when Mayor Richard M. Daley proposed it in all seriousness. Daley argued that the city was in financial difficulties and that the Skyway was not a core city government function, especially considering all the nearby tolled high-ways of the Illinois Tollway. In March 2004 the city government invited bids for the 7.8-mile elevated toll road. When the resulting bids from three prequalified teams were opened late that year, the winning bid for a 99-year concession was for $1.83 billion, all to be paid up front. The win-ning team was a joint venture of the Spanish toll road developer-operator Cintra and the Australian investment bank and infrastructure investor Macquarie.[30]

The lease of the Skyway shined a global spotlight on the United States as a new venue for global infrastructure investment. And the idea of billion-dollar-scale windfalls also inspired governors and would-be gov-ernors to look into whether they had opportunities to do similar deals. These included New Jersey's acting Governor Richard Codey (New Jer-sey Turnpike and Garden State Parkway), newly elected Indiana Gover-nor Mitch Daniels (Indiana Toll Road), and Delaware DOT Secretary Nathan Hayward (US 1 and US 301).

Daniels had campaigned on the idea of leasing the Indiana Toll Road, with the aim of investing all the proceeds not in short-term budget fixes but in other long-lived highway infrastructure projects statewide. He suc-ceeded in 2005, narrowly getting legislative approval for a 75-year lease. The winning bidder, paying $3.85 billion, was the same Cintra/Macquarie team that had won in Chicago.[31] They proceeded to convert both toll roads to interoperable electronic tolling, widen the western section of the Toll Road, and resurface much of its pavement. Daniels used the proceeds to fully fund a 10-year highway investment program called Major Moves. And despite the politically controversial nature of the Toll Road lease at the time it was done, Daniels was solidly re-elected three years later, thanks to having the only fully funded 10-year highway investment program in the country.

The Indiana deal boosted the United States even higher as an opportunity for global infrastructure investors. Steve Steckler, founder and president of the consulting firm Infrastructure Management Group, told the author, "I believe that the Indiana Toll Road and Chicago Skyway fundamentally changed the political momentum for P3s by drawing major investment banks to the table. . . . I believe their entry significantly affected state and national P3 politics."[32] Steckler had worked for Ralph Stanley when he was UMTA administrator, and was an advisor to Caltrans on the financial aspects of the AB 680 concession agreements.

Existing toll roads like the Skyway and the Indiana Toll Road were seen as far less risky investments than brand-new "greenfield" projects like the Dulles Greenway. But with opportunities to lease existing toll roads being rather few, global companies next focused their attention on the nation's fastest-growing state, Texas. Governor Rick Perry, taking advice from his Governor's Business Council on the urgent need to tackle the state's large and growing congestion problem, appointed tolling and P3 advocate Ric Williamson to head the state's Transportation Commission. During 2003 the commission and the Texas DOT carried out a widespread public information campaign targeting congestion and the need for major investment in better highway capacity via tolling and P3s. Recognizing that much of the expertise in both was overseas, they aggressively marketed Texas in Europe and Australia. And they persuaded the legislature to pass landmark legislation, the 2003 Omnibus Transportation Bill (HB 3588), which enabled more widespread use of toll finance not only by the existing toll agencies in Dallas and Houston, but by any urban county that created a regional mobility authority.[33] These new agencies, along with TxDOT, were also empowered to enter into long-term P3 concessions with the private sector.

Perry also announced a grandiose plan to create a number of multimodal north-south and east-west Trans-Texas Corridors to provide an alternative to the state's congested Interstate highways. Each would require a 1,200-foot wide right-of-way, to accommodate not only a toll road but also freight and passenger rail lines, electricity transmission lines, and oil and gas pipelines. The first project put forward was for TTC-35, planned as an alternative to the most congested Interstate, I-35. The competition to analyze and plan the initial toll road portion of TTC-35, from south of San Antonio to north of Dallas, was won in 2005 by a joint venture of

Cintra and the Texas-based road builder Zachry Construction.[34] They estimated the cost of the toll highway portion of the full corridor (rural plus urban) at $7.2 billion. The rest of the corridor—the rail and utility facilities—was assumed to be developed later. Separately from the TTC effort, private sector teams proposed a number of urban toll road and express toll lane projects, based on the favorable provisions of the enabling legislation.

Also in 2005, Virginia received its first true toll concession proposals under its Public-Private Transportation Act (PPTA) legislation. One was from a multicompany consortium that proposed investing $7 billion to add truck-only toll lanes to the 325-mile length of I-81 in that state, a major truck route.[35] Another was Fluor's unsolicited proposal to add express toll lanes to the western half of the Capital Beltway (I-495), discussed in chapter 2. Fluor later added the Australian toll road developer and operator Transurban to its team for this project. Virginia also received two unsolicited proposals for major river crossings in the Hampton Roads area.

In this new climate of investor interest, both Florida and Georgia revised unworkable P3 enabling legislation, drawing on the Texas and Virginia models. They soon began receiving unsolicited proposals, and other states enacted tolling and P3 enabling legislation for the first time. In 2005, Texas tweaked its landmark enabling law to limit toll concessions to 50 years, to prohibit conversion of existing free roads to toll roads without a local referendum, and to clarify some other provisions regarding concession agreements.

The idea of leasing existing toll roads also surfaced in Texas, with serious debate and a major feasibility study on privatizing the Harris County Toll Road Authority,[36] and in Illinois, with legislators authorizing a feasibility study on privatizing the Illinois Tollway.[37] Neither proposal gained traction with pubic officials, in part due to strong opposition from the toll agencies themselves. And in 2007 the Northwest Parkway in Denver, developed by a local toll agency several years before, but not meeting its debt service obligations, was leased to Portugal's Brisa/CCR for 99 years.[38]

The largest controversy arose over Governor Ed Rendell's 2007 proposal to lease the Pennsylvania Turnpike. After receiving much criticism from opponents who disdained the Chicago and Indiana leases, Rendell's original proposal was for a 30-year lease with 100 percent of the proceeds dedicated to transportation via a permanent fund whose earnings would be used for highway and transit projects statewide. With his enabling legislation encountering difficulties in the legislature, thanks in part to all-out opposition from the Pennsylvania Turnpike Commission, in early 2008 Rendell requested bids on a 75-year lease, gambling that a bona fide offer for this very valuable toll road would provide the margin of victory in the legislature. Despite a winning bid of $12.8 billion from Spanish toll-road developer-operator Abertis, the legislature failed to pass the enabling legislation, and Abertis then withdrew the offer.[39]

Florida's enabling legislation permitted the lease of existing toll roads, but the Florida DOT's 2008 proposal to lease Alligator Alley, a tolled portion of I-75 across the Everglades, proved highly controversial and was dropped the following year. The only other lease of an existing toll road took place in Puerto Rico, where the reform government of Governor Luis Fortuno leased PR-22 and PR 5 for 40 years in 2011; the winning bidder was Abertis.[40]

Toll Concessions Mature

As more states tried various versions of toll concessions during the 2000s, what worked and what didn't work became more apparent. Congress actually helped, first by not imposing several proposed restrictions on states making use of this procurement method. More importantly, Congress addressed the disparity between taxable and tax-exempt bond interest rates. First, in 1998 it enacted the Transportation Infrastructure Finance and Innovation Act (TIFIA) to provide subordinated loans, at tax-exempt rates, to any state-authorized transportation project whose primary financing had an investment-grade rating *and* which had a dedicated revenue stream. TIFIA loans were limited to a maximum of 33 percent of the total project budget, emphasizing their role as secondary rather than primary financing. Subsequently, in 2005, Congress authorized federal tax exemptions for private activity bonds (PABs) issued by a public agency on behalf of a P3 project. A total of $15 billion worth of such bonds was authorized, and by the end of 2016 some $6.6 billion worth had been issued and another $4.3 billion allocated, helping to finance 19 projects, of which 14 were highway concessions. One or both of these tools have been used for nearly all the major toll concession projects thus far.[41]

At the state level, it took some additional sturm und drang before a consensus emerged, toward the end of the 21st century's first decade, that concessions were a useful tool for major projects but needed a carefully thought-out legal framework and greater-than-usual state agency expertise both to attract serious investment and to protect the public interest.

The largest controversy erupted in Texas in 2007. First, Governor Perry's concept for the Trans-Texas Corridors had called for right-of-way 1,200 feet wide. Besides being an example of unrealistic central planning (why would a freight railroad want to move its traffic to a government-selected corridor?), it led to massive opposition from ranchers who did not want huge swathes of their property confiscated for such uses. Second, the legacy toll agencies in Dallas and Houston felt threatened by the potential of concession companies poaching the most lucrative new corridors, from whose toll revenues they hoped to cross-subsidize weaker projects. Third, ideological opponents of either tolling or public-private partnerships, from both the left and the right, aligned with the ranchers and toll agencies to oppose toll concessions in particular. When the Texas legislature met that year, it deliberated and decided on a two-year moratorium on any new concession projects, while allowing those already in the early procurement stage to go ahead. It also authorized a study committee to review the issues and make recommendations for policy going forward.

The final report of the Study Committee on Private Participation in Toll Projects, of which the author was a member, made several key findings:

- The highway funding gap in Texas was real, and additional investment via toll finance was needed.
- Start-up toll roads were high-risk, and were better suited to being financed by sophisticated investors willing to take the risk of below-forecast traffic and revenue than by brand-new local toll agencies (the regional mobility authorities).
- In reality, truly toll-viable projects would likely be few, so people shouldn't worry about toll roads appearing "everywhere."
- Most such projects were not lucrative enough to generate large up-front payments, as politicians had been assuming would be the case.[42]

In fact, the report recommended against upfront payments altogether, suggesting that revenue-sharing would better align the incentives of both parties in a long-term agreement. It also argued against the kind of one-sided termination provisions favored by some legislators, as contrary to the spirit of a long-term *partnership* agreement. It recommended against giving the legacy toll agencies first dibs on any proposed toll road, calling instead for using "value for money" analysis (see chapter 6) to determine, case by case, which alternative would produce greater value. It also called for creating a professional P3 office, like those well established in Australia and Canada, to do such analyses.

The 2009 legislature did not accept these recommendations, but apart from adopting the "local primacy" rule for toll agencies, giving them first pick on new toll projects, they did agree to allow toll concessions to continue, subject to the legislature itself approving TxDOT's list of proposed concessions in each legislative session. The result in Texas has been a mixture of toll agency projects, conventional procurements by TxDOT, and selected use of toll concessions. The latter include the huge $2.8 billion LBJ Freeway express toll lanes project described in chapter 2, and an even larger $3.5 billion North Tarrant Express toll lanes project in Fort Worth. By 2016, toll concessions seemed to have become an accepted way of business for highway megaprojects in much of Texas. An article in *Public Works Financing* found that the private investment committed for projects in Dallas and Fort Worth alone totaled $7 billion.[43]

Incidentally, as part of the controversy over concessions, the Trans-Texas Corridor concept was abandoned. The Cintra/Zachry team built only the sections of the toll road now called SH 130, parallel to I-35, between the outskirts of Austin and the outskirts of San Antonio. Its traffic did not live up to projections, and it filed for bankruptcy in 2016. The proposed TTC-69, intended as a substitute for the Texas portion of the yet-to-be-built I-69 from southeast Texas to Indiana, was scrapped in favor of a conventional nontolled I-69 being gradually assembled in the southeastern part of the state.

By contrast, Florida—after improving its previously unused concessions laws several times in the early 2000s, drawing on Texas and Virginia's experience—has emerged as a state where long-established toll agencies are coexisting with concessions without serious conflicts. Two major concession projects have been financed, built, and opened to traffic. One is the $900 million Port of Miami Tunnel, directly linking the island-based port to the Miami expressway system, in particular to shift heavy container trucks off the streets of downtown Miami, where they had been required to go when using the only previous route, over an existing two-lane bridge to the mainland. Because the purpose of the project was to divert traffic away from the existing bridge, charging tolls for the new tunnel was considered counterproductive. So the state, county, and city all agreed to compensate the concession company via availability payments of the kind used in Spain and Portugal (as discussed in chapter 4). This was the first availability-payment concession project in the United States.[44]

The second completed Florida project is a "hybrid" toll and availability-payment concession. The $1.6 billion project's purpose was to reconstruct and modernize east-west expressway I-595 in Broward County near Fort Lauderdale. The project included the addition of three reversible express toll lanes in the middle of the widened corridor, using variable tolling to keep their traffic flowing freely. But toll revenues from just three lanes of traffic were far less than what was needed to finance a project that rebuilt and widened the entire expressway. So the Florida DOT is compensating the concession company via availability payments, covering as much of that obligation as possible from the toll revenues FDOT collects from the express lanes, with the rest coming from traditional highway fuel tax sources. Thus, while the concession company, ACS Infrastructure, is taking on the construction, operations, and maintenance risks, the state is taking on the traffic and revenue risk.[45]

FDOT is also overseeing a similar $2.6 billion concession project to rebuild and widen 21 miles of congested I-4 through Orlando, with two express toll lanes each way added in the middle of the widened expressway. Like I-595, it is a hybrid toll and availability payment concession. FDOT has also begun work on another concession megaproject: the First Coast Outer Beltway around the southern and western parts of Jacksonville. All the while, Florida's turnpike and the three urban toll agencies of Miami, Orlando, and Tampa are moving forward with additions to their own tolled expressways.

Virginia continues as a leader among the states in transportation P3s including toll concessions. The $2 billion I-495 Capital Beltway express toll lanes, already described in chapter 2, opened to traffic at the end of 2012, bringing congestion relief and new express bus service to one of the nation's most congested arteries. And the same Fluor/Transurban team next won the concession to develop express toll lanes on I-95 heading south from the Beltway, with a total project cost of $923 million. With the 95 Express Lanes opening in late 2014, the 495 and 95 Express Lanes constitute the first components of a proposed regionwide network of express toll lanes in the Washington metro area.[46] As of 2017, Transurban is working with VDOT to extend the 95 Express Lanes an additional 10 miles southward, and also to extend the 95 Express Lanes eight miles north along I-395 to the DC line.

Although the Beltway express lanes' first two years of traffic were below projections, both traffic and revenue have since grown smartly. In the first half of 2017, continued growth was observed in both the 495 and

95 Express Lanes. A May 2017 region-wide survey of 1,700 area drivers, conducted by KRC Research, measured nearly 80 percent customer satisfaction with the Express Lanes, and found that 92 percent of car poolers have a positive impression of the lanes.[47]

Another Virginia toll concession project is the $2 billion Elizabeth River Crossings project in the Norfolk/Hampton Roads area. The Skanska/Macquarie team built a third tunnel under the Elizabeth River to relieve congestion in the two existing tunnels, and will operate and maintain all three tunnels for 58 years. This project generated controversy because VDOT and the concession company agreed to charge tolls on all three tunnels to pay for this very expensive improvement, which includes refurbishment and operation of the existing tunnels. Opponents filed suit, arguing that the tolls constituted a tax and that the legislature had unconstitutionally delegated taxing power to VDOT. Late in 2013 the state supreme court ruled unanimously that the tolls are legitimate user fees, not taxes, and that the PPTA-enabling legislation was not an unconstitutional delegation of power to VDOT.[48] Although not directly applicable to P3 enabling acts in other states, this decision heartened supporters of toll concessions nationwide, and might discourage similar litigation elsewhere.

Several states with newer P3 concession legislation are also developing new projects. The Indiana DOT launched two major P3 projects. Indiana and Kentucky collaborated on the Ohio River Bridges project in the Louisville metro area. Each state was responsible for one of two new bridges, both of which are being tolled. Indiana's $1.2 billion East End Crossing was procured as a hybrid toll / availability-payment concession, similar to Florida's I-595 and I-4 projects.[49] Since Kentucky lacked P3 legislation at the time the project began, its Downtown Crossing was procured conventionally. With both bridges completed by the end of 2016, we can expect transportation researchers to compare and contrast the performance of these simultaneous bridge projects in terms of on-time completion, cost overruns, operating and maintenance costs, and so on. Indiana is also using an availability payment concession approach for a new stretch of nontolled I-69 in the southern part of the state.

In 2009, Colorado created a new entity to implement its then-unused P3 legislation: the High Performance Transportation Enterprise within CDOT. Its first concession project was the addition of express toll lanes to US 36, the highway between Denver and Boulder. It is also proceeding with a $1.2 billion project to reconstruct I-70 between downtown and Denver International Airport, adding express toll lanes in the median.[50] HPTE's first toll concession project, US 36, proved to be a learning experience for the agency, legislators, and the public. The legislature enacted a bill adding what many considered deal-killing restrictions on future concession projects, but Governor John Hickenlooper vetoed the bill while adding several policy changes to increase transparency in P3 procurements.[51]

After several years of study of a proposed toll bridge to the Outer Banks, North Carolina's DOT found that project not to be toll-feasible. Its second attempt, an $655 million toll concession to add express toll lanes to 26 miles of I-77 in Charlotte, reached financial close in May 2015, and construction began late that year.[52] Opponents filed suit, claiming that the concession illegally delegated toll-setting to the concession company—a claim similar to what the Virginia Supreme Court rejected on the grounds that tolls are not taxes. The litigation failed, and the project is under way toward a 2018 completion date.

Pennsylvania enacted P3 concession legislation in 2012, after many years of legislative attempts. Its first major use is for a $1 billion project to replace 558 deficient bridges statewide. Since tolling of these mostly small bridges was considered politically unacceptable, the concession company is being compensated via availability payments.[53]

New York is another state with major bridge replacement needs, but it lacks P3 legislation. Consequently, the $3.1 billion replacement of the Tappan Zee Bridge north of New York City is being procured as a conventionally financed design-build contract, even though the new bridge, like the existing one, will charge tolls.[54] The Port Authority of New York and New Jersey does have P3 concession authority, which it used to procure the new Terminal 4 at JFK International Airport in the years between 1999 and 2001, and is using for the replacement of the central terminal at LaGuardia Airport. In the highway area, its first concession is the $1.5 billion project to replace the obsolete Goethals Bridge between New Jersey and Staten Island. The new bridge is being procured as a hybrid toll / availability payment concession, with the Port Authority doing the tolling and compensating the concession company via availability payments.[55]

Arizona's enabling act came about in 2009, replacing an earlier measure that had not led to any feasible projects. Perhaps due to the previous failures, ADOT has proceeded cautiously, developing procedures for procurement and project evaluation and identifying potentially viable projects. Possibilities explored include various express toll lane projects in the Phoenix metro area, a new Interstate highway (I-11) between Phoenix and Las Vegas, a widening of I-17 between Phoenix and northern Arizona, and a possible new toll road between Phoenix and Tucson.[56] In late 2015 ADOT selected the team of Fluor, Granite, and Ames to design, build, and maintain the long-planned $1.9 billion, non-tolled South Mountain Freeway for 20 years. A possible first toll-concession project would create a tolled bypass of congested I-10 through downtown Phoenix.

Georgia has made several false starts with its frequently revised P3 enabling legislation, creating consternation for the companies interested in doing such projects. A planned $1 billion concession to add express toll lanes to I-75 and I-575 in Atlanta's northwestern suburbs was abruptly canceled by Governor Nathan Deal late in 2011, after prequalified firms had been selected and were preparing their proposals.[57] A somewhat scaled-back version of the project is now being procured conventionally, but the apparent lack of toll concessions going forward has called into question the Georgia DOT's ambitious $16 billion plan for a complete network of express toll lanes on the Atlanta freeway system.

Washington State legislators enacted a second-generation P3 enabling act in 2005, repealing the 1994 law that had produced politically controversial proposals for private toll-road projects. Drawing on the Texas and Virginia measures, the 2005 law authorizes P3 agreements with state and private funding, and allows both solicited and unsolicited proposals. But in the decade since then, no projects have been offered by the Washington state DOT, nor have any unsolicited proposals been submitted. That is not for a lack of tolled megaprojects. Two Seattle megaprojects are under way, being procured conventionally: the $2.8 billion Alaskan Way Tunnel, replacing a seismically damaged elevated freeway, and the $4.1 billion replacement of the SR 520 Floating Bridge. WSDOT is also implementing a $1.5 billion set of express toll lanes on congested I-405 on the east side of Lake Washington. Evidently, the political backlash over the failed early-90s private toll road projects still casts a large shadow over WSDOT, many legislators, and private investors.

Finally there is California, a case of enormous potential but many missed opportunities. Its pioneering pilot-project legislation, AB 680, was repealed in 2003. That was partly because two of the four approved pilot projects had been dropped by their proponents (as was discussed earlier in this chapter) but was mostly due to a political battle over the successful 91 Express Lanes in Orange County. The concession agreement for that project had included a "non-compete" clause, under which Caltrans agreed not to build additional free lanes in the canyon through which SR 91 runs. At the time, no one had ever tried to finance toll lanes directly

alongside free lanes, and the financial people insisted that protection of
this kind was needed to get banks to provide the needed debt financing.
But, by the late 1990s, traffic growth was so great that the free lanes had
become as congested as they'd been prior to the addition of the express
lanes. There was great public and political pressure for Caltrans to add
a free lane each way—but the concession company had a legally strong
position against that happening, thanks to the clause in the agreement. The
end result was state legislation authorizing the Orange County Transportation Authority to buy out the remaining 28 years of the company's
concession; the purchase took place in 2002 at a mutually agreed market
value. Political opponents of toll concessions managed to include repeal
of AB 680 in the buyout legislation.[58]

From then until 2009, despite huge transportation funding shortfalls,
California lacked P3 enabling legislation, while many other states were
enacting such laws and attracting investment in billion-dollar-scale projects. After several failed attempts that were backed by then Governor
Arnold Schwarzenegger, including a flawed 2006 law that attracted no projects, the legislature enacted SB-4 in early 2009. With (a) no limits on the
number of projects, (b) allowance for both solicited and unsolicited proposals, and (c) avoidance of the unworkable provision of previous measures
that required legislative approval of negotiated concession agreements, it
appeared that California was joining the P3 mainstream.

But proponents had not reckoned with the political power of the
militant Caltrans engineers' union, Professional Engineers in California Government (PECG). It litigated to stop the first cautious project: an
availability-payment concession to rebuild and maintain the second phase
of an approach road to the Golden Gate Bridge in San Francisco, called the
Presidio Parkway. The project finally began after the state supreme court
rejected the union's appeal of a lower court decision in 2011.[59] Caltrans itself proposed no other projects, leaving it up to county-level transportation
agencies to do so.

The Los Angeles County Metropolitan Transportation Authority announced plans for as many as five billion-dollar-scale concession projects, including the reconstruction of the Long Beach Freeway (I-710)
with truck-only lanes, developing the much-needed missing link on I-710
through South Pasadena as a deep-bore toll tunnel, and adding express
toll lanes to a northern stretch of I-5 in Los Angeles. The latter was included in project that encompassed a set of mostly non-toll projects,
dubbed ARTI, put forward as the easiest concession for LA Metro to

begin with. A major battle ensued over the extent to which Caltrans engineers could micromanage the project, even though the concession approach, by definition, devolves design and project management to the concession company. With that dispute still unresolved, LA Metro announced the suspension of ARTI in spring 2014, calling into question its entire set of planned concession projects.[60]

LA Metro subsequently followed up with a new legislative proposal that would apply solely to Los Angeles County, insulating P3 projects from direct oversight by Caltrans (i.e., by PECG engineers). It failed to gain enough legislative support to be enacted in 2016, and by December 31, 2016—the sunset date of SB-4—the legislature had failed to either extend it for another term of years or replace it with a more flexible enabling act. Thus, California entered 2017 once again lacking P3 legislation.

Conclusion: Lessons Learned

The first two decades of toll concessions in the United States can best be thought of as a learning experience. We've seen successes, partial successes, and failures as elected officials, state DOTs, design and construction firms, toll road operators, and financial institutions learned by trial and error what works and what doesn't. Here are some thoughts on lessons learned.

First, what kinds of projects are not likely to be viable going forward? The pure "private toll road" model represented by the pioneering Dulles Greenway and 91 Express Lanes is not a realistic contender. Highways are seen by nearly everyone as too vested with public-interest concerns to be developed and operated entirely in the private sector. Given the high costs of land acquisition, environmental clearance, taxable debt, and meeting myriad state and federal design and performance requirements—as well as the need to compete with "free roads"—very few purely private projects would pencil out as profitable investments.

Second, the nonprofit corporation model, with no long-term equity ownership, is poorly suited to provide the kind of long-term stewardship required by infrastructure as critically important as highways. What we need for sound 21st-century highways is a better model than today's politicized project selection, with its overemphasis on lowest first cost (rather than lowest life-cycle cost), and frequent shortfalls in ongoing maintenance. The nonprofit corporation alternative, as tried several times in the 1990s, fails on all those counts.

Third, traditional US public utility commission regulation is poorly suited to 21st-century highways, especially those where variable market pricing is needed to manage traffic flow and minimize congestion. Some version of the global practice of contractually based public-sector oversight, via provisions incorporated into the long-term concession agreement, is a much better alternative (as will be discussed in chapter 8).

Fourth, there seems to be little current political interest in simply leasing existing toll roads to the private sector—a practice referred to as "monetization"—even though many of the arguments raised against this idea are spurious (see chapters 6 and 7). On the other hand, there is great potential for long-term toll concessions focused on reconstructing, replacing, and modernizing aging bridges, expressways, and Interstates over the next several decades as they wear out. We'll return to this idea in chapters 9 and 10.

The best opportunities for investing in the US highway infrastructure market in the near term are three types of project: adding express toll lanes to congested freeways, building missing links in existing freeway networks (often using innovative solutions such as elevated lanes or tunnels due to right-of-way constraints), and replacing aging or obsolete highways, bridges, and tunnels. All three types of megaprojects are generally more risky than smaller-scale highway projects, and it is better from a public-interest standpoint that sophisticated investors take such risks, rather than taxpayers.

Risk transfer in megaprojects is one of the most important benefits of concessions (see chapter 6), and elected officials, transportation planners, and state DOTs need to learn more about the risk transfer that can and should be incorporated into concession projects. A well-structured highway concession should assign the risks of cost overruns and late completion entirely to the concession company and its investors. Likewise, the even bigger risk of inadequate traffic and revenue should generally be borne by the private sector, except where there are strong public policy reasons to not charge tolls, as in case of the Port of Miami Tunnel.

We have three examples in the US experience thus far of greenfield toll concession projects going bankrupt: Camino Columbia and SH 130 in Texas, and SR 125 in San Diego. In all three cases, the private sector bore the losses; the highway was acquired out of bankruptcy at a significantly lower price by a public sector highway agency, and it remained in operation to serve the traveling public. The same outcome occurred in the bankruptcy of several P3 toll tunnels in Australia (as we saw in chapter 4).

That country's toll concessions are structured with risk-transfer provisions similar to those of US concessions. Hence, in those bankruptcies only private-sector investors lost money; taxpayers were held harmless, and the tunnels continued in operation under new owners.

A strikingly different outcome occurred with the bankruptcy of the Indiana Toll Road concession company in 2015 and the financial difficulties of the Chicago Skyway concession. Both of these existing toll roads were later acquired by consortia of public pension funds for more than twice the original concession payment amounts. Why? The financial problems of those two concessions were primarily due to highly overleveraged financing, and were exacerbated by short-term reductions in traffic and revenue due to the Great Recession. The pension funds that acquired both concessions saw these tollways' excellent long-term value, and financed the acquisitions with more than 50-percent equity and the rest debt—very conservative financial structures. As pension funds, they seek only high single-digit returns on their equity investment, not the higher returns often sought by infrastructure investment funds.

We have also seen important difference between states that are succeeding with toll concessions and those that are not. The most fundamental of these differences is consistent, bipartisan political support for this method of procuring highway projects. That has not existed in California or Georgia, but it is evident in Colorado, Florida, Indiana, Virginia, and (despite some difficulties) Texas.

Finally, another key difference is the existence of professional staff and advisors that have the expertise to do serious "value for money" analysis to determine when a concession offers greater benefits than traditional procurement. Colorado, Puerto Rico, and Virginia are the only governments that thus far have created dedicated offices of this kind, though other state DOTs with successful concession projects have contracted for specialized legal and financial advice from outside firms. The Federal Highway Administration has also created an entity, called the Office of Innovative Program Delivery, that offers fairly extensive information and advice on best practices in the various kinds of P3s and financing mechanisms relevant to concession projects.

In chapter 6 we will look more closely at the benefits of concession projects, before turning to arguments and concerns raised by critics of highway concessions, from both the left and the right, in chapter 7.

CHAPTER SIX

The Benefits of Long-Term P3 Concessions

The previous chapter explained how long-term public-private partnership (P3) concessions have been introduced into US transportation over the last two decades via toll-financed projects for new highways and bridges, as well as the leasing and refurbishment of several existing highways, bridges, and tunnels. This recent experience offers a preview of the better transportation future we could have if the highway sector were transformed into customer-friendly highway businesses. So our task in this chapter is to look in more detail at what the US record shows, thus far, about the benefits of this new model. What specific benefits are we talking about? And how strong is the evidence that those benefits are real? Needless to say, there are many critics of P3 concessions from both the left and the right in American politics. After reviewing the potential benefits of concessions in this chapter, we will consider the critics' objections and concerns in the following chapter.

Better Incentives

Many of the benefits of concessions stem from the significant differences in the incentives faced by participants in highway projects developed as concessions, compared with the incentives facing participants in traditional highway procurement and operations. These differences include incentives that (1) lead to cost overruns in traditional procurement, (2) contribute to deferred maintenance, and (3) lead to investing in low-priority projects. To understand how these things work, we first need to take a closer look at how US highway development projects are handled under the standard 20th-century model.

Traditional Highway Procurement

State transportation departments (DOTs) are the owner/operators of nearly all US highways, including the Interstates and others labeled as "US" highways (as in US 41). DOTs use a mix of federal and state fuel-tax funds to pay for highway projects. Whether the project involves building a new highway, widening or otherwise improving an existing highway, or rebuilding a highway once it reaches the end of its design life (a maximum of 50 years, if well-maintained), the process involved is basically the same.

First, the DOT decides that the project is one that it should seriously consider doing. Generally it does a preliminary design to get a rough idea what it will cost to build. Then it engages in the environmental review process, to obtain permission to go forward and to flesh out the design concept. Next, it goes out to bid for an engineering company to design the project in detail. Once the detailed design is completed and accepted, the DOT's next step is to go out to bid for a construction contract based on the approved design. The winner will be the qualified company offering to build the project at the lowest construction cost. Once the contract is signed, the contractor proceeds to build it, but often finds aspects of the design to be questionable or difficult to build; this leads to *change orders* which often lead to construction delays and generally increase the total construction cost.

This traditional procurement approach is called design-bid-build (DBB), because of the several steps involved. It has a number of problems, beginning with potential mismatches between the design and its "constructability," often leading to cost overruns and schedule slips. Second, because the contractor is selected on the basis of the lowest proposed construction cost, the companies that bid try to figure out ways to build the project as cheaply as possible. That typically leads to less durable pavement being selected. And that, in turn, leads to considerably higher ongoing maintenance costs during the lifetime of the highway—or to considerable "deferred maintenance" in future years if the legislature fails to appropriate enough money for proper ongoing maintenance, as often happens. In other words, the DBB process focuses on the wrong cost target; it minimizes the *initial cost* at the expense of considerably higher total *life-cycle cost*. And that means highway user tax dollars are being wasted.

In addition, there is no incentive to design the project so as to maximize congestion relief—that's not the contractor's problem.

P3 legal advisor Geoffrey Yarema explained that the DBB process arose as a solution to corruption in the awarding of construction contracts to politically connected builders. But by insisting that everyone bid on a standard, minutely specified design, DBB also "drove out innovation" in large-scale infrastructure. A secondary objective of DBB was to maximize opportunities for local small businesses. But a consequence of that objective was to lose the cost-reduction benefits of economies of scale. Another political objective was to have public employees do as much of the work as possible—which has produced an extreme result at Caltrans, with its militant engineers' union that has fought reforms like design-build and P3s for several decades.[1]

An alternative to DBB that has gradually gained acceptance in most states, at least for large highway projects, is called design-build (DB) contracting. In this approach the DOT does a preliminary design, as before, but then goes out to bid for a team that will work together to *design and build* the highway project, typically for a guaranteed price and a fixed completion date, with per-day penalties and bonuses for late or early completion. The basis for selecting the winning bidder under DB is generally "best value," rather than lowest initial cost. DB addresses the problem of the detailed design being difficult to build, since the designers and construction people work together on the design. In addition, the team can start preliminary construction activity while the final details of the design are being worked out. This overlap of the design and construction phases—and elimination of the time and cost of a separate competition for the construction phase after the design is completed—can reduce the overall procurement schedule by months or even years. In addition, thanks to the fixed price negotiated as part of the DB contract, the risk of cost overruns is shifted from the DOT (i.e., the taxpayers) to the DB team.

The infrastructure finance expert Karen Hedlund pointed out in a 2006 article that DB has also made toll financing easier to obtain. One of its earliest uses for a highway project was the 1993 financing of the $1.1 billion San Joaquin Hills Toll Road in Orange County, California. Early on, the Transportation Corridor Agencies developing the project "received indications from financial markets that their projects would be financeable as an entirety only if they could obtain fixed-price design/build contracts with limited opportunities for cost increases."[2] She went on to quote specific language on this point from Fitch Ratings, one of the principal bond rating agencies.

Among the many studies showing that DB leads to lower project costs and faster completion was one released by the Florida DOT in 2015. It reviewed 58 contracts from 2008 to 2012, of which 11 were DB, selected on a best-value basis, and 47 were DBB, selected strictly on lowest price. In addition to providing somewhat lower costs, often via innovative design features, the DB projects delivered significant time savings.[3]

But for all its merits, DB does not deal directly with the life-cycle cost problem. So it may still produce a highway that is less durable than would be optimal, requiring more maintenance in future years, so that the overall life-cycle cost is not minimized. It may also not provide the best design from the highway users' perspective. Thus, taxpayers and highway users are still not getting the true best value for their dollars.

By contrast, under the long-term concession model, the DOT goes out to bid for a team that not only designs and builds the highway project, but also finances it and maintains it for a period that could be as long as the highway's design life (e.g., 50 years). That dramatically changes the picture regarding minimizing life-cycle cost. Since the same company or consortium of companies will have what amounts to a quasi-ownership interest in the highway for its useful life, it has a powerful incentive to minimize the life-cycle cost by trading off the possibly higher initial cost of a more durable design in exchange for the long-term savings in maintenance costs that the durable design makes possible. And this model can deliver even more value when the concession company's returns are conditioned on customer services and congestion relief.

The Big Dig and its Opposite in Australia

The infamous Big Dig project in Boston was procured via the traditional DBB process and became something of a poster child for that process's shortcomings. The purpose of the project was to replace the aging elevated I-93 through downtown Boston with a tunnel, opening up a large swath of valuable real estate for redevelopment and the resulting property tax revenue. The project concept grew to include extending the eastern end of I-90 (the Massachusetts Turnpike) to I-93, as well as adding a third tunnel between downtown Boston and Logan Airport, across the harbor from downtown. From an initial estimate of $3.2 billion during the design stage in 1987, the cost estimate grew to $5.8 billion in 1991, when the airport tunnel construction began. By the time the I-93 tunnel construction started in 1994, the official estimate was put at $7.8 billion, despite the design contractor's actual estimate of $13.8 billion, which Massachusetts officials deliberately kept secret. The suppressed estimate turned out to be much closer to reality, since the total cost, when the Big Dig was finally completed and all lanes opened to traffic in 2007, was $14.8 billion.[4]

How might a long-term toll concession approach have led to a different outcome? Peter Samuel, longtime editor of *Toll Roads News*, provided a comparison project: Melbourne CityLink, developed and implemented as a toll concession in the 1990s in Australia. Like the Big Dig, it was a megaproject in the downtown area of a major city. The concept was to extend and link together several freeways that stopped short of downtown, enabling faster and uncongested trips *through* downtown as well as improved access in and out of downtown Melbourne. Due to the high density of valuable downtown development, a ground-level freeway was out of the question. So the CityLink was designed as a combination of elevated lanes approaching downtown from the north and tunnels underneath downtown and the river that flowed through it.

Samuel points out many additional similarities between Big Dig and CityLink:

> Both projects had to cope with awful soil conditions, Boston's in bay-edge fill and Melbourne's in river and creek beds of deep muck. Both had to go to Herculean lengths to maintain existing rail transit services and underground utilities, and not interfere with traffic during construction. Boston's tunnels were much bigger, but Melbourne's were much deeper, involving enormous water pressures and uplift. Each encountered significant construction problems. Each included a signature bridge. Both projects had smart, competent engineers and managers. Yet Melbourne's was built in one-third the time and at one-third the cost ($27 million per lane-mile vs. $91 million per lane-mile).[5]

So what, specifically, accounts for the huge differences in outcome? First of all, since CityLink was financed on the basis of toll revenues, there was a major constraint on cost escalation. Politicians might desire all kinds of "nice-to-have" additions, but there was no way to pay for them, so they were eliminated. By contrast, "scope creep" plagued the Big Dig over its several-decade development period, enabled by the political clout of then House Speaker Tip O'Neill (D-MA), who was able to win outsized amounts of federal highway funds for the project.[6] Various interest groups made numerous costly demands for "mitigation," the costs of which were built into the escalating Big Dig budget.

Second, CityLink owner-operator Transurban made use of DB for its construction contract, creating strong incentives to design the project efficiently and to complete it on time; by contrast, the Big Dig was procured under conventional DBB, with all its incentives for costly change orders. Third, unlike the design and construction contractors of the Big Dig, whose job was done once the project was built, Transurban would be the owner-operator of CityLink for the duration of its 34-year concession. So they had that additional reason to be sure the project was built right, minimizing its life-cycle cost.

A more recent US example of a DBB highway megaproject whose cost escalated dramatically is the San Francisco–Oakland Bay Bridge replacement. The original bridge was badly damaged by the 1989 Loma Prieta earthquake. After nine years of contentious debate over a "signature" design for the new bridge, a single-tower, self-anchored suspension design was agreed to, at an estimated cost of $1.5 billion. But after the design phase was concluded and Caltrans went out to bid for construction contracts, the sole bid for just the single tower came in at $1.4–1.8 billion, twice Caltrans' estimate of $750 million for that piece. By the time all the bids were accepted, the total cost had reached $5 billion. And after numerous delays and change orders during construction, the final cost ended up at $6.4 billion.[7]

Who Bears Which Risks?

Large construction projects, such as major highways, bridges, and tunnels, are risky endeavors. There are the Big Dig and Bay Bridge-type risks of cost escalation and late completion. There are risks of natural disasters (floods, earthquakes, etc.). And there are also "traffic risks"—that the actual number of users may be far below what was projected in the studies used to justify going forward with the project.

Transportation "megaprojects"—those costing a billion dollars or more—have a track record as being especially high-risk. In 2003 a team of Danish economists led by Bent Flyvbjerg completed a large-scale study of this problem.[8] They assembled an international database of 258 highway and rail megaprojects, worth $90 billion, in 20 countries. Nearly all these projects (90 percent) experienced cost overruns. The average rail project cost 45 percent more than forecast; the average highway project

20 percent more. And the traffic forecasts were also generally off, with the average rail project getting 39 percent fewer passengers than forecast and the average highway project getting 9 percent more than forecast (though many had less traffic than forecast). Flyvbjerg concluded that the "cost estimates used in public debates, media coverage, and decision-making for transport infrastructure are highly, systematically, and significantly deceptive. So are the cost-benefit analyses."[9]

Flyvbjerg and colleagues spent years thinking about why megaprojects generate such risks, concluding that the conventional procurement approach, in which government is the project promoter and financier, and the private sector is limited to design and construction, creates perverse incentives to create optimistic, "best-case" feasibility studies, produce elaborate designs, and accept construction contracts that builders expect will be rich with change-order prospects. This conventional approach puts the major risks on the shoulders of taxpayers. So Flyvbjerg's remedy is to change to a procurement approach that shifts major risks from taxpayers to the private sector—to parties that have incentives to reduce those risks, as we saw in the case of CityLink. He concluded that the decision to proceed with a megaproject should be based on "the willingness of private financiers to participate in the project without a [government] guarantee." By putting their own money at risk, the investors will be personally and financially involved in monitoring how the project is done, at every step of the way. And if private parties shy away from investing in a proposed megaproject, that fact should be a signal to government that the project is of questionable value, no matter how attractive it looks politically.

While Flyvbjerg's database did not include many toll concession projects, subsequent studies by other researchers have found that long-term concessions have a much better track record on cost overruns and on-time completion than do conventionally procured projects. Allen Consulting Group and the University of Melbourne studied the performance of 54 Australian infrastructure megaprojects, nearly half of which were in transportation. Of the total, 21 were done via long-term concession and 33 via conventional DBB procurement. Cost overruns on the 21 concessions were negligible, averaging just 1 percent, compared with 15 percent for the traditional projects. As for schedule, the average concession project opened early (beating the schedule by 3.4 percent), compared with an average excess duration of 23.5 percent for conventional projects.[10]

Countries such as Australia and Canada in particular, that have decades of experience using long-term concessions, have developed systematic ways of itemizing and quantifying the various risks involved in a mega-project. In Australian states such as New South Wales and Victoria, and in Canadian provinces like British Columbia and Ontario, specialized public-private partnership (P3) units have been created. One of their primary functions is to provide independent analysis of individual projects proposed for procurement as long-term concessions. The specific analysis developed for this purpose is called a value for money (VfM) assessment. The project is first analyzed as being done via conventional procurement, either as DBB or DB, depending on what would be normal within that jurisdiction. The best-case traditional version is called the public sector comparator (PSC). Next, a comparable analysis is made for the project if it is to be done via a long-term P3 concession.

One key part of the VfM analysis defines each of the principal risks presented by the project, and estimates their cost. In the public-sector case, those risks are nearly all borne by the government (except for on-time completion and cost-overrun risks, in the case of DB procurements). The risks that will be transferred to the developer-operator under a toll concession generally include construction cost overruns, on-time completion, operations and maintenance, and traffic and revenue. As a result, risk transfer generally makes a significant difference in the VfM analysis. An additional element in the VfM takes into account other differences between government as owner-operator and the concessionaire as de facto owner-operator for the duration of the concession term, such as as comparison of life-cycle cost. Governments typically self-insure, but the cost to taxpayers of doing so is not traditionally counted as a project cost, though it is included in the VfM. The concession company will pay corporate income taxes if it makes profits, and in a few cases it may pay property taxes to the local government. Those tax revenues would be nonexistent under traditional highway procurement, so they must also be included in the VfM analysis.

An objective VfM analysis will not always conclude that a concession delivers greater value than conventional procurement. But if agreement can be reached on making use of this method, and if it is carried out by unbiased professionals, VfM analysis can help to clarify when a concession is the better alternative, and by how large a margin. As this is written, only Colorado, Puerto Rico, and Virginia have created formal P3 units to do this kind of analysis for US transportation projects, but several other state DOTs (e.g., Florida, Indiana, and Texas) have hired financial consultants to conduct VfM studies on specific projects.

Colorado's P3 unit commissioned a study of the VfM findings for a number of P3 concession projects in the United States and Canada. For six projects, the comparisons were between the transportation agency's best estimate of its initial cost of the project procured conventionally (the PSC), and the actual cost under the P3 concession agreement, as follows:[11]

I-595, Florida	14% lower than PSC
A30, Quebec	33% lower than PSC
FasTracks, Denver	13% lower than PSC
Port of Miami Tunnel	12% lower than PSC
Goethals Bridge, New York	14% lower than PSC
Presidio Parkway, San Francisco	20% lower than PSC.

Four other comparisons in the same report were based on the net present value of life-cycle cost:

SE Stoney Trail, Alberta	63% less than PSC
Five highway projects, Alberta	27% less than PSC
Windsor Essex Parkway, Ontario	15% less than PSC
LBJ Express, Dallas	15% less than PSC.

Competition and Innovation

As the above Colorado study results discovered, even the initial project cost may be lower under a P3 concession approach. That is quite possible if the state DOT permits bidders to offer alternative innovative design concepts. Traditionally, especially under DBB procurement, the state DOT will specify exactly what it wants a new highway, bridge, or tunnel to consist of. It needs to do this so that each of the would-be construction firms is bidding on exactly the same project, with the winner being the one proposing the lowest initial cost. But that process provides little or no incentive for contractors to propose innovative ways of achieving the same outcome.

An alternative way to procure projects is to broadly define a set of performance outcomes and allow companies to come up with their best solutions for meeting those requirements. This could not work under DBB, because comparing the different design approaches would be like comparing apples and oranges, and the DOT could not be selecting the winner solely on the basis of lowest cost of constructing a specified design. But this idea can easily work in a DB procurement, where selection of the winner is generally based on "best value" in meeting the requirements. Some DOTs are now explicitly inviting "alternative technical concepts" when they issue requests for proposals for DB and concession projects.

The greatest scope for innovation comes about when projects are procured via long-term toll concessions, in which a company's success depends on pleasing its customers and getting them to pay to use the facility. This gives the bidders an incentive to focus the design more specifically on providing uncongested travel. So in addition to facilitating proposals that reduce initial cost as well as life-cycle cost, toll-concession proposals may also encourage bidders to produce designs that add additional revenue by offering increased congestion relief.

When the Texas DOT procured the P3 concession projects to rebuild and add express toll lanes to the LBJ Freeway in Dallas and the North Tarrant Express in Fort Worth, it invited innovative approaches from the bidders. In both cases, TxDOT had a limited amount of money to invest in the project as a kind of down payment, since only the new express lanes would be tolled, and the toll revenue from only those lanes would almost certainly not also pay for the refurbishment of the nontolled lanes. For the Dallas project, TxDOT told bidders it had up to $700 million in state funds available to assist with the $2.6 billion project. The winning Cintra/Meridiam proposal was based on using only $445 million of that amount, thanks to its cost-saving alternative design approach of using depressed express lanes rather than putting those lanes in a tunnel beneath the freeway. In the Fort Worth case, TxDOT invited bidders to propose how many miles of the eventually much longer NTE project they could finance and build given the state's estimated $600 million investment in this $2 billion project. The winning proposal committed to building 169 lane-miles as opposed to the 64 lane-miles offered by the other team.[12] A paper presented at a 2015 P3 conference found that the design innovations in the LBJ and NTE projects added up to cost savings of nearly $2 billion.[13]

Even larger-scale innovation can result if the enabling legislation for P3 concessions allows "unsolicited proposals" from the private sector. Most highway projects result from project lists developed by the state DOT (and a state transportation board or commission, if there is one), as part of a long-term plan of highway improvements. But DOTs and transportation boards don't have a monopoly on good ideas. It may take an outside company to spot a potentially viable project that has not been imagined by the powers that be. This kind of creativity was illustrated by the first highway concession effort in California, which we discussed in chapter 5. Caltrans opened its plans and books to the private sector statewide and basically said: Tell us where you see the potential of toll-financed projects to meet significant transportation needs, and we will score all the proposals against a predefined set of criteria and pick the four best ones. Two of the four winning proposals were financed and built, and both involved significant innovation. The express toll lanes on SR 91 in Orange County were the first variably priced toll lanes anywhere in the world. Investors took a significant risk in pioneering this concept, using transponders for the first time to charge different prices at different times of day, and doing so at highway speeds (rather than making motorists go through a toll lane at five miles an hour). Today, express toll lanes are rather common; but when these first ones opened in December 1995, they were revolutionary. Another example of innovation thanks to an unsolicited proposal would be the express toll lanes on the Capital Beltway outside Washington, DC, discussed in chapter 2.

Financial Differences

The use of P3 concessions also involves financial aspects that differ considerably from the 20th-century model. These include deciding how projects get selected, financing major projects rather than paying cash, and increasing the total amount of highway investment.

Sorting Out Good Projects from Bad

One of the biggest problems with the US highway status quo is that most of the recent investments in our highway system don't seem to be making our economy more productive. Quite a few studies by economists have estimated the "return on investment" in the highway sector of the US economy over the years. As noted in chapter 1, in the 1950s and 1960s, when new toll roads and Interstate highways were being built, economists estimated high double-digit annual percentage gains in economic productivity due to the trade and travel facilitated by those new highways.

Similar estimates made for the 1970s and 1980s showed somewhat lower returns. And by the 1990s and 2000s, the newer studies found returns only in the single digits.[14]

The conventional wisdom interprets these results as indicating that we don't need any more highway capacity than we already have. But an alternative explanation is that the ever-increasing expenditure on highways is being channeled into the wrong kinds of projects. It seems counterintuitive that motorists and truckers in our urban areas suffer annual congestion costs in excess of $160 billion a year, but we somehow cannot identify productive investments in congestion-relief highway capacity in those metro areas.

Likewise, today's long-distance Interstates are based largely on maps drawn up in the 1940s and finalized in the 1950s to connect all major cities with limited-access superhighways. In terms of where people and businesses are located, the America of the early 21st century is vastly different from the America of the 1950s. And that suggests scope for at least some additional routes on the Interstate system—with an obvious example being the planned I-11 connecting Phoenix and Las Vegas, two major metro areas that were little more than cow towns in the 1950s. There are dozens of other possible new routes, though many of them might not generate enough traffic and revenue to be good investments. But a 21st-century highway system should be set up to ask—and answer—such questions on an ongoing basis.

The toll concession model offers a way to do this. Instead of highway projects being selected via political horse trading in Congress and state legislatures, new tollway proposals should always be in order. If investors are willing to risk their money on adding express toll lanes to congested freeways, for example, they should have an opportunity to propose such projects and demonstrate their value, as well as their compliance with environmental and other regulations that apply to all highways. Requiring a proposed project to demonstrate toll feasibility provides a screen that helps to sort out potentially viable projects from likely boondoggles.

A recent example of a project propelled more by politics than by financial feasibility was the proposed US 460 toll road in Virginia. The project would provide a second limited-access highway between the Hampton Roads–Norfolk area and Richmond, as a more southerly alternative to the existing (nontolled) I-64. It would be built practically alongside the existing US 460, which goes through many cities and towns, in the manner of pre–World War II highways. The cost was estimated as $1.4 billion and the project was first pursued by Virginia DOT as a toll concession, under the state's Public-Private Transportation Act. But when traffic and revenue studies estimated that only about 15 percent of the cost could be financed via toll revenue bonds, the state, instead of dropping the project, went forward for political reasons, selecting a DB contractor and setting up a nonprofit 63-20 corporation to issue tax-exempt toll revenue bonds to cover part of the cost. This kind of structure replicates the flawed model used for the unviable Pocahontas Parkway in Richmond and for South Carolina's bankrupt Southern Connector, discussed in chapter 5.

With a new governor and DOT secretary taking office in 2014, the project was put on hold, after some $250 million had been spent prior to starting any construction. In July 2015 a settlement was reached with the contractor, terminating the project and recovering $46 million from the company.[15] It's hardly surprising that a "toll road" with two parallel free highways would not attract very much of the traffic between Richmond and the Hampton Roads area. Such low demand is a strong indication that scarce highway resources should not be devoted to a project like this.

The toll-feasibility test should not be *the* deciding factor for every single highway link. Highways generally constitute a network, and for the network to be viable, it may need links that are not self-supporting. The point here is that toll feasibility is an important screening device for separating stronger and weaker projects, in terms of traffic demand. The decision on whether to actually build a "weaker" link should depend on overall benefit/cost analysis. A recent paper by three senior analysts at the Federal Highway Administration explained that benefit/cost analysis should be carried out at an early stage of project development, to see whether the project should be done at all. Only if it passes that basic test, and is large enough to be done as a P3 concession, should a VfM analysis be done to see whether it would make sense for it to be procured as a concession.[16]

Implementing Needed Highway Projects Much Sooner

Under the 20th-century model of highway funding, revenue from the fuel taxes paid by motorists and truckers is accounted for in so-called highway trust funds. The federal money is distributed mostly by formula to each state, and is divided into dozens of different program categories. State DOTs present their proposed budgets to their legislature in each session, with one pot for capital projects (construction, widening, reconstruction, etc.) and another pot for maintenance. Usually every legislator wants at least some capital projects in his or her district, so the capital budget must be divided into many small pieces. That makes it especially difficult to do a megaproject, because (1) that single project would likely soak up most of the capital budget for one or several years, and (2) that project is almost certainly located within just one or two of the state's many legislative districts.

What the above paragraph describes is a system that attempts to pay for capital projects out of annual cash flow—a system that is inherently stacked against the kind of megaprojects that can make a real difference to a more economically productive highway system. Consequently, very few such projects get built. If the project is a major highway, it might be built a few miles at a time over a decade or more, as money can be scraped together each year. But you can't do that with a major bridge or tunnel; it's entirely useless until it is fully completed.

Hardly any other kind of major infrastructure is developed on the basis of annual cash flow and political horse trading. Railroads, airports, electric utilities, pipelines, gas utilities, and even municipal water systems *finance* major capital improvements. That means they go to the capital markets for the large sums needed to build the new facility in a timely and efficient manner, and they pay back the providers of capital out of the operating revenues generated by the new facility. The only US highways and bridges that are financed in this way are toll roads and bridges. Public-sector toll agencies use all-debt financing, in the form of toll revenue bonds. Toll concession companies use a mix of debt and equity, similar to what other investor-owned utilities do.

One of the biggest advantages of financing major projects is that they get built when they are needed, rather than a decade or two later, when enough cash can be amassed and enough political deals can be made. Many long-distance Interstate highways—especially those that are major truck routes—already need additional lanes. But only those early Interstates that were developed as toll roads have a ready means of making timely widening investments. Similarly, the largest 20 urbanized areas in America are plagued with traffic congestion, resulting from both inadequate freeway capacity and a lack of pricing to manage traffic demand. But comparatively little large-scale investment is being made in urban expressway systems, except in those metro areas where express toll-lane megaprojects are being developed under P3 concession agreements (e.g., Dallas–Fort Worth, Denver, Miami, Orlando, and Washington, DC).

A much wider use of toll concessions would provide a way to significantly increase highway investment, allowing timely construction of numerous cost-effective projects that will otherwise stay on the drawing boards for decades in the future, due to the limitations of funding large capital projects out of annual cash flow.

But Do Concessions Actually Add to Highway Investment?

In light of the above discussion about shifting many projects forward in time, it may seem odd to even pose this question. But it's addressed here because some transportation researchers have made the claim that concessions are merely a different form of procurement, not a source of any increased investment. In recent reports on P3 concessions, both the US DOT inspector general (IG) and the Congressional Budget Office (CBO) have made this strange claim. For example, in its 2011 report on the subject, the IG states: "PPPs are not likely to significantly decrease the infrastructure funding gap, because private-sector investment in transportation through PPPs generally does not entail new or incremental funds."[17] A 2012 CBO report makes a similar claim: that toll concessions will not increase the amount of highway investment because the revenue on which they are based must come from the same tolls or highway fuel taxes as in a purely public-sector project.[18]

In an abstract, academic sense, that might seem to be the case. But what we actually see happening in the real world is that the private sector is promoting the use of tolling in situations where there is either no government toll agency to do the project or the project is considered too risky for the toll agency to do. In effect, many decisions to use toll concessions amount to the "outsourcing of political will" to use tolls. In other words, elected officials may have lacked the courage to propose and advocate a toll-financed solution, but the private sector steps forward to make this case to the public and take the risks. That is what happened in the case of the express toll lanes on the Capital Beltway outside Washington, DC, as recounted in chapter 2. There would likely have been no $3 billion Virginia DOT HOV lanes added to the Beltway for decades, if ever; but the private sector stepped forward with a plan to build express *toll lanes* instead of HOV lanes, and it persuaded officials and the public that it could finance, build, and operate the project, on the basis of toll revenues that VDOT had been unwilling to consider on its own.

The United States, in fact, faces a highway funding shortfall, due to the decreasing viability of per-gallon fuel taxes. Once the latest set of federal corporate average fuel economy (CAFE) requirements is fully implemented, requiring the average new car to get 54.5 miles per gallon by 2025, future fuel tax revenues will decline to about half today's level, unless politicians decide to double federal and state gasoline and diesel tax rates per gallon. Since that is unlikely, most transportation experts agree that we need to figure out how to transition from per-gallon taxes to per-mile user fees. Converting major (limited-access) highways to per-mile tolling could be *part of* that transition, and will be explored in chapters 9 and 10. One key to making such a change acceptable to motorists would be to switch to per-mile tolling only as part of rebuilding and modernizing existing nontolled highways. Under that model, highway users would be asked to pay tolls only *after* they get a much better highway or bridge.

What about Taxes Paid by Concession Companies?

Another important difference between highway projects done by the public sector (either by state DOTs or state toll agencies) and concession companies is that the companies are tax-paying business entities while public-sector agencies are not. What difference does that make, in practical terms?

Some critics of concessions argue that because concession companies have to pay taxes and seek to make a profit, that constitutes an "extra cost," which means toll rates must be higher than if the same project were done by a government agency. But that is a very static view of how markets work. If that argument were generally true, the logical conclusion would be that all goods and services should be produced by government, to ensure the price of these things is as low as possible. In the real world, the profit-and-loss system provides powerful motivations to innovate so as to produce the desired output at the lowest feasible cost. So the "cost" of a bridge or highway is not some absolute value, independent of the incentives involved in competing to obtain the contract, delivering the service at a price customers are willing to pay, and designing it to minimize costly and disruptive maintenance during its useful life. Assuming identical "cost" for a government bridge and a private-sector bridge is fallacious. The cost of the latter is the end result of an entrepreneurial discovery process seeking the best solution—such as a CityLink instead of a Big Dig.

The flip side of taxes as an extra cost is tax revenue as an *added benefit* to the state government that is making the decision on procuring the project as a concession rather than doing it in-house. Indeed, that is how tax revenue is treated in value for money analyses, because it is a tangible difference between the two alternatives. What kinds of taxes are we talk-ing about here?

Sales taxes on the materials used in construction are generally not at issue, since nearly all state DOTs contract with construction companies to build highway projects, and those companies already pay sales taxes on their materials. Except in a very few cases of purely private toll roads on company-owned right of way—which do pay property taxes—toll con-cession projects are built on state-owned right of way, and the pavement and bridges are owned by the state, so these companies generally do *not* pay property taxes. But to the extent that their business plans succeed and they make profits, those profits are taxable under state and federal corporate income tax regimes, like those of all other businesses. For ex-ample, the Cintra/Meridiam joint ventures developing the Dallas and Fort Worth express toll-lane projects (the LBJ and NTE) have estimated that over the 52 years of their concessions, they and their investors will pay $3.5 billion (net present value) in federal and state corporate income taxes based on their projected profits on the projects.[19]

If we imagine a future 21st-century America in which most of the ma-jor highways are the responsibility of investor-owned companies under long-term toll concessions, and compare it to a continuation of the status quo in which nearly all major highways are in the public sector and are ex-empt from taxes, the difference, from the government's perspective, could be hundreds of billions of dollars in tax revenue. The large majority of all electric and gas utilities in this country are owned by investors, and pay not only state and federal corporate income taxes but also, in most cases, property taxes. From that perspective, it is odd that the comparably large highway sector receives such different tax treatment.

This point is apparently not understood by the US Treasury, by Con-gress's Joint Committee on Taxation, by the Congressional Budget Office, or by others in Washington. Whenever the subject of making tax-exempt debt available for P3 infrastructure comes up (to level the financial play-ing field between government toll agencies and private sector concession companies), the reaction of these entities is that providing tax-exemption for their revenue bonds deprives the Treasury of revenue it would other-wise be collecting. This view is wrong, for two reasons. First, it completely ignores the corporate income tax revenues that will be generated if a por-tion of the highway sector shifts from state provision to P3 concession provision. Second, it assumes that if tax exemption were not available on these revenue bonds, the same projects would be done by concession com-

TABLE 3. **Simplified comparison of tax-exempt and taxable bond financing**

	Public sector	P3 option 1	P3 option 2
Project debt	100	75	75
Equity	0	25	25
Total funding	100	100	100
Bond interest rate	3.50%	5.50%	5.50%
Target equity return	–	12.0%	12.0%
Weighted average cost of capital	3.50%	7.13%	7.13%
Annual revenue assumed	7.00	7.00	8.00
Annual debt service payment	3.50	4.13	4.13
Debt service coverage ratio	2.00X	1.70X	1.94X

panies using *taxable* revenue bonds. But that is a questionable assumption. Some such projects would likely not be found to be as financially viable if their bonds carried an interest rate that is usually several percentage points higher than the rates on tax-exempt bonds. So those projects either would not be done at all, would be scaled back to a smaller size, would need public subsidies to offset the cost of taxable interest rates, or would be done by state toll agencies—using tax-exempt bonds! So the Treasury would realize little or no extra revenue if concession projects could only be financed by taxable bonds.

Some economists question the wisdom of granting tax-exempt status to P3 project bonds, despite their universal use by state toll agencies. To assess the impact of requiring P3 projects to use taxable revenue bonds, the author consulted a toll feasibility analyst who has worked on numerous public-sector and P3 toll projects. He provided a simplified example comparing a public-sector toll agency and a P3 developer looking at the same toll project. Table 3 shows that the P3 company would have two alternatives, given the two percentage point difference between the tax-exempt (3.5 percent) and taxable (5.5 percent) bond interest rates. Bond rating agencies want a high "coverage ratio," which is the ratio of annual revenue to annual debt service payments, such as the public toll agency's 2.0. In the example shown (P3, option 1), because of the higher interest rate, the coverage ratio would be only 1.7, which the rating agencies would likely translate into a lower bond rating, making it harder to sell the bonds. To increase the coverage ratio (P3 option 2), the company might make a more aggressive revenue forecast, achieving (on paper) a coverage ratio close to 2.0. But that is a risky assumption, and might also lead to a lower bond rating. So the "level financial playing field" rationale for having the same type of revenue bonds available to both state toll agencies and P3 concession companies results in lower-risk projects.

What about Availability-Payment Concessions?

Much of the discussion in this book concerns long-term concessions in which the primary funding source is toll revenues, which provide the basis for raising the large amounts of up-front debt and equity needed to pay for the design and construction of the project. But, as noted in chapter 5, some long-term concessions do not involve tolls. Instead, the government makes a long-term contractual commitment to annual payments, and the winning bidder can take that contract to the capital markets to raise debt and equity. In Europe, on some projects these payments are in the form of shadow tolls paid by the government based on the amount of traffic the highway or bridge attracts each year.

But increasingly, such nontoll concessions are based on annual "availability payments" from the government. In the United States, a state DOT generally has only one principal source of transportation money: existing federal and state fuel tax revenue. Therefore, while pure availability-payment (AP) concessions offer some of the benefits of toll concessions, they do not address the most important problem facing 21st-century US highways: not enough money. To be clear then, when a state opts for an AP concession, it is basically making a long-term commitment to make annual payments out of its already thinly stretched transportation budget—just as if it had issued bonds based on its expected future federal and/or state fuel tax revenues. An AP concession is not a new source of transportation funding; it is a way of financing and managing a transportation project using *existing* funding sources.

The above paragraph refers to what I have called "pure" AP concessions, which are common in Canada and European P3 projects, including many highways. But, as noted in chapter 5, some P3 highway projects in this country are being done as a kind of hybrid, in which the state charges tolls and takes on the traffic and revenue risk, but compensates the concession company by means of availability payments, for which the toll revenues may or may not be sufficient to fund that long-term payment obligation. That is the model used for Florida's I-595 and I-4 projects and Indiana's East End Bridge.

Whether in their pure or their hybrid form, what are the benefits of AP concessions compared with those of traditional highway procurement, either DBB or DB? The answer is that, even when they do not directly address the highway funding problem, AP concessions are a significant improvement over DBB or DB.

One major benefit is that, as with a toll concession, the competition to win an AP concession can generate innovation in design based on the need to minimize life-cycle cost, since the winning team will be responsible not just for construction but for all operating and maintenance costs over the long term of the concession. That can lead to significant overall cost savings, as measured by the annual availability payment that emerges from the competitive process. A good example is the Port of Miami Tunnel concession. Florida DOT had never done a major tunnel project or used a tunnel boring machine. So deciding on a billion-dollar project to bore a highway tunnel beneath a waterway to connect MacArthur Causeway with the island-based port was a highly risky project. FDOT's financial consultants estimated that if they could get a winning bid requiring an annual availability payment of $66 million per year or less, with the company taking on all construction and completion-date risk, it would be a good deal.

Three prequalified companies submitted proposals. When the bids were opened, the three were asking for annual payments, respectively, of $63 million, $38 million, and $33 million per year. Final negotiations with the latter team, the French companies Bouygues and Meridiam, led to a final price of $28 million per year. That was less than half the financial consultants' estimate.[20] The Port of Miami Tunnel also demonstrates the successful transfer of construction cost risk and schedule-completion risk from the state DOT to the concession company. In 2014 the completed tunnel opened, very close to on-schedule and on-budget, with very few change orders. The concession agreement makes the company fully responsible for all operations and maintenance for the entire 35-year term of the concession.

Around the country, several "natural experiments" are unde way which will make it possible within a few years to make side-by-side comparisons of conventional and AP concession procurements: the same type of highway projects, in the same geographic location and political jurisdiction, and carried out in more or less the same period of time. One of these is the Presidio Parkway in San Francisco, under which phase 1 was procured as a DBB project and phase 2 as a pure AP concession. Phase 1 took 48 months, twice its planned schedule, and incurred a 60-percent cost overrun. The P3 approach of phase 2 cost $254 million, which was $110 million less than the state DOT's original estimate—and was completed on time. [21]

Another pair of projects is the Ohio River Bridges effort carried out jointly by the DOTs of Indiana and Kentucky. Both new bridges are tolled to provide the primary revenue source, but Kentucky lacked a P3 enabling law, so its bridge was procured as a DB project while Indiana's was procured as a hybrid AP concession. In each case the state DOT will collect the toll revenue. While the two bridges are not identical, it will be interesting to see how they compare regarding cost overruns, on-time completion, and other performance indicators.

As this book is being written, something of a trend toward AP concessions is under way. In the highway sector, between 1993 and 2016 some 13 toll concessions were financed in the United States.[22] Beginning in 2009, nine AP concessions for highways were financed, including four with state-collected tolls. Since the beginning of AP highway concessions in 2009, nine more toll concession highway projects have been financed, so the AP trend is not an overwhelming shift, but is still a new trend.

There are two reasons for this trend. First, a growing number of construction firms seeking to bid on megaprojects have become comfortable with taking construction and completion risk, thanks to their experience with DB projects, and they are able to contract with asset management companies to handle the ongoing maintenance obligations. But they are leery of, or are simply unwilling to accept, traffic and revenue risk. State DOTs wanting a robust competition are therefore becoming more favorable to AP concessions, since more companies are likely to bid. Secondly, tolling is still controversial in many places, though less so for major bridge replacements. With AP concessions, some projects are being done without tolling, but others have the state DOT doing the tolling and accepting the traffic and revenue risks.

Some states (e.g., Texas and Virginia) do not allow availability payment concessions, since the long-term liability they create is another form of state debt. Florida and North Carolina officials have adopted a limit on the amount of AP liability the state can take on. Other states, such as California, Indiana, and Illinois, are only now embarking on their first AP concession projects and have not formally addressed the liability issue. But the head of Indiana DOT has told the Indiana Chamber of Commerce of his concern about larger-scale use of AP concessions, because "it's a lot like borrowing."[23]

Given both the long-term liabilities created by AP concessions and America's massive highway funding shortfall, my prediction is that pure AP concessions, such as the Port of Miami Tunnel, will turn out to be a niche market. Hybrid AP models, in which tolls provide a major funding source but the concession company is compensated via availability payments, will enjoy a decade or so of popularity before limits on toll risk and total availability payment liability are enacted. The primary longer-term trend will likely be toll concessions.

What about Leases of Existing Toll Roads?

As we saw in chapter 5, the leases of the Chicago Skyway and Indiana Toll Road (ITR) under very long-term concession agreements focused global investor interest on US toll concessions—but also stimulated considerable controversy. While many elected officials and commentators could appreciate the role that concession investment could play in bringing about new lanes or new highways (so-called greenfield projects), they saw no justification for applying the same concept to existing toll roads (brownfield projects).

In May 2007, after Democrats had regained control of the House of Representatives, two powerful members who had opposed the leases of the Skyway and ITR sent a letter to every state governor aiming "to discourage you from entering into public-private partnership (PPP) agreements that are not in the long-term public interest in a safe, integrated national transportation system." The signers were Rep. James Oberstar (D-MN) and Rep. Peter DeFazio (D-OR), at that time, respectively, chairman of the Committee on Transportation and Infrastructure and chair of its highways and transit subcommittee. Although the letter made an unspecific threat of legislation to remove the option of states engaging in long-term P3 concessions, their primary target was brownfield leases. During that same time period, the left-wing magazine *Mother Jones* carried a long article attacking P3 concessions,[24] and the populist TV commentator Lou Dobbs did several segments in which he complained about the "sale" of major highways to foreign companies.

Although Oberstar was defeated for re-election in 2010, his aim of making brownfield leases illegal, or at least less likely, was continued in 2012 by Sen. Jeff Bingaman (D-NM), who introduced several amendments to the then-pending highway bill. Two would have changed the tax treatment adversely for brownfield concessions and the third would have penalized states that leased toll roads by subtracting those miles from the state's total highway miles in the formula for distributing federal highway funding. None were included in the final bill, MAP-21, enacted later that year.

Oberstar and DeFazio criticized the US DOT's failure to question or forbid the leases of the Skyway and ITR (both of which are part of I-90 and are among the many Eastern and Midwestern Interstates developed as toll roads). They argued that these leases "will undermine the integrity of a national system." The head of the American Trucking Associations called this trend the "the piecemeal dismantling of the nation's Interstate highway network." Those critiques are absurd, given that the Interstate highways are owned by the 50 different state governments and that major Interstates in 14 of those states were developed and financed and operate today as toll roads, with their own individually developed toll systems and toll rate schedules.

More substantively, though—what benefits, if any, does the public receive from shifting tolled Interstates to private operation and management for terms of 40 to 99 years? The economist Richard Geddes of Cornell University devotes a chapter in his book *The Road to Renewal* to the subject of brownfield concessions.[25] He points out that the long term of brownfield concessions makes it likely that the concession company will have to rebuild and modernize the toll road at least once during the term of the agreement. That means that it will face construction and completion risks comparable to those encountered in greenfield concessions, but some years later. Both brownfield and greenfield toll concessions face traffic and revenue risks, but those risks are greater for a greenfield project because its traffic is far less certain than traffic on an existing highway. Accordingly, investors require a higher potential rate of return to take on a greenfield concession than a brownfield concession. Conversely, since the overall risk is judged to be lower on a brownfield project, investors have been willing to pay the net present value of 40 to 99 years' worth of lease payments up front for the right to acquire the brownfield concession.

Besides the eventual reconstruction (and widening, when and where needed), among the other potential public benefits from brownfield concessions Geddes cites are the following:

- *Competition in the operation and maintenance of toll roads.* Most existing toll roads are operated by state toll agencies as perpetual monopoly providers. Under a policy favoring long-term concessions, new operators and maintenance teams gain entry into this market, and poorly performing ones are subject to being bought out. Even the potential of new entry is likely to lead to improved performance by existing toll agencies and incumbent concession companies.

- *Improved public control over the toll road.* The concession agreement may increase transparency to the public about the performance standards in effect, and provide a stronger mechanism for holding the tollway operator accountable for meeting those standards. This was definitely true in the case of the Indiana Toll Road concession.

- *Risk transfer to investors.* Even though most of the financing of state toll agencies comes from toll revenue bonds, the risk of default may ultimately fall on the taxpayers. That was potentially the situation when the original Chicago Skyway went bankrupt and the city was sued in 1972 by the revenue bondholders. After five years with no payments, court-ordered toll increases led to resumption of interest payments, but principal payments did not resume until 1991.[26] Had the Skyway been operated by a concession company, the default would have been the company's problem, not the city's. In addition, another risk is that over the very long terms of some brownfield concessions, there could be major changes in transportation technology (e.g., autonomous vehicles), which could change the demand for highway use in ways we cannot foresee today. That kind of longer-term risk is also being shifted to investors via concession agreements.

- *Incentives to maximize traffic flow.* Congestion is not the friend of toll concession investors. Customers will pay to use their highway if they can travel fast and reliably, and investors will be happy if large numbers of customers choose to do that. This gives concession companies incentives to use variable pricing, to keep traffic flowing at high volumes and high speeds even during high-demand periods. State toll agencies have been slow to implement variable pricing.

- *Creation of new investment opportunities.* Pension funds and insurance companies, among other institutional investors, are seeking to make relatively stable long-term equity investments in airports and toll roads to supplement their holdings of utilities, railroads, and pipeline infrastructure. Brownfield toll roads are an excellent fit for such portfolios, whereas greenfield toll roads may be judged too risky. Larger institutional investors seek balanced infrastructure portfolios with a mix of brownfield and greenfield projects. These institutional investors cannot invest equity in government toll agencies.

- *Development of a "thicker" toll operating industry.* Bringing in experienced global operators to the US toll road industry is likely to increase its competence and expertise, drawing on global best practices.

- *Improved governance, transparency, and accounting standards.* Not all toll agencies are run as businesses, using generally accepted accounting principles (GAAP). And as nonprofit agencies, they are not directly accountable to any shareholders.

So there is potential for improved governance via world-class concession management expertise.

- *Incentives to adopt new technologies.* As noted earlier, the first use of transponders for highway-speed variable tolling was accomplished by the concession company that developed California's 91 Express Lanes. And the Indiana Toll Road Concession Company made converting from cash to electronic toll collection one of its first priorities after taking over that toll road. Most US toll agencies are still in the process of converting to all-electronic tolling, despite its lower cost and superior customer service.

I agree with most of Geddes' assessment of brownfield concession benefits. In comparing concession companies with state or local toll agencies, much depends on the caliber of the toll agency in question, and this varies enormously around the country, as will be discussed below.

More broadly, if the basic premise of this book is correct—that the highway sector needs to be rethought and reorganized as a network utility (like electricity, gas, water, cable, telecoms, railroads, etc.)—then whether a major highway is today a traditional "free" road, a state-run toll road, or a planned road waiting to be financed and developed is somewhat beside the point. All such highways would need to be transformed into utility-type businesses, paid directly by their customers and directly accountable to their owners.

As Richard Little, former director of the Keston Institute for Public Finance and Infrastructure Policy at the University of Southern California, has written, "Changing the perception that infrastructure services are a market commodity rather than a public good will not be easy. However, the shift away from the tax-allocation model employed in the US at the federal level for the past 50 years to pay for infrastructure has made such public entrepreneurism a financial necessity."[27]

Why Not Just Use Government Toll Agencies?

Over the past two decades I have often spoken at various conferences of the toll roads' trade group, the International Bridge, Tunnel and Turnpike Association (IBTTA). I have gotten to know many senior people at toll agencies across the country, who are smart, competent, and successful. Some of them have pioneered the transition from cash tolling to early electronic tolling at toll booths, followed by adding bypasses of toll booths (open-road tolling), and finally implementing fully all-electronic cashless tolling at highway speed for everyone.

The IBTTA also represents most of the global toll concession companies, so I have also gotten to know many of their senior people, who are at least equally smart, competent, and successful. But there are important differences between what toll concession managers can do and what government toll agency managers can do. The institutional frameworks differ in some obvious ways, and in many other more subtle ways. So do the external environments in which they operate—and the extent to which politics affects them.

There are also, unfortunately, some toll agencies that have built empires of patronage and pork-barrel, seemingly immune from good-government oversight. My years of contact with the industry lead me to conclude that this latter category is only a small fraction of US toll agencies, despite perceptions in the media and elsewhere that such agencies are typical. But even the well run high-performance toll agencies face limitations and constraints that can prevent them from delivering the same kind of performance that is possible via toll concessions, despite the qualifications and competence of the toll agency management staff.

The Governance Question

How do those who create an enterprise ensure that it is properly run? When economists study business entities, they refer to this as the "principal-agent" problem. Specifically, when shareholders provide the funds for a corporation, they are its principals, and the managers they hire to run the company are their agents. In corporate governance, the larger shareholders are represented on the board of directors, but even smaller shareholders can vote on various measures that are up for consideration. Groups of shareholders—individuals or institutions—can band together to hold managers accountable for implementing strategy to achieve agreed-upon corporate goals.

When economists observe state-owned enterprises, they find a much murkier governance picture—and government toll agencies are a classic example of state-owned enterprises (SOEs). As economist Richard Geddes puts it, "Since a toll authority SOE has no well-defined, active group of owners, its goals remain fuzzy, open to debate, and susceptible to external influence." This leads to an "absence of managerial accountability. . . . When performance is deficient in one area, management can simply claim they were focused on a different goal, with the choice influenced by the group or groups that are more politically effective at any given time—whether unions, environmentalists, consumer groups, or, less frequently, taxpayers."[28] He goes on to say that the absence of a group of shareholder-owners means that "no one bears directly the consequences—through tangible changes in its members' wealth—of managerial decisions." Citizens nominally own the toll agency, but the influence of individual citizen-taxpayers is negligible, compared to that of organized interest groups. Therefore, citizen interest in monitoring the performance of toll agency managers is very weak.

A well-known World Bank report on the problems inherent in state-owned enterprises sums up the problem this way:

> Bureaucrats typically perform poorly in business, not because they are incompetent (they aren't) but because they face contradictory goals and perverse incentives that can distract and discourage even very able and dedicated public servants. The problem is not the people but the system, not bureaucrats per se but the situations they find themselves in as bureaucrats in business.[29]

In what follows we will look at examples illustrating how institutional constraints affect the performance of government toll agencies.

Why Do We Have Government Toll Agencies?

As noted briefly in chapter 3, the model of a government toll agency originated during the Progressive Era in the latter part of the 19th century. Ideas of scientific management and rule by experts, as opposed to politicians,) gained popularity in that period, stimulated by popular disgust with the corruption involved in efforts to develop the Brooklyn Bridge via a traditional government-granted franchise. Two of the earliest toll agencies developed on Progressive Era principles were the Port of New York Authority (which later became the Port Authority of New York and New Jersey) and New York City's Triborough Bridge Authority (which became the Triborough Bridge and Tunnel Authority). These agencies' success in using revenue bonds to build major bridges, tunnels, and parkways led to the model being adopted by the Commonwealth of Pennsylvania to develop and operate the nation's first tolled superhighway, the Pennsylvania Turnpike. And, based on that turnpike's early success, the toll agency model was widely adopted by states during the post–World War II turnpike era.

The toll agency model has remained the principal vehicle for US toll roads through the present day, including the creation of many urban-area toll agencies since the 1960s. Until quite recently, a principal advantage of the toll agency model was that it was able to finance highway projects using tax-exempt revenue bonds. Congress altered that picture in 2005, when the surface transportation reauthorization bill enacted that year authorized up to $15 billion worth of federally tax-exempt private activity bonds (PABs) for use in P3 highway projects. PABs have been used for the majority of P3 concession megaprojects to date, and recent projections indicate that the entire allowed $15 billion in bonding may be allocated to projects before the next reauthorization of the federal highway program.

Despite institutional problems, as illustrated below, the toll agency model so far remains the dominant form for bringing about tolled highways, bridges, and tunnels in America.

Institutional Problems with Toll Agencies

A sampling of the kinds of problems enabled by the current organizational and governance structure of toll agencies includes empire building, politicization, not maximizing in-house talent, accounting system problems, and poor pricing policies. Not all toll agencies have these problems, but most are vulnerable to them, given current arrangements.

EMPIRE BUILDING.   The classic example of a toll agency that became an empire beyond political control was the Triborough Bridge and Tunnel Authority under Robert Moses, its director from 1924 to 1968. The very independence that Moses demanded and obtained, combined with ever-increasing toll revenue, insulated the agency from political challenge for most of Moses's long tenure. Moses wielded unchallenged power to condemn land for his projects during most of his career. The biographer Robert Caro describes the amazing empire Moses created, including its own flag, distinctive license plates, fleets of yachts, automobiles, and trucks, and "its own uniformed army—'Bridge & Tunnel Officers' who guarded its toll booths, revolver-carrying Long Island Parkway Police who patrolled its suburban parks and roads."[30] Thanks to the agency's huge revenues, Moses was able to exert enough political influence to keep it exempt from any oversight by either the state or the city government. Geddes points to this as "a deplorable governance failure due directly to the organizational form of a public authority SOE."[31]

A second example is the Pennsylvania Turnpike, governed by the Pennsylvania Turnpike Commission. Journalist William Keisling is among those who have chronicled this agency's long history of political patronage and excessive spending. In his 1995 book *Helping Hands*, he wrote the following:

> The two political parties for all practical purposes own the Pennsylvania Turnpike Commission. . . . To help facilitate the awarding of jobs, each party since 1985 has employed a patronage boss, officially known as assistant executive directors for the western (currently a Republican) and eastern (currently a Democrat) regions. Their job has been to help the party bosses . . . dole out jobs to the party faithful. The booty is not just jobs. Billions of dollars in all sorts of contracts are awarded.[32]

When Gov. Ed Rendell in 2007 attempted to lease the Turnpike for 75 years, along the lines of the successful leasing of the Indiana Toll Road, he not surprisingly faced bipartisan opposition in the state legislature and an all-out lobbying and PR campaign by the Turnpike arguing against the deal. Ultimately, despite a competitively selected high bid of $12.8 billion from a global toll road concession company, the legislature failed to pass the enabling legislation and the offer was withdrawn.

Geddes points out that this kind of out-of-control management can happen for a short period of time in investor-owned companies such as Enron or Tyco, but that "those failures lasted for weeks or months rather than for decades" because of the ability of shareholders to either oust flawed management or to withdraw their investment, putting the company at risk of collapse. Citizen-owners have no way to withdraw their capital from out-of-control government enterprises.

A third example comes from one of the newer urban toll agencies, the North Texas Tollway Authority. NTTA is generally considered a well-run toll agency which pioneered transponder tolling in the late 1980s and was, as of 2010, also one of the first toll agencies to go completely cashless. But in 2007, under a new board chairman, NTTA engaged in a bizarre challenge to toll concessions. The Texas DOT had run a competitive procurement for a concession to complete the construction of a new urban toll road in the Dallas metro area, SH 121, and operate it for 50 years.

After the winning bidder had been selected, NTTA announced that it would match or exceed that bid. Given that the winning Cintra/J. P. Morgan team had offered an up-front payment of $2.1 billion, NTTA had to abandon its traditional conservative financing policy to match that huge payment. It mortgaged its entire tollway system to pay for this one new project. To pay the projected debt service on the new bonds it would issue, it adopted a much more aggressive toll schedule, to increase the toll rates on all its toll roads by a flat 32 percent in July 2007, and then at the rate of inflation every year for 50 years. In the end, NTTA used its clout in the legislature to override Cintra's (and the Federal Highway Administration's) objections to this intervention into an otherwise completed procurement, and the SH 121 project was given to NTTA.[33] To finance the deal, NTTA issued new debt, increasing its total from $1.56 billion in 2006 to $5.05 billion in 2007 and $7.28 billion in 2008.[34] Needless to say, the agency's bond rating was reduced by the rating agencies Moody's and Standard & Poor's, given its far more aggressive financing approach. In 2010, the NTTA board chairman who had taken this major departure from prudent management was ousted. Unfortunately, the huge new debt and much higher toll rates are still in place.

POLITICIZATION.   The opposite of toll agency empire-building, resulting from too little political oversight, is that the agency becomes a tool of politicians. This most commonly occurs when politicians force the agency to divert revenues away from its business of providing highways, bridges, and tunnels for its toll-paying customers, and instead spends them on politically favored projects. No toll agency has started out with this the idea of funding a wide array of nontoll and nonhighway projects, but over time many of them have been required to do so.

Two of the largest diverters of toll revenues are in the New York metro area. The Port Authority of New York & New Jersey (PANYNJ) operates the George Washington Bridge, several other bridges, and two major tunnels between the two states. Charging among the highest toll rates in the country, the agency uses toll revenue to heavily subsidize the PATH subway between the two states, which it was forced to take over in 1962. That deal came about as part of a bi-state agreement to allow the Port Authority to build the World Trade Center, its first major venture beyond self-supporting highway and airport infrastructure. PATH and the rebuilding of the World Trade Center continue to be major drains on the agency's toll revenue. A recent report on the Port Authority from the Rudin Center estimated PATH's loss in 2012 as about $400 million, and also estimated that between 2002 and 2020 the Port Authority will have put more than $4.6 billion into PATH, not counting nearly $4 billion it spent to replace the PATH station at the World Trade Center.[35]

The regional AAA affiliate sued the Port Authority over using revenues from its latest toll increases for its $15 billion reconstruction of the World Trade Center,[36] but eventually lost the case. In 2015 a new case of revenue diversion came to light: the administration of New Jersey Gov. Chris Christie had lobbied successfully to use $1.8 billion of Port Authority funds to refurbish the Pulaski Skyway, a 3.5-mile elevated highway owned not by PANYNJ but by the state of New Jersey. An investigation into this diversion is under way by both the Manhattan District Attorney's Office and the Securities and Exchange Commission.[37]

A similar change was forced on the Triborough Bridge and Tunnel Authority. In 1967, New York Gov. Nelson Rockefeller championed a plan to merge all the transportation agencies in New York City, including Triborough, into a new Metropolitan Transportation Authority. The plan aimed to capture Triborough's toll revenues to subsidize the increasingly money-losing rail transit lines. Moses, still in charge at age 79, opposed the plan but was eventually bought off by Rockefeller's implied promise to him of a seat on the new MTA's board. Voters approved the merger in November of that year, but Triborough's bondholders proceeded with a legal challenge to the diversion of their toll revenues. But, as Caro recounts the story, the bondholders were represented by Chase Manhattan Bank, then run by David Rockefeller, the governor's brother. After some private discussions, a stipulation withdrawing the suit was signed by both Rockefellers on February 9, 1968, and taken directly to the chambers of the judge who would have tried the suit. The judge approved the deal, based on the nominal agreement of both sides, and the agreement was sealed (not open for public review).[38]

Moses was given only a "consultant" position with the taken-over Triborough, not the promised MTA board seat. Since that time, the renamed MTA Bridges and Tunnels has been the MTA's cash cow. A 2016 report from Moody's Investors Service noted that over the previous five years, MTAB&T had transferred $3 billion to its parent MTA to support its transit services.[39]

Other fairly well-known examples of politically mandated diversion of toll revenues to nonhighway uses include the following:[40]

- The New York State Thruway Authority was required to divert toll revenues to subsidize the Erie Canal and other waterways in the state, until this practice was found to be unconstitutional in 2016.[41]

- The New Jersey Turnpike is required to divert about 20 percent of its toll revenues to other transportation purposes in the state.
- The Atlantic City Expressway must divert toll revenue to various development projects in Atlantic City.
- The West Virginia Turnpike is required to use toll revenues to subsidize economic development and tourism.
- The Delaware River Port Authority (DRPA, originally a toll bridge agency) is required to subsidize a mass transit rail line and ferry using toll revenues, and until recently was also required to spend money on economic development projects.
- The Pennsylvania Turnpike, under Act 44 (enacted in 2007), is required to transfer $450 million per year to the state DOT to use for highway and transit funding statewide. In prior years, the turnpike had been required to build several money-losing toll roads in the Pittsburgh area, widely referred to as "pork pikes."
- In Virginia, the Dulles Toll Road in 2006 was transferred from the state DOT to the Metropolitan Washington Airports Authority for the purpose of using tripled toll rates to heavily subsidize the $5.7 billion extension of the Washington Metro rail line to Dulles Airport and beyond.
- In 2013 the state legislature required the Ohio Turnpike to issue $1.5 billion in new debt, backed by increased future toll rates, to help fund other highway projects in the state.
- The Harris County Toll Road Authority in Houston in recent years has devoted 23 to 28 percent of its revenue to non-toll-road purposes.
- In San Francisco, both the Golden Gate Bridge and the Bay Area Toll Authority (which operates the other toll bridges in the region) use part of their toll revenues for transit subsidies.

These 12 examples are the exception rather than the rule. But many of them are in high-profile cities and states, creating the impression that using toll revenues for nonhighway purposes is common practice. In fact, any use of toll revenues beyond what is needed for the capital and operating costs of the toll facility amounts to a tax that singles out toll payers rather than applying equally to all motorists or all taxpayers.

The lack of external oversight of four federally authorized bi-state toll authorities, including PANYNJ and DRPA, was criticized by the US Government Accountability Office in a 2013 report.[42] The bond rating agencies have also expressed concern about the diversion of toll revenues to nonhighway purposes. In 2012, Moody's Investors Service released a report on the use of toll agencies as cash cows by state and metro area governments.[43] It presented empirical data showing that toll agencies subject to such "external transfers" have weaker financials than those not so burdened.

MANAGEMENT AND PERSONNEL PROBLEMS.   The CEOs of most state toll agencies are appointed by the state governor, and serve at his or her pleasure. That means they are generally replaced when a new governor enters office, especially if there has been a change of political parties. That plays havoc with attracting career professionals who can focus on the medium to long term. It also generally means that senior managers are not paid market-based compensation that accords with the scope of their responsibilities in running what are often billion-dollar-scale enterprises.

In one egregious example, Peter Samuel points out that CEOs of the Massachusetts Turnpike Authority during the decades of the Big Dig's planning and construction served an average tenure of just two years. "Often these people were former legislators or persons aspiring to higher political office. Their preoccupation was to avoid trouble, or more precisely, the perception of trouble, during their time at the helm."[44] As an example, a review of the Big Dig fiasco by the Massachusetts inspector general found that in 1994, "Big Dig managers decreased the [internal] $13.8 billion estimate to $8 billion for public relations purposes in 1994–95 by applying a series of exclusions, deductions, and accounting assumptions."[45]

Suboptimal personnel are a problem that goes beyond top management at many toll agencies. To the extent that they are subject to a state's civil service law, engineers and other professionals will likely have lower pay and benefits at a toll agency than they would doing comparable jobs in the private sector. And while many toll agencies do contract with engineering, financial, and legal firms for various functions, unless they have highly skilled in-house professionals dealing with the outside firms, the agencies may end up paying for more services than they need, or may be taken advantage of in situations where a more highly skilled and knowledgeable staff would not have been.

A former executive director of the previously mentioned toll agency NTTA, Jose Figueredo, provided confidential performance review reports to the board of directors during his one-year tenure. Three such reports from 2008 were obtained by the *Dallas Morning News* in 2012. Among the newspaper's revelations were Figueredo's assessment that "the reality is that the NTTA suffers from a marginally talented workforce, lack of strong internal systems and controls, and a rigid culture that has to be replaced." He also stated that, during the interview process leading to his being hired, board members had made clear to him that "to be successful, major changes had to be made to the organization, its employees, and its culture." But he also reported "serious and systematic resistance to change within NTTA." He laid out a two-phase long-term transformation plan for the agency. But by the end of that year, differences between Figueredo and his board led to his resignation.[46]

Private sector firms increasingly base part of their compensation of key people on performance, which is a way of both motivating people to excel and of holding them accountable for results. Civil service systems do not permit this kind of compensation.

ACCOUNTING SYSTEM SHORTCOMINGS. In 1999, *Public Works Financing* published a short article on the fact that many toll agencies at that time still used cash-based accounting. An excerpt from that article explains the problem:

> U.S. toll authorities vary enormously in the quality of their accounting for the cost and life of their principal assets—their roadway pavement and their bridges and tunnel structures. Some abide by the best commercial practices, using full accrual accounting and realistic asset valuations. Others use cash accounting and report only general fund categories, which makes it impossible to gauge their financial condition, even short-term. Some are often quite opportunistic longer term, too, and make no allowance at all for depreciation of their principal assets, even while outside of the accounts they are saying they will need to do very expensive rebuilding a few years out.[47]

Even as that article appeared, change was on the horizon. The Government Accounting Standards Board had just issued GASB Statement 34, a new set of standards for accrual accounting in state and local governments, including toll agencies. While the original draft required major assets such as highways and bridges to be depreciated, as is required for private-sector assets under generally accepted accounting principles, there was much resistance to this by governments, so that the final published version in 1999 allowed for expensing maintenance costs as long as the reported condition of the facility demonstrated that maintenance expenditures were adequate to maintain asset values. This change brought about increased focus on asset-management strategies, leading to the growth of highway maintenance companies operating under 5- to 10-year contracts.

Besides GASB 34, which included no enforcement mechanism, the other factor pushing toll agencies into adopting accrual accounting has been the evolution of toll collection into fully all-electronic non-cash tolling (AET), a process that is still underway. As Bob Covington of the Washington State DOT put it in a 2013 presentation, "Traditional tolling (toll booths) supported cash basis accounting. Movement to the use of [billing, under AET] requires a change to full accrual or modified accrual basis of accounting."[48] That's because the life cycle of a toll transaction in AET is more complex; it includes debiting of a prepaid account, billing, and subsequent collection activities. Traditional toll-agency cash accounting fails to support self-balancing accounts with double-entry debit/credit subsidiary accounting, and fails to support transactional and financial accountability.

Covington's organization, the Washington state DOT, is a relative newcomer to significant toll operations, and because most of its operations will be AET, they can essentially start their accounting system with a clean sheet of paper. But his 2013 presentation implies that there are still toll agencies still collecting some of their revenue in cash that have not switched to accrual accounting and financial reporting consistent with generally accepted accounting principles.

PRICING SHORTCOMINGS.   In a private business, the pricing of products and services is a subject of ongoing management attention. Offering different prices for different levels of service is increasingly common, as we encounter with airlines and with the surge pricing of Uber and Lyft. Adjusting prices regularly for inflation is common on toll facilities managed under concessions. But most state toll agencies, fearing political backlash over high prices, tend to keep their toll rates unchanged for many years—which means that their rates actually go down over time in real, inflation-adjusted terms. Incoming Indiana Gov. Mitch Daniels, with a long career in the private sector before being elected governor, was astonished to find that toll rates on the Indiana Toll Road had not been increased for 20 years, and that at some toll booths the 15-cent toll cost more to collect than the amount of the toll.

Eventually, of course, the rising costs of staff, maintenance, and repaving catch up with the toll agency and force it to increase the toll rates. But by that point, the increase is large, causing both customer and political resistance. Even larger toll rate increases are needed when the toll road needs major capital investment, such as rebuilding obsolete interchanges or reconstructing major stretches of worn-out pavement. Hardly any toll agencies charge depreciation on their assets or set aside money in sinking funds to replace their assets as they wear out. So the resulting toll increases can be huge when they finally occur. The toll analyst Peter Samuel calls the result "earthquake pricing."

By contrast, toll concession companies typically seek to include in their long-term concession agreements the right to increase toll rates modestly at regular intervals, generally based on an inflation index such as the consumer price index (CPI). Keeping toll rates flat or slightly rising in real terms ensures that the toll road owner-operator can keep pace with the ongoing costs of doing business and set aside money for future capital spending needs, thus reducing the size and cost of future bond issues. In recent years a number of well-run toll agencies (e.g., in Colorado, Florida, and Texas) have received permission for CPI-adjusted toll rates, but they are exceptions to the general rule.

A second problem with the pricing policy of nearly all toll agencies is to ignore the potential of variable tolling to manage traffic flow and reduce the extent of congestion. Ever since the 91 Express Lanes in Orange County, California, began using variable tolling in 1995, numerous HOT lane and express toll-lane projects have been implemented by state DOTs and concession companies on urban freeways in large metro areas. In every case, variable pricing has worked well to ensure free-flowing traffic in these special lanes, even during the worst rush hours.

Only a handful of toll agencies have put a toe into the water of variable pricing for all their lanes. The three suburban toll roads in Orange County, California (run by the Transportation Corridor Agencies); the toll bridges in Lee County, Florida; the New Jersey Turnpike; and the Port Authority of New York and New Jersey are among the few toll agencies that have introduced toll rates that are slightly higher during peak periods than at other hours of the day. And those differential rates have led to modest reductions in congestion—but not to anything like the free-flow conditions in express toll lanes.

Only two toll operators thus far have decided to add express toll lanes to existing urban-area toll roads. The first was the concession company Abertis, which has added such higher-priced express toll lanes to the PR-22 toll road that it is operating under a 40-year concession in Puerto Rico. The new express lanes opened in mid-2013.[49] Florida's Turnpike

Enterprise in late 2012 announced that as part of widening two of its urban-area toll corridors—the Homestead Extension in the Miami area, and the Veterans Expressway in the Tampa area—some of the new lanes will be express lanes with variable toll rates. In the case of Miami, the turnpike's express toll lanes will be part of a network of express toll lanes that is under development by the Florida DOT on most of the region's expressways. The Miami-Dade Expressway Authority, as of this writing, is still debating whether to add such lanes to its highly congested Dolphin Expressway, which would otherwise constitute a missing link in the network plan.

Another problem for some toll agencies is politically mandated exemptions from tolls for various categories of users. This is a major problem in California, where thousands of public officials have legal exemptions from paying tolls on toll bridges, toll roads, and express/HOT lanes.[50] While it is understandable that on-duty emergency vehicles (police, fire, emergency medical) would be exempt from tolls, and no big deal that buses are exempt from express lane tolls, granting exemptions to numerous categories of public officials is both unwarranted and unwise. Their vehicles contribute to wear and tear on the highways and bridges, and contribute to traffic congestion. On express toll lanes in particular, the more vehicles that are exempted from paying the variable toll, the less the pricing power of those tolls to restrain congestion. The same applies to politically granted exceptions to express lane tolls for various kinds of alternative-fuel vehicles.

A related problem is that many special interest groups have lobbied successfully for toll agencies to create special categories for their type of vehicle—such as motor homes or tow trucks—and grant them lower toll rates. As Peter Samuel points out, "As toll collection becomes automated with electronic tolling, vehicle classification is often the biggest challenge because the different classes of vehicle are dictated by politicians with no regard for the feasibility of using sensors—electromagnetic signatures, lasers, video pattern recognition and so forth—to establish vehicle class."[51]

This discussion of the limitations of government toll agencies suggests that the original idea that led to their creation—of professional management insulated from politics—has been largely subverted over the decades, as politics has increasingly intruded into what were intended to be quasibusiness enterprises. The 2014 "Bridgegate" scandal involving the Port Authority of New York and New Jersey has led to serious discussions about fundamental reform. The Rudin Center report chastised the agency for having spent more than $800 million between 2002 and 2012 on "regional projects" selected by the governors of the two states, projects the *New York Times* reporter described accurately as "zero-return projects."[52] An article in the *Financial Times* deplored "a trend toward politicization at some of the US's most important infrastructure managers, which is adding to already significant problems of poor management."[53] It quoted Tom Wright, the executive director of the Regional Plan Association, as saying that agencies such as the Port Authority and Triborough "are no longer non-political, frankly."

To be sure, there is a spectrum of toll agencies, from those that are highly politicized and poorly managed to those that are relatively innovative and well managed. But the inherent constraints on toll agencies as part of the public sector help to make the case for a better organizational and governance model for highways, as proposed in this book.

Summary

This chapter has made a case that the US experience thus far demonstrates that the P3 toll concession model is generating significant benefits compared with those of the 20th-century model of highway funding, procurement, and management, including that carried out by government toll agencies. These benefits include better incentives to minimize cost overruns and late completion of major highway, bridge, and tunnel projects, as well as a greater likelihood of cost-saving and performance-enhancing design innovations. From the standpoint of overall economic productivity, toll financing provides an important tool for screening out highway boondoggles whose costs clearly exceed their benefits. A system based on P3 concessions also offers guaranteed long-term highway maintenance, which would solve a chronic problem of deferred maintenance in a great many states.

This new model would also directly address the serious and growing shortfall in productive highway investment. Financing major projects up front means that many much-needed projects—replacing obsolete bridges and aging Interstates—could be done when needed, not decades later, when cash funding could be scraped together. And using per-mile tolls for these projects would be a large first step toward replacing fading per-gallon fuel taxes with per-mile charges tailored to the cost of the replacement highways and bridges. The toll concession model helps overcome the difficulty politicians have, by "outsourcing the political will" to make greater use of tolling. And with the right kind of performance standards and oversight (to be discussed in chapter 8), it should be possible to have highways that perform better and deliver greater value to highway users than those provided today by either state DOTs or government toll agencies.

That is a large set of claimed benefits. But I am not alone in seeing the value in these institutional changes. The bond rating agency Fitch released an assessment of this trend in 2006, at the height of the controversy over the leasing of existing toll roads. Among the benefits it cited were:

- cost-effectiveness and timely project delivery;
- efficient operations, maintenance, and life-cycle asset management;
- lower government investment;
- higher valuation of highway assets by equity investors;
- ability to have realistic toll rate increases over time, to keep pace with costs; and
- more efficient transport of people, goods, and services.[54]

Bill Reinhardt, founder and editor of the journal of record of the emerging P3 infrastructure industry, wrote a briefing paper on P3 infrastructure in 2014. I will close this chapter with a brief excerpt from that document.[55]

The P3 model is part of the answer to the mega-project cost and schedule problem. By incentivizing private equity to organize and manage large, complex projects (and with sophisticated lenders as the major stakeholders), P3 developers meet deadlines and budgets, or they lose money and someone gets fired. Once the project commitments are signed, there are no construction contract disputes that affect schedule, no excuses for poor performance, no scope creep, and no state senators demanding leniency for a campaign contributor who bends rebar.

Governments demand far higher performance and innovation from their private P3 partners and far stronger financial guarantees than they do from contractors on conventional public works projects. . . . Penalties for underperformance get paid [via warrantees and letters of credit], not litigated.

There is growing evidence that P3 projects are being built for considerably less than public projects. . . . On average, Macquarie found that P3 projects in the U.S. are approximately 15% less expensive than traditional public sector procurements, even for more complicated projects. . . .

To summarize, design-build-finance-operate-maintain delivery of big infrastructure combines the public benefits of accelerated delivery of service improvements, on-time completion, a growing record on first-cost savings, and public budget certainty on both capital and long-term maintenance costs. Public agencies are transferring some risks of ownership, and for the first time are getting valuable information from private bidders on price, schedule, quality, and other aspects of mega-project management. Competition for projects has never been greater, and the availability and price of investment capital is optimal for well-structured projects.

Yet, despite this rousing endorsement, Reinhardt is not optimistic that this model will take a major share of public works delivery in the foreseeable future. That is because there is considerable opposition to the P3 concession model, which is the subject of our next chapter.

CHAPTER SEVEN

Critics and Controversy: Opposition to Tolling and Long-Term Concessions

A s we saw in chapter 6, there can be significant benefits from using long-term concessions rather than traditional methods of developing and operating highways. But this shift from traditional ways of doing things represents a major change. It not only alters the traditional roles of the state DOT and private-sector firms, but it also changes the relationship between highway users and highway providers. Instead of the user paying fuel taxes that are allocated by the legislature, the user becomes a *customer* who pays tolls directly to the highway provider.

Social scientists refer to such major changes as "paradigm shifts." A paradigm is a shared understanding of how things work, whether that be a scientific theory (Newtonian physics versus Einsteinian physics), an organizational form (sole proprietorship versus shareholder-owned corporation), or a new business model (traditional bookstores versus online book sales). It's natural that individuals, organizations, and governments become comfortable with an established paradigm and tend to resist proposed new paradigms. Some resistance results from not understanding aspects of the new paradigm. Other resistance stems from genuine disagreements about the changed roles involved in the new approach. Still other resistance is to be expected from those who see their interests threatened if the new paradigm displaces the old one.

In the short history of US long-term highway concessions, we have seen opposition of all three types. This chapter reviews them and assesses the arguments they are making.

Grass-Roots Populist Opposition

Terri Hall is a self-described home-schooling mother in San Antonio, Texas. Starting in 2005, she became the most outspoken grass-roots opponent of tolling and highway concessions in Texas, and her example has inspired counterparts in other states. Her opposition efforts began locally by creating the "San Antonio Toll Party" (a play on "tea party") to oppose plans by Texas DOT and the local transportation agency (the Alamo Regional Mobility Authority) to develop several planned but unfunded highway improvements using tolls and/or long-term concessions. She tapped into growing statewide opposition to Gov. Perry's grandiose Trans-Texas Corridor vision by creating Texans Uniting for Reform and Freedom (TURF).

Hall has an obvious talent for rhetoric. She's a prolific writer of op-ed articles and a regular speaker at public hearings. She attracted a following that enabled her to organize mass turnouts at such hearings, build effective websites, and create short videos such as *Truth Be Tolled*. One of her practices is to portray tolls as taxes; she regularly refers to them as "toll taxes"—which rhymes with "poll taxes," automatically creating a doubly negative connotation. Many others have picked up on this term, including legislators, editorial writers, and activist groups.

In a 2012 op-ed article, Hall made seven arguments against P3 toll roads in the space of 750 words:[1]

- double taxation,
- the fact that taxpayers brought three-quarters of the money to the table for the NTE project in Fort Worth,
- guaranteed private profits at the public's expense,
- taxpayer bailouts when P3 toll roads go bankrupt,
- government-sanctioned monopolies that leave commuters with only one way to get where they need to go,
- loss of sovereignty and control over the surrounding free routes, and
- managed (express toll) lanes that create scarcity through pricing.

Since these arguments are typical in grass-roots populist opposition to toll concessions, it's worth examining each of them.

"Double Taxation"

Hall and other grass-roots critics argue that unless a proposed toll project can be financed 100 percent on the basis of toll revenue, it should not be built. Thus, any project that requires the state to chip in, say, 20 percent of the total, represents "double taxation" and a subsidy to the private sector. In effect, their view is that only "private toll roads," as attempted by several pioneering states in the 1990s, are legitimate. But, as we saw in chapter 5, very few projects can meet that standard. Given the very high costs imposed by various environmental laws, state and federal design standards (some of which are obsolete), and state DOTs' desire to have new toll projects interface with existing highways exactly as they see fit, the costs of building any new highway project are much higher than most people realize. And especially in urban environments where there are huge networks of nontolled roads, charging tolls high enough to cover all those costs would attract few customers, and hence not generate enough revenues to recover the construction and financing costs, let alone the ongoing operations and maintenance costs.

In this real-world setting, the public-private partnership has emerged as a more feasible alternative to truly private toll roads, and as a way to draw private capital and expertise into the highway sector. In most toll concession megaprojects financed in this country to date, the typical state DOT contribution is 20 to 30 percent of the total project cost. In effect, the state DOT *buys down* the amount that must be recovered from toll revenues to an amount that makes the project financeable with reasonable toll rates. From the DOT's standpoint, this is still a great deal. Instead of having to come up with 100 percent of a megaproject's cost, it can put in 20 percent and have the capital markets finance the rest, based on tolls willingly paid by customers who choose to use the new capacity.

That picture describes what is called the "base case" financial model of the planned tollway. If things turn out worse than the base case (e.g., higher construction costs and/or lower traffic and revenue), the concession company bears those losses. On the other hand, if things turn out much better than the base case, many concession agreements include revenue sharing, in which a portion of the higher toll revenue gets turned over to the state DOT (generally an increasing fraction, the higher the total revenue goes). In this type of agreement, the state will end up getting a return on its up-front investment if things turn out better than projected in the base case.

"Taxpayers Fund the Majority of the Project"

This claim appears again and again, not merely in grass-roots literature but also in newspaper editorials (e.g., the conservative *Washington Times*) and even in a highway industry publication called *Roads & Bridges*.[2] Let's see how people are able to come up with such a claim.

In her 2012 op-ed, Terri Hall used as an example the $2.1 billion North Tarrant Express (phases 1 and 2, financed in 2009). Its financing structure is very similar to that of other toll megaproject concessions. That financing breaks down as follows:[3]

Private equity	$428.8 million	20%
Toll revenue bonds	400.0 million	19%
TIFIA loan	702.4 million	34%
TxDOT money	570.0 million	27%
Totals	$2,101.2 million	100%

Hall and others add up the toll revenue bonds, the TIFIA loan, and the TxDOT contribution to reach 80 percent of the project budget as "government" funding, with only the private equity being counted as private. But the private equity is analogous to the down payment on a house made by the buyer, with the bonds and loan being the equivalent to a first and second mortgage. The toll revenue bonds are tax-exempt private activity bonds, as we saw in chapter 5, thanks to Congress in 2005 agreeing that the federal government should grant the same tax-exempt status to revenue bonds issued for P3 toll projects as it had long allowed for government toll agency projects. TIFIA is a federal program with strong bipartisan support that makes subordinated loans to transportation projects with (1) an investment-grade rating on their senior debt, and (2) a dedicated revenue stream.

The bottom-line point is that, just as you are responsible for your monthly mortgage payments for the entire duration of your mortgage, so is the toll concession company responsible for paying off those bonds and loans during their terms. The bonds and loan, in fact, have priority over the equity in terms of who gets paid when. And in the event that the project goes belly-up, the equity providers stand to lose 100 percent of their equity investment, with the debt providers having first claims on the assets. Thus, the claim that these P3 concessions are largely "funded by government" is simply incorrect.

"Guaranteed Profits"

This claim also appears repeatedly in the grass-roots anti-P3 literature. Yet there is no evidence to back it up. A major part of the value-for-money analysis to decide whether a particular project is better carried out via a concession is estimating the value of risk transfer to the private sector. In a toll concession, the largest risk is that traffic and revenue will turn out to be lower than in the base-case model, putting debt service payments and profits at risk. But that risk is willingly assumed by the winning bidder, and formalized in the concession agreement. Such agreements generally impose limits on toll rate increases—but so does economic reality. The higher the toll rate charged, the fewer the people who will decide that it's worthwhile to use the tollway. So the art of toll road management is to seek the optimum toll rate that will maximize revenue, which may or may not be the highest rate allowed by the concession agreement.

There is nothing in the typical US toll concession agreement that guarantees any profit—unlike typical utility franchises, under which the regulatory body periodically sets a target rate of return consistent with newly approved electricity or gas rates. To be sure, the base-case financial model is agreed to by both parties before the agreement is finalized. But in reality, that is only a best estimate of the likely costs and revenues. The concession company is entirely at risk for the actual project costs and the traffic and toll revenue, whatever they turn out to be. There is no guarantee of any profits.

There is one kind of concession for which the "guaranteed profit" idea contains a grain of truth. As we saw in chapter 6, with availability payment (AP) concessions, the company takes on the risks of construction cost overruns, late completion, and operating and maintenance costs turning out higher than in their base case. But, assuming that they build the project successfully and maintain it in accordance with the provisions in the agreement, they are guaranteed the agreed-upon annual payments during the life of the agreement. They are not guaranteed a profit, but they do avoid the traffic and revenue risk they would have absorbed if the project had been done as a toll concession.

"Taxpayer Bailouts in Case of Bankruptcy"

Grass-roots populists regularly assert that if a P3 toll road fails financially and declares bankruptcy, the taxpayers have to bail it out. There have been a few cases of this kind in Spain, as an outgrowth of the very severe Great Recession afflicting that country starting in 2008. But Spain and several other European countries have a different form of governance for their toll concessions, in which "renegotiation" of concession provisions takes place periodically. That is not how toll concessions work in Australia and the United States. In both of these countries, toll concessions by definition require the company to accept traffic and revenue risk, which makes the company solely responsible for the revenues and costs of the toll road—including in bankruptcy.

In every known case of a toll concession filing for bankruptcy in Australia and the United States, the equity providers lost their investment, and the debt providers took a write-down on the amount of debt they could recover. That has been the case for the Camino Colombia toll road in Texas, the South Bay Expressway in San Diego, and the Indiana Toll Road: zero taxpayer bailouts. It is also the case in Australia for the Lane Cove and Cross-City Tunnel bankruptcies in Sydney, and the CLEM 7 and Airport Link tunnel bankruptcies in Brisbane.

Only two bankrupt US projects, the South Bay Expressway and Segments 5 and 6 of Texas SH 130, had federal TIFIA loans. Even though TIFIA loans are considered subordinated debt (second in line for payment after the primary investment-grade debt), one provision in the law creating TIFIA holds that in the event of a bankruptcy, the TIFIA loan moves to equal standing with the primary debt. In the South Bay Expressway case, the bankruptcy court awarded the banking group, which had provided loans of $340 million, and TIFIA, which had provided a $172 million loan, ownership of the concession in proportion to their investments. Four months after this ruling, the San Diego Association of Governments (SANDAG) negotiated a deal to buy the concession from the banks and the TIFIA office for $344.5 million. This was a great deal for SANDAG, which got an expressway that had cost $658 million to build at a bit over half-price. The deal gave TIFIA $15.4 million in cash, a senior debt loan for $94.1 million at a higher interest rate than the original, and a subordinated loan at 14 percent. According to the Federal Highway Administration's report to Congress, "The TIFIA program is positioned to fully recover the principal balance of the original loan," and rating agency Fitch has given the new TIFIA loan an investment grade rating.[4] Here again, the private sector bore the losses, not taxpayers.

The SH 130 bankruptcy settlement became final in June 2017. In exchange for wiping out the existing loans from a group of banks and TIFIA, those parties became owners of just under half the equity in a new SH 130 concession company, with the balance owned by new investor Strategic Value Investors. SVI has arranged a $260 million credit facility with Goldman Sachs, and has hired Louis Berger Services to operate and maintain the toll road. The TIFIA office is expected to auction off its equity stake in the new concession company, but whether it can recover the full value of its $550 million loan remains to be seen.[5]

"Government-Sanctioned Monopolies"

Hall writes, "When there's only one way to get where you need to go and the state puts that road in the hands of a private corporation who controls the toll rates . . . that's not free choice nor free market—it's tyranny." First, there is virtually no place in America where there is only one road that can get you from point A to point B. If a state DOT holds a competition to add a new toll road that could give you a new and faster way to get from point A to point B, but procures it as a toll concession because there is no money in its budget for a billion-dollar project, that is adding a new choice, just as is adding express toll ("managed") lanes to a freeway. So the new tolled facility is not a monopoly on getting from A to B; it's a new option if you wish to use it.

"Loss of Sovereignty"

What Hall and others appear to mean is that long-term concession agreements are legally enforceable contracts between the state DOT and the consortium that wins the bidding and finances, builds, and operates the toll road. In effect, this means the depoliticization of the tollway during the life of the agreement. Accordingly, neither the legislature nor local officials can unilaterally change the rules 6 or 15 years into the agreement. This does tie the government's hands in some respects, but depoliticization is what makes the capital markets (e.g., infrastructure investment funds that invest equity, and banks and bond issuers that provide debt) willing to put up a billion dollars so that the tollway can get built now, rather than possibly 20 years in the future.

Late in 2011, Georgia Gov. Nathan Deal intervened on the grounds of "sovereignty" in the underway competition for a $1.1 billion concession to add express toll lanes to I-75 and I-575 in Atlanta.[6] By that point in the process, three teams had been prequalified by the Georgia DOT and had devoted several months and millions of dollars to design studies, traffic forecasts, and financial modeling—all of which went down the drain. That kind of political risk has made concession companies steer clear of Georgia since then.

Control over Surrounding Free Routes

One aspect of the "sovereignty" question is provisions in concession agreements about competing facilities. "Non-compete" provisions were not dreamed up by the concession companies to enhance their profits. Some degree of protection has often been granted to toll roads developed by government toll agencies.[7] The purpose of such provisions is to make it possible to sell bonds for a toll road in an environment in which the vast majority of roadways are "free" at the point of use. Ask yourself if you would buy a 30-year bond for a new toll road if the government 10 years from now could build a "free" superhighway alongside it. You'd be foolish to do that, and the financial community long ago persuaded governments that they needed to provide some kind of assurance that it would not take actions that could undermine the ability of the toll road to make the scheduled debt service payments during the life of the bonds. (In chapter 3, we saw how Louisiana Gov. Huey Long put a relatively new private toll bridge out of business by having the state build two "free" competing bridges.)

The classic example, cited repeatedly by critics, is the noncompete provision included in the concession agreement for the 91 Express Lanes in Orange County, California. This was not only the first toll road concession in modern America; it was also the first time anyone attempted to add tolled express lanes to an existing congested freeway. In other words, the free competition was not just nearby: it was only a few feet away. The financial community had never faced such a situation, and insisted on a strong noncompete provision. Caltrans agreed, for two reasons. First, they wanted this pilot project to proceed, in hopes of there being many more like it on other freeways. Second, given their budget situation and the limited room in the canyon through which the Express Lanes were to go, they had no plans to add any more regular (nontolled) lanes to SR 91.

That decision came back to haunt everyone. Traffic and revenue on the new express lanes were robust, but very strong traffic growth in the overall corridor within five or six years led to the return of congestion in the regular lanes. That led to public demand for the state DOT to add more nontolled lanes. But the noncompete provision was legally binding, so the eventual solution was for the Orange County Transportation Authority to buy out the remaining years of the concession at a mutually agreed-upon market value. With the clause extinguished, Caltrans was eventually able to add a regular lane in each direction to SR 91.

Since that time, nearly all toll concession agreements have included *compensation* clauses rather than noncompete clauses (although a few, including the Chicago Skyway, have no such protection at all). A compensation clause generally stipulates that the governments in question have the right to build any and all projects that are in their long-range transportation plans at the time the concession is agreed to. If governments later build other roads that the company can demonstrate are diverting traffic from the tollway and costing it toll revenue, then some degree of compensation is required. Since the specifics of each toll project are different, no cookie-cutter approach can be applied, which means it is not appropriate for a legislature to impose one on all toll concessions.

"Priced Managed Lanes Create Road Scarcity"

In her 2012 op-ed, Hall described express toll lanes, also called managed lanes, as working like this: "The more cars, the higher the price, creating road scarcity through pricing. . . . It makes driving unaffordable and forces the majority of the traveling public out of their cars or stuck in unbearable congestion on unimproved free roads—so those who cannot afford to pay 75 cents a mile to get to work will be treated as second-class citizens without mobility, even though they continue to pay gas taxes for roads." But the express toll lanes developed under toll concessions are *additions to* congested freeways. They draw their customers from those who were formerly stuck in the existing lanes, and give them the option of something better, for a price (which must be high enough to prevent overloading the new lanes). So, in addition to offering those who use them a less congested trip, the new lanes *reduce* congestion in the existing regular lanes. P3 managed lanes add to highway capacity, but in a way that is sustainable in the long term thanks to market pricing. Far from creating scarcity, they expand the amount of highway space and enable it to deliver much higher performance.

"Tolling Existing Corridors"

Another point made by antitoll populists is that toll concessions involve the tolling of "existing corridors." That claim is on the websites of both TURF and the San Antonio Toll Party. The latter recounts Hall's activist career as beginning in 2005 "when she learned that the Texas Dept. of Transportation (TxDOT) was to convert her only [convenient] access to San Antonio, Hwy. 281, into a tollway, which is a double tax to charge taxpayers again and again for what they've already built and paid for." That claim is simply not true. The section of US 281 north of Loop 1604 was an ordinary highway with intersections and traffic signals, not a limited-access freeway. It had three lanes going in each direction closer in, and two lanes going each way further out. The Texas DOT plan was to keep the same number of free lanes, but to move them to either side of the right-of-way, as frontage roads, and build a limited-access tollway in the middle.

Now look again at Hall's claim. First she says that the free lanes would be converted into toll lanes: false. Second, she says the tolls would be charged to drivers for "what they've already built and paid for": again, false. The tolls would pay for the *new* expressway lanes. Yet these claims have been repeated statewide in Texas, and have been adopted by other grass-roots opponents of tolling and P3 concessions. Hall herself has repeated this claim on national TV, including on CNN's former program hosted by the populist Lou Dobbs, and in speeches in Texas and elsewhere.

After many years of litigation in San Antonio, the plan adopted in 2014 is to have the Alamo Regional Mobility Authority, not a concession company, develop and implement the US 281 project as a new nontolled expressway, plus tolled express lanes with frontage roads alongside, as is general Texas practice.

"Tolls as Taxes"

By this point, it should be pretty clear that tolls are fundamentally different from taxes, despite Hall and other activists routinely equating the two. This point was actually litigated in 2013 in Virginia, in a case brought partly by anti-P3 activists and partly by environmental groups. The case challenged the use of tolls to pay for the $2.1 billion Elizabeth River Crossings concession project, which is refurbishing two existing tunnels and adding a third, and which will operate and maintain them for 58 years. The Virginia Supreme Court ruled unanimously that the tolls being used to finance the project are not taxes because[8]

- those who pay the tolls receive a specific benefit not shared by the general public;
- no one is compelled to use the tolled tunnels, since there are other, albeit less convenient, ways to cross the river; and
- the tolls are collected solely to fund the project, not to raise general revenues.

Despite some unique aspects to the Elizabeth River project, the Court's three points could apply equally well to just about any toll project in the country. In the same case, the court also upheld the validity of Virginia's P3 enabling act. The lawsuit had alleged that the act illegally delegated toll-setting powers to Virginia DOT, but that claim actually rested on the plaintiff's prior claim that tolls were taxes—and established law in Virginia says that the taxing power cannot be delegated.

Political Consequences in Texas

More than a decade of activism by Terri Hall and other critics has had political consequences in the Lone Star State. Their arguments contributed to the antitoll, anti-P3 climate of opinion that led to a two-year moratorium on new P3 toll projects being imposed by the legislature in 2007. Although a number of new toll concessions were approved by the legislature after the moratorium expired (as recounted in chapter 5), the activism continued unabated. In 2012, Republican state Sen. John Carona was quoted in *The New York Times* complaining, "The day will surely come when, if you want to go from point A to point B, you're not going to have a choice but to get on a toll road. . . . Well then, suddenly, a toll is just another tax. Let's not kid one another."[9] (On the other hand, the city manager of the relatively low-income border city McAllen in 2014 defended toll financing of a new highway to a *New York Times* reporter as follows: "The feeling is if you want to use it, you should pay for it. That's what I see in McAllen. There's a kind of hesitancy toward 'Let's all go together and pay for it so 20 percent can use it.'"[10]

In July 2014, the Texas Republican Party revised its platform to remove language calling for construction of toll roads in the state. It called on legislators to "adequately fund our highways" without using tolls, and to avoid "the use of taxpayer money to subsidize, guarantee, prop up or bail out any toll projects, whether public or private." The *Texas Tribune* article reporting this news cited Terri Hall as the person who led the effort to change the platform, quoting her as saying, "The grassroots don't want any of this. This isn't a good deal for the taxpayer."[11] *Salon* reported in July 2014 that the leading GOP candidate to succeed the retiring pro-tolling Gov. Rick Perry, Attorney General Greg Abbott, "has said he will build no new toll [roads].[12]

Mr. Abbott was duly elected governor in November 2014. His transportation agenda includes several measures to increase government highway funding by $4 billion per year, and no proposals to expand tolling or

P3s. Legislators introduced dozens of antitoll bills in the 2015 session, but only four passed. The most damaging, HB 2612, as originally written, would have mandated the elimination of all toll roads in the state. After amendments, it ended up only requiring TxDOT to study the possible early retirement of bonds on those toll roads that had been partly funded by the state.[13]

The 2017 session of the legislature was even less friendly to tolling and P3s. It rejected a list of 18 proposed P3 projects worth $30 billion, and banned state equity investments in P3s that had previously been approved but had not yet been financed. Henceforth, only loans may be provided, and the need to repay those loans will make toll concessions harder to finance. Even worse antitoll measures were debated, but rejected.[14]

Other Populist Critics

Terri Hall's efforts have inspired a number of activists in other states where tolling and P3 concessions have become issues for public debate. Diane Cox of the Valdosta, Georgia, Tea Party in 2011 circulated a long Terri Hall piece called "Texas for Sale: New Laws Sell Texas to Highest Bidder," which railed against foreign companies and included the allegation (in bold type) that "PPPs socialize the losses and privatize the profits that amount to horrible public policy. Such contracts are sweetheart deals that eliminate competitive bidding and grant government-sanctioned monopolies (with guaranteed profits) to the well-connected."

In North Carolina, a Charlotte-area activist named Vallee Bubek created an anti-P3 website called P3times.com. On the site, she relates that she "became involved in a P3 toll road battle after learning about a plan to take our existing highway [I-77] in the Charlotte region to build HOT lanes. This plan, *if approved* (stay tuned), will drastically and permanently change the lives of North Carolinians forever." In fact, the project aims to relieve congestion on I-77 in Charlotte by converting a low-performing HOV lane each way and adding an additional tolled lane, providing two express toll lanes each way. Here we see the same pattern of either misunderstanding or deliberately distorting a capacity-increase project. Despite the opposition, the winning concession bidder was competitively selected in 2014, the concession agreement negotiated, and the project financed in May 2015.[15] Construction got under way in late 2015.

Florida's equivalent to Terri Hall is Sally Baptiste, a "blog talk radio" activist who uses lots of bold caps to express thoughts such as "Toll is a four-letter word for tax—toll taxes are very regressive taxes," and "Our national infrastructure is being sold off to foreign corporations." She sends emails along these lines to transportation reporters around the country, with copies to various trucking industry people.

Among the populist conservatives who have picked up and amplified these messages are the aforementioned Lou Dobbs, the late Phyllis Schlafly, Michelle Malkin, Tom DeWeese, and a Townhall.com blogger named Rachel Alexander who, in a 2013 post, mistakenly portrayed Boston's notorious Big Dig as a toll project and appeared to defend those who steal service from toll roads against "vicious enforcement" in collecting their unpaid bills.[16] Terri Hall has done likewise. Even the then executive director of the normally free-market Libertarian Party, Wes Benedict, issued a news release in August 2011 attacking toll concessions in Texas, arguing that they are private monopolies charging whatever they want to, that government would bail them out if they went bankrupt, and that "tolled highways can cost twice as much to build per added lane-mile as non-tolled roads."[17]

The Populist Critique Goes National

Many of the arguments put forth by the network of grass-roots activists have been picked up by national conservative media. *The Washington Times* (not really a national newspaper, but influential with conservative members of Congress) has repeatedly attacked both tolling and P3s on its editorial page.

Even the respectable conservative magazine *The Weekly Standard* repeated some of these arguments. In an April 2014 cover story, staff writer Jonathan Last penned a long attack on express toll lanes and P3 concessions, misunderstanding and mischaracterizing both.[18] Part of his critique was the claim that P3 concessions are a form of crony capitalism, yielding "privatized profits and socialized losses." He misstated the history of how the express toll lanes on the Capital Beltway came to be, failing to explain the project's origin as an unsolicited proposal from Fluor under Virginia's Public Private Transportation Act (as discussed in detail in chapter 2). The procedure for handling an unsolicited proposal is for the Virginia DOT to review it and, if it appears feasible and supportive of VDOT goals, to issue a notice requesting competitive bids. In the case of the Beltway, there were no such bids, so VDOT proceeded to spend several years doing due diligence and then negotiating a concession agreement for the project. Several years later, when Fluor and Transurban made another unsolicited proposal—to convert the HOV lanes on I-95 to HOT lanes—there was a competing proposal, but VDOT's evaluation judged the Fluor/Trans-urban proposal to be superior.

Last also repeated the Terri Hall claim that most of the money in the Beltway project was provided by "taxpayers," ignoring the fact that the concession company is fully at risk to generate enough toll revenues to pay off the private activity bonds and the TIFIA loan, and that the project was financed with a completely normal mixture of debt and equity. He called the $400 million state investment in the project a subsidy, ignoring the fact that it was VDOT's insistence on numerous design changes that boosted the cost from Fluor's original $1 billion to nearly $1.9 billion, a total that was not financeable via toll revenues alone.

As another example of subsidy/crony capitalism, Last cited the provision in the long-term agreement requiring VDOT to compensate the concession company if the volume of nontolled HOV-3s ever exceeds 24 percent of total traffic. The only reason why HOV-3s are entitled to use the new express lanes at no charge is that VDOT *required* the company to offer this. There had never been HOV lanes on the Beltway before, and an unlimited amount of nonpaying customers would make the company's base-case model not financeable. In point of fact, carpooling is in a 30-year downtrend as a fraction of urban commuting, and three-person carpools are far less common than two-person ones, so the 24-percent ceiling is unlikely to ever be reached. This is not a "subsidy"; it's an example of the kind of realistic provisions needed to make a $1.9 billion long-term partnership possible.

Finally, Last also played the egalitarian card, although he never used the odious term "Lexus Lanes." Like other such critics, he calculated an extreme case in which a user of the Beltway express toll lanes used them twice a day, five days a week, and always drove at the peak time when the toll rate was highest. The high, scary-sounding cost leads the reader to see the express lanes as something only affordable by the wealthy. And the cover illustration played to this, with a cartoonish expressway sign listing the toll to use the express lanes and an arrow pointing to the free alternative, designated "Riff Raff." In fact, data on express toll lanes around the country show that the vast majority of customers use them only once or twice a week, for really important trips that must be completed on time. And this is true of people of all income levels. In addition, the types of vehicles using these lanes most frequently are Chevrolets, Fords, Toyotas, and Hondas.[19] But Last's article provided no such context.

Most of these populist conservatives are simply uninformed about 21st-century tolling and how toll concessions actually work. Many also seem drawn to conspiracy theories, and are willing to spread misinformation that furthers their initial uninformed assessment, rather than seek to genuinely learn about this relatively new phenomenon. The activists and arguments profiled here are mostly on the political right. Next we'll look at opposition coming from the political left, where you will see a surprising degree of overlap with arguments from the populist right. But, if you are interested in the conspiracy-theory aspect of anti-P3 activism, take a detour to the sidebar on the NAFTA Superhighway Conspiracy.

SIDEBAR 3 **The NAFTA Superhighway Conspiracy**

One of the lines of attack against Gov. Rick Perry's 2001 Trans-Texas Corridor proposal was the accusation that this project was part of an international conspiracy to politically merge the United States with Canada and Mexico, thus opening the borders to unlimited trade and immigration. The originator of this conspiracy theory appears to have been Jerome Corsi, who wrote a series of columns setting forth the basic case in the conservative weekly *Human Events* in 2006.[1] He expanded the idea into a book the following year.[2]

Like most conspiracy theories, this one is built upon snippets of fact. There was indeed a business coalition called the North American SuperCorridor Coalition (NASCO), aimed at facilitating north-south goods movement, and a map on its website depicted growing trade flow from Mexico northward to Kansas City (a major existing logistics hub), and from there to the north, east, and west. Also, in furtherance of the free-trade aims of the NAFTA treaty, the governments of the United States, Canada, and Mexico in 2005 created a Security and Prosperity Partnership (SPP) to reduce impediments to goods movement among the three countries, especially in the post 9/11 environment. Of course, the Texas DOT had planned the first of its half-dozen Trans-Texas Corridors to run parallel to north-south I-35, already one of the busiest truck routes on the Interstate highway system. Corsi embellished all this with talk of a merged "North American Union" (analogous to the European Union) with its imagined new currency, which Corsi dubbed the "Amero" (analogous to the Euro).

1. Jerome Corsi, "Bush Administration Quietly Plans NAFTA Super Highway," *Human Events*, June 12, 2006.
2. Jerome Corsi, *The Late, Great U.S.A.: The Coming Merger with Mexico and Canada* (World Net Daily Books, 2007).

SIDEBAR 3 **(Continued)**

Many populist conservatives, not just in Texas, became believers in this conspiracy theory, seeing the bits and pieces as adding up to what Corsi imagined. Phyllis Schlafly, founder of the national conservative group Eagle Forum, was among the first to take action, having Corsi conduct a several-day "training session" on the conspiracy for 30 key leaders of the organization in Washington, DC, in November 2006.[3] By early 2007, conservative legislators in a number of states were introducing resolutions opposing any "NAFTA Superhighway System," as well as creation of any trinational entity among the United States, Mexico, and Canada. The Montana legislature passed the first such measure in February 2007 and similar measures were introduced that year in at least 18 other states. In Congress, a resolution along the same lines had 27 cosponsors by the middle of 2007, and that July Rep. Duncan Hunter (R-CA) drafted an amendment to the FY 2008 transportation appropriations bill prohibiting the use of any of those funds for either the SPP or the NAFTA superhighway; it passed by a vote of 362 to 63.[4] Lou Dobbs devoted a segment of his CNN television program to Corsi and the conspiracy theory. Also joining in were the John Birch Society, with articles in its magazine, and the Conservative Caucus, with a major fund-raising mailing attacking the alleged North American Union. *Newsweek* reported late in 2007 that presidential hopeful Ron Paul was "worked up about U.S. sovereignty" because of the NAFTA superhighway and the North American Union.[5]

Needless to say, Terri Hall and her followers picked up on this theme and worked it into their antitoll, anti-P3 arguments. You might think that after the Trans-Texas Corridor was canceled by the Texas legislature, having first been abandoned by the Texas DOT in 2009, the conspiracy talk would have faded away. Not so. Hall and the others now see the larger conspiracy as the United Nations's Agenda 21 (basically an endorsement of various "smart growth" and environmental principles). Hall now writes: "Two of the purposes of Agenda 21 are to abolish private property and restrict mobility, and P3s act as the vehicle to do it."[6] Their target is still the same: tolling and P3s. Only the conspiracy has changed.

3. Phyllis Schlafly, "Is the Sovereignty of the United States at Risk?" Eagle Forum, November 17, 2006.

4. Duncan Hunter, "Superhighway Amendment Passes U.S. House," news release, July 28, 2007.

5. Brendan Smialowski, "Highway to Hell? Ron Paul Has Helped Fan the Flames of a Made-for-Election-Year 'Conspiracy,'" *Newsweek*, December 10, 2007.

6. Terri Hall, "Rick Perry Tied to Agenda 21, Globalist Policies," *San Antonio Examiner*, August 15, 2011.

Critics on the Left

Mother Jones

The first major critique of tolling and P3s from the ideological left appeared in *Mother Jones* magazine early in 2007.[20] It focused primarily on the long-term leases of the Chicago Skyway and the Indiana Toll Road. The authors and several of those they quoted, including Ralph Nader, attacked the deals as "selling" core infrastructure assets. Though acknowledging here and there that the actual transactions were long-term leases, the casual reader could easily miss that, due to the frequent characterizations of the deals as sales.

Amazingly, both deals were criticized for involving a price that was both too high and too low. Early in the article, Schulman and Ridgeway characterized the $3.8 billion up-front lease payment for the Indiana Toll Road as a "fire-sale price," a claim repeated by several others who were quoted in the article, including Nader. But the authors quoted other opponents as lambasting the lease agreement for permitting annual inflation-adjusted toll increases, which those opponents viewed as outrageous. The financial critic Dennis Enright was quoted saying that, if an inflation-adjusted pricing regime similar to that approved for the Chicago Skyway "had been applied to New York's Holland Tunnel for the past 70 years, the toll [today] would stand at $185 rather than the current $6." (Actually, had the original 50-cent toll been indexed to the Consumer Price Index, it would be $6.85 today, only slightly higher than the actual $6.25). But since the amounts the winning bidders offered for the Skyway and Indiana leases were calculated *on the basis of* a CPI-adjusted toll schedule, had the deal been based on a more stringent cap on toll increases, the amount offered would have been significantly *lower*. You can't logically have it both ways, but the same critics ended up making both arguments.

Schulman and Ridgeway also tried to make it look as if Cintra/Macquarie would make an enormous return on their initial $3.8 billion investment in the Indiana Toll Road, by citing an unsourced estimate that the toll road would generate gross toll revenues of "more than $11 billion over the 75-year life of the contract." This comparison ignores two major points. First, the ongoing operating and maintenance costs of a highway are generally two or three times as much as its initial cost to construct, and first-rate maintenance is essential on a toll road to attract and keep customers who would otherwise choose nontolled alternatives. Second, the typical design life of premium highway pavements is 50 years, after which complete reconstruction is usually required. So, even if the Toll Road had been brand-new at the time the lease began, all of it would require reconstruction well within the 75 years of the agreement. In addition, assuming that population and the economy continue growing over the next 75 years, most major highways will need at least some lane additions and possibly some new interchanges. All of these capital and operating costs are the responsibility of the company in a long-term toll concession such as this, with only the toll revenues available for those costs.

Incidentally, a research team from Purdue University carried out a detailed analysis of the Indiana Toll Road lease, using both a value-for-money assessment and a benefit/cost analysis. Their analysis assumed the reconstruction of the entire toll road at year 30 of the 75-year lease. Their overall conclusion was "that it is not likely that a public agency can receive as much benefit as the up-front payment received from privatization, compared with choosing to continue in-house management of a toll road." Moreover, "evidence from the lease documents suggests that proper steps were taken to protect the interests of Indiana residents."[21]

Rep. Peter DeFazio (D-OR) got a lot of space in the *Mother Jones* article, lambasting Indiana Gov. Mitch Daniels at a congressional hearing for "outsourcing political will to a private entity" when it comes to the inflation-adjusted toll caps in the concession agreement. But the authors showed a bit later in the article why that is precisely one of the *advantages* of toll concessions. They pointed out that the federal Highway Trust Fund "is running out of money—in part because lawmakers have not dared to raise the [gas] tax, currently 18.4 cents per gallon, since the mid-'90s" (and still had not done so as of 2017). Only a handful of states index their state fuel taxes to inflation, but the example set by the recent wave of toll concessions has inspired a number of state toll agencies to index their toll rates.

One of the ironies of the article is its prediction that Cintra/Macquirie would make buckets of money from leasing the Indiana Toll Road. The authors quoted DeFazio as telling them that Daniels had "just screwed the state of Indiana and the people of the state of Indiana," because the concessionaire has "a license to print money here." And the authors themselves had presented the misleading comparison of $11 billion in toll revenue versus only $3.8 billion in acquisition cost to imply monumental profits. But as it turned out, in 2014 the ITR Concession Company declared bankruptcy, being unable to service its debts. The deal had been very aggressively financed, with high-interest balloon payments coming due in 2014 that were not possible to make with the reduced toll revenue that had resulted from lower traffic during the Great Recession and several years thereafter. In filing for bankruptcy, the company lost its entire equity investment.

The Indiana Finance Authority, working with the creditors, put the remaining term of the concession up for bids. In March 2015 the winner, from among four bidders, was a consortium put together by Industry Funds Management, one of Australia's largest pension funds. It bid $5.725 billion for the remaining 66 years of the concession. It could afford that high a price because of the very conservative financing structure: 57 percent equity and only 43 percent debt (compared with the ITR Concession Company's 15 percent equity and 85 percent debt). As *Public Works Financing* noted, "the big equity investment made the ITR deal bankable."[22] The lenders ended up recovering close to 99 percent on their loans and bonds.

Nader Group Critiques

The year 2007 also saw the release of a long critique of toll road privatization from the Public Interest Research Group (PIRG), a national federation of state progressive organizations, started by Ralph Nader.[23] That report and a follow-up 2009 report directed the majority of their fire against long-term leases of existing toll roads, despite the fact that by the time of the second report,[24] there had been only four such leases, compared with more than a dozen toll concessions for new highway projects, as the 2009 report's appendix made clear. The discussion was similar in both, with the later report having more citations and an appendix with capsule descriptions of 15 completed P3 toll projects across the country. These reports made many of the same points as the *Mother Jones* article, including the contradictory critique that up-front payments for toll road leases are both too high and too low. But, because they were much longer than a magazine article, these reports went on to discuss a number of other points.

One was that the cost of private toll roads must be higher than that of state-owned toll roads because the public sector has an inherently lower cost of capital. That argument is based on the assertion that companies must issue bonds at taxable rates, despite the fact that Congress had enacted TIFIA in 1998 and private activity bonds (PABs) for P3 highways in 2005, both of which make lower-cost tax-exempt debt available for new-construction P3 projects. Only the cost of a project's equity capital (about

20 percent of the total cost of a new P3 toll road project) needs a rate of return a good deal higher than tax-exempt borrowing rates. So yes, to that limited extent, the weighted average cost of capital would be higher for a PPP toll road than a state-owned toll road, assuming that the amount to be financed was the same in both alternatives.

But, as we saw in chapter 6, the initial cost of a project might be significantly lower if the private sector can figure out smarter ways to accomplish the DOT's objectives, as we saw with both the Capital Beltway in northern Virginia and the LBJ Expressway in Dallas. And that argument also compares only the initial costs, completely ignoring the high likelihood that the private-sector alternative will be designed to have lower total life-cycle costs than the public-sector alternative. It also ignores the value of risk transfer that is an integral part of long-term toll concessions, for both brownfield (existing) and greenfield (new) highway projects. Neither PIRG report dealt with the potential for lower initial cost via design innovations, the likelihood of lower life-cycle costs, or the value of risk transfer from taxpayers to investors.

Another target of the PIRG reports was the long terms of concession agreements. They argued that this inherently results in a loss of public-sector control of transportation, and that terms longer than 30 years are not needed, anyway, and simply permit the concession company to earn higher profits. Taking the second issue first, if the main purpose of a toll concession is to more competently operate and maintain an existing toll road, then a 30-year term might be adequate, especially if the highway in question will not need major maintenance or reconstruction within that time frame (an issue that apparently never occurred to the authors). But for any concession agreement that involves major capital investments in the toll road—such as complete reconstruction of an existing toll road or the creation of a brand-new toll road or set of express toll lanes—the concession duration that makes economic and financial sense will vary considerably, depending on the specifics of the project. This illustrates why a state DOT making the decision on whether to use a toll concession and then negotiating the concession agreement must have expert engineering, legal, and financial advice. Some major new toll bridges and tunnels in France, for example, have concession terms in excess of 70 years, due to the specific base-case financial models developed for those costly and high-risk megaprojects.

To be sure, there are important issues of transportation planning that must be addressed in the long-term concession agreement as well, such as how and when decisions will be made on questions like lane additions and adding new entrance and exit points. Likewise, compensation provisions must be negotiated that permit state DOTs to continue with their long-range plans, but do not put the company and its bond holders at serious risk of default by drawing away too much toll-paying traffic. And all such concession agreements need—and have—termination provisions, both for cause and for convenience. But those provisions, too, must be fair to both parties in what is intended as a long-term public-private partnership.

Of the six recommendations in the 2009 PIRG report, four concern good-government principles such as transparency, proper maintenance, and public control, which in my view are already done pretty well in current concession agreements. (See sidebar on transparency in P3 concession agreements.) The other two, however, are very likely deal killers. One would impose a flat maximum of 30 years for all long-term concessions. The case against that has been presented above.

The second is an absolute deal killer: requiring that the legislature be able to veto or amend a concession agreement that has been negotiated between the state DOT and the winning consortium. As discussed in chapter 6, the costs of competing for a megaproject concession are quite high, both in dollars and in staff time. So are the costs of negotiating a deal. By the time the DOT and the winner have negotiated the hundreds of pages of details of the agreement, they and the state will have spent many months and millions of dollars—which is one reason why long-term concessions are best suited to very large projects, where the costs of getting the deal done are only a small percentage of the cost of the project itself. The risk of all that time and money ending up wasted, if legislators either veto the project or change key provisions, is seen by potential providers as so high as to deter them from bidding. This is not just theory: a number of the early state P3 enabling laws (e.g., Florida's) included a legislative approval requirement, and the result was that no projects were proposed in those states.

"Good-Government" Critiques

Various other progressive groups around the country have picked up on these arguments, and have sometimes made common cause with populist conservatives in activities aimed at preventing concession projects from going forward. But some of their critiques are also being conveyed by more mainstream good-government people writing for entities such as *Governing* magazine and AtlanticCities.com.

In a fairly substantive piece obviously based on background research, *Governing* staff writer Ryan Holeywell asked whether P3s are all they are cracked up to be.[25] Drawing on a highly biased report released earlier that year by the New York state comptroller's office,[26] he asked whether the debt incurred for P3 concessions represented "backdoor borrowing" that would amount to "an end-run around a jurisdiction's debt limits." That would be the case if these were general obligation bonds, secured by the government's general taxing power. But long-term concessions almost exclusively use "project finance," also called "nonrecourse financing," in which the debt is secured only by the project's dedicated revenue stream, such as tolls. Revenue bonds are almost always exempt from voter (taxpayer) approval requirements and state debt limits, because the bondholders have no recourse to taxpayer funds. So an implication that taxpayers are put at risk by toll concessions was either an egregious mistake or a misrepresentation, especially when Holeywell used as his P3 example the Capital Beltway project. That project is a pure toll concession, in which the concession company is fully at risk for the bonded indebtedness.

Holeywell also questioned the idea of risk transfer via P3 concessions. To make this point, he ignored a January 2012 report from the Congressional Budget Office that explains risk transfer as one of the principal benefits of well-structured P3 concessions and discusses how value-for-money analyses quantify the value of such risk transfers.[27] Instead, he relied on a highly political letter from the usually careful California Legislative Analyst's Office, which critiqued the VfM analysis done for two recent California P3 projects and claimed that the risk transfers in those analyses were illusory.[28] Yet we have seen in chapter 6 that in cases of toll concession project bankruptcies in Australia and the United States, including California's South Bay Expressway, the risks of cost overruns and of insufficient traffic and revenues were transferred to the concession companies, which lost their entire equity investments, and in which there were no taxpayer bailouts.

Holeywell also failed to comprehend the difference between lowest initial cost and lowest life-cycle cost, and appeared to accept trade-union arguments defending traditional DBB procurement because it selects contractors solely on the basis of the lowest bid to construct a predesigned project. This ignores a wealth of information both from the DB community (showing better value and earlier completion time from DB procurements compared with DBB) and from the studies showing that P3 concessions lead to lower life-cycle costs, as we reviewed in chapter 6.

Another critique was penned by Eric Jaffe for AtlanticCities.com.[29] Using the then pending, and subsequently approved, toll concession to add express lanes to US 36 between Denver and Boulder, Jaffe used the local opposition to that project as a springboard to discuss potential problems with P3 concessions. He cited noncompete clauses as if they were still common, retelling the Orange County SR 91 Express Lanes story and also noting that the long-term lease of the bankrupt public-sector Northwest Parkway near Denver includes such a provision. He went on to discuss the more relevant compensation provisions in more recent concession agreements, citing the work of the law professor Ellen Dannin, who claims that such provisions amount to revenue "guarantees" for the company.[30] In fairness, he also quoted the economist Rick Geddes, arguing that, given the high risk of toll roads, investors (which increasingly include public pension funds) need some degree of protection for their investments.

Jaffe also drew on P3 critic Elliott Sclar of Columbia University, who maintained that P3 concession projects "tend to interfere with comprehensive approaches to city planning."[31] The example Sclar used was the toll concession for SH 130 between the outskirts of Austin and the outskirts of San Antonio. Jaffe portrayed Sclar as believing that the new toll road "made traffic worse because truckers chose to take the free I-35 through the city rather than pay the toll." That is a serious distortion of reality. First, the Texas DOT itself planned and the built the portion of this toll road in the Austin metro area, where the serious congestion was. When it could not afford to build the rural portion (segments 5 and 6), it awarded that portion to a consortium of Cintra and Zachry as a toll concession. Despite an 85–mile-per-hour speed limit, traffic during the early years of segments 5 and 6 was well below projections. But that was the concessionaire's problem, not that of the Texas DOT. And there is no way that adding highway capacity between Austin and San Antonio could have "made traffic worse." Trucks were on I-35 before the new tollway was built, and they are mostly still on I-35. That's unfortunate, but all the cars that have switched from I-35 to SH 130 have reduced congestion on I-35 from what it would have been without the new tollway.

Jaffe's assessment of the results of a P3 concession suggests either a lack of detailed knowledge of the specifics, or an intent to portray the glass as half- mpty rather than half full. I'd give Jaffe the benefit of the doubt, except that he then recommended PIRG's "six principles for road privatization agreements" without questioning any of them. He described a 30-year maximum term as sensible, since nobody knows what vehicles and travel will be like 30 or more years from now. While that is true, it is also true of any highway built today by the government. The advantage of a long-term concession is that the risk of ending up with a white-elephant highway 30 or 50 years from now—if, for example, fully autonomous cars reduce the amount of highway lane capacity needed in the future—is transferred from the taxpayers to the concessionaire. Given the general slowness of government to change versus the creativity of businesses, my guess is that a concession company stuck with a highway that no longer has enough customers would be more eager than a government to seek more productive uses for that piece of property.

Interest Group Opposition

The opposition to toll concessions discussed thus far appears driven largely by ideology, whether by conservative populism or leftist progressivism. To those of either persuasion, it just isn't right for people to be asked to pay tolls, or for large private companies to make a profit by providing highway infrastructure. Apparently it's all right for large private companies to provide electric power, railroads, natural gas service, telephones, airlines, and so on, but I digress.

Four main categories of interest groups have opposed toll concessions in the early 21st century: environmental groups, public employee unions, some state toll agencies and their municipal bond financiers, and some highway user groups, especially the trucking industry. Let's review their efforts and the arguments they have used.

Environmental Groups

There is a spectrum of environmental groups, ranging from the relatively moderate and economically literate Resources for the Future to the liberal-left Sierra Club to the radical Friends of the Earth and Greenpeace. None of these groups is happy about projects that add capacity to the highway system, but early on it looked as if the Environmental Defense Fund would support some tolled projects. When the concession company that had won the competition to finance, build, and operate the 91 Express Lanes in Orange County was seeking environmental clearance for the project, the California branch of EDF supported it. Even though the project would add four new lanes to the congested SR 91, EDF at that time strongly favored market-based mechanisms such as water markets and highway congestion pricing, and viewed the Express Lanes as an important first step toward the latter. In subsequent years, however, EDF policy changed. While still supporting congestion pricing, the group thenceforth supported only HOT lanes that had been created by converting existing HOV lanes, not those that created new capacity.

The long-delayed InterCounty Connector toll road in the Maryland suburbs of Washington, DC, was to be entirely congestion-priced. EDF was part of a coalition of environmental groups that fought for decades to prevent the toll road from being built. When the road was proposed for construction in 1984, the estimated cost was $216 million. That later increased to $500 million. By 1997, after factoring in EDF-demanded plans to protect trout streams, the cost estimate doubled to $1 billion. A detailed environmental study, adding further environmental mitigation, brought the price tag to an estimated $1.8 to $2.1 billion in 2004. By the time the ICC was built and opened to traffic in 2012, the final cost was $2.56 billion.

As toll concessions became a more important factor for new highway-capacity projects, EDF joined with a dozen other environmental groups in 2008 in issuing 15 principles for such projects.[32] As with the shorter list from PIRG, about half of these are fairly sensible good-government principles that were already being included in most concession agreements: outcome-based performance measures, enforceable compliance measures, provisions to ensure continued facility operation in the event of default or bankruptcy, and clear definition of how tolls/user fees would be set. But most of the others would add costs or limit revenues, putting the financial viability of the projects at risk.

For example, principle 3 calls for active measures to reduce vehicular emissions and greenhouse gases, to protect farmland and open space, and to achieve other environmental goals. Federal and state laws already require all new highway projects to mitigate environmental externalities, but a statement like this implies that projects developed as concessions must go beyond what the law requires of ordinary highways. Number 10 says that concession agreements "must ensure that guaranteed returns to private investors should be reasonable and proportionate to the risk assumed by the investors," which incorrectly implies that concession agreements offer "guaranteed returns." Number 12 says the agreements should improve the provision of public transit in the corridors, by "dedicating [toll] revenues to public transit up front," which implies that toll revenues alone will more than cover the capital and operating costs of the new toll road, something we have seen is rarely the case. Principles 14 and 15 are the obligatory ban on "no-compete clauses" and a maximum concession term of 35 years.

The lawsuit against the toll concession for the Elizabeth River Crossings project in Virginia—which was dismissed by the Virginia Supreme Court, as discussed earlier—had its origins in a 2012 critique from the Southern Environmental Law Center (SELC).[33] The SELC's report was partly an attack on Virginia's pioneering and much-emulated Public Private Transportation Act (PPTA), and partly a poorly informed critique of toll concessions. On the latter, SELC asserted that financing the costs of private projects would be more expensive than doing so on public-sector toll projects because of the difference between taxable and tax-exempt bond interest rates. Yet in 2005, three years before the report was written, Congress had enacted the provision allowing issuance of $15 billion worth of tax-exempt private activity bonds for such projects, so that argument was bogus. The report also ignored risk transfer as a significant benefit of concession projects, and basically argued that anything the private sector could do with tolling, public-sector toll agencies could also do. Yet Virginia's only significant toll agency is the single-project Chesapeake Bay Bridge and Tunnel District, which has been unable to finance a needed expansion of its own facility.

The SELC's critique of the PPTA focused on claims of inadequate transparency of the process and a call for increased legislative (i.e., political) oversight of concession projects. It argued that no steps toward a concession should occur until all environmental approvals were in hand—which would have entirely ruled out Fluor's unsolicited proposal for what became the Beltway's express toll lanes, since the environmental review would have been of VDOT's $3 billion HOV-lanes project, for which no funding was available. The SELC also called for all concession projects to follow a standard model, despite the major differences in cost and risk among megaprojects. It called for canceling a procurement if only one bidder remained at the end of a competitive process—something which would also have ruled out the Beltway project. And, in a final deal-killer provision, the SELC called for the legislature to approve or veto each negotiated concession agreement—as opposed to the current PPTA process, under which the legislature had approved the policies and procedures by which Virginia DOT's P3 unit carries out project procurements.

In Colorado when that state's P3 unit, the Colorado DOT's High Performance Transportation Enterprise (HPTE), was nearing approval of its

first toll concession, for express toll lanes to be added to US 36 between
Boulder and Denver, a coalition of environmental groups and grass-roots
activists created Friends of the Colorado Public Utilities Commission
(FCPUC) to oppose the project.[34] The new organnization's petition to the
legislature called for that regulatory agency to have the final yes-or-no
say on the negotiated concession agreement, contrary to existing law and
realistic practice in states that expected private investment of this kind.
The petition railed against foreign toll road firms (the lead firm in the US
36 consortium was based in Australia) and incorrectly claimed that adding express toll lanes to US 36 would cause traffic congestion in the free
lanes—an echo of Terri Hall in Texas.

The coalition was led by the Drive Sunshine Institute, a local environmental group whose nominal objection was that the concession agreement did not agree to let large numbers of alternative fuel vehicles use
the new lanes at no charge. After the legislature failed to act on FCPUC's
petition and the concession was finalized and financed in March 2014, further agitation led to a bill in the legislature to impose new conditions on
future concession agreements, including a maximum term of 35 years and
a ban on both noncompete and compensation provisions. Although the
legislature narrowly passed the bill, Democratic Gov. John Hickenlooper
vetoed it.

After observing a number of these battles, my assessment is that most
environmental groups are so opposed in principle to new highway capacity that they are willing to make common cause with other opponents
of capacity-creating concession projects. Grass-roots right-wing populists
were very active in the Virginia and Colorado opposition groups discussed
above. Arguments against concessions in both cases have included populist complaints about foreign firms, absurd claims about added toll lanes
leading to increased congestion, and other rhetoric from populist groups
in Southern and Western states. Moreover, with so much now known
about how and why concessions work, it is hard to take such proposals as
arbitrary limits on concession lengths and political veto power over negotiated concession agreements as anything more than attempts to make
concessions impossible to finance and therefore impossible to implement.

Public Employee Unions

Overall, public employee unions have not been prominent opponents of
highway concessions. This may be related to the fact that the states that

have made the greatest use of concessions thus far—Florida, Texas, and Virginia—all have right-to-work laws on their books, as do recent concession practitioners Indiana and North Carolina. Two large states where public employee unions have more political clout—California and New York—have not been friendly to concessions. Although California enacted the nation's first toll concession law (AB 680) in 1989, it was only a pilot program, and was repealed in 2003. It took repeated attempts by former Gov. Arnold Schwarzenegger and the business community to enact a broader concession measure (SB 4) in 2009, allowing an unlimited number of projects. New York state does not yet have a concessions law, despite several recent legislative attempts.

Despite SB 4, only one California transportation concession project has been approved and financed between 2009 and 2014: the Presidio Parkway, an availability-payment concession discussed in chapter 5. It took several years of litigation to enable the project to proceed, due to the efforts of Professional Engineers in California Government (PECG), the union of Caltrans engineers and designers. Their position is that all highway design should be done by Caltrans engineers, period. (Nearly all other state DOTs contract with outside engineering firms to handle much of their design work.) DB procurement gains its savings in cost and time from combining detailed design with construction, as an integrated process. Because DB provides greater certainty that a project will be completed on time and on budget, the financial community is far more comfortable with issuing revenue bonds for a toll project if it is developed via DB.

Over the years, PECG has filed lawsuits against both the original P3 law (AB 680) and SB 4, and has attempted to overturn a voter-approved ballot measure that explicitly legalized contracting out highway design by Caltrans. Although these efforts all eventually failed, in most cases they caused considerable delays and sent signals to potential investors that concessions in California would not have easy sailing. In its public rhetoric against concessions, PECG has employed nearly all the arguments used by opponents in other states, as discussed in this chapter.

A 2012 article about SB 4 and Presidio Parkway by a left-wing investigative reporter presented several of PECG's arguments.[35] It repeated the spurious claim of higher debt-service costs with concession projects, because of the supposed nonavailability of tax-exempt revenue bonds for such projects. It referred to value-for-money analysis as "value-risk analysis," and claimed that such assessments are "rather subjective." It used a lot of space to debunk the 91 Express Lanes project, both for its noncompete clause and for allegedly failing to reduce traffic congestion in the corridor. In fact, it was exceedingly high growth in traffic in that corridor that eventually overwhelmed the congestion relief initially provided by the new express lanes, leading to the return of congestion in the free lanes. In referring to the bankruptcy filing of the South Bay Expressway in San Diego, the article claimed that this event "lost an enormous amount of state and federal money," which is flat-out untrue. (As noted earlier in this chapter, the only federal money in the project was the TIFIA loan, which was refinanced such that FHWA expected to lose nothing on the deal, and California taxpayers lost nothing.) And, after chronicling PECG's ultimately unsuccessful litigation against the Presidio Parkway concession, the piece concluded pessimistically that voter apathy and ignorance of the details might enable concessions to move forward in California.

In 2011, as a bill to enable concessions was pending in the New York State Legislature, the state comptroller's office released a report purporting to be an evenhanded assessment of the pros and cons of concessions.[36] From start to finish, the report adopted anticoncession assessments fostered by public-sector transportation unions. It repeated the claim that P3 concessions only made sense if the initial cost was less than that of conventional procurement. But since private financing was claimed to be more expensive than tax-exempt public financing, no P3s could ever be approved. In the section on P3 financing risks, the report's inflammatory language suggested that private financing could be seen as "a new form of backdoor borrowing," thus implying that taxpayers would be on the hook for the finances of a concession project. This discussion never explained that a toll concession is "project finance," in which only the toll revenues generated by the project service the debt, and taxpayers are not at risk. The report also attacked value-for-money analysis, relying on a critique by the California legislative analyst's office of the Presidio Parkway VfM analysis.[37] That critique was rejected as incompetent by California's Public Infrastructure Advisory Committee, the body created by SB 4 to assess proposed concession projects.

The comptroller's report also misled legislators by telling them that P3-enabling legislation "typically" required "explicit legislative approval" of projects, which invited them to include in the legislation a poison pill that would guarantee zero private-sector interest in concession projects in New York state. It also included a long list of bullet-point red herrings such as community issues, labor issues, environmental issues, and eminent domain—as if these were unique to concession projects, rather than being typical of all transportation megaprojects.

Since this kind of public employee union opposition to concessions seems confined to a small number of states, if it succeeds in preventing serious use of concessions in those states, it will put them at a disadvantage in comparison to the growing number of states that are turning to concessions to tap into the large amounts of private capital now available for transportation megaprojects in states with workable enabling legislation. As noted in chapter 2, the 50 largest infrastructure equity funds raised $250 billion during the most recent five-year period.[38] No definitive total exists for all such funds, but a prudent guess is about $300 billion over the past decade. These funds provide equity investment for projects, which is typically 20 to 30 percent of the project budget, the rest being financed by revenue bonds and/or other forms of debt. If we assume an average of 25 percent equity, the total amount of projects that could be financed by the $300 billion of equity would be $1.2 trillion.

Since the subject of "foreigners buying our highways" is often raised by critics, *Infrastructure Investor* provided a table listing the nationalities of the top 50 infrastructure funds. The largest source of capital (36.8 percent) was the United States, followed by Canada (22.3 percent), Europe (18.1 percent), and Australia (15.7 percent). Thus, North America accounted for 59.1 percent of the total.

Public pension funds, including many union pension funds, have moved into infrastructure as part of their "alternative investment" diversification efforts. While most of the pension funds invest via one or more of the above infrastructure funds (letting the fund select a portfolio of projects, often worldwide), some pension funds make direct investments in specific infrastructure facilities. For example, America's largest public sector pension fund, CalPERS, in 2010 purchased part ownership of privatized London Gatwick Airport. At the other end of the scale, the Dallas Police and Fire Pension System has made direct investments in two Dallas-area express toll lanes projects, the LBJ and NTE projects discussed in chapter 5.

Most state employee pension funds, however, are investing via one or more of the major infrastructure funds. The pension fund for California public school teachers, CalSTRS, in 2012 committed $500 million to Industry Funds Management and $100 million to Meridiam's North America Fund. Other state pension funds investing via infrastructure funds include those of Florida, Rhode Island, Virginia, and Washington state.[39] In the 2015 auction for the remaining 66 years of the Indiana Toll Road concession, about 70 US pension funds joined with Australia's Industry Funds Management to invest in the deal, including the California State Teachers Retirement System, the New York City Employees' Retirement System, the State Board of Administration of Florida, the Arizona State Retirement System, and the Illinois State Board of Investment.

The continued opposition by some public employee unions, such as PECG, to privatized infrastructure is directly in conflict with the growing investment in such projects by public employee pension funds. Even the AFL-CIO seems to be getting more serious about this subject. At the InfraAmericas US P3 Forum in June 2012, AFL-CIO director of policy Damon Silvers said that its members are supportive of investing portions of pension fund assets in US infrastructure—but only if such investment creates jobs.[40] Silvers intended to distinguish between brownfield leases (e.g., the Indiana Toll Road) and greenfield projects that add highway capacity. Yet that distinction ignores the need to reconstruct facilities that reach the end of their design lives during the term of a long-term concession. Silvers also added that union pension funds should invest only in facilities owned and operated by the public sector. That would rule out investments in existing privatized infrastructure, such as Gatwick Airport, as well as greenfield toll concession projects such as the LBJ Express Lanes in Dallas and the I-495 Beltway Express Lanes in northern Virginia.

This union argument also ignores a more basic fact. Infrastructure investment funds invest *equity* in infrastructure—which means a share of ownership. It is not legally possible for a fund to buy a share of ownership in a government-owned toll road or airport in the United States. That is why historical infrastructure investment by US pension funds has been in investor-owned utilities, such as electric companies, railroads, and pipelines. The field of infrastructure investment has broadened considerably, thanks to the privatization of airports, seaports, and highways in many countries over the last several decades, and by the introduction of long-term concessions for highways in the United States. America's public employee unions are still having trouble grasping what this is all about.

Toll Agencies and Municipal Bond Issuers

There has been some degree of tension between portions of the US toll agency community and toll concession companies. The International Bridge, Tunnel & Turnpike Association, based in the United States, has long had many active members from the global toll concession industry—

companies from Australia, Brazil, France, Italy, Spain, and elsewhere. They are accepted as peers by the many US public sector toll agencies, and work comfortably together in planning conferences, developing policy positions, and so on. But as we saw in chapter 6, some US toll agencies have felt threatened by the rise of concessions, whether it is the potential long-term lease of existing toll roads or the competition to develop new urban toll projects.

Likewise, the financial community has been generally supportive and eager to finance large toll concession projects, whether brownfield or greenfield. But some of the municipal finance people who have traditionally issued tax-exempt toll revenue bonds have not always been comfortable with the debt-plus-equity financing needed for toll concessions, which requires people with different expertise and the tapping of different pools of capital. And some smaller municipal bond companies have made common cause with opponents of concessions.

Following the initial concessions for the Chicago Skyway and the Indiana Toll Road, governors and legislators in other states saw the potential of budgetary relief in "privatizing" other existing toll roads, which called into question the continued existence, or at least the future role, of the toll agencies that had developed them. Studies were carried out of potential leases of Houston's Harris County Toll Road Authority system, the Illinois Tollway system, and the Pennsylvania Turnpike, in particular. For the first two there was little serious political support, and the studies ended up justifying the status quo. But, as recounted in chapter 5, Gov. Ed Rendell championed a long-term lease of the Pennsylvania Turnpike, setting off a heated political debate that went on for more than a year.

As noted in chapter 6, the Pennsylvania Turnpike Authority had a long reputation as a source of political patronage jobs and the resulting high administrative costs. Thus, the potential of better management by a professional business ought to have been a major selling point for Rendell. Unfortunately, the campaign to lease the turnpike focused almost entirely on money. One of the most-cited papers opposing the transaction was written by Timothy Carson, then vice chairman of the Turnpike Commission.[41] He drew in part on a critique of the Chicago Skyway and Indiana Toll Road leases by Dennis Enright, the principal of a boutique firm advising state toll agencies on tax-exempt bond financing.[42]

In his paper, Enright relied heavily on numbers. He looked at the annual cap on toll increases built into the Indiana Toll Road concession agreement, and projected that over 75 years, a toll rate that was increased every year by an assumed annual adjustment by GDP per capita would amount to a multi-hundred-dollar toll by the end of that period. This ignores at least two salient points. First, the cap is just that: the maximum annual increase allowed. But no toll road can increase rates beyond what a majority of its customers are willing to pay, as is illustrated by the fact that toll rates on some toll roads *went down* during the Great Recession. Second, the effect of compounding over many decades would mean that all prices would be increasing by similar amounts. Consider the following table, showing the future value of a $1 item after 75 years of annual inflation at several different rates:

Inflation rate	Amount 75 years from now
2%	$4.42
3%	$9.18
4%	$18.94
5%	$38.83
6%	$79.06

Thus, if inflation averaged 6 percent over all 75 of those years, a $1 toll today would be $79 in year 75. But so would a $1 soft drink! Enright's comparisons take advantage of the average person's lack of understanding of compound interest.

Enright's ultimate claim was that any value that could be extracted from a long-term lease of a toll road could also be extracted by "monetizing" the toll road while leaving it in the hands of the existing toll agency. Of course, this alternative rests on the presumption that a government toll agency existing in a highly political environment would be able to stick with a plan of annual toll rate increases over a very long period of time, so that it could issue large new bond issues whose proceeds would be used for other state purposes.

Tim Carson used those Enright arguments in arguing against leasing the Turnpike. But he also asserted many other things that are either misleading or untrue. He claimed that toll concessions overseas seldom exceed 35 years, which is falsified by numerous concessions undertaken in Canada, England, and France since 2000, ranging from 53 to 99 years. He implied that making a profit is incompatible with serving the public's need for good service—ignoring investor-owned airlines, railroads, pipelines, electric utilities, and such. Related to this, he pretended that a for-profit concession company would likely ignore the need for new on-ramps and off-ramps as communities grow—but such contingencies are addressed in long-term concession agreements. And he repeated the false argument about taxable versus tax-exempt debt, ignoring the availability of tax-exempt toll revenue bonds for P3 concessions. These points and more were addressed in a 2007 critique by Peter Samuel and Geoffrey Segal.[43]

Many of the critics of leasing existing toll roads said or implied that they could see the case for using toll concessions to finance, build, and operate needed *new* facilities. But when controversy over that kind of toll concession emerged in Texas, Dennis Enright entered the battle, once again opposing concessions as compared with government toll agencies. When the metro Dallas toll agency, the North Texas Tollway Authority, decided that *it*, rather than the winner of Texas DOT's competition for a concession company (won by Cintra), should build the new SH 121 toll road in Dallas, Enright produced a new report arguing that anything the private sector could do, a toll agency could do, and then some.[44]

The competition that Cintra won, and on which NTTA had declined to bid, was decided on the basis of which bidder would commit to paying the largest upfront fee for the right to build and operate SH 121 for 50 years. Cintra's winning bid offered an unheard-of sum of $2.1 billion up front—essentially 50 years of lease payments in a lump sum. But, since a toll concession is intended to be a long-term public-private partnership, it would have been far wiser for the Texas DOT to have structured the deal on the basis of revenue-sharing over the full term of the agreement. That would have given both the state and the concessionaire a stronger incentive to work together for 50 years. And that, incidentally, is what the Texas Study Committee on Private Participation in Toll Roads subsequently recommended in 2009.

Enright's report presented his calculations showing that NTTA could not only match but even exceed Cintra's winning bid. A think-tank critique of Enright's Texas paper pointed out that his conclusion was based on a number of questionable assumptions:[45]

- unrealistically aggressive traffic and revenue forecasts;
- an unprecedented expectation that a public-sector toll agency would be able to implement 2.5-percent annual toll increases for 50 years, without political interference;

- assumption of the use of *taxable* debt for the concession, despite the ready availability of tax-exempt private activity bonds for such projects;
- assumption, without presentation of any justification, that the private sector's operating and maintenance costs would be 42 percent greater than that of NTTA; and
- use of a different discount rate to calculate the net present value of costs and revenues for the two cases.

In addition to quantitatively stacking the deck, Enright's report falsely claimed that international toll concessions were typically "30 years or less."

Advocates of toll concessions lost both the Pennsylvania Turnpike case and the SH 121 case. In Pennsylvania, the legislature in 2007 passed Act 44, to "monetize" the turnpike. It required the agency to generate enough additional revenue to divert $450 million per year, for 50 years, to the Pennsylvania DOT to pay for highway and transit projects statewide. Because the turnpike was not generating sufficient cash flow to make those annual payments, the agency had to make several large new bond issues to generate cash, and has been required to increase tolls every year since then. In effect, customers of the turnpike are not only paying tolls to cover its capital and operating costs; they alone are also paying a tax generating $450 million a year to help pay for other people's highways and transit systems.

In Dallas, the NTTA also needed several new bond issues to make its $3.2 billion up-front payment for the right to build, toll, and operate SH 121 for 50 years. This required the agency to increase its total bonded indebtedness from $1.56 billion in 2006 to $7.28 billion in 2008, requiring significant systemwide toll increases and leading to a downgrading of its bond rating, as noted in chapter 6. In this case, too, toll payers on SH 121 and the NTTA's other toll roads are now paying not only a toll to cover the capital and operating costs of these toll roads but also a tax to pay for more than $3 billion worth of transit and highway projects throughout the Dallas–Fort Worth region.

Highway User Groups

The American Trucking Associations (ATA) is a federation of state-based trucking organizations. Its primary concern about toll concessions is the tolling, not the concession itself. But because tolling is the principal revenue source for most highway concessions, the ATA has not been supportive of state enabling legislation for concessions. In addition, its more radical counterpart representing individual owner-operators, the Owner-Operator Independent Drivers Association (OOIDA), tends to overlap with right-wing populist positions on transportation issues. The top two issues on the OOIDA's 2015 list of state policy issues were (1) public/private partnerships, and (2) tolling.[46]

The ATA has organized an Alliance for Toll-Free Interstates (ATFI), which includes all its state affiliates, the trucking giants FedEx and UPS, and the National Association of Truck Stop Owners.[47] Its materials raise six primary concerns about the expanded use of tolling. Two of these are obsolete, since they refer to old-fashioned 20th-century tolling, which required tollbooths and toll plazas to collect cash tolls. No new toll road, or Interstate reconstructed with the use of toll finance, would build toll booths or toll plazas when today's all-electronic tolling is dramatically less expensive, more efficient, and far more customer-friendly. So when the ATFI rails against delays, emissions, and accidents at toll plazas, they must be aiming at naive, uninformed people.

As for their claim that toll roads need to use 20 to 30 percent of their toll revenue to cover the costs of toll collection and enforcement, that range of costs was true for 20th-century toll roads with mostly cash tolling. But it is not true for new toll roads designed from the start for all-electronic tolling, using a simplified business model that relies mostly on inexpensive windshield-mounted transponders. A peer-reviewed 2012 study by a team of electronic tolling experts estimated that the cost of toll collection on new toll facilities designed for all-electronic transponder tolling should be in the vicinity of 5 percent of the revenue collected.[48]

But that still leaves four concerns about tolling that ATA shares with other highway user groups such as AAA and the American Highway Users Alliance. First, they are very concerned that revenue-hungry legislatures will simply add tolls to existing highways without making major improvements to them. They have reasons for these worries, based on proposals from half a dozen states over the past 20 years to do just that. When Pennsylvania legislators approved Act 44 in 2007, they were also seeking federal permission to toll I-80 under a federal pilot program and also transfer large portions of its toll revenue to pay for statewide highway and transit projects.

Related to this is the concern over existing diversions of toll revenue to nonhighway and non-transportation purposes. In chapter 6 we saw that 12 significant toll agencies routinely divert revenue, including the Port

Authority of New York and New Jersey, the Dulles Toll Road, and the West Virginia Turnpike. Diversions such as these have been identified as a risk factor by the bond-rating agency Moody's.[49]

Another concern is "double taxation"—having to pay both tolls and fuel taxes for using the same stretch of highway. Only two states, Massachusetts and New York, offer fuel tax rebates to toll road users, based on the number of miles they drive on the Massachusetts Turnpike and the New York Thruway respectively. Everywhere else, toll road users pay both. But offering fuel tax rebates is much easier to do with today's all-electronic tolling, and should be done.

Fourth, highway user groups raise the legitimate concern that high toll rates tend to divert some traffic that would have used the premium highway, if it were nontolled, to parallel surface routes. that might suffer damage from the increased traffic, especially from heavy trucks. The communities through which the diverted traffic travels might also experience congestion, emissions, noise, and accidents due to the added traffic.

In response to these legitimate highway user concerns, a 2014 think-tank study proposed four policies to guide future use of tolling, whether for all-new toll roads or for reconstruction and modernization of currently nontolled Interstates. The following set of policies was termed value-added tolling.[50]

1. Limit the use of toll revenues to the tolled facilities only.
2. Charge only enough to cover the full capital and operating costs of those highways.
3. Begin tolling only after the construction or reconstruction is finished.
4. Use tolls to replace, not supplement, existing fuel taxes (by granting fuel-tax rebates).

Implementation of these principles would address all four of the legitimate ATA concerns put forth in their ATFI campaign. For example, since higher toll rates result in greater traffic diversion, ending revenue diversion would reduce traffic diversion, because the tolls would be lower. These points are addressed further in chapter 8.

Finally, on the subject of toll concessions, as part of my ongoing dialog with highway user groups, Dan Murray, vice president of research at the ATA's research affiliate (the American Transportation Research Institute), in 2012 emailed me a link to the Terri Hall op-ed on "why PPP toll roads won't work," discussed in the first section of this chapter.

He commented that it presented a "logical and well-articulated case." In a subsequent email exchange, he and I had the following dialogue.

DAN: "Private sector firms have an additional operating margin (aka shareholder pressure) that government doesn't."

BOB: "If the idea is that a private firm is worse than government because it seeks a profit, then I guess government should produce and deliver all our electricity, natural gas, water, telecoms—maybe even trucking."

DAN: "P3s attempt to minimize costs (i.e., road maintenance and upgrades) . . . [and use] 'non-compete' requirements to keep the local roads in bad condition to drive vehicles back to the P3 [toll road]."

BOB: "P3s seek to minimize life-cycle costs, since they have a long-term ownership-type interest. State DOTs in this country seek to build as cheaply as possible to make their limited capital budgets go as far as possible, and that ends up meaning a lot more maintenance is needed over the life of the asset."

DAN: "Public-sector discounts/subsidies are always negotiated in the P3 . . . The quick solution here is to make the P3 pay for all support services, including incident/emergency vehicle services. That would make the *true* costs more apparent."

BOB: "When you add up the capital and operating costs of the proposed P3 project, and do an investment-grade traffic & revenue study, the revenue-maximizing toll often does not cover all of the project's life-cycle costs. So the state DOT must decide: Does adding this project produce enough transportation benefits to justify the state buying down the amount that must be financed based on toll revenues or not? If not, the project does not proceed. If yes, the deal is done with a state contribution of capital."

DAN: "Since the government (aka taxpayer) is no longer financially liable (see subsidy exception above), then the US DOT must reduce state formula funds by those miles that the state is no longer maintaining."

BOB: "You and Sen. Bingaman can make such an argument, but that will certainly reduce a state's incentive to get into the P3 business, so that is only 'reasonable' if your goal is less investment in the highway system."

I did not persuade Dan in that exchange, and he did not persuade me, needless to say. But I am guardedly optimistic that the value-added tolling policies outlined above and discussed in the next chapter will make tolling (and hence toll concessions) far more beneficial to highway users than many of them currently realize.

Some good news on this score emerged in 2016. The major membership organization for individual motorists, the AAA, made two important policy changes, adopted by its national board in late 2015 and announced at its national conference in spring 2016. In addition to being open to proposals for replacing per-gallon fuel taxes with per-mile charges (mileage-based user fees), AAA will henceforth also be open to driver-friendly toll projects in which the tolls are used solely for the benefit of the tollpayers and (ideally) in which the tolls replace fuel taxes in the corridors in question.[51]

Conclusions

In this chapter we have reviewed the principal arguments raised by opponents of concessions, from right-wing populists to left-wing progressives on the ideological spectrum, as well as the arguments put forth by interest groups that prefer the status quo. The main message in this book is that the status quo, which worked pretty well in the last century to develop a national network of paved highways, is not sustainable in the 21st century. In the next chapter we will compare the status quo more directly with the idea that highways are, in fact, better thought of as another network utility, analogous to electricity, telecommunications, and pipelines.

CHAPTER EIGHT

Highways as Network Utilities

Origins of the Idea

The basic thesis of this book—that we have an obsolete model for funding and managing our highway system—has several founding fathers. One of them is former World Bank transport economist Gabriel Roth. Back in 1967, when he was working for Britain's Road Research Laboratory, he wrote a book called *Paying for Roads*, which made the case for road pricing as a way not only to pay for the capital and operating costs of highways, but to reduce or eliminate traffic congestion.[1] The copy he sent me in 1987, after I'd gotten to know him at meetings of the Transportation Research Board, helped inspire my 1988 Reason Foundation policy paper on privately financed express toll lanes.

A decade later, after he'd retired from the World Bank to do transport consulting, Roth published *Roads in a Market Economy*,[2] which argued that we've made a fundamental mistake putting government in charge of roads. As the Nobel laureate in economics James Buchanan wrote in the foreword to this volume, "The author starts from the proposition that roads, being part of the 'command economy,' exhibit the typical command economy characteristics of congestion, chronic shortage of funds, and insensitivity to consumer needs. As an alternative, the book presents a market-economy framework, employing the tried and tested concepts of ownership, market pricing, and profitability, for the commercial provision of roads on the model of telecommunications."

Roth's book also included a 22-page epilogue written in 1952 by the future Nobel laureate economist Milton Friedman and the historian Daniel J. Boorstin, titled "How to Plan and Pay for the Safe and Adequate Highways We Need." One of this paper's main conclusions is as follows: "The provision of highway service is a socialized industry removed from the test of the market. The result is that the total expenditures on highways have been too small, that these expenditures have been improperly distributed among different kinds of roads, and that we have too little highway services per dollar spent." Writing in an era long before the development of today's all-electronic tolling, Friedman and Boorstin could not envision a model for privatizing anything other than long-distance toll roads (such as the Pennsylvania Turnpike), and reluctantly envisioned government as having to play the major role in ordinary highways and urban roadways. But they said that were a low-cost charging system to be developed, that conclusion would be very different.

Another inspiration was a series of papers and presentations developed in the 1990s by Stephen Lockwood, when he was associate administrator for policy in the Federal Highway Administration in 1989–92. Lockwood was a prime mover in getting FHWA comfortable with a larger role for tolling and pricing in the US highway system, support for which was included in the surface transportation reauthorization law called ISTEA, enacted in 1991.

The best summary of Lockwood's vision of highways as utilities may be a presentation he gave at the University of Minnesota Center for Transportation Studies in 1995.[3] In the presentation, he referred to the current highway framework as a "dumb" system, "handicapped by fragmented jurisdictions, undercapitalization, limited technical capacity, and often politicized priorities"—little of which has changed two decades later. He also opined, "The curious thing is that most of us as consumers accept this situation as the best our transportation agencies can do. [But] imagine living with hand-cranked, wall-mounted operator-manned telecommunications today, as we still live with 1950s highway technology. What we accept in transportation, we don't accept in other services."

Lockwood went on to point out that "highway transportation is the last great government-provided public utilities monopoly, still surviving in an age of increased government downsizing, deregulation, devolution, and privatization." He then sketched out a scenario for major change, looking back from an imagined future of the year 2050. By 2025, he posited, "progressive states had already moved quickly to develop priced toll networks on the upper-level [limited-access] highway system. . . . Some of these were private franchises [concessions] and others were publicly operated."

As the scenario continued, after that came "consolidation of highway agencies and technology companies into regional 'transcorps' on a multi-

jurisdictional basis." Since he was speaking in Minnesota, his example involved the merger of the Minnesota and Iowa DOTs, which then joined
with Bell, IBM, and Chrysler to form the Midwest Transcorp, "whose
shares are traded on the stock market to raise capital for [highway] automation." Congestion was made obsolete, thanks to variable pricing and
active management of traffic flows. Technology also made it possible to
reserve road space in advance for high-priority trips with guaranteed arrival times. Some highways were automated, permitting platooning and
speeds up to 105 miles per hour. "Customers receive their transportation
bills consolidated with their communications bills," and most "believe the
higher speeds and delay-free travel are worth the price."

This was just one possible vision of the transformation of highways
into a network utility. It was another inspiration for the thinking that led
to this book.

The Basics of Public Utilities

A public utility is an enterprise created to build and operate infrastructure
to deliver an essential public service, such as electricity, natural gas, telecommunications, or water and wastewater. Utilities are capital-intensive
and often exhibit significant "economies of scale," which means that the
cost per unit of service delivered gets lower as the scale of the enterprise
gets larger. Because of this, many utilities have been organized as legally
sanctioned and regulated monopolies, on the grounds that prices will be
lower, on average, with a single large utility than with two or more smaller
ones in the same territory. However, within the past several decades in
the United States, telecommunications has been largely deregulated, as
technological change has made competition more feasible. AT&T was
broken up, required to spin off its local and regional companies, and its
long-distance service was opened to competitors. At the local level, technology made it feasible for cable providers and telephone providers to
compete with one another. Likewise, in many states, electricity has been
partially deregulated, with local distribution of electricity separated from
long-distance transmission and from competing power plants that generate the electricity.

In the United States today, we have three alternative ways to organize
utilities. The most common is investor ownership, in which the company
is a for-profit business, traded on the stock exchange and regulated by a

state public utility commission. A second alternative is government ownership and operation, usually in the form of a municipal utility owned by a city or county government and operated on a nonprofit basis. (The federal government also owns several electric utilities, the best known of which is the Tennessee Valley Authority.) The third alternative is the user cooperative. These are basically nonprofit corporations owned by their customers. As a general rule, only for-profit, investor-owned utilities are subject to formal external regulation by a state regulatory agency. Municipal utilities are presumed, not always wisely, to be operating in the public interest. And utility co-ops are intended to be self-regulating, since the governing board represents the customer-owners.

In electricity, to take one category, in 2013 investor-owned utilities sold 59 percent of all US electricity by value, compared with 15 percent by municipal utilities and 11 percent by electricity co-ops.[4] But the co-ops play a larger role than most people realize. The 877 mostly rural co-ops serve nearly 19 million people and operate 42 percent of the miles of electric distribution lines.

Nearly all categories of public utilities operate networks to distribute their services to customers. In many cases these networks interconnect, as in electricity, railroads, and telecommunications. An interconnected network is still a network, even though its component parts may have different owners, different organizational forms, and different pricing policies. Thus, the idea of highways as a network utility could encompass many subnetworks owned and operated by different enterprises. What makes interchange among separately owned networks feasible is common technical standards. In highways, this could include standards for lane widths, overhead clearance heights, bridge load limits, and electronic toll collection for particular categories of highways. The existing Interstate highways, though owned and operated by individual states, are a network with uniform federal technical standards.

In the US tolled highway sector today, we see two of the three types of utility enterprises. Nearly all tolled highways in the 20th century were built and are operated by nonprofit government enterprises: toll *agencies*, both regional and state-specific. Beginning largely in the 21st century, as recounted in chapter 5, we have a growing number of investor-owned concession companies operating in a for-profit mode under long-term concession agreements with the state DOT. Although several authors have recently suggested transportation co-ops as a third alternative (discussed later in this chapter), I am not aware of any functioning examples in the highway area.

The transportation economist David Levinson, of the University of Minnesota, is a longtime researcher on the performance of US transportation agencies. In a recent policy paper he concluded that "the organizations that built U.S. highway networks are ill-suited to the task of maintaining them, let alone rejuvenating them." This is because they lack the resources needed to properly do their job, are overly politicized, and are constrained by law and bureaucratic culture. Levinson therefore concluded that they should be converted into highway public utilities.[5] He also noted that these utilities could take any of the several forms noted above: investor-owned, state-owned, or co-op owned.

In the same policy paper, Levinson reported that both New Zealand and Australia have taken some modest steps in this direction. As part of sweeping reforms of the New Zealand government and economy carried out by a Labour government in the 1980s, the New Zealand Transport Agency (NZTA) was separated from the Ministry of Transport and converted into a "Crown agent" charged with carrying out government transport policy. This change left policymaking with the government ministry, but gave the NZTA the charge, as a state-owned corporation, to deliver transportation infrastructure and services. The Ministry of Transport, which had 5,000 staff in 1986 before the change, was down to just 50 by 1995 in its slimmed-down policy-making and regulatory role. The NZTA receives transportation user-tax revenues collected by the government, and is responsible for the provision of roads and highways throughout a small nation. Its decisions on which projects to invest in must be justified via benefit/cost analysis, but its decisions and operations are its own business decisions, not decisions made by legislators. This approach has delivered large efficiency gains, compared with the traditional state agency approach, Levinson reported.

Australia's highway commercialization has gone somewhat further. Each Australian state now has its own road enterprise, such as the Roads and Traffic Authority (RTA) of New South Wales, VicRoads of Victoria, and RoadTek in Queensland. Each operates as a government-owned business, making decisions about services and projects with far more autonomy than a typical US state DOT. For example, the RTA has marketed worldwide its Sydney Coordinated Adaptive Traffic System (SCATS), a traffic-signal coordination system now in use in 146 cities in 24 countries. The RTA's roads and fleet services division provides services to transportation agencies in other parts of Australia. VicRoads has a consulting branch with clients overseas. David Hensher of the University of Sydney found that the country's commercialized road enterprises are evolving a corporate culture that resembles private firms operating in the marketplace.[6] In recent years, several developing countries have gone much further, proposing the privatization of their major highways. The most recent proposal, in September 2017, came from India. At a meeting of the Indo-American Chamber of Commerce, union minister Nitin Gadkari suggested the possibility of an initial public offering (IPO) of shares in the National Highways Authority of India, estimating it might raise $150 billion.[7]

In his 2013 paper, Levinson argued for reform of the ownership, regulation, and funding of US highway agencies. As he noted, ownership options include state corporations, investor ownership, and co-ops. Because in many cases highways will have aspects of monopoly, some form of regulation needs to be considered. Levinson cited a British study of potential highway privatization that would be accompanied by the same kind of price-cap regulation now applied to the UK's privatized airports, air traffic control, electricity, and water utilities.[8] As for funding, Levinson recommended direct user charges that were proportional to use, such as miles driven.

Although Levinson's study was basically theoretical, the transportation utility idea has begun to attract attention among longtime transportation professionals.

- A 2011 think piece by the engineering firm HNTB suggested that the way to end gridlock over proper highway funding and stewardship would be to "take the bold step of transforming our transportation assets into functioning public utilities," like electricity, gas, and water utilities.[9]
- The 2013 annual report of the Toll Division of the Washington state DOT included nearly a full page on the topic of "transportation as a utility."[10] The state's secretary of transportation, Lynn Peterson, told the National Congestion Pricing Conference, held in Seattle in July 2013 and sponsored by the Federal Highway Administration, "Transportation must be thought of as a utility."[11]
- Eric Peterson, the former deputy administrator of the USDOT's Research and Innovative Technology Administration, has concluded that "the transportation system is the most important utility, since it supports the supply of all the necessities to the human population. . . . When it is not functioning properly, these essential needs are delayed and sometimes not available."[12]
- Former West Virginia Secretary of Transportation Samuel Bonasso is quoted by Peterson as follows: "Transportation is a utility essential for our access to basic necessities. . . . It should be treated like sewage, water, electricity, waste disposal, natural gas, telephone, etc. The user of the system should be paying

for the use of the system at an appropriate rate that reflects the cost of constructing, operating, and replacing it."

- In Britain, the chairman of the Royal Auto Club (RAC) Foundation in 2012
  proposed that the UK highway assets base be converted into an investor-owned
  utility regulated like other British utilities (in airports, electricity, gas, and
  water).[13]

Thus, it appears that the general concept is starting to gain traction among
people with experience living and working within the constraints of politicized bureaucracies.

What Do Americans Pay for Utilities?

Americans have a very clear idea what they pay for conventional utilities,
because they get a bill every month from each one. The typical bill item-
izes how much of each service you have used, the rate per unit of each
(e.g., local or long-distance phone calls), and hence the amount owed. But
hardly anyone knows what they pay for the roads and highways that they
drive on—and which bring to their door the mail, UPS and FedEx, pizza
delivery, and possibly the paramedics or fire engines. That's because the
charges for road use—mostly the federal and state taxes on gasoline—
are hidden in the price of fuel. This lack of transparency gives most people a false idea of how much they pay for highways compared with other
utilities.

Many people think that when the price of fuel goes up, so does their
gas tax. That would be the case if the gas tax were a sales tax, because a
sales tax is levied as a percentage of the purchase price. (The retail sales
tax is 6 percent where I live.) But the gas tax does not change when the
price of fuel changes, because it is a fixed amount *per gallon purchased*.
The federal gas tax is 18.4 cents a gallon, regardless of whether the price
at the pump is $2.50 or $4. And because neither the federal gas tax nor
most state gas taxes are indexed for inflation, if politicians leave the rate
unchanged for a decade or two, the purchasing power of the gas tax revenue decreases every year, especially when the annual inflation rate is
high. The federal gas tax has not been increased since 1993.

So how much does the average person or household pay per year in
fuel taxes? It's a bit tricky to figure out. Basic energy use data are available from Oak Ridge National Laboratory. Their data for 2011 showed

that there were 118.7 million households and 248.9 million personal vehicles, for an average of 2.1 vehicles per household. There were 211.9 million licensed drivers, which gives us 1.78 drivers per household. Americans drove 2.946 trillion miles in 2011, which means the average driver accounted for 13,900 miles of travel. With 1.78 drivers per household, that means 24,815 annual miles per household.

The Federal Highway Administration reports that the average (federal plus state) fuel tax paid per household is $46 a month, or $552 a year. (These numbers enable us to calculate that the average driver paid 2.22 cents per mile in federal plus state fuel taxes, as of 2011.) The Florida Transportation Commission in 2012 produced a four-page handout called "Florida's Transportation Infrastructure Scorecard." It took the total revenues available to FDOT from federal and state fuel taxes plus state license tag fees, and divided that total by the number of licensed drivers. The result was $335 per driver per year. Assuming that Florida has the national average number of drivers per household (1.78), this works out to $598 per household per year, close to the $552 national average.[14]

Now let's compare that $550 to $600 per household per year to typical bills for other utilities. In a presentation at the 2014 transportation finance conference organized by the Transportation Research Board, Caltrans director Malcolm Dougherty presented figures showing that the average California household pays $1,032 per year for cable television, $852 per year for phone services, and $540 per year for Internet services. California is a costly state, so for our purposes, national averages are better. Table 4 presents national average household data for the most common utility services.

TABLE 4. **Average cost of utilities per household**

Utility	Average monthly Bill	Annual cost	Year
Electricity[1]	$107.28	$1,287	2012
Telephone[2]	$102.17	$1,226	2011
Cable[3]	$80.00	$960	2012
Natural gas[4]	$83.00	$996	2006
Water[5]	$71.06	$853	2008–9

1 Energy Information Administration, "2012 Total Electric Industry Consumers," http://builder.hw.curationdesk
.com/files/2013/12/Screen-Shot-2013-12-04-at-2.48.16-PM.png, accessed January 30, 2014.
2 Brad Tuttle, "$47 a Month? Why You're Probably Paying Double the 'Average' Cell Phone Bill," Time.com,
October 18, 2012. Citing US Department of Labor figures.
3 Alex Sherman, "Bundled Cable TV Withstands Consumer Opposition," *Bloomberg Businessweek*, November 14,
2013.
4 Energy Information Administration, "Average Monthly Residential Natural Gas & Electricity Bills," 2006.
5 Circle of Blue Urban Water Pricing Survey (for family of four, 150 gal./person/day), www.circleofblue.org
/waternews/wp-content/uploads/2010, accessed January 30, 2014.

By comparison, the national average annual gas tax bill of $552 is something of a bargain (though this figure does not include the cost of local roads, which are typically paid for out of local taxes on sales and/or property). Perhaps if people's monthly or annual highway bill were as transparent as their other utility bills—and if they were only paying for the highway services they used—they would consider paying more for better service, such as less congestion and fewer potholes.

How Would People Be Charged?

The best and fairest way to pay for utilities is based on how much of the service you use. In the early days of municipal water supply, there were no meters; the technology had not yet been invented. So the costs of the system were covered by local property taxes. Predictably, this led to considerable waste of "free" water, so cities began charging by the number of outlets, faucets, toilets, and so on. That helped a bit, but it was the invention and use of mechanical water meters for each property that led to efficient use of water, once it was charged for on the basis of the number of gallons used. There are still places today that lack water meters (e.g., portions of Sacramento and some other cities in California's Central Valley), and statistics show much greater water use per capita than in similar communities with water meters.

Historically, the development of fuel taxes, beginning with Oregon in 1919, was seen by some as a second-best way to charge for highway use. There was no "highway use meter" technology available then, comparable to mechanical water meters. But since gasoline had become the dominant motor vehicle energy source by the 1920s, having beat out steam and electricity; since the paved roads themselves were similar two-lane corridors; and since all cars had roughly similar fuel economy measured in miles per gallon, charging for highway use on the basis of gallons consumed was a reasonable proxy for highway and road use. But in a 21st century that will feature a growing array of propulsion alternatives—full electric, gasoline/electric hybrid, hydrogen fuel cell, natural gas (CNG/LNG), diesel, and others—charging per gallon will soon be obsolete. Indeed, the need to begin the change to a per-mile system was documented by a special committee on which the author served, created by the Transportation Research Board in 2005.[15] That was also a primary recommendation of a national commission created by Congress to address this issue several years later.[16]

Today we have simple, low-cost all-electronic tolling (AET) technology that is well suited to limited-access highways (expressways and Interstates). Because there are limited numbers of entry and exit points on these highways, tolling equipment installed only at entrances and exits can charge you the posted rate for the exact number of miles you travel on those highways. It would be hugely costly to install such equipment on ordinary open-access streets and roads, so AET will not be used there. Instead, low-tech solutions, such as annual reading of today's electronic and largely tamper-proof odometers, will permit charging a basic rate for miles driven on the rest of the roadway system. (Other alternatives for local roads are discussed in a sidebar in this chapter.)

Shifting from per-gallon to per-mile charging would be a major change, and people are having a hard time getting used to the idea. The subject has been needlessly confused by some transportation researchers proposing "vehicle-mile taxes" (VMTs) to be collected by a mandatory box in every car that "tracks" every single trip you take (when and where)—a prospect many people recoil from as privacy invasion by a Big Brother government. Unfortunately, many media portrayals of a shift to per-mile charging have uncritically adopted this model, which is far from what most serious transportation researchers are envisioning. This book proceeds on the premise that a mandatory tracking device in every car idea will be judged both politically and economically unfeasible. Current pilot projects in Oregon and other states are proceeding on the premise that motorists should be able to choose among methods for paying mileage-based user fees, which will likely include a GPS alternative for those who are less concerned about privacy and want other services that the GPS link makes possible. (See the further discussion in the sidebar in this chapter).

A recent Reason Foundation policy paper identified 10 ways in which a per-mile charge is a better way to pay for highways than a per-gallon tax.[17] Here we can see how a highway utility funded by per-mile charges would be better than the status quo of politicized highways.

1. *With highway utilities, per-mile tolling is a direct, rather than indirect, user fee.* This means paying the fee directly to the highway provider, rather than to a political body—a far more transparent approach that does not allow politicians to redirect monies to pet projects.
2. *Per-mile tolling provides the highway utility with a sustainable, long-term funding source for its long-lived infrastructure.* Paying per mile is independent of

unpredictable changes in future propulsion sources, so it is far more likely to remain viable as a long-term funding source. And the reliable stream of user-fee revenues provides a means for issuing long-term revenue bonds for large-scale investments.

3. *A per-mile toll can be tailored to a highway or bridge's cost.* Fuel taxes generate 2.2 cents per mile no matter whether you drive on a gravel country road or a six-lane Interstate. That makes it hard to accumulate enough money to pay for major new or replacement projects. A highway utility system could charge lower rates for inexpensive local roads and higher rates for expensive premium highways and major bridges and tunnels.[18]

4. *Per-mile charging means increased fairness to highway customers.* Someone who drives only on local streets would pay a per-mile charge based on the costs of those roadways. Those who use Interstates would pay on the basis of the higher costs of those highways.

5. *Monthly highway bills would be self-limiting.* With a highway utility, the purpose of highway bills is to pay for the highways, period. That's a sharp contrast to politicians inventing numerous ways to spend gas taxes on things other than highways.[19]

6. *Highway utilities would ensure proper ongoing maintenance.* The utility's asset value would depend on the condition of its highways and bridges. Smooth pavements would also help attract and keep paying customers. This is standard practice for toll roads, whose roadway conditions are better, on average, than comparable nontolled highways.

7. *The highway utility model provides the means to expand a highway when needed.* Cellphone customers would be outraged if their provider failed to add more towers or bandwidth to keep up with demand for the service, so the companies add needed capacity as a matter of course. By contrast, there are usually political battles over increasing gas taxes, even to pay for new projects that are clearly needed.

8. *Highway utilities would bring a shift from "funding" to "financing."* With gas taxes, highways are paid for out of the annual cash flow from those taxes. But toll roads generally finance major projects by issuing long-term toll revenue bonds. That is also how other utilities pay for large capital projects. This means that the capital is raised up front, when the project is needed, and that users pay for it over its useful life. Financing major projects is more efficient and more equitable than pay-as-you-go funding. It is like using a mortgage to finance a home purchase, rather than waiting to buy the house until you have saved up the entire purchase price.

9. *Highway utilities would reduce traffic congestion.* Where serious congestion

exists, as on many urban freeways, shifting to a highway utility model would help in two ways. First, as we know from express toll lanes, variable pricing can limit the number of vehicles attempting to use the same lane during rush hours, and transponder tolling is the low-cost technology that permits variable pricing. Second, the utility model should make it easier to add more lanes where feasible, just as electric utilities add more distribution lines, or a water utility increases the size of its wastewater treatment plant to accommodate growth.

10. *Per-mile tolling on expressways and Interstates will likely begin the needed transition from per-gallon taxes to per-mile charges.* That's because the greatest need for highway investment today is to rebuild and replace aging freeways, bridges, and Interstates with state-of-the-art facilities. Financing these megaprojects with per-mile tolls collected via all-electronic tolling is the most plausible way to do this (see chapters 9 and 10 for specifics).

To underscore these points, think about what a battle typically ensues over proposals to increase the federal gas tax or the gas tax in your state. Although these taxes began as a kind of user fee (actually, a user tax), instead of being paid to a highway provider, the money goes to the government treasury. The next year a legislative body meets and, in addition to addressing a hundred other subjects, it decides how much of the highway fund money to appropriate and where to spend it. The state DOT may present its priority list of projects, but it also knows that the legislators are politicians who each want to have projects in their districts. So, to be realistic, their priority list will have to take that into account. Because construction (either a new project or replacement of a worn-out project) gets legislators more good PR than a large maintenance budget, all too often maintenance gets the leftovers, leading to deferred maintenance—which means roads and bridges wear out prematurely and must be replaced sooner. And because usually all projects must be paid for in cash (no financing!), big-ticket items that are needed now may have to be put off for a decade or two.

Can you imagine if your cellphone or electricity provider worked like that? Those services, as well as your natural gas, cable TV, and water supply, are all run as businesses. You pay for what you use, and the money goes directly to the company. There are no politicians between you and the service provider. When the system starts to run short on capacity, the company can issue bonds and perhaps implement a rate increase to cover the new debt service costs. Their mantra is providing reliable, high-quality service to you, the paying customer. Converting the highway system into a network utility aims to bring similar improvements to this last government utility monopoly.

SIDEBAR 4 **Paying for Other Streets and Roads**

Over the next several decades, America will transition from per-gallon fuel taxes to mileage-based user fees. This book proposes that for *highways*—here defined as limited-access highways such as Interstates, urban freeways, and any other intercity highways that may be upgraded to limited-access—the replacement institution should be a highway utility industry paid for by per-mile tolls charged electronically for the use of those highways. But how would the rest of the roadway system be paid for?

The simplest alternative for non-limited-access highways—urban arterials (major thoroughfares) and local streets and roads—would be to leave existing institutions (state DOTs, and county and city public works or transportation departments) in place, with the state DOTs collecting a basic per-mile charge and distributing the proceeds among the current roadway providers: state, county, and city. This basic charge could be collected via something as simple and no-tech as annual odometer readings required for renewal of one's vehicle registration. Another no-tech option, offered in California's road charging pilot project, is an unlimited number of miles per year.[1] People choosing this option can pay a flat annual fee for unlimited miles driven in the state. Somewhat higher-tech options would be available for those desiring a more detailed basic-roads bill, or for those who live and work in a metro area that straddles a state boundary line (the two adjacent states would each be entitled to the payment for the number of miles driven on its side of the border, and the car's onboard computer could keep track of how many miles were in each category via a plug-in gadget that used cell phone towers to determine which side of the state line the car was on). Others might welcome a GPS option that included other useful services, such as emergency assistance like that provided by GM's GPS-based OnStar system.

It is also possible to create roadway utilities to deal with these state and local roads. One possible model is the user co-op, discussed elsewhere in this chapter. All licensed drivers or adult residents in a city or county could be designated as the owners of the open-access roadways within that jurisdiction (exempting the

1. "California Road Charge Pilot Goes Live," *Road Charging News*, June 2016.

limited-access highways that have transitioned to the highway utility or utilities serving that part of the state). The local roadway user co-op would have the responsibility to manage the mileage-based user fee revenues attributed to the vehicle miles of travel in that jurisdiction for the previous year. As the owner of these roadways, the co-op could contract with the jurisdiction's transportation or public works department, or with commercial providers that offered more cost-effective proposals, to operate and maintain those streets and their traffic control devices. The co-op would also need to hire a small professional staff to assess needs, monitor contractors, and carry out competitions for ongoing services.

Another way to pay for local streets and roads, which already exists in several dozen US cities, is transportation utility fees (TUFs). Under this model, the local government retains ownership of the streets, but charges residents and business occupants for the benefits of roadway access to their properties. The underlying basis for this approach is that people and businesses benefit not just from their use of local roads but also from the access they provide. In the case of individuals, this includes receiving mail and packages, access by repair people, and so on. This is the same rationale under which most local governments pay for local streets and roads out of property tax revenues. But in those cases, it is the property owners who pay, as opposed to the residents or business occupants who pay TUFs.

Transportation utility fees are calculated on the basis of the land-use intensity of the property, translated into estimated trip generation rates. Many TUF cities use rates provided by the Institute of Transportation Engineers (ITE). The TUF amount is typically added to monthly city utility bills, along with water, sewerage, and any other local utility services.

TUFs originated in La Grande, Oregon, in 1985. According to research by UCLA urban planning PhD candidate Carole Turley, more than a dozen cities in Oregon now have TUFs.[2] Only four cities outside Oregon currently have them: Austin, Texas; Loveland, Colorado; Mission, Kansas; and Provo, Utah. Four other cities that tried TUFs discontinued them due to legal challenges. Those challenges hinged on whether the TUF was structured as a tax or as a fee. Austin has avoided this kind of challenge by allowing residents who do not own or drive cars to opt out of paying the TUF.

At the neighborhood level, private streets exist in a number of neighborhoods around the country. Some of the best-known examples are the private places of

2. Carole Turley, "A TUFF Sell: Transportation Utility Fees as User Fees for Local Road and Streets," working paper, UCLA Luskin School of Public Affairs, October 2014.

SIDEBAR 4 **(Continued)**

Saint Louis, which date back to the mid-1800s. A 1984 study by the Advisory Commission on Intergovernmental Relations identified 427 private streets in the Saint Louis metro area.[3] Many of these dated back to the previous century, but a 1981 article in *Reason* magazine found that residents concerned about crime and vandalism in their neighborhoods were able to purchase their (typically several-blocks-long) streets from the city and limit access via gates, while assuming full responsibility for ongoing maintenance.[4] There are also 181 private streets in San Francisco, many dating back to the early 1900s.[5] The architect and urban analyst Oscar Newman wrote extensively about the benefits of private neighborhood streets in his book *Community of Interest*.[6] Whether residents of a much larger neighborhood could feasibly purchase and maintain their neighborhood streets is an interesting question.

A much larger trend in recent decades is that of new residential developments with deed-based homeowner associations (HOAs) that provide various "municipal" services such as landscaping, park and recreational facilities, and often ownership and maintenance of the streets. The most comprehensive assessment of this trend was researched and written by Robert Nelson of the University of Maryland.[7] Nelson cites 1999 data from the *Community Associations Factbook* indicating that, as of that time, 54 percent of HOAs provided basic street maintenance and 53 percent were responsible for street lighting; the percentage of HOAs that actually owned their streets was not stated. Nelson also cites a 1989 study by the Advisory Commission on Intergovernmental Relations concluding that local private ownership of neighborhood streets "offer[s] a number of advantages that their members value highly."[8] In short, a number of options exist for the management and operation of local streets and roads that could be adapted to a future in which most or all road use is paid for on a per-mile basis.

3. Roger B. Parks and Ronald J. Oakerson, *Metropolitan Organization: The St. Louis Case*, Advisory Commission on Intergovernmental Relations, 1984.

4. Theodore J. Gage, "Getting Street-Wise in St. Louis," *Reason*, August 1981, pp. 18–26.

5. Phillip Matier and Andrew Ross, "Rich SF Residents Get a Shock: Someone Bought Their Street," *San Francisco Chronicle*, August 7, 2017.

6. Oscar Newman, *Community of Interest* (Doubleday, 1980).

7. Robert H. Nelson, *Private Neighborhoods and the Transformation of Local Governments* (Urban Institute Press, 2005).

8. US Advisory Commission on Intergovernmental Relations, *Residential Community Associations: Private Governments in the Intergovernmental System?* (Washington, 1989).

What about Utility Regulation?

When most people hear the term "highway utility," their first reaction is negative. They immediately think of bureaucratic regulatory agencies like the one that imposed the Bell System's telephone monopoly for 71 years, or about hassles with their local cable company (which in many cities still faces no competition, by law). Yet the concept of regulation seems to go hand-in-hand with the idea of public utilities. Why is this, and would it apply to highway utilities, too?

The key factor in traditional public utility regulation is monopoly, generally considered when a capital-intensive utility has significant economies of scale, whereby the cost of each unit delivered (kilowatt-hour, gallon of water, BTU of gas) is lower if one large utility serves an area instead of two smaller ones. Transportation economists are divided over whether highways possess such economies of scale. The authors of the classic Brookings book *Road Work* reported that "the best-fitting equation gives a ratio of average to marginal cost of 1.03, which is statistically indistinguishable from 1.00 (constant returns)."[20] In a more recent paper the economist Richard Geddes concludes, "The research that is available has concluded that road infrastructure exhibits a constant returns-to-scale production technology, which at a minimum calls the road network's natural monopoly characteristics into question."[21]

The other factor economists cite is "market power"—the ability to charge above-market prices because it is not feasible for another provider to compete. That might be true for the only bridge or tunnel across a major body of water for many miles in each direction, but it is seldom true for highways or roads. There are nearly always alternative ways to get from A to B. As Ralph Erickson and Richard Geddes have pointed out, "Unlike water, electricity, and many other utilities, the degree of market power is likely to vary significantly across different transportation facility segments. . . . A particular highway may face intense competition both from other modes of travel and from competing routes."[22] This suggests, they conclude, that on average, highway regulation should be less "tight" than that applied to traditional utility monopolies, and should not be of the "one-size-fits-all" variety.

But the emergence of investor-owned companies introduces a factor that has been largely absent from the US highway sector until recently. Except for the handful of long-term concession highways, bridges, and tunnels recently brought into existence, all our experience has been either with state-run nontolled highways or public-sector toll roads. The public-sector providers are presumed, by their status in the public sector, to be operating in the public interest and in the most efficient manner—and hence not in need of regulation (although we saw in chapter 6 that this is not always a valid assumption). But once for-profit players enter the highway sector, concerns arise over the extent of profits they might make, and whether the tolls they charge will be seen as price gouging. However valid those concerns may or may not be, the question of regulation of highway utilities must be explored.

There is an array of possible regulatory approaches. One, of course, is the traditional state public utility commission (PUC). Another approach—which has been applied in most European, Canadian, Australian, and Latin American concessions—is to include regulatory provisions in the long-term concession agreement, tailored to the specifics of the project. A third alternative is to rely on nonprofit providers, such as state toll agencies or user co-ops. A fourth alternative is to adopt what Australia has done with its privatized airports: light-handed regulation in which no specific regulation is applied at the outset, but the normal competition laws, which we refer to as antitrust laws, will be applied if and when price gouging or other monopolistic behaviors occur. Let's look briefly at each alternative.

Traditional Public Utility Commission Regulation

As applied to US electricity, telephone, and other utilities for most of the 20th century, PUC regulation assumes a geographic monopoly based on economies of scale, and sees the job of the PUC as that of setting rates that allow the utility, if run well, to achieve a targeted rate of return (ROR) on its investment in the facilities (which are referred to as the "rate base"). There is a large academic literature detailing the problems and limitations of ROR regulation, beginning with the high administrative costs of the agency and its rate-setting process. One of the major problems is the perverse incentives of the utility with its guaranteed monopoly and almost-guaranteed ROR. Because the dollar amount it can earn each year is the defined rate of return (e.g., 10 percent of the value of its rate base), the utility has an incentive to maximize the rate base rather than seek to invest as efficiently as possible.[23] In addition, because rates are typically set for a period of years, they may not keep up with changing conditions (e.g., rapid changes in energy prices for an electric utility).

Another well-known problem is regulatory capture, in which the regulated industry figures out how to make use of the regulatory structure to

reduce entry by competitors and increase its profits. The historian Gabriel Kolko was one of the first to document this problem, arguing that US
railroads in the late 19th century actively worked for the creation of the
Interstate Commerce Commission for this purpose.[24] The University of
Chicago economist George Stigler studied a number of regulated markets
and concluded that, "as a rule, regulation is acquired by the industry and
is designed and operated primarily for its benefit."[25]

Traditional PUC regulation is clearly overkill for the highway utility
situation. It's a one-size-fits-all approach, whereas case-by-case assessment is needed, since few highways are actually monopolies or possess
significant economies of scale. It sets fixed prices for companies that in
many cases need to use variable pricing to provide the low or zero congestion desired by their customers. It is also a poor fit for a new toll road
or bridge that may operate in the red during its early years, as customers
take several years to figure out whether the value provided is worth the
toll, while annual debt service payments must be made on schedule.

The only case I know of in which the PUC regulation approach has
been used for an investor-owned toll road is the Dulles Greenway, whose
birth and early years were described in chapter 5. Once the Greenway finally started making money and had to go to the Virginia utility regulator
to request a rate increase in 2007, local politicians turned the process into
a populist circus, railing against what seemed to them to be too-high tolls.
The eventual result of that battle was a shift to seven years of price-cap
regulation, but with toll rates after that period left undecided. As the end
of that seven-year period approached, a Republican legislator asked Virginia's PUC (called the State Corporation Commission) to investigate the
Greenway's toll rates, which he claimed were unreasonable and discouraged use of the tollway. In September 2015 the SCC closed its investigation, concluding that the tolls were "reasonable in relation to the benefit
obtained" and "will not materially discourage use of the roadway."[26] But
the kind of risk and uncertainty created by such a process holds up a large
stop sign to investors, and, as a result, no other toll projects in Virginia
have been developed under that model. No other state has authorized
investor-owned toll roads subject to PUC regulation.

Concession Agreement Regulation

As discussed in chapter 6, the concession agreement is a very detailed
long-term contract, typically negotiated between a state DOT and the

concession company that has won the competition to do the project. Its hundreds of pages deal with a large set of topics intended to govern the long-term public-private partnership in ways that are fair to both parties. From the regulatory standpoint, it deals with questions such as required performance standards, pricing, hand-back conditions (at the end of the concession term), early termination by either party, competing facilities, and amendment of the agreement to take into account unforeseen developments.

When it comes to toll rates, in the US experience so far we see two different approaches. For long-distance toll roads such as the Indiana Toll Road, the concession agreement typically provides a cap on annual toll rate increases, such as the previous year's increase in the consumer price index (CPI). That approach should work reasonably well, assuming that the concession company is able to add lanes in future years to cope with traffic growth and prevent future congestion. But urban toll roads are far more likely to need the ability to use unregulated variable pricing to deal with congestion, especially in situations where it is either politically impossible to add lanes or so costly that a major addition, such as elevated express toll lanes, cannot be made immediately. In Toronto, the concession agreement for urban expressway Highway 407ETR puts no limitations on toll rates, but instead requires the concession company to achieve certain traffic-flow performance standards that may require lane additions in future years.

In Texas and Virginia, concession agreements for express-toll-lane projects, such as the I-635 LBJ Express Lanes in Dallas and the I-495 Beltway Express Lanes in northern Virginia, provide for revenue sharing. The idea is that if the toll lanes perform significantly better than the base-case financial model included in the concession agreement, revenues above predefined levels are shared with the state DOT. Rather than having the DOT or a regulatory commission attempt to monitor the concession company's rate of return, the concession agreement can spell out in advance how gross toll revenues will be divided between the company and the DOT. In such agreements, a sliding scale is generally agreed to, with increasing shares of the toll revenue paid to the DOT the more that revenue exceeds the base-case level. Gross toll revenue is easy to measure, so this is a transparent, inexpensive way to deal with what some might consider above-market profits. For the LBJ Express Lanes project, the agreement defines five bands of gross toll revenue. In the lowest band, zero revenue is shared with the state. If revenue falls into band 2, then

12.5 percent of it is shared with Texas DOT. The percentages for bands 3, 4, and 5 are 25 percent, 50 percent, and 75 percent.[27]

Another question is how long a concession agreement should last. There has been much debate over this question, with some arguing for terms no longer than 20 or 30 years and others defending terms as long as 99 years, as apply to the Chicago Skyway and Toronto's 407ETR. Advocates of the shortest terms cite the typical planning horizon for state DOT and urban-area MPOs of 20 to 25 years, and the typical competition provisions of concession agreements that may require compensation for highway projects other than those in the long-range plan that take traffic away from the concession highway. Concession companies respond that the length of the concession cannot be one-size-fits-all, since the base-case financial model can be substantially different from one project to the next, which is why some high-risk megaprojects—such as the world's highest bridge, the Millau Viaduct in France—have concession terms in excess of 70 years.

An alternative approach to this question is called present value of revenue (PVR) and has been advocated by the Chilean economist Eduardo Engel and colleagues. Under this approach, the competition to become the concession company is based on which bidder offers to do the project for the lowest present value of toll revenue over the life of the concession.[28] The DOT sets the maximum toll rate it will allow and the discount rate to be used in the net-present-value (NPV) calculation. Thus, the term of the concession is not specified, but lasts as long as it takes for the company to achieve the net present value of revenue specified in its bid. The idea of the PVR approach is to reduce the traffic and revenue risk that the company assumes in a toll concession, by giving it more time to earn a total sum that it has accepted as its return on investment, even if this takes many years longer than it had hoped. Engel reports that both Chile and Colombia have used PVR auctions to award concessions, with this method becoming standard in Chile for highway concessions in 2008.[29]

Nonprofit Providers

There are several other possibilities for avoiding regulation motivated by concern over excess or above-market profits. One would be to simply avoid the use of for-profit companies and expand the scope of urban and state toll agencies. Another would be to adapt the nonprofit user co-op idea to the provision of highways. A third possibility is the idea of a "public-public" partnership.

In chapter 6 we discussed some significant governance problems with the current US toll agency model. While some state and local toll agencies have been innovative (e.g., in pioneering competitive contracting of highway maintenance, converting to fully all-electronic toll collection, and adding premium express toll lanes to their existing tolled facilities), others have become politicized bureaucracies overstaffed with political hires, diverting large fractions of their customers' toll revenues to politically favored projects—both in transportation and outside transportation. In addition, while some new toll agencies have been created in urban areas in recent years, especially in Colorado and Texas, there has been a countertrend of state DOTs absorbing formerly separate state toll agencies. This has occurred to varying degrees in Florida, Kansas, Massachusetts, North Carolina, and Texas, which suggests some degree of political dissatisfaction with the independent state toll agency model.[30] In Florida there was even an attempt in the legislature in 2011–12 to consolidate the urban toll agencies into the Florida Turnpike Enterprise, itself now a "district" of the Florida DOT.[31] Given the mixed record and governance problems with public-sector toll agencies, this model will not be considered further.

The transportation user co-op is an approach we have not yet seen in the highway field, but there are a number of examples in aviation. The original US air traffic control system was begun by a nonprofit user co-op created by several airlines: Aeronautical Radio, Inc. (ARINC). After the federal government took over air traffic control in 1936, ARINC expanded its membership and took on what became a global role in providing various communications services for airlines (e.g., linking cockpit crews with airline dispatchers by radio).[32] It also helped launch the air traffic control systems of Cuba and Mexico on a similar nonprofit user co-op model. After World War II, a competitor user-owned nonprofit based in France, called Société internationale de télécommunications aéronautiques (SITA), emerged and grew to global status providing similar services. And in 1996 the Canadian air traffic control system was separated from Transport Canada and set up as a nonshare, not-for-profit corporation funded entirely by user charges and governed by a board of aviation stakeholders—basically a user co-op.[33]

At the Transportation Research Board's 2014 transportation finance conference, David Ungemah and Chris Swenson gave a presentation on transportation co-ops as a potential new way to manage and govern roads and highways.[34] They argued that the main challenge in transitioning from per-gallon fuel taxes to per-mile charges is political, stemming from public distrust of the current owner-operator models—state DOTs, toll agencies, and P3s alike. After reviewing the surprisingly large role of user co-ops in agriculture (e.g., Sunkist, Ocean Spray) and utilities (e.g., rural electricity and telephone co-ops), they argued that applying this model to surface transportation could resolve concerns over distrusted institutions, taxes, and tolls. Such a co-op could be formed to be the investment vehicle and operational owner of either a new or a reconstructed highway, bridge, or tunnel funded by tolls (per-mile charges), with investment dividends (from net revenue after covering all costs) paid to the owners.

Ungemah and Swenson presented two possible models: the direct-user model, in which the paying customers are the owners, and the public-public model, in which local municipalities became the owners of local roadways. They identified a number of issues that would need attention to flesh out such models, primarily questions of liability and of ownership: Who would be the owner-members? And how would governance work? In 1999, Gabriel Roth suggested a user co-op approach, using as an example a hypothetical Los Angeles Freeway Travelers Association to operate and manage the freeway system on a commercial basis, funded by road pricing revenues.[35]

A different "public-public" model has been proposed by Richard Geddes and Dimitar Nentchev as a way to change the incentives of governments so as to embrace direct pricing of their roadways.[36] Under this approach, ownership of the highways within a particular jurisdiction would be granted to the taxpayers of that jurisdiction. To refurbish and maintain that set of roadways, the owners would seek bids for a toll concession similar to those for the Chicago Skyway and the Indiana Toll Road, with the winner being determined by the highest upfront payment. Part of the payment would be used to create a permanent fund, comparable to Alaska's Permanent Fund based on its oil revenues from the North Slope. This fund would pay an annual dividend to each taxpayer, like what is done in Alaska. The other portion of the upfront payment would be used to renovate and expand the roadway network.

Light-Handed Regulation

Australia privatized all its major airports in the late 1990s, mostly via long-term concessions. For the first few years it employed a form of price-cap regulation of the airports' charges to airlines. But since 2003, its policy on airports has instead been "light-handed regulation." This means that airports are subjected only to the normal competition laws affecting all other industries, with mandated disclosure of costs and prices. Thus, the only airport regulator is the Australian Competition and Consumer Commission (ACCC), roughly equivalent to the antitrust division of the US Department of Justice.

In 2010 the ACCC's annual report noted airline concerns over Sydney Airport's profits, and suggested that this particular airport might need more explicit regulation. In response, the government ordered a report by its Productivity Commission, an independent body that reports to the government's treasurer. The commission found that light-handed regulation of airports was working well, with significant investment by the concession companies, high service quality, and no indication of "inappropriate exercise of market power."[37] Tellingly, despite the airline concerns over Sydney, following release of the Productivity Commission's report, "no party sought a return to regulatory price setting, given past experiences with its associated costs."

Highways are not airports, to be sure. But, given that metro areas in Australia and most of the United States have only a single commercial airport, airports would appear to have more market power than highways, when both are operated by for-profit companies under long-term concession agreements. Thus, a conceivable alternative, at least for some highway utilities, is to avoid explicit regulation of prices or revenue, and to rely instead on appeals to antitrust law in the event a highway utility misuses the market power it does possess.

Designing Concessions to Protect Customers

Given the discussion above, in my judgment the most realistic approach for protecting customers in a highway-utility world is some form of concession-based regulation. Going with that option would avoid the high administrative costs of traditional utility commission regulation and the skewed incentives for the regulated entity to overinvest in physical facilities that are inherent in traditional ROR regulation. Existing state and urban toll agencies would continue as examples of government utilities, as is the case with municipal water and electric utilities, though many would be candidates for governance reforms and increased transparency or conversion to another ownership model. User co-ops would be another option where the political climate was not favorable to investor-owned highway utilities. While I would be willing to try light-handed regulation of otherwise non–price-regulated highway utilities, I doubt that this option would be politically acceptable, at least in the near term.

So our next topic is to consider what kinds of provisions should be included in the legal framework needed for the emergence of a thriving highway utility industry in which the long-term toll concession is the primary model.

Let's begin by understanding why the primary model should be the toll concession, rather than the kind of availability payment (AP) concession we encountered in chapter 6. AP concessions are used worldwide and, to some extent recently in the United States, for a wide array of public infrastructure, including courthouses, school buildings, prisons, and increasingly highways, such as portions of the new I-69 in southern Indiana. For highways, toll concessions are preferable for several reasons.

First, a major problem facing America's highway system is insufficient investment—in new capacity, and especially in replacing worn-out capacity. The remedy is per-mile charges (tolls) to replace the increasingly inadequate system of fuel taxes. An AP concession is a *financing* tool, but not a means of adding new funding to the highway system, since it generally relies on existing tax revenue to make the availability payments. It does not increase the total amount of money going into highway capital investment.

Second, AP concessions create new debt on government balance sheets, whether that is acknowledged or not. As Australia's Productivity Commission has put it,

> If a PPP involves non-contingent obligations to make future payments to private sector providers, then this creates a liability that needs to be funded from taxes and/or user charges, and has an impact similar, perhaps greater, to direct government borrowings. Some forms of availability payments have been developed for road projects that are of this kind. Ultimately, ratings agencies see all claims on government as the same. There is no magic pudding.[38]

Most state governments have legal or constitutional debt limits, so their ability to make large-scale use of AP concessions will be quite limited. A few states have created explicit limits on the amount of availability payment liability they will take on. For example, a 2013 Florida statute requires that no more than 20 percent of all state and federal transportation revenues in any year can be devoted to debt and debtlike obligations, including availability payments. The Florida Division of Bond Finance includes AP obligations in its benchmark debt ratio calculations.[39] North Carolina has a 6-percent cap on debt payments as a fraction of its transportation tax revenues; availability payment obligations are included.[40]

Another reason for toll concessions rather than the AP kind is the need to shift from per-gallon taxes to per-mile charges, and tolls are a well-understood form of per-mile charging. Since the Interstate Highway System (rural plus urban) handles 25 percent of total US vehicle miles of travel, converting that portion of the highway system to per-mile tolling will be a large step toward replacing per-gallon fuel taxes.

Finally, highways and bridges require owners, who are charged with the responsibility of providing excellent services to their paying customers, as is the case with other network utilities. There will still be a role for government in deciding where a highway route will go, in ensuring proper performance standards and interoperability among portions of the network operated by different companies, and in setting the rules for dealing with externalities such as noise and emissions. But the highway sector has lacked (1) owners willing to invest their own capital in projects that make business sense, (2) a direct customer-provider relationship between highway customer and highway provider, and (3) a robust funding and financing system that is insulated from politics. AP concessions, including hybrid toll/AP concessions in which the state DOT does the tolling, do not provide this kind of business model. Yet the functional equivalent of the toll concession is the business model that has delivered the world's best utilities in electricity, gas, water, and telecommunications.

Creating Trustworthy Highway Utilities: Value-Added Tolling Principles

Although toll roads are statistically safer and better maintained than equivalent limited-access nontolled roads (such as Interstates),[41] many Americans don't have a high level of trust in toll agencies, which are the only forms of toll provider they know. Many Americans have a kind of love/hate relationship with toll roads, and trucking organizations almost always oppose any further expansion of tolling in America. Many of these concerns are historically legitimate, and they will have to be addressed credibly in order to bring about an investor-owned highway utility industry.

Two of these concerns have been made obsolete by 21st-century all-electronic tolling, but because most people don't yet realize this, the trucking industry continues to use them as arguments against increased tolling or implementation of mileage-based user fees. The first concern is about congestion, accidents, and increased emissions as vehicles wait in long lines to pay their tolls at toll plazas. This ignores the fact that existing toll roads are steadily converting from cash tolling to all-electronic tolling (AET) with no toll booths or toll plazas at all. By the end of 2014, this transition had been completed on toll roads in Dallas, Denver, Miami, and Orange County, California, and it is now beginning to take place elsewhere. If and when currently nontolled Interstates are rebuilt and widened on the basis of toll finance, nobody will build toll plazas on them. They will be designed and built from the outset for cashless AET.

The second obsolete concern is that tolling is very inefficient compared with paying for roads via fuel taxes. Gasoline and diesel taxes are collected at the wholesale level, not at the retail gas station. The widely believed figure is that collecting fuel taxes costs about 1 percent of the revenue generated, which sounds very efficient. Actually, when a recent Transportation Research Board study looked more closely at the additional costs due to fuel tax evasion and exemptions, the real number appears to be closer to 5 percent—but that still seems pretty efficient.[42] By contrast, studies based on data from the past 15 years or so put the cost of toll collection by legacy toll agencies at 20 to 30 percent of the revenue collected, which is very inefficient.

Fully cashless AET changes that picture dramatically. A team of electronic toll collection experts in 2012 researched new toll roads whose systems were designed from the start for transponder-based AET, using a streamlined business model aimed at maximizing the use of transponders (versus more expensive billing based on license plate images). The result was that such systems are approaching a collection cost as low as 5 percent of the revenue collected.[43] And since toll collection does exhibit economies of scale, the fact that the three small toll roads in the study were able to get their collection costs down to near 5 percent suggests that this target is more achievable on larger toll roads, where fixed costs can be spread over much larger numbers of customers.

Further evidence comes from a system called PrePass Plus, used by trucking companies to enable transponder tolling in the 15 E-ZPass states in the Northeast and Midwest. The service is provided by the nonprofit HELP, Inc., and billing service is operated for HELP by a division of Xerox. The cost to a trucking company for getting a consolidated bill (all tolls charged anywhere in those states) is just $5 per month, which covers all of Xerox's billing costs. For a truck that incurs toll charges of $150 per month, the collection cost is just 3.3 percent of the associated toll revenue. In other words, AET for trucking is already generating revenue at a collection cost comparable with fuel taxes.[44]

The other four concerns raised not only by trucking groups but also by groups representing ordinary motorists, such as AAA, are in need of serious consideration. They are as follows:

1. *Adding tolls to existing highways without adding value for drivers.* The most notorious example of this was when Pennsylvania twice applied to the US DOT for permission to put tolls on I-80, which parallels the tolled Pennsylvania Turnpike, about 85 miles to the north. The nominal purpose was to rebuild aging I-80 via toll finance, but the PennDOT plan was to charge rates far above what was needed for I-80, so as to generate half a billion dollars a year for highways and transit systems around the state. The excess tolls would have been the equivalent of a tax imposed solely on I-80 users to pay for nontolled highways and transit systems. Fortunately, the US DOT turned down this proposal. Highway user groups have considerable fear that a shift to per-mile tolling would lead to that kind of situation: of toll road customers being turned into cash cows.

2. *Diverting toll revenues to other uses.* This concern points not to hypotheticals, but to actual practices of about a dozen toll agencies, mostly in the Northeast, that are already using revenues from ever-increasing toll rates to fund mass transit and the World Trade Center in New York City; "economic development" in Atlantic City, the Delaware River Valley, and West Virginia; and transit projects in northern Virginia and San Francisco. As with Pennsylvania's rejected proposal for tolling I-80, for the dozen or so agencies that regularly divert toll revenue in this way, significant portions of their tolls are not really tolls but taxes imposed in a discriminatory manner only on those who use those toll roads, rather than all taxpayers or all motorists in the state in question.

3. *Double taxation.* On nearly every existing tolled road, bridge, and tunnel in America today, motorists and truckers pay fuel taxes and tolls on the same facility. Since tolls are supposed to be the funding source for the toll facilities, highway users have a legitimate complaint that the miles they drive on the toll road should be exempt from gasoline or diesel taxes. Actually, two states— Massachusetts and New York—do have fuel tax rebate programs under which those who use the Massachusetts Turnpike and the New York Thruway can apply for a refund of the estimated amount of fuel tax they paid for the miles driven on the tolled highways. To the best of my knowledge, these little-known rebate programs are used almost exclusively by trucking companies.

4. *Diverting traffic to parallel routes.* Those experts who do toll road traffic and revenue studies know that if a new highway is opened as a toll road, some fraction of the traffic that would have used it if it were not tolled will instead opt to drive on parallel routes to avoid paying the toll. That may subject businesses and residences along those routes to increased noise, emissions, and accidents—and possibly to damage by heavy trucks to pavements not designed to take their weight. There is no question that this impact is real.

As we look to create a framework for a highway utility industry that highway customers can trust, how can these four concerns be addressed? A recent policy paper advanced a concept called value-added tolling.[45] It consists of four key points that should be among the core principles for the highway utility industry framework. These principles would apply to all new uses of per-mile highway charging, to be consistent with the way other utilities keep faith with their customers. They would also be incorporated into long-term concession agreements.

First, limit the use of toll revenues to the tolled facilities. This is the basis of all other utility pricing. When you pay your phone bill, water bill, or electricity bill, you are paying just for the services delivered by the utility's facilities, not for a variety of unrelated projects dreamed up by politicians. This would not preclude a highway utility company from using its toll revenues wherever in its network they would add the most value, just as electric utilities do.

Second, charge only enough to cover the full capital and operating costs of the tolled facilities. In a for-profit model, this would have to include a reasonable return on investment to the concession company and its investors who (as we saw in chapter 6) take on significant risks that in 20th-century highways were borne by taxpayers.

Third, begin tolling only after the facility's construction or reconstruction has been completed and it has been opened for use by paying customers. Thus, a rebuilt Interstate would be treated just like a brand-new toll road (the toll-finance community is used to seeing no revenue until a project is finished). This is also standard practice in public utilities; new capacity cannot be charged for until it is actually ready to be used to serve customers.

Fourth, use tolls instead of, not in addition to, current highway user taxes. With all-electronic tolling, it is simple to create software that identifies the vehicle make and model, looks up the relevant EPA miles per gallon figure, and calculates the fuel tax paid for the number of miles driven on the tolled highway. That file would be transmitted to either the state DOT or the Department of Motor Vehicles to inform them of the amount of fuel-tax rebate they must pay out to specific toll road customers.

Taken together, these policies would create a genuine value proposition for highway users, both motorists and truckers. They would convert an underfunded, congested, poorly maintained, and politicized highway system into a network utility in which the charges were purely payments for use, to cover the capital and operating costs of the network, as in all our other public utilities. The provision prohibiting revenue diversion to outside uses would mean toll rates lower than are typically seen on many of today's best known tolled Interstates that divert revenue (e.g., the Pennsylvania Turnpike). And lower toll rates mean less traffic diversion, since we know that the higher the toll rate, the more traffic will divert to parallel routes.

Additional Customer Protections

Would the value-added tolling provisions, embedded in law and included in concession agreements, be sufficient to gain highway users' trust in the highway utility model? Two other factors could assist with this task: the financial markets and the way in which the term of a long-term toll concession is determined.

FINANCIAL MARKETS. The investment funds and financial institutions that provide the debt and equity to pay for construction or reconstruction would have a strong interest in maintaining the viability of the highway utility business on an ongoing basis, including protecting its revenues from being diverted to other purposes. Various covenants have long been included in revenue bond agreements for this purpose. One type of covenant requires debt-service reserve funds to be established and maintained, so that funds are available to ensure that debt-service payments can be made to bondholders even during recession years when traffic and toll revenue typically decline. Maintenance reserve funds are also nearly always required as a high-priority use of toll revenue, since the toll facility must be kept in excellent condition in order to attract and keep customers that might otherwise divert to nontolled alternatives.

These covenants have a long history of being enforceable in court. In addition, the bond rating agencies play an important guardian role. They review the financial plans of every revenue bond issue before it is offered to investors, and provide their estimate of how risky they judge the bond to be, via a letter grade. The interest rate on a toll revenue bond is lower if it achieves a high letter grade such as AA, which means that the annual debt service payments will be lower. A higher-risk bond, as evidenced by a worse letter grade (e.g., B) must pay a higher interest rate to persuade investors to buy it, and that means the toll road company's debt service payments will be higher. In recent years, as more legislatures have required toll agencies to divert revenue to non-toll-road purposes, the rating agencies have expressed concern over the use of toll roads as "cash cows." In 2012, Moody's Investors Service issued a report on this subject, which included research findings showing that toll agencies that diverted revenue in this manner ended up with lower bond ratings and, therefore, higher debt service costs.[46]

SETTING A TERM OF THE RIGHT DURATION. Electric utilities generally have long-term franchises ranging from 50 to 99 years. Those are essentially long-term concession agreements, except that they are far less comprehensive than toll concessions, because electric utility rates are regulated by a separate regulatory commission. A long term is important for both highways and electricity, because the intent is to have a long-lived business operating, maintaining, adding to, and refurbishing long-lived infrastructure that provides an essential public service.

Major highways are designed to last 50 years or so, with proper ongoing maintenance. But traditional toll revenue bonds have terms of 30 to 35 years. If the concession term for a new highway or an about-to-be reconstructed highway is set to match the expected pavement life of 50 years, what happens during the later years of a toll concession after the initial bonds are paid off, if no new investment is needed during the concession's remaining years? In a fast-growing state or urban area, this problem might not arise, because most highways will need additional capacity to cope with growth during such a long period of time. But in a slow-growing jurisdiction, no such additions might be needed. In those cases, the out-years would be a period of large profits far in excess of operating and maintenance costs and a reasonable return on investment. That means that the customers would be paying far more than the capital and operating costs of the facilities, which violates the second value-added tolling principle. If the facility in question is an urban expressway using variable tolling to manage traffic—reducing congestion in regular lanes, eliminating it in premium lanes—then reducing tolls would lead to serious degradation of service levels.

One way to deal with this would be for the financial community to agree to significantly longer-term toll revenue bonds. If the bonds were to be paid off over 50 years, and the useful life of the facility were also 50 years, then before the expiration of the 50-year concession a new competition would be held for a concession to rebuild and modernize the facility for another 50 years (or however long new technology by then would make feasible). The incumbent provider would be free to compete for the new concession, of course, as is generally the case when an electric utility franchise expires. Another possibility would be for the surplus revenues, beyond the agreed-upon equity return, to be transferred to the DOT but set aside in a sinking fund to go toward the eventual reconstruction and renovation of the facility beyond the term of the concession.

Making the concession term match the highway's useful life is contrary to the concept of variable-length concessions, as proposed by Eduardo Engel and discussed earlier in this chapter. That model seems better suited to an environment in which highway concessions are used opportunistically rather than as the basis of an ongoing highway utility industry.

As the highway utility industry develops and matures, creative new models will undoubtedly emerge.

Other Public Interest Protections in Concession Agreements

Many other details must be addressed in concession agreements. In recent years, several very good policy papers have emerged on how to protect the public interest in such agreements. Among those making such recommendations have been the Transportation Research Board, the Brookings Institution, and the Federal Highway Administration.

The broadest and most comprehensive report is a product of the National Cooperative Highway Research Program, managed by the Transportation Research Board in cooperation with the American Association of State Highway and Transportation Officials (AASHTO), the membership organization for state DOTs. Its 2009 report provides a comprehensive primer on long-term concessions.[47] This includes advice on deciding how and when to use concessions. It then devotes considerable attention to basic public interest issues and on how to address them in concession agreements. Topics addressed include control of the highway asset (division of responsibility between the DOT and the company), tolling policy, competition provisions, use of proceeds and revenue sharing, maintenance standards and hand-back provisions, labor relations, length of the agreement, termination and buyouts, safety and enforcement, liability and insurance, and transparency. (For more on transparency, see the sidebar.)

The Brookings Institution report makes a persuasive case for states to create P3 units: specialized entities with the high-level legal and financial expertise to carry out benefit/cost and value-for-money analyses, so as to determine when it makes sense to use long-term concessions.[48] The P3 unit would also serve as the entity within the state government that manages the procurement process, including the final step of negotiating the detailed concession agreement itself. P3 units are well established in Australia, Canada, and the United Kingdom, but have not yet been widely adopted in the United States. As this is written, such units are in operation only in Colorado, Puerto Rico, and Virginia.

More recently, a team of analysts from the Federal Highway Administration (FHWA) and the US DOT's Volpe National Transportation Systems Center produced a first-rate report on how to use benefit/cost analysis to decide whether a project is worth doing, and then how to use value-for-money analysis to decide whether it is best done as a long-term concession.[49] And in 2014, the FHWA's Office of Innovative Program Delivery produced a model contract guide for toll concessions.[50]

In this chapter we have reviewed how a highway utility industry could operate, and how highway users could be protected by a form of regulation that avoids the high costs and perverse incentives of traditional public utility regulation. But how could the United States transition to highway utilities? That is the subject of the next two chapters. In chapter 9 we will look at how the transition could come about for major highways such as long-distance Interstates. And in chapter 10 we will do the same for urban freeways.

SIDEBAR 5 **Transparency in P3 Concession Agreements**

The idea that P3 concessions are some kind of "crony capitalism" is something of an urban legend. I encountered it when testifying before a congressional committee back in 2007, when some members of the House Transportation and Infrastructure Committee were outraged by the long-term leases of the Chicago Skyway and Indiana Toll Road.

The need for transparency during the entire P3 concession procurement process, as well as during the course of these long-term agreements, is well understood by the agencies using this relatively new approach for major US highway projects. The US Department of Transportation, via the FHWA's Office of Innovative Program Delivery and US DOT's relatively new Build America Transportation Investment Center (BATIC), have produced model concession agreements and guidelines for how to do these procurements transparently. A recent example is BATIC's *Successful Practices for P3s*, a 64-page guide (with three appendixes) whose underlying theme throughout is transparent practices.[1]

For this book, I contacted the seven state DOTs that have completed one or more highway or bridge P3 concession (design-build-finance-operate-maintain) projects to ask about specific policies that would reflect a meaningfully transparent approach to procuring and managing such projects. All seven responded, and the results are summarized in table 5. One of the first responses was from Kome Ajise at the Caltrans headquarters in Sacramento. It is reflective of the views of respondents from the other six agencies: "I think this [nontransparency allegation] is one of the most overstated claims against P3 agreements. Because of the political nature of P3 projects, they tend to be the most transparent agreements we do, in terms of how they have to be in the public domain."

For table 5, I selected five key indicators of transparency and asked each of the seven state DOTs to explain how it dealt with each one:

1. **Public meetings.** From start to finish, the project is explained to the public via a series of public meetings, generally held in the portion of the state where the proposed project is to be located.
2. **Written P3 procurement manual.** Because P3 concessions are quite different from traditional DBB procurements or newer DB procurements, a state DOT needs to develop detailed guidelines so that all relevant staff, as well as prospective bidders, understand all aspects of the process.
3. **State "open records" law.** This goes directly to the mistaken view that P3 documents are not fully disclosed. These state statutes, which differ somewhat from state to state, generally offer limited exceptions for proprietary information and trade secrets. This is no different for P3 agreements than for any other contracts the state DOT may enter into.
4. **Value-for-money analysis.** As noted in chapter 6, a VfM analysis is intended to weigh the benefits and costs of using a DBFOM procurement instead of a conventional DBB or DB procurement. It is a powerful tool with a long

---

1. Build America Transportation Investment Center, "Successful Practices for P3s," US Department of Transportation, March 2016.

TABLE 5. **Transparency indicators at state DOTs with P3 concession programs**

	California	Colorado	Florida	Indiana	North Carolina	Virginia	Texas
Public meetings	yes	yes	yes	yes	yes	yes	yes
P3 procurement manual	yes	yes	yes*	yes	yes	yes	yes
Open-records law	yes	yes	yes	yes	yes	yes	yes
VfM analysis	yes	yes	yes	yes	yes	yes	no***
Concession agreements online	yes	yes	yes**	yes	yes	yes	yes

*Guidelines, not mandated procedures
**Upon citizen request
***Other analysis method used to decide best procurement model

SIDEBAR 5 **(Continued)**

track record in Australia and Canada, only recently becoming common in P3 decision-making in the United States. Its use is recommended by US DOT.

5. **Concession agreements posted online.** In some respects, this is the acid test of P3 transparency, since these multi-hundred-page documents are intended to cover every aspect of the long-term agreement.

The response from all seven state DOTs was very forthcoming, and these programs are highly transparent to legislators and the public. I will close with a representative comment by Leon Corbett of the Comptroller's Office of the Florida DOT: "We have benefited from being open about our projects because it stimulates helpful interactions with all sectors, public and private, about the projects. The impact of these projects is far-reaching. There is a lot of interest from the citizens, government leaders, news media, and industry. We want to take the best path forward to deliver a major project, P3 or not. That starts with being transparent with your stakeholders."[2]

2. Leon Corbett, FDOT, email to the author, October 28, 2016.

CHAPTER NINE

Transforming the Interstate Highways

Chapter 8 explained, in general, how highway utilities would work. In this chapter we will explore how the transformation of current highways into highway utilities could begin. A change of this magnitude would not happen all at once, in a kind of Big Bang scenario. It is almost certainly not something that would be led or mandated by the federal government, in an age where Congress ranks lower in public esteem than most other institutions in our society. The change will be an evolutionary process, taking advantage of our federalist structure of government, with the 50 states as laboratories of democracy, trying new approaches and learning from each other.

My thesis, explained below, is that the first highways to make the transition will be long-distance Interstate highways. This chapter will first explain *why*, and then turn to the question of *how* this could come about.

Why Begin with the Interstates?

The Importance of the Interstate System

If you grew up in the 1970s, 1980s, or 1990s, the Interstate highways seem to have always been there. But, as recounted in chapter 3, there were no Interstates at all prior to the 1960s. Congress enacted the legislation in 1956 after years of debate. While a few of these long-distance corridors were completed by 1960, the vast majority were constructed and opened to traffic in the 1960s and 1970s, with some of the more difficult stretches completed in the 1980s, and the last major project, I-105 in Los Angeles, not completed until the mid-1990s.

Transportation experts correctly view the Interstate system as America's most important and most valuable highways. They are much safer than the previous intercity highways with US route numbers (US 1, US 27, etc.), due to their superhighway design features: wide medians to separate traffic going in opposite directions, gentler grades and wider, banked curves, breakdown lanes, and so on. The ability to go long distances at high speeds with no traffic lights led to a huge growth in long-distance trucking, and ultimately to the creation of a freight logistics system that became the envy of the world. The increased ease of longer-distance personal travel led to greatly expanded horizons for family vacations, which led to the birth of national chains of hotels, motels, and restaurants, as well as the invention of new categories of vehicles such as campers and motor homes.

Did construction of the Interstates have a measurable economic impact? Economists tend to be cautious about such matters. A 1991 study by the Congressional Budget Office noted conflicting results among studies that attempted to measure the economic impact of "public investment" or overall infrastructure investment.[1] But it did note that "carefully chosen federal investment in physical infrastructure such as highway and aviation projects would yield economic rates of return higher than the average returns on private capital." Equally cautious was a literature review by the Federal Highway Administration the next year, finding that "a consensus that public capital has a weak, positive effect on private economic activity is emerging among researchers involved."[2] It was not until 1996 that a definitive study of the impact of the Interstate system itself appeared. In a peer-reviewed study done for the FHWA's Office of Policy Development, Ishaq Nadiri and a colleague estimated that the economic returns from Interstate highway investment from the 1950s through the 1970s was in excess of 50 percent per year, and produced productivity gains for nearly all sectors of industry.[3] The Nadiri study is frequently cited, and its findings were reinforced in a later study by John Fernald of the Federal Reserve Bank of San Francisco, who found even higher returns for the years before 1973.[4] A later study by Nadiri and a coauthor found lower rates of returns on highway capital investment between 1990 and 2000.[5]

Today the 47,182 miles of Interstates (both rural and urban) handle 25 percent of all vehicle miles of travel in the United States, on just 2.5 percent of the roadway lane-miles. That is due to a combination of selection of routes that would serve a high volume of traffic (with a few political exceptions) and the ability to maintain high volumes of traffic on uninterrupted highways at high rates of speed (except during rush hours on urban Interstates in the largest metro areas).

Reasons for Concern

We cannot take all these benefits for granted as going on indefinitely, for two reasons. First, all highways eventually wear out. Premium highways like the Interstates have a maximum pavement design life of 50 years, if they are properly maintained. But at the end of that lifetime, the pavement must be replaced—not resurfaced, but torn up and replaced. And that is very expensive. The few Interstates built in the late 1950s needed reconstruction by 2010—or sooner, if they had not been properly maintained—and a small amount of this reconstruction has taken place. For the much larger number built in the 1960s, the decade of the 2010s should be reconstruction time, as the 2020s will be for those built in the 1970s, and the 2030s for Interstates built in the 1980s. So we are on the verge of needing several decades of massive reconstruction projects.

The second reason for concern is that some of these long-distance Interstates need—or will likely need, in the next decade or two—additional lanes. That is especially true of those Interstates that have become major truck corridors in America's freight logistics system—such as east-west routes like I-40 and I-70 and north-south routes like I-35 and I-81. That means not only selective widening of the pavement, but also the widening of many of the system's bridges and overcrossings (except for the few cases in which those were built with enough extra capacity for the future). Well designed bridges can generally last 75 to 100 years, but for bridges without enough lanes, it may be wiser to replace them rather than figure out how to add extra lanes (which is often not as cost-effective as building a higher-capacity and longer-lasting replacement bridge).

The largest problem facing America's state DOTs is how to pay for the reconstruction and selective widening of their portions of the Interstate system. It is *their* problem, because the states are the owners and operators of these vital highways. (The federal government owns none of this system; federally owned roads are mostly within national parks and on other federal lands.) Estimates of the investment needed to revamp and modernize the Interstate system range from $1 trillion to several times that amount. But as we also saw in chapter 3, the federal fuel taxes that provided 90 percent of the money to build the Interstates are now being spent on a vast array of highway, transit, safety, bike path, recreational trail, sidewalk, and beautification programs, all of which have vocal constituencies. There is little support for a large increase in federal gasoline and diesel tax rates, which were last increased in 1993. So there is no identified source of federal funding for a trillion-dollar-scale Interstate modernization program. If this challenge is to be taken on, it will probably have to be done largely by the states and their DOTs.

Per-Mile Tolling as the Funding Source

A revolution in tolling technology has taken place during the last 25 years. It began with the introduction of windshield-mounted transponders using short-range radio-frequency communication to provide a customer's account number to an antenna mounted at the toll booth. That meant cars and trucks could roll through those toll lanes at five miles per hour instead of having to line up and stop to pay with coins. This electronic toll collection (ETC), beginning around 1988, reduced congestion at toll booths and toll plazas. The next step occurred when some toll road operators realized that transponders could be read accurately at highway speeds, and began creating high-speed lanes to bypass toll plazas. This was called open-road tolling (ORT), and it had become widespread by 2010 on most major toll roads, with toll booths increasingly located off to the side and the majority of tolls collected electronically in the high-speed main lanes.

The third step, being implemented today by a growing number of toll operators, is elimination of cash tolling altogether to create all-electronic tolling (AET). Since the toll gantries used for ETC and ORT already required video cameras to take images of vehicle license plates for enforcement purposes (to identify vehicles trying to steal service by driving without an account or transponder), the AET model seeks to get 90 percent or more customers to have accounts and transponders, and to bill the rest by license-plate imaging. (Transponder tolling is much less costly than billing based on license-plate images.) Entire toll systems have converted or are in the process of converting to AET, including Dallas's North Texas Tollway Authority, the toll roads in Denver and Miami, the southern portion of Florida's Turnpike, and The Toll Roads of Orange County, California. AET is also standard practice on America's growing number of HOT lanes and express toll lanes. Nobody is building toll booths or toll plazas today, and nobody will build them in the future.

In recent years, the idea of using toll finance to pay for the reconstruction and widening of the Interstate highway system has occurred to many transportation experts.[6] Since AET is a relatively inexpensive way to do tolling, nearly all such proposals include doing the tolling via AET. This lends itself very well to a limited-access highway system such as the

Interstates, because there are relatively few places to get on and off. With AET equipment (antennas and video cameras) located only at on-ramps and off-ramps, vehicles can be charged a stated rate per mile, based on the number of miles they have driven between entry point and exit point.

Another advantage of using toll finance to reconstruct and widen the Interstates is that the toll rates can be selected to cover the capital and operating costs of *these specific highways*. With federal and state fuel taxes, everyone within a state pays the same rate per mile, which for passenger cars averages 2.2 cents per mile, whether those miles are driven on two-lane country roads or eight-lane superhighways. That overcharges those using low-cost basic roads and undercharges those who use premium highways, as a 1995 economic analysis of California highways documented.[7] As discussed in more detail later in this chapter, for most long-distance Interstates a toll rate of 3.5 cents per mile for cars (in 2010 dollars) would be adequate, if all the toll revenues were used solely for the capital and operating and maintenance costs of the tolled Interstates—and if that base rate were adjusted annually for inflation. That 3.5-center-per-mile starting toll rate is 60 percent more than what the average motorist pays in today's fuel taxes (2.2 cents per mile).

Transition to Mileage-Based User Fees

Another reason to use per-mile tolling to rebuild the Interstate system is to begin solving the problem of the obsolescing fuel taxes. Two key factors make the fuel tax a poor long-term source of dedicated highway revenue in the 21st century. First, there will be large increases in vehicle fuel economy (miles per gallon) in the next decade alone. Current federal law mandates that by 2025 each auto company's new-vehicle fleet-wide average must be 54.5 miles per gallon, which is more than double the 23.5 miles-per-gallon average of all such vehicles on the road in 2010. Unless federal and state fuel tax rates were doubled by then—which nobody thinks is remotely likely—the revenue from fuel taxes would soon be cut in half. That would decimate highway funding at a time when it is already barely enough to maintain the existing capital stock of highways, not counting any new construction or major reconstruction.

The second reason for fuel-tax obsolescence is that many new sources of vehicle propulsion are either in production or likely to be during the next decade or two. Hybrid vehicles that use electric motors supplemented by a gasoline engine are growing in popularity, and the technology of pure electric vehicles, such as Teslas, continues to improve. Research and development continues on hydrogen fuel cell propulsion for motor vehicles. And the trucking industry is experimenting with medium and heavy trucks fueled by natural gas, either compressed (CNG) or liquefied (LNG). Nobody can predict the mix of propulsion sources for cars and trucks in 2030 or 2040, but virtually the entire transportation community believes that increasing fractions of them will not be powered by gasoline or diesel fuel. That implies the need to replace per-gallon fuel taxes with propulsion-neutral sources of highway funding.

As of now, the transportation community has reached consensus that (1) the United States does need to transition to a more sustainable, propulsion-neutral highway funding source, and (2) the best replacement approach is to charge per mile rather than per gallon. Hence, the term "mileage-based user fee" (MBUF) is increasingly accepted as the goal. There is as yet no consensus on how the transition could or should take place, but there is general agreement that this, too, will be a process led by the states, not by the federal government. There is also growing support for the idea that a one-size-fits-all approach is probably not the best way to go.

One strand of this thinking is to give highway users a choice of methods. The California and Oregon MBUF pilot programs have included a number of choices, including a no-technology option based on periodic odometer readings or a high fixed rate for unlimited annual miles. Other options include one based on using cellphone towers to distinguish between in-state and out-of-state miles, and another based on GPS. Pilot programs of this kind are a good way to learn which methods are popular (or not), which ones are costly or inexpensive, and which work well or poorly.

Another possibility is to have different charging systems for different categories of roads. In a paper for the 2013 Transportation Research Board annual meeting, Chris Swenson and David Ungemah proposed a business model for MBUFs using several different systems—such as AET for limited-access highways (Interstates and urban expressways) and other systems for rural roads and local streets.[8] That model has the advantage of enabling the transition to per-mile charging to take place on one portion of the highway system—such as the Interstates—before consensus has been reached on how to do this for other highways, streets, and roads.

Hence, in this chapter we will explore the use of AET as (1) the method used to finance the reconstruction and selective widening of long-distance

Interstates, (2) the first step in the transition from paying for highways per gallon to paying for them per mile, and (3) the first step in transitioning to highway utilities.

What the Interstates Need

What would a modernized 21st-century Interstate highway system look like? In 2013 the Reason Foundation published detailed research on this question, which was dubbed Interstate 2.0.[9] This section reviews the five major aspects of this revamped system, focusing in this chapter on just the long-distance portions; urban Interstates and other expressways will be discussed in chapter 10. The five components of Interstate 2.0 are

- reconstruction
- selective widening
- truck-only lanes
- no toll plazas
- real service plazas

Reconstruction

Prior to the Interstate 2.0 report, there was no detailed estimate of the cost of reconstructing the entire Interstate highway system. The only figures were top-down estimates for rebuilding the system as a whole, based on extrapolation from estimates of its original construction cost adjusted for construction-cost inflation. Yet it was possible to make a far more detailed estimate, which is what this study set out to do.

The analysis started at the state level, because construction costs vary considerably among states, partly due to differences in terrain (mountains versus flat) and partly due to large regional differences in construction costs. The Federal Highway Administration (FHWA) maintains a large array of highway statistics tables online, which include the number of route miles and lane-miles of all the existing Interstates, broken down by state and with separate figures for rural (long-distance) and urban Interstates. Its cost tables provide national average cost figures for various categories of highway, including the Interstates, of (1) rebuilding existing lanes and (2) adding new lanes. For long-distance routes, these unit costs (per lane-mile) are provided for three types of terrain: flat, rolling, and mountainous.

This information provided a way to estimate the reconstruction cost of the long-distance Interstates in each of the 50 states. The methodology took differences in terrain into account, and also adjusted the FHWA's national-average unit costs by creating a state-specific cost factor based on data from R. S. Means Company's *Heavy Construction Cost Data* volume. It also included an estimate of the cost of adding AET gantries and antennas, based on electronic toll expert Daryl S. Fleming's estimate of $250,000 per route-mile for long-distance Interstates. The estimated net present value of the cost of reconstructing all the existing rural Interstate lane-miles between 2020 and 2050 was $148 billion, in 2010 dollars. The cost per state varied from a low of $85 million for Hawaii to a high of $8.2 billion in California.

Selective Widening

Widening is generally more costly per lane-mile than reconstruction, because additional right-of-way may need to be acquired. Since the original Interstates were built, a number of corridors have had lanes added due to traffic growth that exceeded the capacity of the initial design, which was typically two lanes in each direction. Widening has been especially needed in key truck corridors.

Figuring out which long-distance Interstates would need additional lanes required estimating future traffic growth, corridor by corridor, over the next 40 years. There has been considerable discussion since the Great Recession about growth rates of highway travel. The long-term uptrend in annual vehicle miles of travel (VMT) stopped and actually decreased slightly during the depth of that recession, and only began growing again in 2011 and 2012. By 2015, VMT had clearly resumed the pre-recession uptrend. The amount of driving *per person* (VMT per capita) appeared to have maxed out during this time period, after having grown steadily each decade since World War II. Yet FHWA data released early in 2017 showed that VMT per capita had also resumed upward growth since 2014.[10] For these reasons, VMT will likely continue to be grow in coming decades, though possibly at more modest rates than the historical trend since World War II.

Inquiries among transportation research colleagues identified a new VMT projection methodology developed by the US DOT's Volpe Center in Cambridge, Massachusetts.[11] To greatly oversimplify, it projects personal-vehicle VMT conservatively as a function largely of population growth (consistent with the view that VMT per capita may have topped out). But it projects truck VMT on the basis of other factors including economic growth, consistent with extensive research on freight movement that forecasts continued robust growth for truck traffic in coming decades. The result was a detailed state-by-state table, giving for each state an estimated annual percentage growth rate for personal vehicle travel and a separate growth rate for truck travel. For personal travel, these rates ranged from a low of 0.3 percent per year in Connecticut to a high of 2.2 percent per year in Arizona. And for truck traffic, they went from a low of 1.8 percent per year in Wisconsin to a high of 3.4 percent per year in Arizona.

Autonomous vehicles (AVs) are likely to affect future VMT growth, but opinion in the transportation community is divided on the direction of this impact. One view is that autonomy will lead to people foregoing car ownership and relying on "mobility as a service"—summoning shared robo-taxis for all their automobility needs. Under this view, even though VMT per vehicle would increase, the size of the needed vehicle fleet would shrink, and urban VMT in future years would be less than at present.

However, the majority of AV researchers expect that future VMT in an AV world will increase at a faster rate than historical trends. This view expects that most people will continue to own cars, and that three key categories of people—those below driving age, those too old to drive, and the disabled—will gain new mobility via AVs, thereby increasing total VMT. A 2015 study by KPMG made quantitative estimates of VMT from these new users and projected that total US VMT in 2050 could reach five trillion, compared with around three trillion today.[12] An overview report on the implications of AVs by Parsons Brinckerhoff reached this conclusion: "VMT will likely increase as the cost of travel decreases and more people choose to drive."[13] We will return to the subject of autonomous vehicles in chapter 11.

Using the conservative VMT growth rates from the Volpe table, the study estimated annual car and truck traffic on each state's long-distance Interstates from 2010 through 2050. But the statewide growth in overall Interstate travel was not sufficient to determine which specific Interstate highways in that state needed more lanes. For that, more detailed data were obtained from the FHWA on each individual Interstate highway in each state, giving the number of lane-miles and route-miles of each (e.g., I-95 in North Carolina), along with its 2010 average daily VMT. The research then used standard state DOT traffic engineering factors to determine how many lanes would be needed on each corridor, in each decade of the 2010s, 2020s, 2030s, and 2040s, to provide uncongested travel—technically, at what traffic engineers define as Level of Service C. The large overall spreadsheet that resulted identified 96 state-specific corridors that would need lane additions. Of those, 41 already needed one or more additional lanes each way in the 2010s, five others will need lane additions in the 2020s, another 27 will need lane additions by the 2030s, and another 23 by the 2040s.

Using the FHWA data for the cost per lane-mile for long-distance Interstate lane additions, again modified by each state's cost factor, the study derived a preliminary cost estimate for widening these Interstates. Once again, the results varied considerably by state. But a further analysis of truck traffic would be needed before this task was complete.

Truck-Only Lanes

Some of the most truck-intensive corridors in the above widening analysis did not appear to need more than one new lane in each direction, to judge from the Volpe Center VMT truck growth rates. That result seemed counterintuitive, and it led to a more detailed analysis. The FHWA maintains a separate research effort known as the Freight Analysis Framework (FAF), which collects and analyzes detailed data on goods movement by all modes of transportation, including trucks on highways. The FAF office provided a detailed Interstate Highways data set, which researchers at the Civil Engineering School at Georgia Tech analyzed for the Reason Foundation using special geographic information system software. This yielded detailed projections of truck traffic for each separate Interstate corridor in each of the 50 states as of 2040.

The FAF data for 237 high-truck-traffic Interstate corridors were compared with the previous 2040 truck traffic projections for the 96 corridors identified as needing lane additions by then. In many cases the FAF data identified a need for adding more than one lane each way. It also identified 16 state corridors not in the original spreadsheet that would also need additional lanes by 2040.

Since all the corridors identified from the FAF analysis were projected to have trucks constituting 40 percent or more of all traffic by 2040, they were flagged as warranting truck-only lanes. Those corridors are as follows:

- I-10 from California to Mississippi (six states)
- I-30 in Texas and Arkansas

- I-40 from California to Tennessee (seven states)
- I-65 in Tennessee, Kentucky, and Indiana
- I-69 in Indiana
- I-70 from Missouri to Pennsylvania (five states)
- I-71 in Kentucky
- I-76 in Colorado
- I-80 from Nebraska to Ohio (five states)
- I-81 from Tennessee to Pennsylvania (four states).

As explained in an earlier Reason Foundation study, truck-only lanes would offer an array of benefits.[14] For motorists on Interstates that are major truck corridors, driving on lanes without heavy trucks would be less stressful, probably somewhat faster, and definitely safer. For trucking companies, in addition to safety benefits and lower driver stress, truck-only lanes that are barrier-separated from regular lanes would make it feasible for them to use so-called LCVs—longer combination vehicles (long doubles and short triples). With LCVs a single driver could in many cases haul up to double the cargo, using considerably less fuel per ton-mile. Fuel consumption and tailpipe emissions per ton-mile would be reduced by using LCVs, adding to trucking company cost savings and reducing the industry's environmental footprint. The Environmental Protection Agency's SmartWay Transportation Partnership has noted the environmental benefits of multiple-trailer rigs, and can analyze these factors using its FLEET performance model.[15] But due to safety concerns about mixing LCVs with other traffic (combined with anti-LCV lobbying by railroads), LCVs are currently allowed only on selected turnpikes and on rural Interstates in the mountain West.

Another reason for dedicated truck lanes is the potential value to the trucking industry of truck platooning on long-haul Interstates. Semi-automated trucks—using collision-avoidance and lane-keeping technology, and linked by real-time communications—could operate at around 50-foot spacing, far closer together than is currently allowed. This close spacing would reduce the air drag on all the trucks, especially the ones following the lead truck, thus leading to reduction in fuel use and greenhouse gas emissions. The benefits would increase as the number of trucks in the platoon increased. But a line of four 18-wheelers only 50 feet apart could pose a major problem for cars that need to change lanes (e.g., to get to an exit ramp in time). So dedicated truck lanes would be a safer corridor for truck platoons than regular general-purpose highway lanes.

When the widening costs of the truck lanes analysis were added to the previously estimated cost of the ordinary widening, the *total* widening cost came to $74.9 billion, again with considerable variation from state to state. A handful of states—including Alaska, Hawaii, Maine, Montana, the Dakotas, New Hampshire, and Vermont—turned out to not need any additional lanes through the 2040s. States with truck-only lanes typically had higher than average widening costs. But those costs are all based on conservative projections of the likely growth in car and truck travel in coming decades.

Altogether, for the long-distance Interstates, the combined costs of reconstruction and widening would total $223 billion.

No Toll Plazas

Motorists in the Northeast and Midwest, where some of the existing Interstates are tolled, are now experiencing the benefits of open road tolling (ORT) on some of these corridors, but so far only the Massachusetts Turnpike has converted completely to cashless all-electronic tolling (AET), which eliminates all toll booths and plazas. The first long-distance toll road to begin the transition to all-AET was Florida's Turnpike, which is not an Interstate. It extends from south of Miami to northwest of Orlando, where it connects to nontolled I-75. The turnpike first eliminated all toll booths and plazas in Miami-Dade County, after which it began a northward transition through the urban areas of south Florida (Fort Lauderdale, West Palm Beach) that will eventually extend all the way to the interchange with I-75 northwest of Orlando.

In converting the nontolled majority of the Interstate system to AET to pay for reconstruction, widening, and ongoing operations and maintenance, no one would base the new toll collection on 20th-century cash tolling. It will certainly be carried out via cashless AET, which avoids the large capital costs of adding toll plazas to these several hundred corridors, as well as the ongoing labor costs of an army of toll collectors.

The toll industry is hard at work today developing nationwide electronic tolling "interoperability." This would mean that motorists and trucking companies would need just one transponder and one toll account to use tolled highways nationwide. A preview of this kind of interoperability is the E-ZPass system in place for toll roads, bridges, and tunnels in 16 states in the Northeast and Midwest, as far west as Illinois, as far north as Maine, and as far south as North Carolina. Florida is working to make its statewide SunPass system interoperable with E-ZPass, beginning with interoperability with the electronic tolling systems of Georgia and North Carolina, and extending thereafter to South Carolina and Texas.

With nationwide electronic tolling interoperability and AET used on the entire Interstate system, many of the things motorists and trucking companies dislike most about toll roads will be gone: long lines at toll plazas, accidents at or near toll plazas, added tailpipe emissions at toll plazas, and the need to carry a supply of coins in passenger cars. With AET, trucking companies will get monthly electronic invoices that can identify specific trips, allowing them to bill their customers for toll costs as part of the cost of truck transportation (as they do now with fuel surcharges). Two service providers endorsed by the American Trucking Associations, Bestpass and PrePass Plus, already provide this kind of interoperable, single-transponder, single bill to trucking companies in the E-ZPass states and additional locations.[16]

Real Service Plazas

One additional feature of a toll-financed Interstate 2.0 is the addition of modern, well-supplied service plazas to the large majority of long-distance Interstates that currently lack them. Travelers on nontolled Interstates today must rely on gas stations, fast-food restaurants, and truck stops that are generally, but not always, clustered near exits. By contrast, turnpikes (including those that were grandfathered into the Interstate system) all include service plazas at regular intervals where motorists and truckers can refuel, purchase refreshments, sit down to a meal, and even buy souvenirs.

The reason why there are no service plazas on non-tolled Interstates is the lobbying clout of an organization representing those businesses near the exits: the National Association of Truck Stop Owners (NATSO). Its efforts have made it against federal law for Interstates funded by federal highway grants to provide any retail activities of the kind provided at toll road service plazas. Instead, all you get are "rest areas" that provide a place to park, rest rooms, and junk-food vending machines. In lobbying to keep this ban in place, NATSO makes two arguments. First, it says it would be unfair competition for Interstate operators to create service plazas when such services are already available from its members at or near exits from the Interstates. That kind of protectionism should be laughed out of court in a country whose economy is based on free-market competition.

Second, NATSO argues that if service plazas were available, toll-road customers would no longer patronize its off-Interstate members, because it would cost motorists more to get off the toll road and then get back on. That might be the case for the cash-based toll systems of 20th-century toll roads. But it would not be the case for 21st century toll roads using per-mile tolling, with the toll amount being based on the actual number of miles driven on the tolled Interstate. Whether or not you got off to get gas or buy a Coke would make no difference to the number of tolled miles you drove, measured from on-ramp to off-ramp. Moreover, experienced NATSO member companies would be well qualified to bid to offer their services on the hundreds of new service plazas that would be added to the 21st-century Interstates.

Another feature of the new service plazas would be ample parking for trucks, so that drivers can find safe places to park when they must cease driving and obtain needed sleep, to comply with federal hours of service rules. The lack of safe and conveniently located truck rest areas is yet another example of inadvertent customer-unfriendliness of an Interstate system that conceives of its patrons as "users" rather than as "customers."

Yet another feature of the service plazas would probably be refueling/recharging stations for the alternative-fuel and all-electric vehicles of coming decades. As an example, Tesla is developing a national network of "Supercharger" locations spanning the Interstate system. But since it will charge customers for the electricity, they cannot be located at today's Interstate rest areas. Instead, drivers must leave the Interstate and navigate to an off-highway location. And since it currently takes 75 minutes to fully charge a Tesla, the driver would presumably like other things to do during that time—such as have a meal or do some shopping. Doing this would be far more convenient at a normal toll-road-type service plaza.

Toll Feasibility

What would it cost to use the reconstructed and modernized Interstates? And would the toll revenues actually be enough to pay for the huge revamping of this national network of superhighways?

To get a first approximation required a very large number-crunching exercise. It used the traffic projections from the widening analysis described above to estimate the toll revenue that could be collected on each state's modernized Interstates. As in any such calculation, several assumptions had to be made at the outset. First, since the value-added tolling principles described in chapter 8 call for per-mile tolls to be true user fees, the toll rate should be as low as possible, consistent with fully covering the capital and operating costs of the rebuilt and modernized corridors. Second, to make this funding source sustainable on a long-term basis, unlike fuel taxes, the toll rates must be indexed to inflation, so that the revenues do not lose purchasing power over the many decades of an Interstate's useful life. Third, the maintenance budget should be built into the financing model, as is typical of toll road practice worldwide—and in sharp contrast to typical state highway practice today, which leaves maintenance needs to the whims of future legislatures. Fourth, because Interstates are the most costly of all highway types, the toll rate per mile would likely be somewhat higher than the de facto revenue per mile produced by today's fuel taxes.

Since state plus federal fuel taxes on average yield about 2.2 cents per mile for passenger cars, the starting point was a baseline toll rate for cars of 3.5 cents per mile, in 2010 dollars. National figures for long-distance toll roads showed that large trucks pay about four times the rate per mile of cars, since heavy trucks cause the vast majority of wear and tear on pavement and bridges, so the baseline rate for trucks was set at 14 cents per mile. (Those rates are lower than the average long-distance toll rates in place as of 2010, which were 4.9 cents per mile for cars and 19.9 cents per mile for large trucks, but those rates reflect both the higher costs of largely cash toll collection and some degree of diversion of toll revenue to non–toll-road purposes.)[17] Both of these rates were indexed for inflation, using an estimated average annual consumer price index of 2.5 percent per year.

The next step was a 35-year spreadsheet for each state's long-distance Interstates, with the first rebuilt corridors opening to traffic in 2020 and various projects continuing through the 2040s. In each year of tolled operation, the *gross* toll revenue is that year's car traffic (vehicle miles of travel) multiplied by the CPI-adjusted car toll rate for that year, and a comparable calculation for truck VMT times the truck toll rate.[18] To get the *net* toll revenue that is available (1) to pay the annual debt service on toll revenue bonds and (2) to provide a return on the equity investment of the toll road utility company, the gross revenue had to be adjusted for operating and maintenance costs. Annual maintenance expense was estimated at 10 percent of gross revenue, and costs of all-electronic toll collection were estimated at 5 percent of gross revenue.[19] Both of these estimates were vetted as realistic by highway industry professionals, in a version of the Interstate 2.0 paper that was peer-reviewed and accepted for presentation at the Transportation Research Board's annual meeting.[20]

The financial feasibility of each state's toll-financed Interstate modernization was assessed by comparing the net present value of the stream of net toll revenue with the net present value of the reconstruction and widening costs, using a 6-percent discount rate. The results of this assessment were surprisingly positive. For all 50 states as a group, the net present value (NPV) of toll revenue was 120 percent of the NPV of cost, even though the basic toll rates had been selected arbitrarily (i.e., as an educated guess). Looking at the individual states, 36 of them had revenue and costs that would permit car toll rates to be lower than the baseline 3.5 cents per mile, and in some cases quite a bit less (see table 6). Ten other states, generally ones with somewhat lower traffic levels and hilly or mountainous terrain, would need baseline car toll rates of 4.1 to 5.8 cents per mile to pay for Interstate reconstruction and widening. Those rates are higher than in the first 36 states, but are clearly in the ballpark of today's national average long-distance car toll rate of 4.9 cents per mile.

Only three states would require significantly higher toll rates to pay for reconstructing their Interstates: Montana (8.5 cents per mile), Vermont (9 cents per mile), and Alaska (20.6 cents per mile). Especially in the latter case, toll rates that high could lead to significant diversion of traffic to other roads, and may be judged politically unacceptable. None of these three states need road widening, and given their relatively low traffic levels, their Interstates may not require reconstruction for several more decades. In the case of Alaska, its rural "Interstate" mileage consists of two-lane highways that do not comply with normal federal Interstate standards.[21] Hence, the standard FHWA cost numbers for rural Interstates significantly exaggerate the cost of rebuilding them. Thus, a separate analysis of modernizing these Alaska routes would be needed.

TABLE 6. **Rural Interstate highway modernization costs and estimated baseline toll rates (for cars)**

State	NPV of reconstruction and widening cost, 2010 (in millions of dollars)	NPV revenue/NPV cost (@ 3.5¢/mile)	Estimated value-added toll rate (for cars)
Alabama	$2,452	234%	1.5¢/mile
Alaska	$3,748	17%	20.6¢/mile
Arizona	$9,183	104%	3.4¢/mile
Arkansas	$3,321	189%	1.9¢/mile

TABLE 6. (*continued*)

State	NPV of reconstruction and widening cost, 2010 (in millions of dollars)	NPV revenue/NPV cost (@ 3.5¢/mile)	Estimated value-added toll rate (for cars)
California	$19,933	103%	3.4¢/mile
Colorado	$4,858	78%	4.5¢/mile
Connecticut	$479	103%	3.4¢/mile
Delaware*	0	0	none
District of Columbia*	0	0	none
Florida	$5,481	171%	2.0¢/mile
Georgia	$5,694	190%	1.8¢/mile
Hawaii	$85	79%	4.4¢/mile
Idaho	$3,873	66%	5.3¢/mile
Illinois	$7,825	125%	2.8¢/mile
Indiana	$5,281	162%	2.2¢/mile
Iowa	$3,952	135%	2.6¢/mile
Kansas	$2,806	123%	2.8¢/mile
Kentucky	$4,087	171%	2.0¢/mile
Louisiana	$2,750	185%	1.9¢/mile
Maine	$1,477	119%	2.9¢/mile
Maryland	$2,145	142%	2.5¢/mile
Massachusetts	$847	113%	3.1¢/mile
Michigan	$4,235	103%	3.4¢/mile
Minnesota	$4,384	74%	4.7¢/mile
Mississippi	$2,085	193%	1.8¢/mile
Missouri	$4,513	169%	2.1¢/mile
Montana	$6,261	41%	8.5¢/mile
Nebraska	$4,085	85%	4.1¢/mile
Nevada	$2,971	75%	4.7¢/mile
New Hampshire	$790	110%	3.2¢/mile
New Jersey	$988	108%	3.2¢/mile
New Mexico	$6,366	102%	3.4¢/mile
New York	$4,536	106%	3.3¢/mile
North Carolina	$5,913	120%	2.9¢/mile
North Dakota	$2,520	66%	5.3¢/mile
Ohio	$7,084	140%	2.5¢/mile
Oklahoma	$4,389	143%	2.4¢/mile
Oregon	$3,932	129%	2.7¢/mile
Pennsylvania	$8,004	148%	2.4¢/mile
Rhode Island	$140	221%	1.6¢/mile
South Carolina	$3,825	189%	1.9¢/mile
South Dakota	$3,075	60%	5.8¢/mile
Tennessee	$6,704	152%	2.3¢/mile
Texas	$17,038	126%	2.8¢/mile
Utah	$4,849	103%	3.4¢/mile
Vermont	$2,498	39%	9.0¢/mile
Virginia	$6,858	139%	2.5¢/mile
Washington	$4,379	98%	3.6¢/mile
West Virginia	$3,556	77%	4.5¢/mile
Wisconsin	$3,006	161%	2.2¢/mile
Wyoming	$4,055	80%	4.4¢/mile
Total or average	$223,296	120%	

*Delaware and the District of Columbia have no rural Interstate highways.

How to Make the Transition

If toll-financed reconstruction and modernization of the Interstates is such a good idea, why is it not already underway? The one-word answer is Congress. As we saw in chapter 3, when Congress created the Interstate highway program in 1956, it rejected the idea of continuing with the toll-finance model pioneered by the Pennsylvania Turnpike and emulated by 14 other states. It created the federal Highway Trust Fund, and dedicated the revenues from federal gasoline and diesel taxes to it as an alternative to toll finance for constructing the Interstate system. In addition, Congress banned the use of tolls on any federal-aid highway. So it is currently against federal law for states to embark on the program outlined in this chapter.

That description slightly oversimplifies matters. Beginning with the 1991 legislation reauthorizing the federal program (called ISTEA), Congress began to liberalize the prohibition on tolling. First, the ban was removed from all federal-aid highways except Interstates. Then a pilot program was created to allow poorly performing car pool lanes on Interstates to be converted to toll lanes, as long as car pools could still use them for free. Subsequent legislation allowed for the replacement of Interstate bridges and tunnels with toll-financed bridges and tunnels. Congress later "mainstreamed" the ability to convert car pool lanes to toll lanes, allowing all states to do that.

In the TEA-21 reauthorization of 1998, Congress created a pilot program that allows three states to apply to the FHWA for permission to use toll finance to each rebuild a single Interstate highway, as long as the toll revenues are used only for the capital and operating costs of that Interstate. Pennsylvania applied (for I-80), but was rejected because its plan did not comply with the revenue restriction. Three other states eventually were awarded the three slots: Missouri (for I-70), North Carolina (for I-95), and Virginia (originally for I-81 but later switched to I-95).

Unfortunately, none of the three states has been able to reach a political consensus on actually doing its proposed toll-financed reconstruction. Missouri selected I-70 as its proposed Interstate to rebuild with toll finance. The state had previously taken part in a separate, federally funded four-state "Corridors of the Future" study that addressed the I-70 corridor from Kansas City on the west to eastern Ohio. All four state DOTs (Missouri, Illinois, Indiana, and Ohio) worked together with the engineering firm HNTB and tolling experts Wilbur Smith Associates (now CDM Smith), along with the active participation of the trucking association of each state. The resulting feasibility study of this truck-intensive corridor concluded that the best alternative for reconstruction and widening was to expand I-70 from four lanes to eight, with two of the lanes each way being dedicated truck lanes that could safely handle long-double rigs.[22] Given the high cost of the project, toll financing was recommended as the only realistic way to pay for it, and P3 toll concessions were envisioned as the procurement method. Of the four states, only Missouri had a slot in the pilot program. Unfortunately, its legislature failed to enact tolling legislation and P3 legislation that would permit the Missouri DOT to move forward on its portion of this planned four-state corridor.

The North Carolina DOT selected I-95 as its candidate for reconstruction and widening because it is among the oldest Interstates in North Carolina and also needs additional lanes along most of its 182 miles. It produced a fairly detailed modernization plan, but ran into considerable local opposition. Residents along much of the I-95 corridor, which is largely rural and somewhat lower-income, and which lacks any of the state's large metro areas, objected to being "singled out" to pay tolls for their Interstate when North Carolinians who use the Interstates in other parts of the state (I-40, I-77, I-85) would continue to drive without having to pay tolls. When a new governor of the opposite party was elected in 2012, the I-95 toll-financed reconstruction plan was put on the back burner.

As recounted in chapter 5, Virginia got into a major battle with the trucking industry over its original plan to reconstruct and widen I-81 under the pilot program by adding truck-only lanes but only charging tolls to trucks. In addition to maintaining their long-standing opposition to tolls, the truckers objected to being singled out as the only ones who would have to pay for modernizing I-81. Virginia DOT eventually gave up on that plan, and got permission from the FHWA to switch its slot in the program to I-95, so that Virginia and North Carolina could both modernize their portions of this important route. But having been burned by trucking opposition over its I-81 plan, the Virginia DOT omitted truck-only lanes from its I-95 toll-financed reconstruction plan. And as it encountered similar opposition from rural residents along the corridor, it scaled back its plans to only partial reconstruction, with tolling to take place only at the border with North Carolina. This plan reduced local opposition but, with the change of governor and DOT secretary in 2014, this plan, too, was put on a back burner.

Analysis of these failures leads to two conclusions. First, the trucking industry and other highway user groups opposed the pilot program because they feared that the tolling, once allowed, would evolve into a general funding source to bail out cash-strapped state DOTs—as Pennsylvania attempted to do with its twice-rejected pilot-program request to toll I-80, but succeeded in doing with Act 44 for the Pennsylvania Turnpike, as discussed in chapter 6. Without the support or at least the acquiescence of highway user groups, implementing any of the projects proposed under the pilot programs is unlikely. A study of the specific concerns about tolling of the AAA, the American Highway Users Alliance (AHUA), and the ATA led to formulation of the value-added tolling principles discussed in chapter 8, and a more detailed follow-up study addressing the concerns of the trucking industry.[23] These efforts included not just reading the groups' material, but having serious discussions with their senior research and government affairs people. As noted in chapter 8, the AAA changed its policy in late 2015 to be open to proposals based on value-added tolling principles.

Second, since it will be a political challenge to forge a coalition in a single state to actually begin moving forward with toll-financed Interstate modernization, a three-state pilot program is insufficient. What is needed to jump-start the transition is to maximize the likelihood that at least one "pathfinder" state emerges whose governor and state DOT can develop and market a credible, customer-friendly program for toll-financed Interstate reconstruction and modernization. To maximize the odds of this happening, the opportunity should be open to far more states (ideally all 50), to avoid the situation in which three states that had not found an acceptable way forward could sit on the three available slots, precluding others with better plans from going ahead.

Congress took a small step toward fixing this in 2015. In the FAST Act that reauthorized the federal highway program, Congress added a "use-it-or-lose-it" provision to the pilot program. Any current slot-holder that did not demonstrate significant progress toward implementation by the end of 2016 had to forfeit its slot. That will make such slots available to states whose political and DOT leaders are interested in toll-financed Interstate reconstruction. Under this provision, North Carolina and Virginia gave up their slots; Missouri asked for and received an extension but failed to enact tolling legislation. As of mid-2017, therefore, three slots were available. Serious interest has been expressed by legislators and other public officials in Connecticut, Indiana, Rhode Island, and Wisconsin, so it appears quite possible that one or more of the open slots will be requested during 2017.

Whichever state serves as the pathfnder should develop and market a credible 20- to 25-year plan to reconstruct and modernize all of that state's Interstate highways using toll finance. The plan would explain that all the Interstates will be wearing out during that time frame and will need replacement, so they will all be reconstructed, and widened where needed, in a systematic and prioritized manner. Everyone's turn will come as the program is rolled out over several decades, so no portion of the state will be "singled out" to pay tolls. And no one will pay tolls on an Interstate corridor until it has been rebuilt and, if necessary, widened. The Interstates that get done first will have much better pavement and enough lanes to significantly reduce congestion, so those who use them will get real value for the toll money they spend. If the full set of value-added tolling principles is applied, they will also get rebates on their state gas taxes for all the tolled miles they drive on the new second-generation Interstates.

The idea of a pathfinder state leading the way is not mere wishful thinking. In chapter 5 we learned the story of the first two toll concession projects in modern America—the 91 Express Lanes in Orange County, California, and the Dulles Greenway in Virginia. By allowing those projects to be implemented, California and Virginia became pathfinder states for toll concessions, and the 91 Express Lanes project became the prototype for a whole generation of HOT lanes and express toll lanes (ETL) projects in urban areas across the country. Under the then-new Value Pricing Pilot Program created by the 1991 ISTEA law, the FHWA held workshops around the country in cooperation with state DOTs and local transportation planning bodies, explaining how variable pricing had been demonstrated to keep special lanes flowing freely during rush hours. HOT and ETL projects were implemented in the late 1990s and ever since then, based on the example of the 91 Express Lanes project. A pathfinder project that works has a powerful demonstration effect.

What Congress needs to do, then, is to "mainstream" the toll-financed reconstruction pilot program by making three changes:

1. Expand it from three states to all 50 states, even though some states might never use it.
2. Allow each participating state to use toll financing to reconstruct and widen all of its Interstates, not just one.
3. Impose value-added tolling restrictions as a requirement, to ensure that the new toll revenues are true user fees and do not become a general state transportation funding source.

If these changes are made, at least one pathfinder state will step forward and gain political consensus for the kind of several-decade reconstruction and modernization program outlined above. And after one state shows the way, many more will follow.

As this chapter was being finalized, Indiana unveiled an alternative route to toll-financed Interstate reconstruction and widening. Its legislature and state DOT are studying an approach that would make use of the existing authority to use toll revenue to finance replacement of non-tolled bridges on existing Interstates. Since every overpass or underpass is a bridge, their studies suggest enough tolling potential points on the first two Interstates they have studied so as to generate enough revenue to pay for the reconstruction and widening of each corridor.[24] Their case is based in part on the approval by FHWA of Rhode Island's plan, now underway, to charge tolls to heavy trucks for using bridges on certain of its Interstate highways.

Who Will Be the Providers?

Assuming that the above scenario comes about, how will this lead to the development of Interstate highway companies? The two existing organizational models for US toll roads are government toll agencies and long-term toll concession companies, as discussed in previous chapters. So those are the likely initial choices facing legislators and state DOTs when they begin to implement the reconstruction and modernization of their long-distance Interstates.

States with well-run, efficient state toll agencies (e.g., Florida's Turnpike) will likely see that agency as the default option for this program. States with a history of troubled toll agencies (e.g., the Pennsylvania Turnpike Authority) might decide to turn to the private sector for at least two reasons. First, their state toll agencies might not be comfortable complying with the federal value-added tolling conditions that require lower toll rates that can be used only for the capital and operating costs of the newly tolled Interstates. Second, the credibility of a commitment to highway users that the new tolls will not be a piggy bank for statewide transportation funding may be greater if a different institution has the responsibility for the Interstate modernization program.

Many states do not have experienced state toll agencies, including large states like Arizona, California, Colorado, and Minnesota, as well as numerous smaller states. Georgia, Illinois, and Texas have nominal state toll agencies that have done only urban toll projects. Most or all of these states would be wise to opt for inviting experienced toll concession companies to become their Interstate modernization providers, under the supervision of their state DOTs, as Indiana is now considering.

From an investment perspective, rebuilding and modernizing estab-lished Interstate highways should be highly attractive to infrastructure in-vestment funds as well as to global concession companies such as Abertis, ACS Infrastructure, Cintra, Cofiroute/Vinci, Macquarie, Plenary, Skan-ska, and Transurban. Brand-new (greenfield) toll roads and new express toll lanes are high-risk endeavors, since traffic and revenue, in particular, are difficult to predict accurately. By contrast, every existing Interstate corridor has a long and well-known traffic history. That makes these proj-ects a kind of hybrid of greenfield projects (new construction in corri-dors without existing toll roads or lanes) and low-risk brownfield projects (takeover and operation of existing toll roads). Therefore, Interstate re-construction and modernization will be considered medium-risk projects that should be financeable at moderate interest rates. Lower financing costs will help to keep the toll rates modest. And modest toll rates will mean that less traffic diverts to nontolled routes.

We can only speculate about the relative proportions of investor-owned Interstate toll concessions and Interstate modernization done by state toll agencies willing to abide by the value-added tolling provisions. The outcome might resemble the electric utility sector, in which investor-owned utilities account for 59 percent of all electricity sales. Alternatively, it might look more like the water utility sector, in which municipal utilities account for 85 percent of customers served.[25] With either outcome, the nation's premium long-distance highway system will be transformed into a set of customer-serving businesses.

Implementation Issues

One practical question concerns the scope of concession contracts for a state's long-distance Interstates. Projected traffic on the various corridors within a state (e.g., North Carolina's I-26, I-40, I-73/74, I-75, I-77, and I-95) may differ considerably from one another. Assuming that they all handle enough traffic to continue as part of the Interstate system, the legislature and state DOT may face the question of whether those corridors with the most robust traffic should help to pay for those with weaker traffic. The case for doing that is twofold. First, it might be more appealing to high-way customers to have the same per-mile toll rate apply everywhere on this state's long-distance highway network. Second, requiring the weakest corridor to be fully self-supporting from its own toll revenues might lead to toll rates so high as to discourage use of that corridor, creating a kind of vicious cycle in which insufficient traffic and hence insufficient revenue leads to higher toll rates, which leads to even less traffic and greater diversion of traffic to parallel routes. By that logic, it would appear to make better sense to finance the long-distance Interstate system of the state as a single enterprise—a strategy that state toll agencies, as well as some urban ones, refer to as "system financing." Under that approach, it would appear that having the state toll agency, if there is one, run the entire system is preferable.

However, there are many benefits to the investor-owned approach using toll concessions, as we saw in chapter 6. There are ways to address the "weak corridor" problem in a toll concessions context. To see how this might work, we first need to consider that in most states with a number of long-distance Interstates, some may be a decade or two older than others and will need reconstruction much sooner. Second, some may already need widening (lane additions), while others may not need more lanes at all, or may only need them 20 or more years in the future. A competitive process could be devised that would bundle a strong corridor with a weaker corridor, so that the winning concession company would become responsible for both, on a defined schedule. In most cases the stronger corridor would likely need reconstruction and widening sooner, due to more accumulated wear and tear, and would therefore be modernized before the weaker corridor, thus ensuring tht healthy toll revenue flows by the time the weaker corridor needs reconstruction.

Network Additions and Deletions

In the previous discussion, the implicit assumption was that the current set of Interstate highways is the optimum number of routes, connecting all the key locations in a state, as well as linking to comparable routes in adjacent states. But in developing a revamped Interstate system for 21st century America, we should not be constrained by the map drawn up in the 1940s for a vastly different country. The major changes in population distribution, industry, and shipping patterns over nearly three-quarters of a century call for taking a fresh look at the network as part of Interstate modernization. For example, there are no Interstate routes linking several of the largest metro areas in the West and Southwest—Las Vegas to Phoenix, Austin to Houston, and Raleigh to Norfolk. Between these fast-growing metro areas there are only undivided four-lane highways that go through many small towns with traffic signals and low speed limits.

A second national network was designated by Congress in 1991: the National Highway System. In addition to the Interstates, the NHS contains another 116,000 route-miles of highway in both urban and rural America. In creating the NHS, Congress asked state governments for recommendations of routes to be included. Some states, concerned about the additional costs required on federal-aid highway projects (Buy America, Davis-Bacon, etc.), nominated only highly traveled highways that might have qualified for Interstate status. Others, seeking to maximize federal aid, nominated a much larger number of routes. Hence, the NHS as defined is a mixture of high-traffic and lower-traffic routes, only some of which would make sense as additions to the 21st-century Interstate system. One virtue of a toll-financed system is that a toll feasibility analysis of possible additions would rather easily weed out those corridors that were included in NHS for political rather than serious transportation reasons.

By the same token, the toll-feasibility study that would have to be carried out for every one of a state's existing Interstate corridors may identify some corridors that simply do not have either current or projected traffic sufficient to make toll financing a realistic proposition. Those corridors, which by definition would not be candidates for lane additions, could be down-selected and made into ordinary highways.

The result would be a revamped Interstate network that would likely increase the fraction of all vehicle miles of travel that it handled from the current 25 percent to a larger fraction of the total.

What Role for the Federal Government?

The premise of this chapter is that the federal government (meaning Congress and FHWA) is not going to be the key player in rebuilding and modernizing the Interstate highway network. That would be a profound change from the original system, in which FHWA's predecessor came up with the basic route structure and Congress created the Highway Trust Fund and dedicated federal fuel taxes to pay for 90 percent of the initial cost of those highways (Interstate 1.0). Yet the conversion of the Highway Trust Fund and federal fuel taxes into a general-purpose transportation fund, combined with nearly a quarter century of inability and/or unwillingness to either reduce the scope of the program or to increase its user-tax revenues, means that Congress has basically abdicated its role in sustaining and modernizing this vitally important network. So the states will take the lead responsibility for creating Interstate 2.0.

This shift in basic responsibility does not leave the FHWA and Congress without a role to play. As noted earlier in this chapter, the transition laid out here can only happen if Congress grants tolling flexibility to the states, and does so in a way that can gain the support, or at least not the opposition, of the key highway user groups.

A second federal responsibility is to retain the role of setting standards so that Interstate 2.0 remains a *system*, with compatible lane-widths, curve radii, maximum grades, and numerous other performance standards. To facilitate more efficient nationwide trucking, these standards should include the same maximum truck size and weight standards everywhere— including those for longer combination vehicles (LCVs) in truck-only lanes, wherever states choose to include them in the reconstructed Interstate corridors.

Since this revamped network would be financed by tolls, the federal government should continue its work with the toll industry to ensure nationwide interoperability of all-electronic tolling. Under that approach, motorists and trucks would need only a single toll account and a single transponder to operate nationwide (just as your MasterCard works everywhere nationwide). States would be required to provide for enforcement across state lines, by granting access to vehicle registration information to permit billing of out-of-state vehicle owners who evade paying tolls.

One other possible federal role is to assist the three outlier states (Alaska, Montana, and Vermont) whose toll feasibility is far below the level at which realistic toll rates could generate enough funding to support reconstruction and ongoing operations and maintenance. Those three have always been "donee" (cross-subsidy recipient) states in the federal program, and would not even have Interstates if not for the built-in cross-subsidization in the original Interstate program. All three states have mountainous terrain (hence higher construction costs) and considerably lower traffic on their Interstates than do other states. Charging tolls high enough to pay for the reconstruction of their Interstates would likely have the adverse consequence of shifting considerable traffic to lower-quality roads, further reducing toll revenues and creating significant negative impact on the local roads. Interstates in Alaska and Vermont link up with Canadian highways, and Montana's I-90 is a key east-west link in the network. So there is some network-continuity justification for assisting those states in maintaining their portions. The federal assistance should be made conditional on their implementing all-electronic tolling at a basic level that would at least cover ongoing operations and maintenance costs.

This chapter has shown why and how long-distance Interstates will likely be the first major highways converted to the network utility model. This prediction was echoed in a presentation by Ed Regan, senior vice president of CDM Smith, at the annual meeting of the International Bridge, Tunnel & Turnpike Association in 2014.[26] A major portion of the presentation concerned "the Interstate tolling era." Regan projected that by 2020, between two and four states will have used toll financing to reconstruct and modernize their Interstates, with five to eight more doing so by 2025, and 10 to 15 more following suit by 2030. The result would be 17 to 27 states replacing their worn-out Interstate 1.0 with brand new Interstate 2.0 facilities by 2030.

In chapter 10 we will explore the more complex transition involving urban expressways, including urban Interstates.

CHAPTER TEN

Transforming Urban Freeways

The urban freeway system is a far more complex subject than the rural Interstates discussed in chapter 9. Initially hailed as an urban version of the superhighway—promising faster trips, increased safety, and the revitalization of downtowns—freeways came to be seen as destroyers of neighborhoods, as contributors to the decline of mass transit, and ultimately as the locus of chronic traffic congestion.

Yet the kinds of freeways that we built in the second half of the 20th century were not what urban transportation planners had envisioned in the 1930s and '40s. The early vision was for a smaller-scale, multimodal form of parkways and expressways. In this chapter we will examine what might have been, assess recent proposals for changing the freeways, and then consider large-scale revisions to current expressways, how to pay for their conversion to something better, and how to manage them in a more-sustainable manner. As in previous chapters, there are some lessons to be drawn from other countries as well.

What Might Have Been: A Grid of Urban Parkways

As Jeffrey Brown, Eric Morris, and Brian Taylor explained in a 2009 journal article, early urban transportation planners reacted to the explosive growth of automobiles by "calling for a hierarchical system of interconnected types of streets, grade separations at particularly busy intersections, and acquiring rights of way in advance of future development in outlying parts of the city."[1] These ideas were reflected in a major transportation plan for Los Angeles in 1924, as well as in plans for Oakland in 1927 and Vancouver in 1928. Only portions of each were implemented.

The rapid increase in automobiles and trucks in the 1920s and 1930s led to the next major urban roadway concept: expressways. These were inspired in large part by the parkways developed in that era in the Northeast, including many in the metropolitan New York area under the leadership of Robert Moses. As Brown, Morris, and Taylor related, the new urban expressway concept took two key ideas from the Eastern parkways: limited access and grade separation. These features would permit larger volumes of traffic and higher speeds than on local streets and boulevards, enabling the expressways to relieve a significant amount of local congestion.

The first conceptual plan for an urban-area parkway/expressway system came from the Regional Plan Association of New York. In 1936 it published a plan for a system of parkways and freeways in the counties surrounding New York City.[2] It was inspired by the early parkways developed by Robert Moses as a way for city dwellers to gain easy access to open space and recreational areas outside the city. They were intended for cars only, mostly two lanes each way, and were generally contoured to follow natural terrain features.

Similar ideas were put forth on the West Coast. In 1939 the Transportation Engineering Board of the city of Los Angeles proposed a system of expressways. Unlike the freeways that were built in the 1950s and '60s, the proposed expressways had mostly two lanes, or at most three, in each direction. They were designed for speeds of 40 to 50 miles per hour, not the 65-to-70-miles-per-hour design standard of the freeways ultimately built. And many were laid out in something like a grid network, enabling most of the population to be within a few miles of an expressway for the longer-distance portions of their trips. The first of these to be constructed was the Arroyo Seco Parkway, linking Pasadena with downtown Los Angeles. With two lanes each way, it followed the natural contours of the arroyo and was very similar to New York's suburban parkways, except for the absence of tolls. The Auto Club of Southern California in 1937 had produced a plan for an 800-mile parkway system, estimated to cost $800 million.[3]

Following the opening of the Arroyo Seco Parkway in 1940, the Los Angeles County Regional Planning Commission adopted a version of the Auto Club plan in 1943.[4] Though called "freeways," nearly all the routes described in the plan were identified as parkways. At the time of publication, initial portions of four had been built or were in the final planning stages.

As Brown, Morris, and Taylor pointed out:

> If these plans had been built, they would have had important traffic service
> benefits; for example, now that cities have just a few large [freeway] facilities,
> more drivers must travel long distances on local streets just to access the free-
> way network, thereby increasing vehicle miles of travel. Also, a denser network
> would have balanced traffic flows between the [expressway] and the surface
> street systems. The 1939 [Auto Club] plan for Los Angeles reflects this vision;
> it proposed a dense grid pattern as opposed to a sparse ring-radial system, in
> order to spread traffic across the city instead of concentrating it in and through
> the [Central Business District].

These expressway plans from the 1930s and '40s were explicitly focused on handling trips within the urban region, as opposed to making
it easier for long-distance trips to get to or past the urban area. Many of
these plans were also multimodal, aiming to facilitate region-wide express
bus service or to accommodate existing streetcar lines in the medians,
to get the streetcars off mixed-traffic local streets. A few even proposed
truck lanes in the median.

Some aspects of these early expressway concepts were initially embraced by the federal Bureau of Public Roads (BPR). In its 1939 report
that dismissed toll financing for what would become the Interstate Highway System, the urban portions were proposed as a way to revitalize
downtowns that by the 1930s were already losing residents and businesses
to their suburbs. BPR engineers proposed that each large urban area include a circumferential beltway linked to downtown by radial expressways
connecting to a downtown hub route, with much of the system built either
depressed or elevated from grade level.[5] The beltway was intended to let
through traffic bypass the city, but also to link the radial expressways to
one another, so as to prevent the kind of "ribbon" development that had
accompanied long streetcar lines from downtown to the suburbs.[6] These
urban expressways were further elaborated upon in the 1941 report *Interregional Highways*, which became the original planning document for
the Interstates. BPR chief Thomas MacDonald, presenting the report to
Congress in 1944, described the urban expressways as a way to reverse, or
at least slow down, the kind of patchy suburbanization that had occurred
along streetcar lines.

But when Congress enacted the Federal-Aid Highway Act of 1944, the
urban component of the planned Interstate Highway System was scarcely
mentioned. For the next several years the BPR worked with state highway

departments to select the primary intercity routes. Those were announced in 1947, along with an initial 3,900 miles of an eventual 9,200 urban expressway routes. The BPR had wanted the urban expressway program to be coordinated with a new federal program to replace the slums that would be torn down to make room for the urban expressways. But President Harry Truman did not want the government involved in slum clearance, and he denied that request in 1949. With that, opined FHWA historian Richard Weingroff, the "vision of expressways as the centerpiece of urban revitalization came to an end for all practical purposes."[7]

While the Interstate program was being debated in Washington, states were beginning to take their own actions on urban expressways. The large-scale plans for such networks in Los Angeles and San Francisco were unaffordable from the traditional local property tax revenues that had paid for most local streets and roads, especially since the Great Depression had devastated property values. So cities turned to the state government for gas-tax funding. In California and a number of other states, legislatures agreed to expand the use of gas taxes to major urban highways—but typically on condition that these projects be managed by the state highway department and be designated as state highways. By 1956, before any federal Interstate funding had reached the states, there were 480 miles of urban freeway either completed or under construction in the 25 largest cities.[8]

By turning over the development of freeways to state highway departments, cities lost control of their purpose and design. With that transition, the vision of a dense grid of moderate-speed parkways or expressways vanished, and Los Angeles's original Arroyo Seco Parkway was converted into the higher-speed Pasadena Freeway. Nearly all the others were redesigned to meet state highway standards. As Brown, Morris, and Taylor put it, "The highway engineers who dominated state departments of transportation espoused a narrower, more technical view of transportation planning [than did their urban counterparts]. They aimed to maximize traffic flows and to minimize costs while adhering to uniform design standards. Shifting control over urban highways to the states imposed this perspective on metropolitan as well as rural freeways."

These changes were amplified when Congress finally enacted the funding plan for the Interstate Highway System in 1956. The bill had failed dismally in 1955, but proponents made an all-out effort to gain support from members of Congress from urban areas the following year. Within eight months of the 1955 defeat, the BPR mapped out all the remaining routes for urban Interstates, and published maps showing these systems in a "Yellow Book." The book's effect on urban Congress members was profound. The lure of getting all these projects, plus the new federal funding formula requiring only 10 percent of the project cost to come from the state highway budget, as opposed to the traditional 50/50 federal/state matching requirement, changed the outcome for the Interstate bill when it was reintroduced in 1956.[9] The bill passed almost unanimously.

As a result, all urban Interstates had to be developed to the high-speed, high-volume design standards of the state highway departments. This included a design speed of 70 miles per hour, broader sweeping curves, generous breakdown lanes on either side, higher overhead clearances for large trucks, nd so on. This "upscaling of freeway design" significantly increased the cost of the new freeways, partly due to the significantly greater right-of-way required by greater widths (more lanes, wider left and right shoulders, larger curve radii, etc.). Congress limited the number of urban Interstates and their length (route miles), but not their cost. And because it had implicitly rejected a dense grid of smaller expressways, the incentive for urban freeway builders was to build as many lanes as possible in the relatively few urban corridors Congress (and state highway departments) had designated.

The result of all these factors was far more extensive taking of land by eminent domain to build the giant freeway corridors. As Brian Taylor points out, "The expressways envisaged by most early planners in cities like Los Angeles would have required some displacement of existing homes and businesses, but far less than for the massive freeways eventually built."[10] In addition to major negative effects on neighborhoods, the giant freeways concentrated traffic noise and vehicle emissions to a much greater extent than would have occurred if the original grid of modest expressways had been built. It is hardly surprising that "freeway revolts" broke out in many urban areas in the 1960s, as various community groups decided that enough was enough and engaged in protests and litigation to stop a number of planned components of the freeway systems in many urban areas, leaving many with missing links that reduced their overall transportation value.

Tear Down Urban Freeways?

One legacy of the freeway revolts is that groups opposed to our auto-intensive urban transportation system have been calling for tearing down, rather than replacing, aging urban expressways. This position is championed nationally by the Congress for a New Urbanism, and is often supported in specific instances by pro-transit and bicycle/pedestrian groups.

These organizations point to a handful of cases in which freeways (actually, only portions thereof) have been torn down and replaced by boulevards. The largest and best known of these is the West Side Highway, a 4.6-mile elevated freeway down the west side of Manhattan. It was built in stages between 1929 and 1951 and, due to its narrow lanes and sharp S-turn exit ramps, was considered obsolete by many transportation planners by the time it was completed. It was poorly maintained, and it experienced serious deterioration due to the salt used to de-ice it in the winter. After a car and a truck fell through it(!) in 1973, it was shut down, and after years of debate the structure was torn down in 1989 and replaced with a six- to eight-lane boulevard.

In 2002 the initial section of a never-completed freeway in downtown Milwaukee was torn down. The Park Freeway was intended to link I-43 with the Stadium Freeway to the west and the Lake Freeway to the east and south. Only three-quarters of a mile of the freeway was built and opened to traffic in 1971; local opposition defeated plans to build the rest, and eventually led to the replacement of the short existing segment with a surface street and bridge over the Milwaukee River.

In Portland, an early limited-access route through downtown, US 99W or Harbor Drive, opened to traffic in 1950. When I-5 was subsequently completed through Portland in 1966, running parallel to Harbor Drive, the latter's function as a limited-access through route became obsolete, and the one mile that had approximated a freeway was replaced with a boulevard named Naito Parkway.

In San Francisco the 1989 Loma Prieta earthquake damaged two partially completed elevated freeways, the Central and the Embarcadero. After much debate, the one-mile Central Freeway was torn down and replaced with the new, nonelevated Octavia Boulevard. The Embarcadero Freeway, similar to the Park Freeway in Milwaukee, was only the first leg of a planned several-mile SR 480 freeway along the city's eastern and northern waterfront. The approximately one-mile elevated structure was demolished and replaced with a tree-lined boulevard that included a median streetcar line.

Several themes emerge from these cases of urban freeway replacement. All the built freeway segments were very short, and none was a key component of its city's limited-access network. Two, West Side Highway and Harbor Drive, were obsolete at the time they were replaced by boule-vards. And the stub-ends of freeways that would never be built in Milwau-kee and San Francisco had little reason for being.

Alternatives to Teardowns

A different case is being debated in Syracuse, New York. Like that of Los Angeles, the city's original urban expressway plan called for a north-south and an east-west expressway, both at grade and with partial access from local streets, plus a beltway around the city for through traffic. Those plans were abandoned after Congress created the Interstate program with up to 90 percent federal funding and state highway department control.[11] What resulted instead was the new north-south I-81 going through the city on a 1.4-mile elevated structure known as the Viaduct. Today the aging Viaduct needs to be replaced, and controversy has raged over how to do that. One faction calls for replacing the Viaduct with a ground-level bou-levard, complete with signalized intersections. That might work for those making local trips in and around Syracuse, but it ignores the needs of long-distance travelers on what is, after all, an Interstate highway that extends from Tennessee to Canada and is a major truck route for most of its length. Syracuse does have a partial beltway, I-481, that allows through travelers to bypass downtown at the cost of traveling about 50 percent farther, which is what those travelers would likely do if the Viaduct were replaced with the proposed four-lane, tree-lined boulevard. A tunnel was the first choice of many, but has been rejected by the state DOT as unaf-fordable, though toll financing was apparently not considered. As of late 2016 the remaining alternatives were either a rebuilt viaduct or the bou-levard option.[12]

A similar controversy is underway in Hartford, Connecticut, where I-84 goes through its downtown on a three-quarter-mile elevated viaduct. This section of I-84 has the highest traffic volume in the state—175,000 vehicles on an average day—so replacing it with a boulevard has little support. A 2010 study by the Capitol Region Council of Governments re-viewed five alternatives and concluded that a replacement freeway, mostly at ground level but with some stretches depressed below grade, would probably be most cost-effective.[13] As of fall 2016, the state DOT has se-lected the below-grade replacement, which would permit portions of the freeway to be decked over.[14]

Two major metro areas, Boston nd Seattle, have opted to replace aging elevated freeways with tunnels. As discussed in chapter 6, Boston's project was the very complex and extremely costly ($14.8 billion) Central Artery/ Tunnel project, commonly known as the Big Dig. It replaced the aging elevated north-south I-93 through downtown Boston with a 1.5-mile, eight-lane tunnel. The project also included extending east-west I-90 across I-93 to connect to a new (third) tunnel to Logan Airport, plus a new I-93 bridge across the Charles River to Cambridge. Thus, although considerably inflated due to the dysfunctional incentives of conventional design-bid-build contracting (see chapter 6), the $14.8 billion price tag included far more than just the I-93 tunnel that replaced the elevated freeway.

A much simpler project is underway in Seattle: replacing the two-mile elevated Alaskan Way Viaduct with a 1.7-mile deep-bore tunnel. While any new tunnel in a major urban downtown must confront myriad potential obstacles (water and sewer lines, subway lines, power and telecommunications cables, etc.), the Seattle project intended to minimize those problems by excavating the tunnel deeper than the Big Dig, and by using "Bertha," a state-of-the-art tunnel-boring machine like the one used for the A86 tunnel that constructed the missing link on the A86 Paris ring road. Alas, after only five months of tunneling, the tunnel-boring machine hit a still-unknown obstacle and stopped moving. Efforts to repair the cutting head were more costly and time-consuming than expected, and the tunneling did not resume until 2016. "Bertha" finally broke through at the other end of the route in early April 2017. Work remains to build the roadway decks, install ventilation equipment, and so on, so the project will not be ready for traffic until 2019.[15] The full cost of the project is not known, but it is certain to be a lot more than the planned $3 billion.

Another aging elevated expressway is the Gowanus (I-278) in Brooklyn. In 1995 residents welcomed a serious proposal from the Regional Plan Association to replace the elevated expressway with a major tunnel, estimated at the time to cost $2 billion. Despite two decades of effort by the Gowanus Tunnel Coalition, the New York DOT opposed the plan, proposing instead to replace the elevated expressway with a comparable structure. Advocates were dismayed by the DOT's January 2015 announcement that it plans to spend $344 million to redeck the elevated expressway.[16]

Decks and Lids

Elevated freeways divide communities, but so do the many freeways built below grade in trenches. A less costly alternative than a tunnel can be to build a deck over the freeway, converting the former barrier into a park and opening up the valuable immediately adjoining land to compatible development.[17]

One of the earliest projects of this kind took place in downtown Seattle. Freeway Park was created by decking over several blocks of I-5, creating more than five acres of urban park back in 1976. That project has inspired others, including 17-acre Hance Park, built over I-10 in Phoenix; a 28-acre park over I-90 on Mercer Island near Seattle; three decks over portions of I-35, in Duluth, Minnesota; freeway parks in Atlantic City and Trenton, New Jersey; and most recently the 5.2-acre Klyde Warren Park, built over the Woodall Rogers Freeway in downtown Dallas in 2012.

Several larger projects are currently underway in Saint Louis, Denver, and Hamburg, Germany. In Saint Louis, I-70 was built alongside the Mississippi River, which meant that it creates a barrier between downtown and the iconic Gateway Arch on the riverbank. After many years of planning, construction is underway, as this is written, to create the "Park over Highway," a $380 million project set for completion by the end of 2017.[18] In Denver, the $1.2 billion long-term concession project that will reconstruct 12 miles of I-70 between I-25 downtown and I-225 east near Denver International Airport includes replacing an aging two-mile viaduct section with a below-grade corridor, including express toll lanes, topped by a four-acre park. The park will help reunite communities on either side of the busy freeway, and the below-grade design and deck will reduce its noise impact (figure 1).[19] In Germany, work has begun on a project to deck over 2.2 miles of the congested A7 autobahn in Hamburg, which will provide 62 acres of new park land.[20] Other projects along these lines have been proposed for the Hollywood Freeway in Los Angeles, the I-10 in Santa Monica, the I-35 in Austin, the I-30 in Dallas, and the I-395 in Miami.

Avoiding Short-Sighted "Removals"

In thinking through the future role of urban expressways, we should not lose sight of the value of the existing freeway networks, despite what many thoughtful people agree were mistakes made in building massive "high-speed" freeway projects rather than the dense grid of lower-impact expressways originally planned. Replacing a freeway through downtown carrying 175,000 vehicles a day with a signalized boulevard could create even worse congestion than what now plagues many urban freeway systems.

FIGURE 1. Planned park on new deck over I-70, Denver. Source: Colorado Department of Transportation.

Advocates of freeway removals extrapolate from a handful of mile-long examples to much larger proposals. Peter Park, who ran the Milwaukee project that tore down the Park East Freeway stub, told a reporter in 2014, "There's not been a single city in the world that's taken a freeway out and things haven't gotten better for everybody."[21] That's an example of hasty overgeneralization. The fact that something works on a tiny scale does not necessarily mean that it will work the same on a much larger scale.

Consider irresponsible proposals such as *Streetsblog USA*'s 2014 article implicitly calling for removal of "eight monster interchanges that blight American cities."[22] Its discussion of the eight projects, each with a brief description and an aerial photo showing lots of concrete, entirely ignores the benefits of these interchanges and the potentially massive negative impacts that would occur were they to be torn down. One of them, the Circle Interchange (I-90, I-94, and I-290) in Chicago, is the third-worst traffic bottleneck in the country, according to separate studies by the American Highway Users Alliance and the trucking industry's American

Transportation Research Institute. Seattle's I-5/I-90 interchange is number 18 on the AHUA national bottlenecks list. Instead of being removed, these interchanges, obsolete in their design and safety features, need to be replaced with state-of-the-art designs, as has been done in recent years for the Springfield Interchange in northern Virginia and the Marquette Interchange in Milwaukee.

Urban Interstates, which constitute the large majority of US urban freeways, handle 24 percent of all urban vehicle miles of travel on just 3.8 percent of all urban highway lane-miles. To argue that if freeways were "torn down," this traffic would somehow melt away, as many teardown advocates claim, is ludicrous. Replacing a one-mile stub-end in Milwaukee with a surface street had a negligible impact on traffic flow. But replacing the nearby Marquette Interchange (I-94, I-93, and I-794) with signalized surface streets would have caused massive displacement of traffic and significantly reduced access to downtown Milwaukee. In fact, the $810 million redesign and reconstruction of the Marquette in 2008 significantly reduced the congestion caused by its poorly designed and less capacious predecessor.

People continue to travel on urban freeways because using them is less bad than the alternatives. The 2015 American Community Survey data on commuting show a continuing increase over the past decade in the fraction of commuters driving to work alone, an option chosen by 76.6 percent. Another 9 percent of commuters carpooled, meaning that 85.6 percent of commuters got to and from work by automobile. The average share of commuting by public transit was 5.2 percent, and in most metro areas the majority of public transit riders ride buses. Hence, including bus riders, more than 88 percent of Americans get to work on our roadways and freeways.[23]

There are many reasons for the overwhelming preference for driving in most of the country (apart from a handful of major cities with traditional central business districts and pre-auto-era rail transit: New York, Boston, Chicago, Philadelphia, San Francisco, and Washington). For the past three or four decades, the predominant commuting pattern has been suburb-to-suburb, notwithstanding the outdated misconception that most people commute suburb-to-downtown.[24] This has occurred as job locations have followed residents to the suburbs. This phenomenon also explains why the average commuting time by automobile has remained essentially stable at about 25 minutes for 40 years or so, as the urban economists Peter Gordon and Alex Anas have separately documented.[25]

The challenge, then, is to figure out how to reconfigure the urban high-way/expressway system for the future, rather than "tear it down." That is what we will explore in the rest of this chapter.

Repurposing Freeways

If we could start over, prior to the creation of today's massive freeways, I would aim for something far closer to the original concept of a grid of much smaller parkways and expressways, many of them depressed below grade to minimize their noise impact. Since starting over is not really practical, the challenge is to try to reuse or repurpose the existing urban highway infrastructure to make it work better for individual motorists, bus transit, and trucks. Several serious transportation professionals have given a lot of thought to these questions, and we will explore their ideas in this section.

One of those experts is Brian Taylor of UCLA, who first brought to my attention the pre-Interstate city expressway plans based largely on Eastern parkways. In a 1995 paper he used California freeway history to compare the impact of the shift from pre-Interstate expressway designs to the federally mandated standards adopted by the California highway department (now called Caltrans). The pre-Interstate expressways were designed for 55-miles-per-hour design speeds rather than the later 70-miles-per-hour standard. That change had a major impact on various dimensions, as is summarized in table 7:[26]

Taylor points out that 46 percent of the increase in inflation-adjusted freeway development costs during the 1960s and '70s was due to the "upscaling" of designs, as typified by the data in table 7. Most of these changes were aimed at increasing the safety of motorists traveling at the new 70-miles-per-hour design speed, but the significant increase in cost was an important factor in limiting the number of planned freeways that could be built with the available federal and state gas-tax money. Of course, in hindsight we know that, for the large majority of their users, most of California's urban freeways regularly fail to operate at anything close to the 70-miles-per-hour design speed.

A transportation researcher who has taken seriously the point about unrealistically high design speeds is Ken Small of the University of California, Irvine. In a 2008 research paper, Small and coresearcher Chen Feng Ng criticized US freeway design standards as not cost-effective, given the

TABLE 7. **Upscaling of freeway design standards**

Design feature	1955 minimum	1985 minimum	% difference
Left shoulder width	2 feet	10 feet	+400%
Right shoulder width	8 feet	30 feet	+275%
Urban curve radius	1,100 feet	3,000 feet	+173%
Rural curve radius	2,200 feet	5,000 feet	+127%
Left bridge shoulder width	2 feet	5 feet	+150%
Right bridge shoulder width	8 feet	10 feet	+25%

realities of how urban freeways are used.[27] These Interstate-era design standards are codified in the *AASHTO Design Standards-Interstate System*, produced by the American Association of State Highway and Transportation Officials. The two key assumptions on which these standards are based are (1) safe design for high speeds, and (2) all lanes designed to handle all types of traffic, including heavy trucks. In this and follow-up papers, Small and Ng suggested that there could be benefits from rethinking both assumptions. That would mean working out the implications for cost and performance of lower design speeds and of having some lanes or highways configured for cars only, and others for trucks only. Those revisions harken back to the parkway concepts of the 1930s, which inspired the pre-Interstate concepts for urban expressways.

Small and Ng examined what could be done with an existing freeway if the lane widths were reduced from 12 to 10 feet and the shoulders reduced proportionally. New cars-only expressways could be designed to this "narrower" profile, and some existing freeways could be converted to cars-only operation without widening. For example, a current freeway with three 12-foot lanes going each way and the 10-foot and 30-foot shoulders shown in table 7 (36 plus 40 totals 76 feet wide in each direction) could be converted to five lanes each way if the lanes were each 10 feet wide and the shoulder widths were reduced by half: 50 feet for lanes plus 20 for shoulders equals a total width of 70 feet in each direction.

In a 2012 article, Small and Ng presented an example of a new parkway designed for lower speeds. Using standard freeway dimensions, a right-of-way 40 feet wide would accommodate only two lanes each way, but with reduced dimensions (lanes 10 feet wide, and narrower shoulders) could handle three lanes each way. They next analyzed the speed and capacity performance of the two alternatives, finding that the total capacity in vehicles per hour was 47 percent greater with the "narrow" design, despite the slightly lower speed when operating at capacity (51.2 versus 52.3 miles per hour).[28] In follow-up work, using data from seven large and very large metro areas, they found that in many large urban freeway systems, investment has been overly focused on achieving a high design speed at the expense of greater throughput capacity, and they suggested "giving greater attention to the possibilities of low-footprint roads which offer considerable capacity even though speeds are only moderate."[29]

The arrival of large numbers of autonomous vehicles in coming decades will strengthen the case for narrower lanes—at least for cars-only roadways. Fully autonomous vehicles will be able to drive more closely together than conventional vehicles, thanks to their automation systems (including automatic braking and more precise lane control). Existing highway "capacity" manuals and standards will have to be revised accordingly. This is not a near-term need, however, since most experts think fully autonomous vehicles are several decades away from being introduced, and if the large majority of people replace their existing vehicles with AVs on a normal schedule, it will take about two decades for the entire fleet to be replaced—if that's what people choose to do (see chapter 11).

In 2016 the Federal Highway Administration released a document aimed at assisting transportation planners who are considering lane-narrowing options. It includes design and safety guidelines, as well as case studies of narrow lanes and shoulders.[30]

The potential of cars-only expressways has also been explored by other transportation researchers and designers. In his excellent book *Transport in Europe*, Christian Gerondeau proposed a new design for compact highway tunnels in cases where cars-only routes would be acceptable.[31] He showed that with 10-foot lanes and 8.4-foot overhead clearance comparable to that in most parking structures, six travel lanes could be included within a circular tunnel just 34 feet in diameter. The design used two decks, with travel in one direction on the lower deck and travel in the opposite direction on the upper deck—an arrangement that inherently increases safety. This concept was used as the basic design for the toll concession project for the A86 tunnel outside Paris (figure 2).

In a 1992 presentation to the American Society of Civil Engineers, the highway engineer Gary Alstot proposed adaptive reuse of congested freeways based on converting the inner lanes to cars-only. He showed that with lane widths of 10 feet and a clearance height of 7 feet, cars-only lanes could be double-decked within the standard 16.5-foot vertical clearance

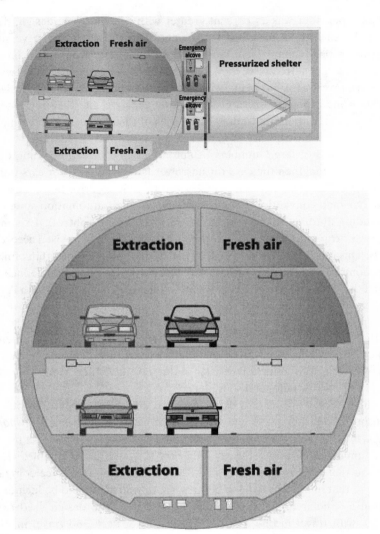

FIGURE 2. Reduced-dimensions double-deck cars-only A-86 tunnel. Source: Cofiroute USA.

used on urban Interstates, as shown in figure 3, which contrasts his design
with the double-decking that was actually applied to the Harbor Freeway
(I-110) in Los Angeles. Alstot's design would add four new cars-only lanes
to the freeway, above four of the existing lanes also reserved for cars only,
while reserving the two outer lanes either for a mix of cars and trucks or

for trucks only. Under this design concept, buses would not fit within the 7-foot clearance heights, since urban buses are typically 10 feet, 8 inches high, requiring a clearance height of 12 feet. Thus, unlike today's practice of mixing buses and cars in express toll lanes, buses would have to share the outer lanes with trucks and possibly other cars.

These approaches to repurposing the lanes on existing major freeways would not return us to the lower-impact expressways proposed prior to the Interstates. However, they do suggest ways of getting greater effective use out of the rights-of-way and structures that are already there, without widening, in the limited urban freeway corridors that already exist. The Alstot concept would preserve truck access on these repurposed freeways, but would limit trucks and buses to the outer lanes. If and when new cars-only parkways were developed to flesh out the original grid concept, those new roads would supplement the existing arterials and freeways and would not take away any truck access that already exists in the urban roadway system.

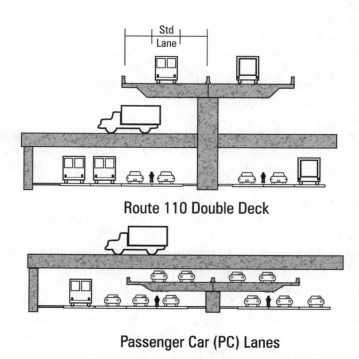

Route 110 Double Deck

Passenger Car (PC) Lanes

FIGURE 3. Old versus new way to add second level to freeway. Source: Reason Foundation.

Supplementing Freeways with Managed Arterials

Arterials are urban highways, generally with two, three, or occasionally four lanes in each direction, that typically have posted speed limits of 35 to 45 miles per hour and traffic signals at intervals of about one per mile. These arterials supplement the freeways, providing a pale approximation of the grid of parkways envisioned by the pre-Interstate planners. Compared with the original parkway plans, today's arterials suffer from two serious problems: they have open access, as opposed to limited access; and they have signalized intersections instead of grade separations where they cross other important roadways. Both these deficiencies restrict major arterials from providing the level of service envisioned for the pre-Interstate parkway grid.

Traffic engineers have used two design features to reduce the problems caused by these deficiencies. First, when possible, they have reduced fully open access to these major arterials. The most common approach is to provide a raised median that prevents left turns except at signal-controlled locations. This improves traffic flow and significantly reduces the risk of a rear-end collision or side impact into the left-turning vehicle. In some cases, the engineers have worked with adjoining businesses to limit entrances and exits to those businesses' parking lots, sometimes relocating entrances and exits to side streets.

But the biggest limitations of today's major arterials are the signalized intersections. Wherever two major arterials intersect, the total time at which a motorist might be stopped for the complete light cycle (including left-turn arrows) can be up to three minutes in many cases. Hence, the throughput (measured as vehicles per lane per hour) of a six-lane arterial with traffic lights can be about half that of an equivalent six-lane highway without traffic lights. Traffic signal synchronization can reduce those delays and increase the arterial's throughput in one direction, if the signals are timed so that those driving at the posted speed limit get a series of rolling green lights. But rolling greens cannot be simultaneously provided in both directions, and many motorists drive slower or faster than the posted speed limit.

Civil engineer Chris Swenson appears to be the first to come up with the idea of using tolled grade separations (underpasses or overpasses) at today's major urban arterial intersections. In a study funded by FHWA's Value Pricing program in 2003, Swenson adapted the principle of HOT lanes—you pay a toll if you wish to use the faster alternative—to arterial intersections. The idea was to offer motorists and buses a choice: stay on the existing lanes and risk a long red-light delay, or pay a modest toll (estimated at 25 cents) to use a new underpass or overpass.[32] The study was carried out for Lee county, Florida, which had already built several nontolled arterial overpasses and was interested in trying a tolled overpass on Colonial Boulevard, one of its most congested arterials.

In a subsequent Reason Foundation policy study, Swenson and Poole proposed a network of arterials for Lee County, Florida, that would be retrofitted with tolled overpasses or underpasses, depending on location. The study included preliminary cost and revenue estimates suggesting that toll revenues might be sufficient to finance the construction of these grade separations.[33] Cost estimates were developed for each grade separation (overpass or underpass) for a sample arterial, and the toll rates ranged from 20 (off-peak) to 45 (peak) cents per intersection. Making assumptions about what fraction of through trips would opt to use the underpasses at various times of day, the study estimated the toll revenue as at least in the ballpark of being able to pay for the costs of these infrastructure improvements.

In a more detailed study of the major arterials in southeast Florida (Miami-Dade, Broward, and Palm Beach counties), the same authors proposed a more extensive network of what were dubbed managed arterials, on the basis of this tolled underpass concept.[34] Figure 4 illustrates the concept proposed there. This study included calculations of the vehicle throughput of a managed arterial (MA) compared with that of a typical Florida six-lane arterial with signalized intersections. The MA design concept offered two lanes in each direction on the underpass, along with four nontolled lanes each way at the traffic signal: two through lanes, one left-turn lane, and one right-turn lane. The existing six-lane arterial has a throughput of 51,800 vehicles per day; reconfigured as a managed arterial, its throughput is increased to 87,600 vehicles per day.

This study also compared the person-moving capacity of these MAs to that of two other possible improvements. First, if the six-lane arterial were widened to eight regular lanes, its throughput would be 67,000 vehicles per day, far less than the 87,600 of the MA configuration. The second comparison was with widening the arterial and using the extra lane each way for buses only. In this case, the person-moving capacity of the MA was greater at all percentages of bus usage than the person-moving capacity of the eight-lane arterial with one lane each way restricted to

FIGURE 4. Optional tolled underpass for managed arterials. Source: Reason Foundation.

buses only. This study's results were presented at the 2012 Annual Meeting of the Transportation Research Board, and the paper was published in TRB's journal of record that year.[35]

The managed arterials concept offers a way to convert selected major arterials into a smaller-scale version of the grid of parkways envisioned by the early planners. It's a second-best idea, since we cannot go back in time and undo the mistakes that were made in concentrating existing freeways in overly large, nominally high-speed corridors. But we can repurpose those freeways with lower design speeds and more lanes by making some of the lanes for cars only. And we can supplement the repurposed freeways with a grid of upgraded arterials with tolled grade separations at major intersections and traffic signal timing for all signalized intersections.

Rebuilding and Modernizing Freeways

Pricing versus Capacity Expansion

For several decades, transport economists and highway engineers have debated how best to deal with the enormous problem of freeway congestion. The economists diagnose freeway congestion as the predictable result of a system that fails to price its services in a sensible way. They point to what happens in cities without water meters, where per-capita water use is double the use in comparable cities with meters (where people pay on the basis of how many gallons they use, rather than paying for the cost of the water department via their property tax bill). They also point out that nearly all other network utilities charge people for what they consume, in proportion to their use, as discussed in chapter 8. But they also cite the many examples of basing the price structure in part on the level of demand:

- With smart meters, electric utilities can charge lower rates at times of day when demand is low, to encourage people to shift some uses (e.g., running dishwashers) out of the times of peak demand. That enables the utility to make better use of its existing capacity without having to build as many new power plants as otherwise.
- Before the prevalence of mobile phones, traditional telephone service charged day, evening, and weekend rates corresponding to times of high, medium, and low demand for long-distance service. This enabled the phone company to provide good service with less total capacity.
- Airlines use "value pricing" to offer lower fares to those who purchase far in advance or who travel on days of lower demand, to help fill their planes to their target "load factor" of about 85 percent of seats filled.
- Even restaurants and movie theaters use variable pricing—with lower-priced happy hours at bars and restaurants, and matinees at movie theaters—so as to fill seats at times of lower demand, and ease overcrowding at peak times.

Thus, many transport economists say the solution to highway congestion is variable pricing, charging rates that will limit the number of vehicles on the road during peak periods to the amount consistent with keeping traffic flowing at modest speeds rather than degenerating into stop-and-go conditions.

Figure 5 helps to explain what variable pricing does to reduce congestion on priced lanes. The curve shows what happens to speed (vertical axis) as the flow of vehicles increases (horizontal axis). As flow increases, speed declines to the point at the far right side of the graph; this is the maximum flow rate the lane can handle. As more vehicles attempt to use the lane, speed drops further and the flow becomes seriously congested—a combination of lower flow and lower speeds. This region, called level of service (LOS) F, is shown as the lower portion of the curve. What variable pricing does is raise the price as flow increases, to keep the traffic on the upper portion of the curve. Most priced-lane facilities aim for LOS C,

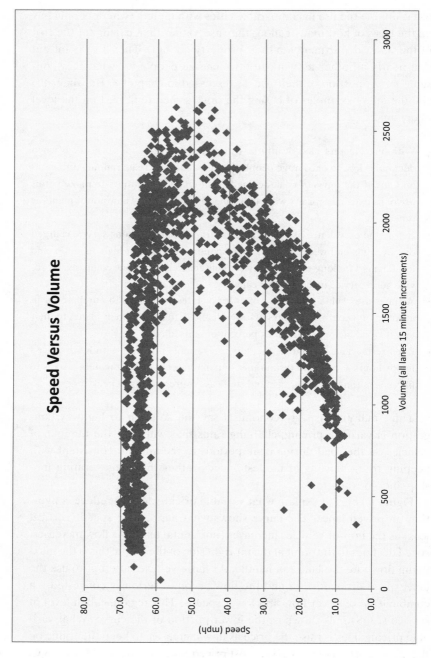

FIGURE 5. Freeway traffic speed versus throughput. Source: WSP USA.

which is the best combination of speed and flow along the upper side of the graph without congestion. More than 20 years of experience on the SR 91 Express Lanes in California has been validated by more than two dozen other priced-lane projects implemented since then. Variable pricing works.

By contrast, highway engineers generally argue that the solution to traffic congestion is to add capacity, either by widening existing highways and freeways or by adding additional links to the overall network. They, too, have empirical evidence to support this approach. In most years the Texas A&M Transportation Institute produces a highly detailed *Urban Mobility Report* that quantifies the level and extent of traffic congestion in America's largest hundred or so urban areas. Figure 6 is extracted from the 2012 report, and comparable figures have appeared in previous reports. Of the 101 urban areas analyzed in this report, 17 have attempted to keep their highway capacity growing in step with the growth in vehicle miles of travel—on average, to within 10 percent of traffic growth. Another 28 urban areas added some capacity, but their traffic growth outpaced capacity growth by as much as 30 percent. The majority, 56 urban areas, added even less capacity. The figure compares the average congestion in each set of urban areas from 1982 through 2011. As you can see, the 17 urban areas that increased capacity the most have had by far the smallest increases in traffic congestion. For further thoughts on capacity addition, see sidebar 6.

The conclusion I draw from this debate is that the economists and the engineers are both correct. We do need a pricing system that reflects the time-varying demand for highway use, but we also need to provide a level of capacity that produces good service to highway users—just as other network utilities do. It's not either/or; it is both/and.

What Kind of Capacity Should Be Added?

Given the large value provided by variable pricing, a first principle is that all new capacity for the urban freeway network should be priced. Following that principle accomplishes two things simultaneously. First, it enables the new lanes to be operated as express lanes, giving road users, including buses, at least some capacity that is virtually guaranteed to be uncongested during times of peak demand. Second, the revenue will help pay for what we know will be very costly projects, few of which are possible with today's stagnating fuel-tax revenues.

Percent Increase in
Congestion

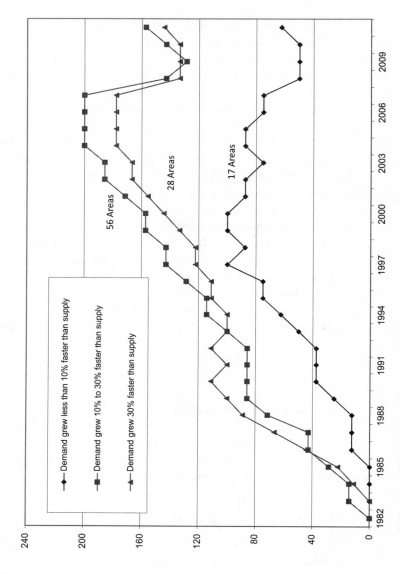

FIGURE 6. Capacity additions lead to lower congestion. Source: Texas A&M Transportation Institute.

SIDEBAR 6 **The Iron Law of Freeway Congestion?**

Is adding freeway capacity futile? Some years ago, Anthony Downs of the Brookings Institution postulated that adding capacity to a congested highway leads to a "triple convergence" of responses.[1] When the freeway is expanded, some drivers shift to it from other roads, some drivers shift to using it from other times of day, and some commuters shift to it from other modes of transportation (e.g., riding the bus). The predictable result is that after some interval, the expanded highway ends up just as congested as before. This has been called the "iron law of freeway congestion," and antihighway groups have used it as a reason to lobby against adding capacity, especially to congested urban freeways.

In 2011 the *American Economic Review* published a quantitative analysis of this phenomenon by Gilles Duranton and Matthew Turner, titled "The Fundamental Law of Road Congestion: Evidence from U.S. Cities."[2] Using FHWA highway statistics data and National Household Travel Survey data, their econometric analysis found evidence that VMT (vehicle miles of travel) on urban Interstates increases in proportion to highway capacity. In effect, they claimed, highway supply creates its own demand.

Tanya Snyder of Streetsblog USA published a blog post that year, based on the Duranton and Turner paper, called "Building Roads to Cure Congestion Is an Exercise in Futility."[3] Like a 2011 *Wired* article about the same paper, it claimed stronger results than Duranton and Turner's analysis had produced: a purported one-for-one correlation always and everywhere between highway capacity growth and VMT growth. That post was resurrected in 2014 shortly after a billion-dollar northbound HOV lane was opened to traffic in Los Angeles on I-405 through the Sepulveda Pass. When, after the first month, before-and-after traffic comparisons showed negligible changes in rush-hour travel speeds on that stretch of the 405, even though the duration of the peak period had been shortened, antiauto and antihighway writers declared that outcome a vindication of Duranton and Turner. Joseph Stromberg wrote a post on Vox.com headlined, "The 'Fundamental Rule' of Traffic: Building New Roads Just Makes People Drive More."[4]

1. Anthony Downs, *Stuck in Traffic: Coping with Peak-Hour Congestion* (Brookings Institution, 1992), pp. 27–30.

2. Gilles Duranton and Matthew Turner, "The Fundamental Law of Road Congestion: Evidence from U.S. Cities," *American Economic Review* 101, no. 6 (2011).

3. Tanya Snyder, "Building Roads to Cure Congestion Is an Exercise in Futility," Streetsblog USA, May 31, 2011.

4. Joseph Stromberg, "The 'Fundamental Rule' of Traffic: Building New Roads Just Makes People Drive More," Vox.com, October 23, 2014.

There are a number of problems not only with popularizations of the Duranton and Turner paper, but with the authors' own analysis. First, their detailed analysis is for urban Interstates only. Analytically, they treat arterials and all other roadways in the metro area as a large blob. That leaves them unable to analyze, as opposed to only speculating about, the extent to which drivers shift trips from parallel arterials to the newly expanded urban Interstate—a switch that would represent not new driving, but simply a reallocation of existing driving.

Second, the authors' premise that all such freeways have a "natural level of saturation" implies that all urban Interstates should fill up to the point of serious peak-period congestion. But in fact, actual congestion levels vary considerably, in both extent and duration, among each metro area's freeways, and among large metro areas overall. Randal O'Toole's Antiplanner blog provides data on daily VMT per lane-mile on urban freeways, finding a range from as low as 9,000 to a high of 22,000.[5]

Third, since most metro areas have added relatively little freeway capacity in recent decades, the authors' analytical results, even if correct, tell us only that making marginal increases in freeway capacity produces little in the way of congestion reduction. In fact, the relatively small number of urban areas that have made capacity additions much larger than average have had considerably less congestion thereafter than the majority that have done only incremental additions. Exhibit 13 in the 2012 *Urban Mobility Report* from the Texas A&M Transportation Institute is a graph showing that, as compared to the 84 urban areas that have made only modest capacity additions, the 17 that have kept capacity growth to within 10 percent of VMT growth have on average experienced decreasing congestion since 1997.[6] Duranton and Turner's methodology does not capture differences of this kind.

O'Toole also provides data, for the same time periods that Duranton and Turner cover, showing significant differences among the 30 largest metro areas in the relationship between capacity expansion and VMT growth.[7] If their finding was correct that the elasticity between capacity increase and VMT increase is always close to 1.0, those large elasticity variations among congested urban areas would not exist.

5. Randal O'Toole, "*Wired* Gets It Wrong Again," *Antiplanner*, June 23, 2014.
6. David Schrank, Bill Eisele, and Tim Lomax, "Exhibit 13: Road Growth and Mobility Level," *TTI's 2012 Urban Mobility Report*, December 2012, p. 20.
7. O'Toole, "*Wired* Gets It Wrong Again."

SIDEBAR 6 **(Continued)**

The commuting expert Alan Pisarski provided some additional perspective in a 2014 presentation on this subject.[8] If some version of Downs and Duranton and Turner's "fundamental law" were correct, would the "futility" conclusion of the antiauto people follow? On Downs's triple convergence, Pisarski suggests looking at why more motorists show up on the expanded freeway: some switch from parallel routes because they find the expanded freeway an improvement over their former route. Those who shift from other travel times do so because it increases their utility to be able to drive at that hour. The same goes for those who shift from other modes of transport. Hence, the expanded freeway "improves and expands choice for both previous and new users."

This gets back to the question of how a highway provider should respond to increased demand from its customers. Should it tell the customers they are wrong to prefer personal mobility? Should an electric utility tell its customers they should switch to woodburning stoves rather than add generating capacity? Should a school district not add schools to serve a growing population of families with kids? Infrastructure providers are supposed to provide the vital facilities that people are willing to pay for, not tell them their preferences are wrong.

To be sure, there are locations where the cost of adding freeway capacity may significantly exceed the benefits to highway customers. When that is the case, I agree with Anthony Downs and with Duranton and Turner that the solution is to implement congestion pricing. And in some of those cases, the pricing revenue may be high enough to make the capacity addition feasible.

8. Alan Pisarski, "VMT and Its Causes," presented at the Heritage Foundation, October 21, 2014.

A second principle is that we should avoid any large-scale condemnation of right-of-way through urban areas. Proposing a whole new freeway through established residential or commercial areas is a recipe for decades of litigation, huge additional costs for relocation and mitigation of those adversely affected, and a serious possibility that the project will end up not getting built. The last freeway built in Los Angeles, the 19-mile Century Freeway, exemplifies this process: it took 21 years between design and opening, following extensive litigation, negotiations, and mitigation. That ballooned the cost to $2.2 billion, making it one of the costliest freeways ever built in the United States.[36]

Where does that leave us in terms of feasible ways to add needed (priced) expressway capacity? Back in 2006, Peter Samuel, the longtime editor of *Toll Roads News*, suggested an array of alternatives.[37] In addition to the cars-only lanes that could be squeezed into existing freeways per Gary Alstot, Samuel proposed

- elevated express toll lanes built in the medians of existing freeways;
- tunnels to fill in missing links in freeway networks;
- new cars-only (or cars-and-buses-only) parkways using former railroad rights-of-way, flood plains alongside rivers, and shared use of electric utility rights-of-way.

Each of these ideas is worth considering in individual cases. No single solution would work everywhere.

One of the best examples of elevated toll lanes is in Tampa, Florida. As noted in chapter 2, the Selmon Expressway is an important commuter toll road from the eastern suburb of Brandon into downtown Tampa. When the Tampa Hillsborough Expressway Authority decided that it needed more lanes, they rejected the idea of condemning additional land to widen the expressway. Working with engineers at Figg Bridge, they came up with the concept of installing pillars in the median to support three reversible elevated lanes. Since commuter traffic was highly directional (inbound in the morning, outbound in the afternoon), the real need was for reversible lanes, which meant that three new lanes could do the work of six. With the pillars needing only six feet of width in the median, the project's nickname became "six lanes on six feet." By precasting segments of the elevated structure off-site and erecting them from above, the project could be built economically and with minimal disruption of daily traffic. The elevated express toll lanes opened in 2006, using all-electronic tolling. The cost was surprisingly low at $420 million, about $16 million per lane-mile (figure 7).[38]

We have already discussed tunnels as one alternative for replacing worn-out and unsightly elevated freeway viaducts in downtown areas. But tunnels can also play a key role in filling in missing links in freeway networks that were never built due to freeway revolts. A classic example is the Long Beach Freeway (I-710) in Los Angeles, which was supposed to extend from the Port of Long Beach in the south to the Foothill Freeway (I-210) in the north. The last section of I-710 was mapped as bisecting the upper-middle-class community of South Pasadena, which became the site of a major freeway revolt in the 1960s. Even though Caltrans condemned land for the right of way and purchased all the houses, litigation and

FIGURE 7. Elevated express-toll lanes on Tampa Expressway. Source: Tampa Hillsborough Expressway Authority.

politics prevented the freeway from being built for more than 40 years, and the houses remained in place.

In 1996 came the first proposal to transportation planners for a double-decked cars-only tunnel similar to the one then underway to fill in the missing link on the A86 Paris ring road. Engineers at Jacobs Engineering in Pasadena provided some pro bono assistance in suggesting the best route, along with some input on tunneling costs. Caltrans headquarters expressed some interest as well. Although the idea attracted some publicity, it was not until about 2010 that the Southern California Association of Governments (SCAG) and the Los Angeles County Metropolitan Transportation Authority (LA Metro) decided that completing that missing link was a top transportation priority, and put the tunnel project on their list of potential toll concessions. A 2015 Reason Foundation study identified several other missing links in the SCAG region that could be filled in via toll tunnels.[39]

Indeed, LA Metro became so enthusiastic about the potential of such tunnels that it proposed an even larger tunnel to relieve massive traffic congestion on the San Diego Freeway (I-405) through Sepulveda Pass, the principal freeway route between the West Side of Los Angeles and the San Fernando Valley. It is among a handful of mega-projects that the

MTA is considering for development as long-term toll concessions.[40] The
Reason Foundation's 2015 mobility study of the Los Angeles metro area
agreed with the need for this additional link in the freeway network, but
proposed locating it further west, tunneling under Topanga Canyon to
link US 101 in the Valley with the western end of the Santa Monica Freeway (I-10) in Santa Monica. This would spread out traffic flow, rather than
further concentrating it along the I-405 corridor.[41]

Other possibly "neglected rights-of-way" suggested in Peter Samuel's
paper are flood plains along rivers, especially in dry Western states where
the amount of water in such rivers is minimal 95 percent of the time. In the
early 1990s, one of the proposals selected by Caltrans under its AB 680
private toll road pilot program would have built an urban cars-only tollway along the concrete channel of the Santa Ana River in Orange County,
extending the SR 57 freeway south to connect with I-405. Local opposition doomed that project. The Trinity River flood plain in Dallas is the
site for a long-proposed Trinity Parkway toll road. The latest plan called
for building four lanes initially, with possible future expansion to six. The
project was very controversial, and after years of debate, the city council
voted against it in August 2017.[42]

Many urban areas include little-used or no-longer-used railroad rights-
of-way. Current transportation planning orthodoxy sees these mostly as
sites for light rail lines, which transit agencies often do not have the money
to build. But many of these rights-of-way would be ideal locations for cars-
only parkways with narrower lanes and 50 miles-per-hour design speeds.
Samuel's 2006 paper identified candidate locations in Brooklyn, Chicago, and Los Angeles where such conversions could be done—though
the corridor he proposed in Los Angeles is now being devoted to a new
light rail line being constructed between downtown and Los Angeles International Airport.

Paying for Freeway Modernization

In chapter 9 we reviewed the results of the 2013 Reason Foundation study
on reconstructing and selectively widening the rural Interstates in all
50 states, and the feasibility of financing this modernization via modest
per-mile tolls. That same study also analyzed modernizing urban Interstates, which constitute the large majority of urban areas' freeway networks. While the rural Interstate study was complicated to a minor extent
by differences in terrain (e.g., mountainous versus flat), rural Interstates

are otherwise very similar, so the cost and revenue estimation was fairly straightforward.

When it comes to urban Interstates, however, the kinds of solutions discussed in this chapter—urban tunnels, elevated lanes, managed arterials, and parkways to supplement the Interstate/expressway network—make generic cost estimation for scores of urban freeways far more complex. Such estimation was, in fact, far beyond the scope of that 2013 study. Any such overall revamping of a specific urban area's expressway system would have to be tailored to the specifics of that location, as the Reason Foundation has proposed for selected large urban areas including Atlanta,[43] Chicago,[44] Denver,[45] Miami,[46] and Los Angeles.[47] For purposes of this chapter, however, we will use the generic approach from the urban Interstates portion of the 2013 Interstate 2.0 study. The purpose is to get some idea of the magnitude of the costs of reconstruction and selective widening, as well as to see what sort of toll revenue might be needed to finance such costs.

The first task, as with rural Interstates, was to estimate the cost of reconstructing all of the existing urban Interstates in each state. Data from the Federal Highway Administration's highway statistics tables provided the number of lane-miles in each state. The FHWA's Highway Economic Requirements System (HERS) cost data provided national average costs for reconstructing urban Interstate lane-miles in four urban-area size categories: small, medium, large, and very large. Using the size categories from the latest *Urban Mobility Report*, the study estimated the fraction of each state's urban lane-miles in each of the four size categories, and applied the relevant reconstruction cost to each subset. The total for all 50 states was $440.8 billion (net present value, in 2010 dollars), considerably more than the cost of reconstructing all 50 states' rural Interstates.

The more complicated analysis was to figure out where widening is needed, when (by decade), and how many lanes. This was done using the same state-by-state car and truck growth rates (Volpe Center Methodology) for vehicle-miles of travel to project future traffic volumes for each specific urban Interstate. Knowing the number of existing lanes on each one, it was possible to calculate how overloaded those lanes would be for each of the next three decades. Use of level of service D (high throughput with some, but not severe, congestion) indicated a maximum of 18,000 daily vehicle miles of travel per lane-mile as the threshold for lane additions. This analysis identified 97 urban Interstates in 30 states that will need additional lanes at some point between 2020 and 2050.

Since it was not possible to spell out the specific nature of these lane additions in a generic study of this kind, the methodology simply used FHWA's HERS unit cost figures for urban Interstate lane additions to arrive at a ballpark cost estimate. The net present value of that set of new construction projects was another $318.9 billion. Altogether, the net present value of reconstruction and widening came to $759.7 billion.

The final task in this exercise was to estimate the toll revenue. This is where the need for variable pricing came into the picture. Two kinds of variation were needed. First, the rates during peak periods should be significantly higher than during off-peak periods. Second, since congestion is generally worse the larger the urban area, different rate schedules were needed for small, medium, large, and very large areas. Also, since trucks always pay much higher rates than cars, taking up more road space and doing a lot more pavement damage, separate rate schedules were needed for cars and for trucks. Table 8 is the set of generic toll rates used for this analysis.

Note that the off-peak rates for cars and for trucks in small urban areas are the same as the baseline rates used in chapter 9 for rural Interstates. Like the generic rates used in that exercise, the toll rates in table 8 were selected simply as figures that might be in the right ballpark to pay for the costs of rebuilding, widening, and maintaining a revamped urban Interstate system. Both the costs and revenues generated by this exercise exclude the costs and potential revenues of (1) any other non-Interstate expressways in the urban area, and (2) any upgrades to existing arterials or creation of new parkways to supplement the expressway network, as discussed previously in this chapter.

The end result of this exercise is summarized in table 9, which provides a state-by-state listing of the estimated costs of urban Interstate

TABLE 8. **Per-mile urban Interstate toll rates, in 2010 dollars**

	Peak rate	% of traffic	Off-peak rate	% of traffic
Cars				
Small urban	5¢	30%	3.5¢	70%
Medium urban	6¢	40%	4.5¢	60%
Large urban	7.5¢	50%	5.5¢	50%
Very large urban	10¢	60%	7¢	40%
Trucks				
Small urban	20¢	35%	14¢	65%
Medium urban	24¢	40%	16¢	60%
Large urban	30¢	40%	18¢	60%
Very large urban	40¢	35%	20¢	65%

reconstruction, widening, and net toll revenues. All the numbers are net
present values in 2010 dollars. As you can see from the last line in the table, overall these "ballpark" toll rates from table 8 provide nearly enough
revenue, on average, to cover the reconstruction, widening, and operating and maintenance costs of the modernized urban Interstates across the

TABLE 9. **Urban Interstate highway modernization costs and toll revenues, net present value
(NPV), in millions of 2010 dollars**

State	NPV of reconstruction cost	NPV of widening cost	NPV of net toll revenue	NPV of total cost	Revenue/cost
Alabama	$4,158	$169	$8,011	$4,327	185%
Alaska	$1,024	$0	$501	$1,024	49%
Arizona	$6,575	$3,875	$12,755	$10,450	122%
Arkansas	$2,217	$318	$5,028	$2,535	198%
California	$62,116	$105,735	$103,922	$167,851	62%
Colorado	$4,714	$1,373	$9,837	$6,097	162%
Connecticut	$5,767	$3,685	$9,175	$9,452	97%
Delaware	$1,824	$229	$2,298	$2,053	112%
District of Columbia	$578	$554	$819	$1,132	72%
Florida	$18,602	$11,837	$39,823	$30,439	131%
Georgia	$22,219	$16,983	$35,755	$39,202	91%
Hawaii	$964	$666	$1,564	$1,630	96%
Idaho	$1,042	$526	$2,100	$1,568	134%
Illinois	$30,158	$19,092	$37,484	$49,250	76%
Indiana	$8,757	$2,636	$16,543	$11,393	145%
Iowa	$1,704	$188	$3,004	$1,892	159%
Kansas	$3,273	$0	$4,256	$3,273	130%
Kentucky	$4,210	$1,977	$8,353	$6,187	135%
Louisiana	$5,045	$1,053	$10,468	$6,098	172%
Maine	$698	$0	$678	$698	97%
Maryland	$8,532	$6,570	$17,822	$15,102	118%
Massachusetts	$17,306	$19,729	$19,429	$37,035	52%
Michigan	$20,392	$3,098	$22,123	$23,490	94%
Minnesota	$6,115	$2,716	$9,916	$8,831	112%
Mississippi	$1,992	$36	$3,273	$2,028	161%
Missouri	$9,367	$5,154	$16,977	$14,521	117%
Montana	$644	$0	$342	$644	53%
Nebraska	$781	$188	$1,322	$969	136%
Nevada	$2,475	$1,661	$5,240	$4,136	127%
New Hampshire	$2,541	$0	$2,343	$2,541	92%
New Jersey	$18,608	$12,193	$21,622	$30,801	70%
New Mexico	$1,740	$286	$4,091	$2,026	202%
New York	$33,086	$12,782	$26,972	$45,868	59%
North Carolina	$8,948	$5,812	$22,504	$14,760	152%
North Dakota	$560	$0	$444	$560	79%
Ohio	$16,593	$6,482	$26,930	$23,075	117%
Oklahoma	$2,674	$267	$5,464	$2,941	186%

TABLE 9. (*continued*)

State	NPV of reconstruction cost	NPV of widening cost	NPV of net toll revenue	NPV of total cost	Revenue/cost
Oregon	$3,193	$981	$6,063	$4,174	145%
Pennsylvania	$18,151	$8,012	$19,156	$26,163	73%
Rhode Island	$1,222	$352	$1,887	$1,574	120%
South Carolina	$3,017	$952	$6,060	$3,969	153%
South Dakota	$871	$0	$537	$871	62%
Tennessee	$7,310	$3,415	$19,198	$10,725	179%
Texas	$33,996	$38,564	$74,263	$72,560	102%
Utah	$4,200	$854	$10,183	$5,054	201%
Vermont	$415	$0	$279	$415	67%
Virginia	$10,195	$6,157	$20,452	$16,352	125%
Washington	$13,072	$11,226	$18,366	$24,298	76%
West Virginia	$1,960	$0	$2,727	$1,960	139%
Wisconsin	$4,148	$520	$5,878	$4,668	126%
Wyoming	$1,003	$0	$652	$1,003	65%
Total	$440,752	$318,903	$704,889	$759,655	93%

country. But, as you can also see, the state-by-state results vary widely. A few mostly rural states don't need any widening, but most of those still cannot cover total costs with the rate schedule of table 8. Overall, 38 states could cover 90 percent or more, and sometimes much more, of the costs via the toll rates in table 8. And most of the others could do so with somewhat higher rates.

Making the Transition

In chapter 9, the rationale for the transition of rural Interstates to being tolled was the need to pay for rebuilding and widening them. While that would be a big change, it would occur gradually over several decades in each state. And there is at least a US precedent for many portions of the rural Interstate system in the Northeast and Midwest to be operated as toll roads. But, since America has few urban toll roads, and only a handful of those with even modest price differences between peak and off-peak hours, the transition from freeways to priced urban expressways would be a bigger change than toll-financed reconstruction of rural Interstates. How could such a transition come about?

Getting Used to Urban Road Pricing

In a paper for the annual meeting of the Transportation Research Board in 2011, the author suggested a pricing transition plan, with the rationale being primarily to provide people with relief from ubiquitous freeway congestion.[48] It first reviewed various attempts, mostly in Europe, to implement congestion pricing either in central business districts of cities or on freeway systems, all but a handful of which have failed politically. The average motorist-voter viewed the pricing proposal not as offering a benefit, but as only imposing a cost.

The one major success in America has been the implementation of variably priced HOT lanes and express toll lanes. As of 2017, such lanes are in operation on one or more freeways in the metro areas of Atlanta, Baltimore, Dallas, Denver, Houston, Los Angeles, Miami, Minneapolis, San Diego, San Francisco, Seattle, and Washington, with projects proposed or under construction in a number of other metro areas including Austin, Charlotte, Chicago, Jacksonville, Orlando, Phoenix, Tampa, and Washington, DC. Although the first such project in a metro area is often controversial, once people try these lanes and see that they work, the projects generally are well accepted.

The logical next step—already in the long-range plans of Atlanta, Dallas, Denver, Houston, Miami, Minneapolis-Saint Paul, San Diego, San Francisco, and Seattle—is a whole network of express toll lanes. The network benefits in such cases can be profound. If the entire metro area freeway system hosts a seamless network of express toll lanes that are priced to ensure uncongested travel at all times, then time-urgent trips by individuals and emergency responders can be made via that network from more or less any origin in the region to any destination, assuming that the freeway network itself adequately spans most of the metro area. Likewise, this kind of uncongested network is an obvious "guideway" for region-wide express bus service. Compared with building a rail transit network of comparable scope, the infrastructure of the express toll network would be paid for not out of the very limited supply of federal transit New Starts grants, but via toll revenue initially supplemented by fuel-tax revenues. Public transit providers would be getting this huge, uncongested guideway at no cost to them.

Since no metro area has yet built—or even designed in detail—a complete express toll-lanes network, we do not know if such networks can be self-supporting from toll revenues over the long term. Once more individual express toll-lane projects have been in operation for a decade or more, it will be more feasible to estimate their long-term viability as fully toll-supported infrastructure.

A key hypothesis in the paper is that once much of the express toll network is in place, and people come to appreciate its benefits, over time they will understand that pricing works for expressways just as it works for electricity, water, natural gas, telephones, and movie theaters. To the extent that the unpriced lanes on the freeways remain congested, or become more congested over time as the metro area continues to grow, people will be more receptive than they are today to proposals for some form of pricing on the non-express lanes. If it is then proposed that the freeway with the most remaining congestion could be improved by adding a modest charge to drive on it during the most congested hours of the day, they might well consider that it could improve their individual travel, especially their daily commute.

In thinking this over, it's important to understand something that has only recently come to be appreciated by transport economists. *There is no single "correct" price for freeway lanes.* Detailed studies of people who commute in corridors where express toll lanes are an option find that few people use them every day, morning and afternoon. There is a small minority of well-off commuters for whom a peak price of $1 or more per mile, which actually exists during some afternoon hours on the 91 Express Lanes in Orange County and the I-95 Express Lanes in Miami, is no big deal to pay every day. But the large majority of motorists use express toll lanes only for specific trips that are very important, and worth paying a high price for. Those who choose this option are paying for two benefits, not just one. Yes, they pay for the time savings involved in using the uncongested express lane. But solid research shows that they are also paying for the reliability involved.[49] When you're in the congested regular lanes, your actual arrival time is something of a crapshoot, varying a lot from day to day. But in an express toll lane, your arrival time is much closer to the time when you need to be there—to catch a plane, to make a critical meeting on time, or to pick up a kid from day care before five dollar-a-minute late fees kick in.

So the suggestion is to implement a modest peak charge to use the regular lanes—something that a majority of commuters would feel comfortable paying if it meant that congestion was reduced somewhat and travel times were made more predictable for them. And for those at the margin between yes and no, the availability of fast and reliable express bus service on the express lanes network would be a far better alternative than most of the slow-moving transit available today. With a modest charge only at peak hours, those whose trips did not have to be made during those hours would be motivated to travel earlier or later in the day.

What about Paying for Reconstruction?

Paying for the widening of urban freeways by designating the new lanes as express toll lanes addresses the problem of widening, but it does not deal with the need to reconstruct the existing lanes. That problem is just as real for urban Interstates as it is for rural ones, and is especially needed for obsolete interchanges that are major bottlenecks for cars and trucks. In chapter 9, the premise for the rural Interstates was that developing a toll-financed reconstruction plan based on tolls that are true user fees (i.e., strictly limited to paying for the costs of the greatly improved highways, with rebates of fuel taxes for the miles driven on the replacement lanes) would lead people to accept that as the best, or least bad, way forward.

During the time period when states are in the midst of a several-decades-long program of rebuilding and modernizing their long-distance Interstates, they will also very likely be adding express toll lanes to their urban Interstates. As the revenue from fuel taxes gradually declines over time, leaving state DOTs strapped for funding to do more than basic maintenance, it will become evident that some urban Interstates are reaching the point where it is far wiser to reconstruct them than to just keep patching them. At that point, state DOTs should be able to point to their initial successes in reconstructing and widening *rural* Interstates with toll financing. This will allow them to propose a comparable several-decade program for their urban Interstates. In this case, too, it will be important to propose toll rates that distinguish between high-value trips at high toll rates on the growing express toll network, and all other trips that will use the reconstructed regular lanes at toll rates akin to those suggested in table 8. It will also be important to provide rebates of people's fuel taxes for all the miles they drive on newly tolled expressways.

The toll revenues in table 9 were based entirely on the peak / off-peak toll schedule from table 8. For small and medium-size urban areas, which may not need separate express toll networks, rates like those listed should suffice to cover freeway reconstruction and widening. The very large urban areas—like Chicago, Los Angeles, New York, San Francisco, and some others—will need express toll networks and their much higher toll

272   CHAPTER TEN

rates to generate enough additional revenue to reconstruct and expand their expressway networks.

The Role of Toll Concessions

In chapter 9 we saw that the private sector should be keenly interested in the business opportunity presented by reconstructing, modernizing, and then operating and maintaining long-distance rural Interstates. Those projects represent a low- to medium-risk kind of concession—far less risky than a brand-new toll road with no established traffic history, but still one with the usual construction risks of megaprojects. Would the private sector also be willing to take on the even larger megaprojects involved in reconstructing and modernizing urban expressways? We have several strong indications that the same kinds of companies would see the urban projects as solid business opportunities.

First, the highest-risk elements of a revamped urban expressway system would be the initial projects to add express toll lanes, and eventually express toll networks, to existing freeways. As this book is being written, long-term concessions have been awarded for 12 express toll lane projects, as shown in table 10. Nearly all of these are toll concessions, in which the concession company takes on not only the risks of construction cost overruns, late completion, and operation and maintenance, but also the risks of inadequate traffic and revenue. The latter risk is especially high on variably priced express toll lanes, since under current conditions they compete directly with the unpriced lanes right next to the express lanes. Yet the private sector is taking on those risks, due to these

TABLE 10. **Current US express toll lane concession projects**

Project	Location	Cost	Status
SR 91 Express Lanes	Orange County, CA	$130 million	Opened 1995
I-495 Beltway Express	Northern VA	$1.99 billion	Opened 2012
I-95 Express Lanes	Northern VA	$940 million	Opened 2014
I-595 Express Lanes	Fort Lauderdale, FL	$1.6 billion	Opened 2014
I-635 LBJ Express	Dallas, TX	$2.8 billion	Opened 2014–15
N. Tarrant Express 1 & 2	Fort Worth, TX	$2.05 billion	Opened 2015
US 36 Express Lanes	Denver, CO	$208 million	Opened 2016
N. Tarrant Express 3	Fort Worth, TX	$1.4 billion	Under construction
I-77 Express Lanes	Charlotte, NC	$655 million	Under construction
I-4 Express Lanes	Orlando, FL	$2.3 billion	Under construction
SR 288 Express Lanes	Houston, TX	$1.05 billion	Under construction
I-66 Express Lanes	Northern VA	$3.5 billion	Under construction

projects' longer-term revenue potential. Since the risks of reconstructing, operating, and maintaining the existing freeways with known traffic histories should be lower, it is reasonable to expect the private sector to be even more strongly attracted to those megaprojects—as well as to other megaprojects such as tunnels to fill in missing links in the existing freeway systems.

In the early days of reconstructing urban Interstates, before there is a political consensus on the need for per-mile tolls to finance such projects, there is an opportunity for what in chapter 6 were termed hybrid concession models, in which both tolls and availability payments play a role. Two examples can be found in Florida: I-595 in Fort Lauderdale and I-4 in Orlando. In both cases, the entire freeway needed reconstruction in addition to widening with the addition of express toll lanes. But the toll revenue from only the new lanes would likely not generate enough revenue to finance these megaprojects ($1.6 billion for I-595 and $2.3 billion for I-4). For these two projects the Florida DOT decided to do the tolling of the new express lanes itself, compensating the concession company via 35 and 40 years of availability payments, respectively. Both projects generated serious competition, indicating strong private-sector interest in this lower-risk concession model (because FDOT itself is taking the traffic and revenue risk).

That hybrid model is not generalizable to the $759 billion task of reconstructing and widening America's urban Interstates. Why? Because state governments are in no position to assume $759 billion in liabilities, given their very large unfunded pension liabilities as well as state debt limits. Therefore, just as with rural Interstate modernization, the vast majority of urban Interstate modernization will have to involve toll financing, and will therefore be carried out as toll concessions.

A second piece of evidence that the toll concession industry would be interested in reconstructing, modernizing, and operating urban expressways comes to us from overseas. As we saw in chapter 4, most or all of the urban expressways in Australia, Chile, and Spain have been developed as toll concession projects. Since most of these were greenfield projects— brand-new tolled expressways—they were higher-risk than the reconstruction projects needed to modernize America's urban expressways.

The overseas urban tollway experience also addresses the question of monopoly versus competition. A central-planning mentality would likely envision a metro area's tolled expressways as a single system, operated as a monopoly. Yet what we have seen in other countries are multiple concession companies developing and operating individual components of the network. To be sure, government has played an important role in ensuring common standards, not only for the physical infrastructure but also for the interoperable all-electronic tolling.

Santiago, Chile, is an excellent case in point. In the early 1990s, Santiago was plagued by high and increasing traffic congestion. It had only a small amount of freeway capacity. In 1993, the Ministry of Public Works launched a nationwide program to procure new infrastructure via concessions, with a Santiago tollway network as one of its top priorities. The project led to competitions for four initial tollways, with the first concessions awarded in 2000 and the first segments opening to traffic in 2003. All four tollways were in operation by 2006.[50] In line with standard global practice, these are pure toll concessions, with the companies taking on traffic and revenue risk and other risks parceled out between the ministry and the concessionaire, based on which party can best deal with the risk in question. Two additional concession projects added new links to the system in the late 2000s.

While these new tollways have certainly increased mobility for Santiago residents, they experience congestion during peak periods. The concession agreements permit a higher peak toll to be charged if congestion reaches a specified level, but that rate applies only for a preset period and at a preset markup from normal tolls.[51] This is a far cry from the dynamic, real-time market pricing that applies on nearly all US express toll lanes.

Chile has undergone several changes of government since the concession program was launched in 1993, but the program has continued with only minor changes. In 2014 the new Socialist government unveiled a new $9.9 billion infrastructure program that includes new concessions for airports and toll roads. Two of the biggest components are for two more additions to the Santiago tollway network: the $1.98 billion Costanera Central in mid-Santiago, and a $726 million project to complete the Vespucio Oriente ring road, joining up with a $1.3 billion tunnel already under construction there.[52]

The ministry established the basic specifications for the electronic toll system; each concession agreement requires the concessionaire to participate in the interoperable Santiago toll system, and to provide transponders to its customers at no charge. The business model includes seven basic features:

- Any customer can open an account with any concessionaire and receive a free transponder for each owned vehicle.

- All contracts grant the customer the right to use any toll road in the network, and the obligation to pay invoices issued by any concessionaire.
- Each concessionaire sends customer account details to a government-sponsored customer database, which could be contracted out to a commercial firm.
- Each concessionaire can retrieve from that database information regarding customer accounts opened with other concessionaires.
- There are no roaming fees or any other kinds of fees between the concessionaires.
- Each concessionaire directly invoices a transponder user for the use of its toll road, regardless of who has issued the user's transponder.
- Each concessionaire bears its own user risks, including those of unpaid invoices.[53]

This is only one possible model for interoperability. Under America's E-ZPass system, whose members include nearly all the toll roads and bridges in the Northeast and Midwest, interoperability is structured so that a customer has a single toll account with the toll operator that has issued his or her transponder, and receives a single bill or account statement. This is analogous to the credit card systems operated by Master-Card, Visa, American Express, and others. You can use your Amex card at any participating merchant in any state and receive a single monthly bill. That is the direction in which electronic tolling interoperability is heading in the United States.

New technologies that may be developed for comprehensive mileage-based user fees may go beyond today's transponder/gantry system and make use of multifunction on-vehicle devices or smartphone apps. Bern Grush and Gabriel Roth explored some of these options in a paper presented at the 2013 annual meeting of the Transportation Research Board.[54]

In this chapter we have seen that today's sparse network of very high-capacity, chronically congested urban freeways can be reinvented to provide less congested and more reliable service for cars, buses, and trucks. This network also can and should be supplemented by an improved grid of arterials, in the spirit of the original vision for lower-impact express-ways throughout urban areas. As was the case with the long-distance Interstates discussed in chapter 9, per-mile charging is a critically important change that will make it possible to finance the revamping of the urban expressway system. Such variable charges can be a powerful tool for reducing congestion, and for opening up uncongested arteries throughout the urbanized area.

The closing chapter of this book will pull together all the pieces of this new vision for America's highways. It will also look at various trends in both government and transportation that suggest that the time is ripe for changing from the 20th-century highway paradigm to the 21st-century vision outlined in this book. But first we need to pause and consider several factors that have led some to argue that highways will be less and less relevant as we move further into the 21st century. That's the subject of chapter 11.

CHAPTER ELEVEN

Challenges to the New Vision for US Highways

I n this chapter, we will examine challenges to the highway future sketched out in this book. Does it really make sense to plan for a future in which highways will still be key transportation arteries? What about the impact of the millennial generation, whose members are said to shun cars and driving? Will the advent of autonomous vehicles (AVs) radically change how we get around? Will AVs enable two or three times as many vehicles to use our highways without congestion, thereby making it unnecessary to increase highway capacity? What about the threat of global climate change? Will government policies to greatly reduce the use of petroleum mean a shrinking role for cars, trucks, and highways? And doesn't a vision of revamped urban expressways conflict with current trends toward "smart growth"—reshaping urban areas to have much higher density, far less urban sprawl, and greatly increased use of alternatives to driving? These are all real issues that deserve a careful assessment.

Millennials and Driving

You have probably read a number of articles about how different millennials are from previous generations. Definitions of this generation vary, with the most common one consisting of those born between 1982 and 2004,[1] but others include those born as early as 1976. Studies cited below use varying definitions of millennials. Many popular articles tell us that, unlike baby boomers and Generation X, millennials do not rush to obtain driver's licenses as soon as they reach legal driving age. They have lower rates of auto ownership than previous generations, and they tend to live in or near city centers, getting around mostly by walking, bicycling, and using public transit. They also tend to be renters rather than homeowners. At least that is the mass-media portrayal.

This description has penetrated far enough into American culture since the Great Recession to be influencing transportation planning. Since the millennial generation is larger than even the baby boom generation, if this picture of the millennials' travel and housing behavior is correct, it implies that traditional highway planning, which rests on long-established methods of forecasting the growth of vehicular travel, will need to be rethought. Projections of vehicle miles of travel, such as those relied on in chapters 9 and 10, would have to be revised downward. In fact, during the Great Recession, the long post–World War II upward trend in total driving (vehicle-miles of travel, or VMT) reversed and declined somewhat below its 2007 peak. Driving-miles per person (VMT per capita) appeared to have reached a plateau several years earlier, and declined during the Great Recession.

The Public Interest Research Group (PIRG), a progressive, Nader-inspired organization that we met in chapter 7, released a major report in 2013 on changing trends in mobility.[2] The report attributed these changes to different attitudes and behavior among people between the ages of 16 and 24, its definition of the millennial generation. Citing limited data, the report portrayed this generation as not very interested in getting driver's licenses or living in the suburbs, as wanting to live downtown, and as preferring to get around by walking, bicycling, and using public transit. By making a number of assumptions, the PIRG report projected future VMT through 2040 at drastically lower levels than projections from nearly all transportation agencies.

The commuting expert Alan Pisarski questioned this thesis.[3] He cited a 2010 Pew Center study that found that 37 percent of young respondents were either out of work or underemployed. He also cited figures from the National Highway Transportation Survey showing that annual VMT per capita differs dramatically by employment status. For people ages 16 to 24, employed males drove 12,000 miles in 2009, compared with about 6,000 miles for unemployed males of that age group. He also noted that in the last two decades nearly all states have enacted "graduated licensing" schemes that restrict driving by those 16 to 18 years of age. Yet, despite this obstacle, from 2001 to 2009 the fraction of those under the age of 19 with driver's licenses remained essentially constant.

Pisarski's claim was that what PIRG and others portrayed as fundamental changes in attitudes and values were mostly temporary negative impacts from the Great Recession. Not only were numerous millennials without jobs, but their parents were buying fewer new cars and hence not passing along their old ones to their offspring. Derek Thompson assembled data on millennials in 2013, finding that the number of people between the ages of 15 and 34(!) who were living with their parents had soared from 0.5 million in 2008 to nearly 2 million in 2011.[4] Fewer young people than usual were getting married, having children, or buying homes, and this wsas leading to what Thompson described as "stagnation" in household formation since 2007.

As for the alleged shift of millennials and others from driving to walking, biking, and public transit, there was very little evidence in the data. David Price and Don Pickrell of the US DOT's Volpe Center in Cambridge, Massachusetts, compared reductions in driving during the Great Recession to increases in use of alternative modes of transportation.[5] They found that increased use of public transit accounted for only 1 percent of the decrease in automobile travel, with bicycle and walking trips accounting for only a few percent more. These findings were reinforced in a paper by several researchers published in the *Journal of the American Planning Association* in 2017.[6] They found that between 2004 and 2013, highway passenger miles of travel decreased by 561 million, but public transit passenger miles of travel increased by only 9.6 million, indicating little evidence that most of the reduced driving trips had been replaced by public transit trips. Likewise, there were only very small changes in the amount of trips made via bicycle or walking.

What about the choice of where to live? The demographer Wendell Cox compared US Census data for 2000 and 2010, finding that people between the ages of 20 and 29 in 2010 were less inclined toward urban living than their predecessors.[7] In 2000, 19 percent of people then in this age group lived in the core municipalities of major urban areas, but this decreased to 13 percent in 2010. Cox also compared commuting data for people of the ages 16 to 24, using data from the US Census Bureau's American Community Survey (ACS) for 2000 and 2011. The results are shown in table 11. These trends mirror overall national trends in commuting, which show slight increases in drive-alone commuting, a long-term decline in carpooling, and only modest changes in use of public transit, biking, and walking.

But facts did not seem to discourage those with a preconceived story to tell. *Fortune* magazine's Leigh Gallagher got extensive media coverage

TABLE 11. **Change in millennials' commuting modes, 2000–2011**

Commuting mode	ACS 2000	ACS 2011
Drive alone	66.9%	69.7%
Car pool or van pool	17.4%	12.6%
Public transit	5.4%	5.8%
Other (bike, walk, etc.)	8.9%	9.3%
Work at home	1.4%	2.6%

for her 2013 book proclaiming the death of suburbs.[8] According to Gallagher, it was not just millennials who hated the suburbs; it was also empty-nest baby boomers. Both groups were forsaking suburbia for the central city where they could walk, bike, and use public transit to get around, she maintained. What Gallagher had actually identified was a temporary glut of new housing on the fringes of suburbia, lacking buyers due to the Great Recession. When the urban geographer Joel Kotkin and demographer Cox reviewed the data on baby boomers' migration patterns, they found just the opposite of what Gallagher claimed. Using census data for the 51 largest metro areas, and comparing 2010 with 2000, they found net out-migration of boomers from most metro-area core cities, with roughly a million fewer boomers in 2010 within five miles of the centers of the 51 largest metro areas than had been the case a decade earlier.[9] Overall, the share of boomers living in core cities declined by 10 percent over that decade.

As the economic recovery took hold, new data on millennials' housing preferences became available. A 2014 survey for John Burns Real Estate Consulting obtained the housing preference views of a million Americans, sorted by generation.[10] Among millennials, only 16 percent preferred to live in an urban core, while 55 percent preferred an inner suburb, and the remainder preferred either an outer suburb or an exurban location. Demographer Cox analyzed census data on housing trends between 2000 and 2010.[11] For millennials (here defined as people between the ages of 20 and 29), the number living in urban cores did increase slightly from 4.3 million to 4.6 million during that decade. But because of their rising total numbers, the *fraction* of millennials in urban cores decreased from 20.2 percent in 2000 to 19.3 percent in 2010. The biggest change over that decade was in newer, further-out suburbs, which went from housing 20.6 percent of millennials in 2000 to 24.4 percent in 2010. And another 14.3 percent of them in 2010 even resided in exurban areas.

As the recovery continued, millennials turned to car-buying. A *Bloomberg News* story in spring 2015 found that millennials accounted for 27 percent of US new car sales in 2014, up from just 18 percent in 2010.[12] Reporter Jing Cao also noted that as the recovery took hold, the employment rate for people of the ages 25 to 34 had reached 76.8 percent by March 2015, the highest rate since 2008. A 2014 global survey report by the accounting firm Deloitte found that 80 percent of US millennials planned to purchase a vehicle within the next five years (as compared with 83 percent of other generations).[13] In 2015, J. D. Power reported that millennials were the fastest-growing category of car buyers.[14] And a 2016 study of car-buying intentions by Bankrate.com found that 24 percent of millennials were planning to buy a car: a higher percentage than in any other demographic group.[15] Early in 2017, data for 2016 from J. D. Power found that millennials had actually purchased 29 percent of all new cars.[16]

So the real question boils down to this: Do the speculations about millennials' driving and housing behavior reflect fundamental changes in attitudes and preferences, as PIRG and others alleged? Or do they reflect temporary consequences of the millennials' age and employment status, and the disparate impact of the Great Recession? This question was addressed in some detail in a 2015 PhD dissertation from the UCLA School of Urban Planning. Kelcie Mechelle Ralph analyzed years of detailed travel data and macroeconomic trends.[17] Her conclusion was that recent changes in young adult travel demand and housing choices are not statistically significant. The reported reduction in driving by millennials between 2000 and 2010 can be explained primarily by the steep fall-off in travel by the *segment* of this population that was not employed. "It's all about whether you're working or not working," she told *Public Works Financing*. "We're [now] back to normal historical patterns."[18]

The urban planner Noreen McDonald reached similar conclusions in a 2015 article in the *Journal of the American Planning Association*.[19] She found that millennials are indeed traveling somewhat less than previous generations at this point in their lives, but this applies to all modes of travel, not just cars. To the extent that the millennials are driving less, it is because they do not have jobs.

Similar conclusions were reached by UCLA analysts in research first published in 2012 and further refined since then.[20] In an early 2017 webinar, UCLA's Evelyn Blumenberg and Brian Taylor summed up their half-decade of research into four principal findings:

1. Through 2009 (and the recession) there was a significant decline in travel among youth.
2. The decline was largely explained by the downturn in the economy.
3. Youth and others travel fewer miles in dense urban areas, but those areas comprise less than 5 percent of all US neighborhoods.
4. Those young adults who don't drive much increased by about 50 percent between 1995 and 2009, but others of that generation are highly mobile.

Overall, they concluded, it is premature to argue that driving among youth is passé, or that recent trends in millennial behavior will persist.[21]

Those findings were further reinforced by a 2015 survey on Americans' housing and travel preferences, conducted by Associated Press-GfK.[22] The AP reporters summarized the findings thus: "Contrary to the widely held notion that the millennial generation is flocking to cities and giving up their cars, younger people are not significantly more or less likely than older people to prefer urban living with a shorter commute and access to public transport." The article's headline stressed the finding that a slight majority of all age groups favored suburban or rural living.

Millennials are now participating in the revived growth in VMT. Every month the Federal Highway Administration releases its "Traffic Volume Trends," reporting on changes in VMT. Total VMT peaked at 3.02 trillion miles in 2007 and then slightly declined, bottoming out at 2.95 trillion miles in 2010. Since then, as the economy has recovered, VMT has resumed an upward trend. The increase was slow at first, but VMT reached 3.095 trillion in 2015. The growth during 2016 increased by 2.9 percent nationwide, with the FHWA reporting the year's total at 3.2 trillion.[23]

Correspondingly, urban traffic congestion reached new highs in 2014, as measured by the Urban Mobility Scorecard produced by the Texas A&M Transportation Institute and INRIX.[24] Table 12 is a summary of key national congestion indicators for 1982 (the first year these data were collected), the initial recession year 2007, and post-recession 2014. With the renewed growth in VMT, congestion is now at all-time high levels.

Alas, despite solid data refuting the idea that Americans are retreating from suburbs and from driving, there is a time lag in book publishing. Books researched during the Great Recession years have only recently got into print, building their arguments on the temporary travel changes caused by that recession. The 2014 e-book *Curbing Cars: America's Independence from the Auto Industry* was written by Micheline Maynard, former Detroit bureau chief of the *New York Times*. It cites a "clear trend that driving is dropping" and quotes PIRG's Phineas Baxandall as saying,

TABLE 12. **Congested commutes, post-recession**

Measure	1982	2007	2014
Travel time index	1.09	1.21	1.22
Average delay per commuter, in hours per year	18	42	42
Total delay, in billions of hours	1.8	6.6	6.9
Wasted fuel, in billions of gallons	0.5	2.8	3.1
Total cost of time and fuel wasted, in billions of dollars	$42	$154	$160

"We shouldn't assume a return to past travel habits when Americans are persistently driving less and using other forms of transportation." A similar message was conveyed by New York-based Sam Schwartz, a former chief engineer of the New York City Transportation Department, whose book claims that "a quiet revolution is under way. Americans drive fewer miles every year, preferring instead public transport or a move back into the heart of downtown."[25]

But recent data tell us otherwise. The idea that we have witnessed a fundamental move away from driving and suburban living, by millennials or other generations, has little support in the data,. And what had appeared to be a plateau and even a decline in VMT per capita has reversed since 2014, reaching 10,065 miles per capita in 2016, just a bit less than the previous high of 10,117 reached in 2014. Whether this signals a longer-term uptrend in per-capita driving remains to be seen. But what does seem likely is that the historic upward trend of total VMT has returned. This reflects well on the conservative projections of car and truck VMT growth rates used in the analyses in chapters 9 and 10 of this book. Personal VMT growth will likely reflect overall population growth, while truck VMT will likely be correlated with economic growth measured by GDP. Consequently, we very much need to modernize not only our highways but the institutional framework in which they will exist.

Autonomous Vehicles

One of the hottest issues in surface transportation today is autonomous vehicles (AVs), popularly referred to as self-driving cars. Thanks in part to the pioneering work of Google, all the major automobile companies are now working on AVs, and the popular media are full of visions of a radically different future.

In the mass-media version of this future, within a decade or two AVs will dominate the vehicle fleet because they will remove the drudgery of driving (both long-distance and in congested commuting) and because they will be much safer than ordinary cars, with automated systems to avoid impending collisions. And because an AV could be summoned when a driver needs it, people would no longer need to buy and own cars; they could simply pay for transportation on demand, as a service, using "robo-taxis" without human drivers. There will still need to be streets and highways for the AVs to operate on, of course; but thanks to automation, the AVs could safely travel much closer together. According to some estimates, this would mean that existing highways could handle two or three times more vehicles than they do today, without congestion.

If this vision is more or less realistic, it could significantly alter projections of future highway capacity needs, like those discussed in chapters 9 and 10—depending on how soon AVs could actually be implemented. They would not reduce the need to reconstruct aging bridges and highways, but they could reduce the need for widening them. They would also radically disrupt urban public transit by enabling personalized door-to-door transportation without requring people to go to a transit stop and wait for the bus or train to show up.

But is this AV future realistic? And if it is, how many decades away is it? Serious transportation researchers are looking into all aspects of a possible AV future, and few of them share the mass media version summarized above.

We need to begin this discussion with some basics. First, researchers recognize five different levels of vehicle automation, as defined by the Society of Automotive Engineers. They are as follows:

- level 1: driver assistance (adaptive cruise control or lane-keeping assistance)
- level 2: partial automation (multiple driver-assistance features)
- level 3: conditional automation (self-driving capacity that requires the driver to take control in certain situations)
- level 4: high automation (full self-driving capacity on some types of roads and in some weather conditions)
- level 5: full automation (full self-driving capacity on all types of roads and weather conditions, with no driver controls provided or needed).

Many new cars today are at level 1, and a few high-end cars have several driver-assists such as lane-keeping and emergency braking (level 2).

Human-factors researchers are dubious about level 3, partly on the basis of their analysis of aircraft pilots failing to maintain "situational awareness" while in autopilot mode, such that they are unable to resume control and take proper actions quickly enough. Some researchers therefore argue that it might be wiser and safer to skip level 3 altogether—a position Ford Motor Company has publicly taken. Hence, what AV researchers mean by automated vehicles is level 4 or level 5.

The major societal changes portrayed in popular media—such as fully automated cars becoming ubiquitous within the next 10 years, slashing accident and death rates and leading to major changes in urban land use—are rejected by serious researchers as unrealistic. This is due partly to a number of technical problems in vehicle automation that are a long way from being solved, uncertainty about how auto insurance will be handled, the length of time it takes to replace the entire vehicle fleet (typically about 20 years), and the huge unknown of what fraction of autonomous vehicles (AVs) will be owned by individuals and what fraction will exist as various forms of on-demand robo-taxis—"mobility as a service." The impact of AVs on the amount and type of roadway infrastructure needed in the future depends on all of these factors.

One thoughtful AV policy analyst is Bern Grush, an entrepreneur and researcher based in Toronto. In a 2016 report for the Residential and Civil Construction Alliance of Ontario, Grush summarized his findings as follows:

> Since the premature forecast of peak car in 2008 and now the hype surrounding the automated vehicle, we are often told that we have enough road capacity; that shared robotic taxis will optimize our trips, reduce congestion, and largely eliminate the need for parking. This advice implies we need wait only a few short years to experience relief from our current infrastructure problems given by decades of underinvestment in transportation infrastructure. This is wishful thinking. Vehicle automation will give rise to two different emerging markets: semi-automated vehicles for household consumption [level 4] and fully automated vehicles for public service such as robo-taxi and robo-transit. These two vehicle types will develop in parallel to serve different social markets. They will compete for both riders and infrastructure.[26]

Technology Challenges

Achieving level 4 or 5 automation is still very much a work in progress. Among the points made by researchers are the following:

- Automation is inherently "brittle" and subject to failures.
- Hence, at least for a long time from now, a driver must be able to take over on short notice (level 3).
- We don't really know how to provide for such transitions, and our experience with cockpit automation in aircraft is troubling.
- There are ambiguous situations, where we may not want the automation to make the decisions.[27]

In a cautionary article in *MIT Technology Review*, Will Knight focused on human factors that make full automation "a distant destination."[28] He discussed MIT researcher Bryan Reimer's analogy with increasingly automated aircraft cockpits, in which pilots have sometimes become so accustomed to letting the automation fly the plane that they have difficulty responding quickly and properly when something goes wrong. He also cited cognitive scientist Don Norman's concern that fully automated systems with no driver override can lead to unsafe maneuvers, such as the car speeding up when moving into a freeway exit ramp if there is no car immediately ahead of it.

There are at least three different ways in which AVs could be designed to navigate. Google's method relies primarily on detailed maps of all streets and highways, which must be updated essentially in real time in order to account for construction zones, accidents, water main breaks, and so on. That map guidance is supplemented, of course, by sensors on the vehicle that spot the actions of other vehicles, road signs, pedestrians, and obstacles in the road. A second model relies mostly on detailed rules of behavior in response to real-time inputs from sensing devices about the roadway, other vehicles, and obstacles. This approach is typified by the system developed by Mobileye, and depends less on maps, relying primarily on algorithms that aim to interpret real-time video data the way a driver does.[29] A third model would feature the equivalent of an air traffic control system for all roadways, in which that control system communicates in real time with fleets of fully autonomous vehicles, using two-way communications. This model is assumed by those focusing on fleets of robo-taxis. Any researcher seeking to simulate the performance of a large roadway system must make assumptions about which model of automation would be employed, and there seems to be no consensus yet on which model is most feasible, cost-effective, and politically acceptable.

Then there is the issue of how reliable the automation must be. Steven Shladover of UC Berkeley has pointed out that there is one fatal-crash injury for every 3.3 million hours of vehicle operation today. So, in order for an AV to be at least as safe as that, the automation system's "mean time between failure" (an engineering statistic measuring a system's reliability) must be at least that high.[30] Shaldover told *Thinking Highways* that the automation system "is a consumer product that is software-intensive. It has to operate under incredibly complicated and diverse conditions. This far exceeds the complexity of what a laptop computer or a smartphone needs to do, but can you imagine a laptop or a mobile phone that can go 3 million hours without crashing?"[31] That works out to about once every 342 years.

Due to such problems, for the foreseeable future there will very likely be driver controls (steering wheel and pedals) and some way to very quickly hand back control to the driver under certain circumstances (i.e., level 3). But we know from human-systems-engineering research that automated systems can lead to boredom, which encourages distraction. So, at the very time when the human must quickly resume control, "the operator may be unaware of the state of the vehicle . . . and may not be able to respond quickly and appropriately" to avoid an accident.[32] Several recent airliner crashes occurred when pilots relied too heavily on automation and failed to respond quickly and appropriately when conditions suddenly changed. The researchers M. L. Cummings of Duke University and Jason Ryan of MIT conclude that the design of vehicle automation must ensure that the driver understands the system's limitations and maintains full awareness of the system's state in real time. That is completely at odds with the mass-media image of people holding business meetings or playing computer games while the vehicle drives itself. And, as noted earlier, these difficulties have led some AV researchers, such as Princeton University's Alain Kornhauser, to argue against implementing level 3 at all.

Among the most difficult questions are whether or when to let the automation make decisions in ambiguous situations. As of now, humans are much better than machines at interpreting a traffic cop's gesture at a construction zone, or at distinguishing between harmless debris in the road and an object that the vehicle must swerve to avoid. Cummings and Ryan point out that "avoiding a car calmly changing lanes is entirely different from anticipating the actions of a reckless and irrational driver." Shladover is concerned about "ethically ambiguous situations," such as letting the automation make the decision about whether to swerve to avoid a possibly fatal accident, such as when pedestrians are on one side and an oncoming car is on the other. Cummings and Ryan suggest that perhaps "machines should not be allowed to take the lives of humans under any circumstances, which is similar to one of the three laws of robotics drawn up by [science fiction] author Isaac Asimov."

More likely than an all-AV future within the next few decades is a continual increase in driver-assist tools such as adaptive cruise control, lane-keeping, and automatic braking to avoid crashing into a vehicle or object ahead. This is the scenario Bern Grush projected in his report for the province of Ontario. We may also see level 4 cars operating without driver interaction in specialized lanes on expressways and within retirement communities, which are far more constrained environments than busy and unpredictable city streets. Automated trucks, including trucks that can operate very close together in "platoons," so as to reduce fuel consumption by lowering air drag, would be far more likely to gain acceptance if they were to operate in dedicated truck lanes (discussed in chapter 9) than in regular highway lanes.

Shared versus Owned AVs

Even if the automation dilemmas discussed above are eventually resolved to make possible vehicles without any driver controls, the mass-media vision of cars being summoned on demand, making ownership irrelevant, is unlikely to emerge over the next several decades, if at all. Assuming that people still work in large numbers in specific locations—whether in downtowns, office parks, or factory complexes—most of them will work standard daylight hours, meaning there will still be morning and evening rush hours. The idea that nearly everyone in the office park could summon a roving AV to come pick them up all within the same 30 to 45 minutes, with little or no waiting time, simply does not work mathematically. A team of MIT and Stanford researchers simulated a fleet of "robo-taxis" as a replacement for all modes of personal vehicle travel in Singapore, using actual travel patterns and the current road network.[33] They found that a fleet of 250,000 robo-taxis would do the job, but with a maximum wait time of *30 minutes* for people to be picked up. The maximum wait time for your own personal vehicle is the time it takes you to walk to where it is parked.

Some initial computer modeling scenarios have generated unexpected consequences. Most such models assume that a very large fleet of AVs would be in motion most of the day, rather than being parked most of the time. That leads to large projected land-use savings due to the elimination of most urban parking lots and parking structures. In a simulation of on-demand AVs replacing personal cars for just 5 percent of daily trips in Austin, Texas, the researchers found that "instead of [each AV] driving 100,000 miles over 10 years [like today's cars], they're [each] driving 100,000 miles every year."[34] If the entire vehicle fleet (instead of just 5 percent) were replaced by on-demand AVs, the impact on total urban-area VMT could be much larger.

It is unclear what effect this kind of on-demand "mobility as a service" would have on total VMT, but this simulation suggests the potential of larger total VMT than many people would have expected. That would also lead to more wear and tear on streets and highways than in naive AV visions, and possibly to greater vehicle emissions as well. The policy researchers Bern Grush and John Niles point out that results from such urban simulations "cannot be reasonably extrapolated to suburbs and rural areas, or [to] work/service vehicles," and that there is no evidence that all or most humans will prefer to give up vehicle ownership.[35]

In a 2017 article, Grush and co-author Blair Schlecter (who favor shared rather than owned AVs) discuss the many categories of people who will likely prefer to own an AV rather than using a shared, on-call AV.[36] These include

- travelers with non-routine needs, including those with children;
- travelers who are elderly or disabled;
- retiring baby boomers;
- travelers who smoke;
- those concerned about communicable disease; and
- those requiring carrying and storage capacity.

The think tank Resources for the Future released a discussion paper in 2016 reporting on a 1,200-person survey on AVs. On average, households indicated a willingness to pay $3,500 extra to purchase a vehicle with partial automation, and $4,500 for one with full automation. But many were not interested at all. Overall, participants "split approximately equally between high, modest, and no demand" for AVs.[37] The Texas A&M Transportation Institute carried out a similar survey of residents of Austin. They found that 52 percent of current auto commuters were not likely to opt for an AV, while 57 percent of those who currently walk, bike, or use public transit expressed positive interest. And of those who favored an AV, 59 percent preferred to own it.[38] Morgan Stanley did an international study of the potential market penetration of shared-use vehicles, in the context of the emergence of shared-use AVs. Their *global* estimate was that shared-vehicle use would increase from 5 percent today to 25 percent by 2030—but the largest increases would be in developing countries where conventional vehicle ownership is low; not in the United States or Europe. The shared-mobility market share for the United States was projected at just 7 percent by 2030.[39]

Urban planners who favor the "mobility as a service" paradigm have adopted the term "CAVs," meaning "connected automated vehicles." This term has spread to mass-media articles, leading people to think that communication—either between vehicles (V2V) or between the vehicle and the roadway infrastructure (V2I)—is essential to an automated vehicle future. V2V communication is important for truck platooning, in which the trucks following the leader at close spacing must have real-time communications linking their automation systems. To achieve level 4 automation for personal vehicles, most AV researchers see little or no need for such "connectivity." But this communications capability would be essential for a company or agency managing a large fleet of roving robo-taxis (level 5).

Greater or Fewer Vehicle Miles of Travel?

Until recently, the AV research community had reached no consensus about whether the realization of an AV future would increase or decrease the total amount of VMT. But as of 2017, the majority view is that under most plausible scenarios of how an AV future will evolve, there will be increased VMT.

In addition to the impact of urban level 5 robo-taxis circulating most of the day rather than being parked, many researchers think that if people no longer have to actively drive their level 4 vehicles, many will choose to live farther from their workplace, increasing their average daily commuting distance. At the third annual Automated Vehicles Symposium, cosponsored by the Transportation Research Board, several transportation modelers from metropolitan planning organizations predicted that AVs would increase annual VMT by between 5 and 20 percent, with freeway VMT increasing by 30 percent.[40] At the fifth such conference, UC Berkeley researcher Joan Walker provided an overview of various studies on the impact of AVs on VMT. One set of studies showed increases of between 4 and 15 percent, assuming that individuals in owned AVs multitask while traveling in them. Studies that focused on a shared-vehicle context estimated 8 to 10 percent greater VMT because the shared vehicles would be in motion most of the day, with this effect largely offsetting the reduction in individual miles driven. As noted in chapter 9, a study by consulting firm KPMG on the impact of level 5 AVs on the mobility of those too young, old, or disabled to drive, estimated that VMT in the United States would grow to five trillion per year by 2050, compared with three trillion today.[41]

Researchers increasingly see the VMT outcome as depending considerably on what fraction of AVs end up being individually owned. Grush and Niles expect that if large numbers of people choose to own AVs, that will expand the vehicle fleet to those not currently able to drive—young, old, and disabled people. On the other hand, if the on-demand model predominates, there could be a significant reduction in the overall vehicle fleet.[42] But these are just speculations; no one can reliably predict how people will behave with new technologies decades from now.

Most research to date on the impact of AVs on VMT has focused on urban areas. But there are also potential impacts on intercity highway VMT. In a recent conference presentation, Alan Pisarski and Richard Mudge suggested that both freight and passenger travel would likely increase once level 4 vehicles were on the market.[43] An academic paper in 2015 estimated that for trips of less than 500 miles, AVs would attract trips from both airlines and conventional personal vehicles.[44] For passenger travel, the ability to be productive while traveling will affect people's trade-offs between using a motor vehicle and opting for an intercity bus, train, or airline flight, especially for trips of up to several hundred miles. The implications for freight are potentially even larger. If the driver of a long-haul truck is needed only for the non-Interstate portions of the trip (referred to as the first mile and the last mile), that will significantly reduce the operating cost for truck freight, which should increase its volume as compared with current projections. Thus, the AV future implies greater intercity VMT than in conventional forecasts.

What Impact Will AVs Have on Urban Form?

There have been a number of academic exercises in modeling a simulated urban future based on AVs and mobility as a service. The OECD's International Transport Forum has done a series of these exercises using Lisbon, Portugal, as the site of its modeling. The 2016 simulation was announced in its newsletter as having demonstrated that replacing all conventional car and bus trips in Lisbon with automatically dispatched door-to-door services "would provide the same level of mobility to citizens using only 3% of the current number of vehicles," and would also "cut emissions by one-third, and on-street parking would become superfluous."[45]

A newer version in 2017 expanded the scope to the entire Lisbon metro area. The study report spelled out the many assumptions on which the above outcomes depended. The researchers used detailed data on the Lisbon metro area's current daily travel, and assumed that all cars and buses were replaced with shared robotaxis and AV minibuses. Although per-vehicle VMT was increased tenfold, total VMT was reduced by more than one-third, and there was significant reduction in CO_2 emissions. But what did it take to achieve these outcomes? Privately owned cars would be banned. A centralized dispatch system would assign individuals to vehicles. The study asserted that shared robotaxi rides provided the "same level of mobility" as car owners now have, but that assertion ignores (1) the extra time needed to pick up and drop off other passengers, and (2) many people's desire to make stops to or from work to run errands. A similar but US-focused study by the Boston Consulting Group estimated that by 2030, up to 25 percent of VMT in the United States could be handled in urban areas by self-driving electric vehicles operated in shared fleets.[46] The study assumed that level 5 robo-taxis would be in widespread use by then—something that hardly any serious AV researchers think is likely.

The idea that AVs can or will transform urban areas relies on far more than market forces, as the Lisbon study made clear. In a guide for government agencies produced by the consulting firm Parsons Brinckerhoff, its author presents two possible scenarios—a "driverless nightmare" in which individually owned AVs enable people to live in the exurbs and travel longer distances while working productively en route, and a "driverless utopia" of compact smart-growth urban areas. Leaving no doubt as to her preference, the author writes, "This guide assumes that local, regional, and state governments will want to take actions that encourage moving toward the 'driverless utopia' standard."[47]

Timing of the AV Transition

To sum up, for the foreseeable future the mass-media vision of totally driverless cars replacing all personal vehicles seems unlikely, especially over the next several decades. The more likely scenario for this time frame is that increasingly more advanced driver-assist features will be added to new vehicles. These features will increase highway safety and permit vehicles to operate somewhat closer together, increasing the throughput of expressways to some degree—but they will not permit a doubling or tripling of vehicle volume on existing highways.

Once level 4 (highly autonomous) technology is perfected and gains approval from safety regulators and insurance companies—something projected by UC Berkeley's Shladover as likely to happen in the 2030s[48]—it will take about two more decades for most or all non-AV vehicles to be replaced by highly autonomous ones (since complete fleet turnover typically takes about 20 years). That means it will likely be more than 30 to 40 years from now until anything like the mass-media vision of a driverless future could arrive. Even in that scenario, most transportation researchers expect the impact to be an increase, not a decrease, in VMT.

Therefore, it is likely that the kinds of highway capacity additions discussed in chapters 9 and 10 will still be needed over the next several decades, to cope with increased personal and freight traffic due to population growth and a growing economy. However, it is also conceivable that when the truly driverless vision eventually comes to pass, we might find ourselves with excess highway capacity. If that comes about, who should bear the risk of dealing with possibly unneeded highway infrastructure? If we continue with the 20th-century model, with all highways owned and operated by government, then it is taxpayers who will bear those risks. But if we shift to the network utility model of highway companies, as proposed in this book, those risks will be shifted to investors in the highway companies. This approach will give us the improved highways that we need for the next 30-plus years, without sticking taxpayers with the possible burden of coping with eventual excess highway capacity.

Global Climate Change

How will policies aimed at reducing greenhouse gas emissions affect the future of highways? Many environmental groups and urban planners argue that government policy must dramatically reduce the use of motor vehicles, since air, land, and sea transportation powered by petroleum-based fuels is responsible for about one-third of all human-caused greenhouse gas emissions. Gasoline, diesel fuel, and jet fuel are all derived from petroleum, and emissions of CO_2 are directly proportional to fuel use. But the alternative

to reducing use of cars, trucks, trains, and airplanes is to significantly reduce the CO_2 output of these vehicles.

There is no question that the earth is in a long-term warming cycle that
will produce both negative and positive effects over the next century.[49] It
is also true that the energy density of petroleum-based fuel is far greater
than that of any other known vehicular power source, which is why in the
20th century those fuels displaced first electricity in automobiles and then
steam power in railroads, and why they continue to be the only currently
viable source for aircraft propulsion.

The industries that produce aircraft, railroad locomotives, trucks, and
automobiles are all investing considerable sums researching new fuels,
new types of engines, and other ways of reducing energy consumption
in order to reduce both the cost of fuel and the carbon footprint of these
vitally important modes of transportation. But since climate change is a
global problem, unilateral action by the United States, or even by the
United States and Europe, cannot solve the problem. China already emits
twice the greenhouse gases per year as the United States does, and that is
with a far lower, though rapidly increasing, amount of vehicle ownership
and electricity use. Any serious effort to reduce the carbon footprint of
transportation will have to be global to be effective.

Looking more narrowly at the future of cars, trucks, and highways in
this country, we need to consider the benefits provided by cars, trucks,
and highways in addition to the costs and feasibility of reducing transportation's carbon footprint. Those who downplay the benefits of the highway
system advocate US government policy aimed at doing the following:

1. shifting a large fraction of urban auto trips to public transit,
2. shifting a large fraction of intercity highway trips to passenger rail, and
3. shifting a large fraction of freight from trucks to freight railroads.

Making a serious dent in transportation's carbon footprint via those policies would be very difficult. Currently, some 86 percent of US commuting trips are by car, mostly in single-occupant vehicles but also in some
carpooling. Trends over the last three decades show carpooling in a long
decline and single-occupant commuting in a continued modest increase.
This is the case despite a large-scale federal and state investment in adding carpool lanes to freeways and devoting 20 percent of federal Highway Trust Fund monies to public transit. Only about 5 percent of daily
commuting is by public transit, overall—though in six legacy-transit cities

TABLE 13. **US commuting mode share, 2015 vs. 2006**

Mode	ACS 2006	ACS 2015
Drive alone	76.0%	76.6%
Car pool or van pool	10.7%	9.0%
Public transit	4.8%	5.2%
Walk	2.9%	2.8%
Bicycle	0.5%	0.6%
Taxi or other	1.2%	1.2%
Work at home	3.0%	4.6%

Sources: US Census Bureau, 2006; and American Community Survey, 2015

(New York, Chicago, Boston, Philadelphia, San Francisco, and Washington) public transit's share is significantly higher. In all but those legacy-transit cities, the lion's share of public transit's 5 percent is bus, not rail; so public transit, too, depends heavily on highways.

The reason for the car's very high share and public transit's low share is the suburbanization of jobs over the last 50 years. Most people's mental model of cities envisages a central business district surrounded by suburbs, with commuting defined as radial trips from suburb to center. But every decennial census since the 1960s has shown that the predominant form of commuting is suburb-to-suburb, as companies of all kinds have followed their employees to suburban locations.[50] For example, the report *Commuting In America 2013* finds that the largest fraction of commuters (30 percent) go to work either within their own suburb or in another suburb. The second-largest category is commuting within the metro area's principal city or between two principal cities (25 percent). The traditional suburb-to-city work trip is true of only 16 percent of commuters. This pattern has occurred all over the world, driven in part by increasing affluence.[51] It is highly unlikely to be reversed by any conceivable set of government policies compatible with a free society.

Intercity passenger rail is basically a nonplayer in the United States. Amtrak, the government-owned passenger railroad, carries 0.1 percent of all intercity passenger travel, and except in the Northeast Corridor (Boston to Washington), Amtrak is all diesel-powered. Even if a massively funded government effort managed to increase that share tenfold, that would still accomodate only 1 percent of passenger travel, not enough to make a meaningful difference. In any case, careful research by a number of different groups shows that the carbon footprint per passenger mile

TABLE 14. **Carbon footprint of various trips (pounds CO$_2$ per trip)**

	Bus	Train	Car	SUV	Plane
Solo traveler					
100 miles	15	45	110	140	75
250 miles	40	110	270	345	160
500 miles	85	215	540	695	300
1,000 miles	170	430	1,085	1,385	514
2,500 miles	420	1,075	2,710	3,465	925
Family of four					
100 miles	65	170	120	150	305
250 miles	170	430	300	375	630
500 miles	335	860	605	755	1,205
1,000 miles	670	1,720	1,210	1,505	1,665
2,500 miles	1,680	4,300	3,020	3,660	3,705

of Amtrak is significantly greater than that of intercity motor coach.[52] A detailed study by M. J. Bradley & Associates for the ABA Foundation found that the per-passenger CO$_2$ emissions for typical motor coach trips were 45 to 66 percent lower than for Amtrak trips, both diesel and electric. Another study, by the Union of Concerned Scientists on alternative modes for vacation travel, produced comparisons of the carbon footprints of five modes of travel.[53] Table 14 here is derived from that report's table 4. As you can see, from a carbon footprint standpoint, buses beat trains for trips of every length, whether by a solo traveler or by a family of four. For long trips, airplanes beat trains as well. So shifting intercity passengers from motor coach to rail would make CO$_2$ emissions worse, not better. And, needless to say, intercity motor coach relies on the highway system as its infrastructure.

As for freight movement, prior to the Interstate highway system's creation, the US rail network was much larger than what exists today. According to the US DOT's Bureau of Transportation Statistics, in 1960 there were more than 207,000 miles of railroad in operation. By 2011 that total had decreased to 95,500. Urban areas used to have rail lines and sidings serving factories, warehouses, and other freight customers, but those lines are long gone and they won't be coming back; those customers today are served by truck. The entire "just in time" freight logistics system depends on the speed and flexibility of trucks to haul freight to regional distribution centers, and from there either to assembly plants or to retail locations. The major railroads have achieved modest success in shifting a small fraction of longer-distance freight from truck to what is called "rail intermodal" service—mostly shipping containers on specially designed rail cars. But most freight experts, including those at the US DOT, project little change in market share between rail and truck in coming decades.

So for all of these reasons, we will still need a large, well-maintained, and modestly expanding highway system for the foreseeable future. From a carbon footprint standpoint, though, there is good news to report. Both automakers and truck producers are working hard on reducing the carbon footprints of their vehicles. For personal vehicles, current federal Corporate Average Fuel Economy (CAFE) standards require nearly doubling the average miles-per-gallon of the new personal vehicle fleet by 2025. In that year, the average new car must get the equivalent of 54.5 miles per gallon, compared with the previously required new-car average of 27.5 miles per gallon as of 2009.[54] So future cars will have a much lower carbon footprint than those in the vehicle fleet today. Calculations by Wendell Cox using assumptions from the US Department of Energy's *Annual Energy Outlook* documents for 2008, 2012, and 2014 show that CO_2 emissions from light-duty vehicles (cars, vans, and pickups) will decrease by 32 percent from the level projected in 2008, and by more than 50 percent from what DOE projected in 2005.[55] Thus, instead of light-vehicle CO_2 emissions increasing from 1.2 billion tons in 2005 to 1.9 billion tons by 2035 (under the 2005 projection), that number is now projected to decrease to only 0.75 tons by 2035. And that is despite increased population and VMT between now and 2035.

Larger emission reductions may eventually be possible if automated robo-taxis become commercially feasible between 2030 and 2050. For example, researchers from the Lawrence Berkeley National Laboratory have estimated that small one- to three-person robo-taxis could have CO_2 emissions 87 to 94 percent below conventional motor vehicles in 2030, in part by being optimized for small size and light weight and by lacking the need for drivers and associated controls.[56] The current federal CAFE standards do not require any fuel-economy improvements after 2025, largely due to uncertainties about future technologies that would be needed to accomplish even higher fuel economy at an affordable cost. But given the ongoing research in alternative propulsion technologies as well as automated vehicles, it seems quite plausible that technology developments will permit further carbon footprint reductions in the decades between 2030 and 2060.

One likely result of the changes in personal vehicles brought about by the 54.5-miles-per-gallon requirement is that they will be considerably lighter than today's new vehicles, since moving less weight consumes less fuel. Yet the trend for trucks is likely to move in the opposite direction, since EPA calculations show that longer, heavier big rigs reduce carbon emissions per ton-mile. Mixing heavier trucks with much lighter cars is a recipe for disaster. This mismatch strengthens the case discussed in chapters 9 and 10 for greater use of cars-only and trucks-only lanes and roadways as existing expressways and Interstates are reconstructed and modernized.

Smart Growth and Public Transit

Overlapping the concerns about greenhouse gas emissions is a widespread movement by urban planners, large urban property owners, environmentalists, and advocates for bicycling, walking, and public transit that generally goes by the name of smart growth. The premise—which long predates concerns over climate change—is that cars and roadways have blighted cities and that suburbanization, referred to as "urban sprawl," has consumed green space and the countryside. Our settlement and transportation patterns, therefore, should be dramatically overhauled, smart-growth proponents urge. In their view, ideally, there should be no more suburban development, and all of the need for additional housing and commercial use should be filled by densifying already developed land within the urban area. Use of cars should be discouraged, with government shifting highway-user-tax money from roads to public transit, bike lanes, and sidewalks. The ideal is that most people would be able to walk, bike, or take public transit to work and for recreation.

These policies have been gaining adherents for decades, since long before climate change became a political issue. They have resulted in measures such as urban growth boundaries, which greatly restrict conversion of undeveloped land outside a defined boundary to any form of development; upzoning to increase density in existing neighborhoods; "Safe Routes to School," a federal program using highway money to fund more sidewalks; and "complete streets" policies that seek to mandate that nearly all streets have sidewalks and bike lanes. The more extreme version of the latter is "road diets," under which the objective is to reduce auto use on multilane arterials by converting, say, a four-lane arterial into two through lanes plus a center turn lane, using the remaining space for wider sidewalks and bike lanes. A related measure is to convert regular traffic lanes into bus-only lanes, significantly reducing the capacity of an arterial to handle peak-period traffic flows of the large majority of commuters.

There have been many serious critiques of smart-growth policies. Among them is a book on suburbanization by Robert Bruegmann of the University of Illinois,[57] *Smarter Growth* by Randall Holcombe and Sam Staley (both at Florida State University),[58] a policy paper by the Cato Institute's Randal O'Toole,[59] a book by demographer Wendell Cox,[60] and a book by my former Reason colleagues Ted Balaker and Sam Staley.[61] They cite considerable research showing that urban growth boundaries, by curtailing the supply of affordable housing at the fringe, lead to higher housing costs and distortion of the normal demographic profile of an urban area (with more rich and poor people than prior to the boundary, but a much smaller middle-income population). They find no evidence that smart-growth policies lead to reduced traffic congestion or to significant increases in transit use.

The negative impact of urban containment on housing affordability is not fully understood by most of the advocates of smart growth. Curtailing the supply of suburban and exurban land and requiring new housing to be built on expensive urban land has sharply increased housing costs in metro areas that have consistently applied such policies. Demographer Wendell Cox provided a global overview in 2015.[62] He reported data on the ratio of median house price to median household income for 86 metro areas of one million or more population. Historically, a "median multiple" of 3.0 has been considered affordable. In 2014, highly restrictive US metro areas had much higher median multiples: 9.2 in San Francisco and San Jose, 8.3 in San Diego, and 8.0 in Los Angeles. By contrast, metro areas that do not practice urban containment—such as Atlanta, Dallas–Fort Worth, and Houston—still had multiples in the 3-to-4 range.

There are other inherent flaws in the smart growth approach, beginning with the idea that it makes sense for people in a large urban area to be forced by poor auto transportation to live and work in the same small portion of that area. That idea flies in the face of why we have urban areas to begin with—what economists call urban agglomeration benefits. The larger and more diversified the population of an urban region is, the more positive-sum transactions can take place. This is especially important for employment relationships. The economic productivity of an urban area will be higher if a job seeker has access to a large number of potential employers, because she will then have a greater likelihood of finding one that can make the best use of her unique talents and skills. The same is true for employers; in a very large metro area the employer has a much better chance of finding people who are the best (highest-productivity) match for the skills it needs.

Transportation turns out to be a key factor in enabling such positive-sum, wealth-increasing transactions. Imagine drawing a circle around the location of your residence, to define how far you are willing to commute to get a satisfying job. The larger the radius of that circle, the more potential job opportunities you have. Likewise, for a company located in a specific place, its prospective-employee circle is defined by a similar radius, representing how far potential employees are willing to travel to and from that company's location. Most people measure that radius in time rather than distance. It turns out that, even though there are always some outliers, most people are unwilling on a long-term basis to spend much more than 30 minutes each way getting to and from work. So the size of their opportunity circlein a given metro area is critically dependent on the quality of the transportation system.

Helping us to understand transportation's role is what some have termed the travel-time paradox. For several decades, transport economists such as Peter Gordon and Harry Richardson of the University of Southern California have documented, using census data on commuting, that average commute times in various metro areas have hardly changed at all—despite urban sprawl and ever-increasing congestion.[63] More recently, Alex Anas of SUNY Buffalo did a detailed modeling analysis of the Chicago metro area, to explore possible increases in travel time due to a projected 24-percent increase in metro area population between 2000 and 2030.[64] Anas's model, unlike most transportation planning models, included changes in land prices that influence location decisions over time. The model also included additions of highway and public transit capacity during that time period. The result showed that by 2030, auto commute times would increase only by 3 percent, and public-transit trip times hardly at all. The reason, Anas concluded, was that people relocate where they live or work in order to keep their commute times about the same. But this happy result comes about only if the transportation system expands accordingly.

If the transportation is not improved, the metro area's economy is likely to suffer. The economists Remy Prud'homme and Chang-Won Lee studied the relationship between urban travel time and regional gross domestic product for cities in France and South Korea.[65] When the size of opportunity circles expands, thanks to transportation system improvements that enable a person to cover a greater distance within an acceptable commute time, the economic productivity of the metro area increases. Specifically, when the effective size of the labor market (the area of the circle) increased by 10 percent, the urban region's economic productivity increased by 1.3 percent. Similar results have been obtained by other transportation analysts. Glen Weisbrod studied the impact of congestion on the economic performance of Chicago and Philadelphia.[66] David Hartgen and Gregory Fields applied the analysis of Prud'homme and Lee to the transportation systems of Atlanta, Charlotte, Dallas, Denver, Detroit, Salt Lake City, San Francisco, and Seattle, finding similar results.[67]

A recent empirical study from the Marron Institute of Urban Management at New York University provided further insight into the relationship between transportation access and the productivity of urban economies. In "Commuting and the Productivity of American Cities," Shlomo Angel and Alejandro Blei found that the labor market of an urban area, defined as the number of jobs reachable within a one-hour commute, nearly doubles when the workforce of the metro area doubles. But across the 347 metro areas they studied, the commute time increased only 7 percent despite the doubling.[68] They found that an efficient region-wide transportation network is a key factor in this result, and their policy recommendations for higher economic productivity were therefore to foster

- speedier, rather than slower, commuting;
- more, rather than less, commuting; and
- longer, rather than shorter, commutes.

These policies would expand the opportunity circles of employers and employees, enabling more positive-sum transactions, and hence a more productive urban economy. But they are exactly the opposite of the policy prescriptions of smart growth.

This Marron Institute analysis illustrates the absurdity of seeking to confine people's economic activity to a small portion of a large metro area. One early manifestation of this was the attempt by urban and transportation planners to promote "jobs-housing balance," measured by having each portion (e.g., each county) of a large metro area have comparable percentages of the region's jobs and of its housing. The rationale was that this would reduce "excessive" commuting by enabling people to find jobs close to where they live. But from urban agglomeration economics, you can see why that is a recipe for a low-productivity urban economy. And while it is true that recent census data show that many suburban areas are now approaching jobs-housing balance on their own—and not because of specific government policies—this does not necessarily reduce commute distances, because people commute across boundaries.

A fascinating example is Fairfax county, Virginia, which is highlighted in brief 15 of *Commuting in America 2013*.[69] Since the year 2000, the number of jobs and the number of working residents in this county have been approximately equal. But it turns out that only 52 percent of those working residents actually have jobs in the county. Out of 582,000 resident workers, 280,000 commute to work in adjacent counties or the District of Columbia. And out of 574,000 jobs in Fairfax county, 272,000 are filled by workers from other counties in Maryland and Virginia, and from the District of Columbia. This happens because of urban agglomeration effects: companies and employees finding specific matches that produce greater value. And it makes Fairfax county one of the most economically successful counties in the United States.

The less extreme version of smart growth is one in which cars and roads are so obnoxious by definition that transportation policy should discourage car travel and shift resources heavily toward public transit. People should be encouraged to live in high-density transit villages where they can easily obtain public transit service to their jobs elsewhere in the metro area. The problem with this vision is the inability of public transit to compete very effectively with the automobile-highway system, despite today's traffic congestion. Several important studies in recent years have documented the extent of this problem.

First came a major Brookings Institution study in 2012, analyzing data from 371 transit providers in America's largest 100 metro areas. The good news was that more than three-fourths of all jobs are in neighborhoods with public transit service, but the bad news was that only 27 percent of those jobs can actually be reached by public transit within 90 minutes.[70] That is more than three times the national average commuting time of 26 minutes. A subsequent study by Andrew Owen and David Levinson of the University of Minnesota reviewed job access via public transit in more detail in 46 of the 50 largest metro areas.[71] Their travel time estimates combined actual in-vehicle time with estimated walking time at either end of the transit trip, to approximate total door-to-door travel time. Their data tables showed how many jobs in each metro area could be reached by public transit within 10, 20, 30, 40, 50, and 60 minutes. It turns out that only five of the 46 metro areas have even a small percentage of their jobs accessible within 30 minutes, door-to-door, via public transit. All the others have 1 percent or less, with Atlanta and Dallas in last place at 0.3 percent. Within 60 minutes, door-to-door, the best five have only between 15 percent and 22 percent of jobs reachable by public transit. And that simply does not cut it.

The previous year, Levinson had done a comparable study of accessibility to jobs via automobile commuting in the largest 51 metro areas.[72] His data showed that in 2010, in 31 of those areas, 100 percent of jobs could be reached by car within 30 minutes or less. Within 40 minutes, all jobs could be reached by car in 39 of the 50, and within 60 minutes, essentially 100 percent of the jobs could be reached by car in all 51 metro areas. The contrast with accessibility via public transit is profound. The roadway network is ubiquitous, connecting every possible origin to every destination. By its very nature, the public transit system is not and cannot be ubiquitous in the same way.

Because the cost of building something much closer to a ubiquitous public transit system is so enormous, some smart growth advocates instead now attack the dispersed nature of jobs as the real problem. In addition to their term of opprobrium "urban sprawl," meaning suburbia, they have coined the additional term "job sprawl" to stigmatize the now universal dispersion of job locations across entire urban regions. Brookings itself published two reports going after "job sprawl," one in 2013 and another in 2015. The first report tortured early data from the Great Recession to argue that job dispersion was being reversed (it wasn't).[73] The second report measured proximity to any job of any kind, regardless of whether it would be a conceivable fit for anyone within public transit commuting distance.[74] As I wrote in my newsletter at the time, "I suspect the reason smart-growthers [now] disparage the emerging jobs-housing balance as 'job sprawl' is that it torpedoes their model of downtown as *the* major employment center, reachable by rail transit."[75] With the reality of dispersed employment, "there is no conceivably affordable rail transit system that could solve that problem." In a free society, people choose where they live and work, and employers choose where to locate.

Finally, we turn to what some advocates of smart growth consider their ultimate rationale: greenhouse gas reduction. The first serious effort came from the Urban Land Institute, which released a report called *Moving Cooler* in 2009.[76] It recommended a bundle of transportation and land-use policies as the best way to reduce motor-vehicle greenhouse gases by reducing the amount of driving. It proposed new taxes on miles traveled and on parking, densification of urban land use, and doubling of public transit subsidies, while ignoring the potential of vehicle technology improvements. In estimating cost, it ignored the cost of new public transit subsidies and the costs incurred by those who switch from a 20-minute car commute to a potentially 45-to-60-minute walk/bike-plus-public transit commute in all kinds of weather.

That report was followed by a far more analytical special report from the Transportation Research Board, *Driving and the Built Environment*.[77] In attempting to quantify the effects of the smart-growth strategy, it produced two scenarios. The "moderate" scenario assumed that 25 percent of all new and replacement housing is produced at twice today's densities, and that residents of the new housing will drive 12 percent less. The result was that greenhouse gas emissions reduced by just 1 percent by 2030. The completely unrealistic "upper bound" scenario, under which 75 percent of new and replacement housing would be high-density and its residents would drive 25 percent less, still produced only modest greenhouse gas reductions. (*MIT Technology Review* summed up the report's findings in an article headlined "Forget Curbing Suburban Sprawl: Building Denser Would Do Little to Reduce CO_2 Emissions.")

Both of these reports were critiqued by Wendell Cox and Adrian Moore in a 2011 study.[78] Their review of this and other research concluded that the compact development approach is unlikely to achieve more than a 5-percent reduction in automobile CO_2 emissions by 2050. They showed that higher density would lead to more congestion in the compacted areas, which in turn would lead to higher CO_2 emissions than driving at steady speeds; and they also cited evidence of much higher social costs due to the impact of compact development policies on housing prices. By contrast to this behavioral strategy, Cox and Moore estimated the reductions in CO_2 that would happen thanks to the technological improvements to vehicles due to federal CAFE standards. Their projection showed that, as more efficient cars replace older ones in the fleet, the CO_2 reductions would be between 18 and 33 percent by 2050. And these calculations were done assuming the then-current 35-miles-per-gallon requirement for new vehicles, rather than the subsequent increase to 54.5 miles per gallon. Cox's follow-up analysis in 2015 estimated that greenhouse gas reductions produced via improvements in vehicle fuel efficiency by 2040 would dwarf reductions produced via smart growth measures by between 17 and 50 times,[79] without any need for people to change their travel or housing behavior.

California, alas, has opted to go full-bore for the behavioral approach to greenhouse gas reductions. In 2008 its legislature enacted AB 375, which requires the metropolitan planning organizations of the four major urban

areas in the state (where 87 percent of people live) to implement densification and travel-reduction policies. An early indication of the flaws in
this plan was provided by the air quality analyst Sarah Siwek in 2011. Her
calculations estimated that if the law were fully implemented, its measures
would contribute only 1.75 percent of the required statewide greenhouse
gas reductions by 2020. Technical improvements to vehicles and fuels
would dwarf the reductions made through AB 375's behavioral approach.[80]

The San Francisco Bay Area's Metropolitan Transportation Commission adopted an aggressive plan to implement AB 375, called Plan Bay
Area. It would shift much transportation funding from roads to public
transit, impose new costs on driving, limit construction of single-family
homes, and require that the majority of new housing be multi-family and
be located near public transit centers. A careful analysis by the transportation analyst Thomas A. Rubin in 2013 showed that, thanks to vehicle
fuel economy improvements, the Bay Area was by then already close to
achieving the 2020 target for greenhouse gas reductions—without implementing the draconian restrictions on driving and housing.[81]

In short, as more people realize that large-scale efforts to densify urban
areas and restrict driving will not meaningfully reduce greenhouse gases but
will seriously constrain people's choices of where and how to live and work,
these behavioral approaches are likely to be rejected in most urban areas.

Conclusions

In this chapter we have reviewed the most widely heard arguments against
a future that will continue to require large and robust urban and long-
distance highway systems. These include the arguments

- that we are now seeing fundamental change in travel and housing preferences
  that will lead to significantly less driving in coming decades;
- that autonomous vehicles will soon replace individually owned vehicles
  with "mobility as a service," leading to significantly less need for highway
  infrastructure;
- that the need to address climate change will require drastic shifts in both personal
  and goods-movement transportation, leading to less need for highways; and
- that cars and driving should be heavily deemphasized in urban areas, in preference to people living at much higher densities and getting around via biking,
  walking, and public transit.

We have seen considerable evidence that all four of these perspectives are seriously flawed. First, the alleged change in housing and transportation preferences were mostly short-term impacts of the Great Recession, especially for younger people. Total driving, as measured by VMT, seems very likely to continue growing along with population, and truck travel seems likely to continue in pace with economic growth. For both reasons, we will continue to need a robust urban and long-distance highway network to support a free and open economy.

Second, while autonomous vehicles hold great promise for significantly reduced accidents and deaths on our roadways, as well as for increased mobility for those who cannot drive, the visions of ubiquitous, fully autonomous vehicles *and* of people switching from owning vehicles to using robo-taxis on demand are both uncertain as to feasibility and timing. If either or both of these visions eventually comes to pass, it will likely be 30 or 40 years in the future. Their implications for VMT are also highly uncertain, with increases beyond business-as-usual projections now considered more likely than decreases. Hence, it would be unwise and irresponsible not to modernize and expand our highway networks where it is justified.

Third, the idea that to reduce greenhouse gases from transportation we must reduce driving and truck shipping has been shown to do far less to reduce CO_2 emissions than the very powerful impact of major, achievable improvements in propulsion efficiency. Current federal miles-per-gallon standards through 2025 will yield significant reductions from today's CO_2 emission levels in the 2030–35 time frame, with further technology improvements quite likely thereafter.

Finally, reconfiguring our large metro areas to reduce suburbanization of housing and jobs would reduce the economic productivity of those urban areas. That is especially true if the policy seeks to constrain people to work in close proximity to where they live. Even the milder version that would rely on public transit instead of highways to get people to optimal job locations would fail, on the grounds of unaffordable transit capital and operating costs and unacceptably long commuting times.

None of this argues for business as usual in the highway sector. As previous chapters have explained, the 20th-century highway model is failing, and needs to be replaced by the kind of highways-as-network-utility model explained in these pages. The final chapter makes the case that the time is ripe to begin the transition to this new model.

CHAPTER TWELVE

A New Future for US Highways

In this book we have taken a critical look at the US highway system as it evolved over the 20th century. While this top-down, centralized approach—first at the state level, and since 1956 at the federal level—did succeed in giving America a nationwide system of paved roads, today hardly anyone is satisfied with our highway system.

The problems are legion, beginning with the huge direct cost of traffic congestion in the 200 or so urban areas—a whopping $160 billion per year just in wasted time and fuel. And while our highways and bridges are not "crumbling," there are chronic problems of deferred maintenance, leading to many rough roads and a surprisingly large number of bridges that are either structurally deficient or at least functionally obsolete.

The 20th-century highway funding system that was predicated on per-gallon fuel taxes as a good approximation of a highway user fee is breaking down, for several reasons. Because a growing share of the proceeds is no longer spent on highways, people have come to view gas taxes as just another tax, which politicians are therefore leery of increasing. Yet as cars continue to get more efficient, using fewer gallons to go a given distance, revenues from per-gallon fuel taxes do not keep pace with either the growth in driving or the cost of building and maintaining highways.

Moreover, with decisions on how to spend the money collected for transportation being largely political at both state and federal levels, the billions raised and spent each year are often not spent on projects that would produce the most bang for the buck. Most federal highway and transit money is doled out by formula, and although members of Congress are no longer allowed to single out pet projects for dedicated funding ("earmarks"), the overall process is based far more on politics than on sound economic principles such as ensuring that the benefits of a project exceed its costs.

In light of these failures of the 20th century highway model, this book argues that a far better model would be to reconceive highways as another category of network utility, in addition to the familiar examples of electricity, water supply, telecommunications, and natural gas. For the most part, those network utilities are not run by government agencies, with key decisions made by legislators. Instead, the providers are organized as companies that sell services to customers. That is true regardless of whether those companies are owned by investors or are government enterprises (such as municipal electric and water utilities).

If highways were provided by highway utility companies—investor-owned concession companies, government toll agencies, or nonprofit user co-ops—a great many things would be different. For example:

- People would pay for highways based on how much they used, just as we pay for water by the gallon and for electricity by the kilowatt hour.
- People would be just as familiar with what highways cost, on the basis of their monthly bill, as they are with the cost of cable, cell phones, and electricity.
- Per-mile highway charges would be subject to some form of regulatory oversight, based on the extent to which the highways and bridges in question had competitors or were essentially monopolies.
- Large-scale investments for new highways and for replacing worn-out ones would be *financed* via the capital markets—just as individuals do in buying a home and as other utilities do in building new facilities—rather than being paid for piecemeal out of annual appropriations.
- Major highway investments would be primarily business decisions, not political decisions—subject, of course, to the same kinds of land-use and environmental constraints faced by all other commercial developments.
- Highway operations would be managed in real time, to provide customers with the quality of services they were willing to pay for.
- Highway companies would have strong incentives to keep their facilities in excellent condition, so as to attract and keep customers.

This is a profoundly different model for highways than what we assumed, in the last century, was the only or the best way to obtain highway services. Yet, as we saw in chapter 4, many other countries followed a different path for highways in the second half of the 20th century, developing large portions of their highway systems using direct user fees (tolls), and highway corporations that were initially government-owned but later privatized. Comparing the tolled highways of France, Italy, Spain, Chile, and Australia with our very flawed system suggests that a highway utility model could be a viable alternative to the US status quo.

In this closing chapter, we will examine the prospects for this vision of our highway future to become reality. With the major highway funding challenges facing Congress and the states, where would the money come from for a highway utility industry? And is there any reason to think that public and political opinion could support such a major change in how we provide highways in America?

Why the Time Is Right for a New Highway Model

The change proposed in this book would be a radical departure from the 20th-century status quo that legislators, transportation agencies, and the public generally accept without question. But we are at a point in time when a number of factors together will provide the motivation for major change. Those factors include

- the looming insolvency of the federal government,
- the dire fiscal problems facing state and local governments, and
- the obsolescence of per-gallon fuel taxes as the primary highway funding source.

Those three problems mean that the 20th-century status quo cannot and will not continue. The key question is: What will replace that failing status quo? Three new factors point the way toward the vision set forth in this book. Those are

- the growing worldwide and US track record of toll concessions;
- the emergence of global infrastructure investment funds, willing and able to invest in transportation infrastructure; and
- the need and desire of US pension funds to diversify their portfolios via infrastructure investments.

Together, these six factors create the preconditions for the shift to the proposed 21st-century highways model.

Three Major Causal Factors

Looming Federal Government Insolvency

Since the closing years of the Clinton administration, when the federal budget produced a small surplus for several years in a row, annual budget deficits have increased to previously unthinkable levels. In every year that the government operates at a deficit, the amount of that deficit gets added to the national debt. Between 2000 and 2016 the national debt held by the public increased from $3.4 trillion to $14.4 trillion.[1]

This could not have happened at a worse time, because we are at only the beginning of several decades during which the entire baby boom generation will retire. In addition to leaving the tax-paying workforce, they will all draw Social Security and Medicare payments for the rest of their lives. Those entitlement programs, by definition, operate on automatic pilot, increasing each year in accordance with the growth of the fraction of the population entitled to receive those benefits, which are inflation-adjusted. The government also faces large unfunded liabilities for its growing student loan program and the Pension Benefit Guarantee Corporation.

Both the Congressional Budget Office (CBO) and the Government Accountability Office (GAO) continually warn that the government is on an unsustainable path. In 2012 congressional testimony, a senior GAO official warned that "GAO's long-term simulations show that, absent policy changes, the federal government faces unsustainable growth in deficits and debt."[2] That dire fiscal outlook was repeated in April 2015, in the GAO's annual Federal Fiscal Outlook. To restore long-term fiscal balance, the GAO estimated that either revenue would have to be 17 to 27 percent higher or noninterest spending would have to be 17 to 27 percent lower on average each year over the next 75 years.[3]

The seriousness of the ballooning national debt has been somewhat masked since the Great Recession by the Federal Reserve's policy of forcing interest rates far below historical averages. In 2011 the retired banker George Christy used projections from the CBO to show how annual interest payments on the national debt could produce a major crisis by the early 2020s.[4] The CBO's January 2016 budget forecast projected that the annual budget deficit will triple to $1.37 billion by 2026, and that interest payments on the accumulated debt will nearly quadruple from $223 billion in 2015 to $830 billion in 2026. As Christy predicted, once normal interest rates return, interest on the national debt will require a larger and growing share of the federal budget, squeezing out other priorities, including highways.

The late economist Herb Stein, a former chairman of the President's Council of Economic Advisors, is noted for saying, "If something cannot go on forever, it will stop." This maxim has become known as Stein's Law, and at some point it must take hold regarding the out-of-control federal budget. It will be hugely difficult, politically, to take entitlement programs off their current autopilot. It will be somewhat easier, politically, to re-think the federal role for "discretionary" spending of all kinds—which includes transportation.

With the declining after-inflation yield from federal gasoline and diesel taxes, between 2008 and 2016 Congress added $140 billion in general fund money to the Highway Trust Fund, so as to prevent decreasing the annual amounts made available to state and local transportation agencies.[5] In a climate of federal fiscal retrenchment, there will be little or no room for such discretionary spending. Indeed, with this eventuality in mind, the bipartisan 2010 Simpson-Bowles Commission recommended that all infrastructure now receiving federal funding be made 100-percent self-supporting from user taxes and/or user fees.[6] Neither the Congress nor President Barack Obama implemented any of the commission's recommendations; they instead enacted a 10-year sequester to limit both defense and nondefense discretionary spending, leaving entitlements untouched.

But the Simpson-Bowles recommendation of self-supporting infrastructure was wise, and will eventually be heeded. Transitioning highways from tax-supported government programs to self-funded highway corporations follows logically from this change. And in the case of highways, the transition can follow recognized models for other US utilities, as well as other countries' highway experiences, thus making the transition much easier to implement.

Dire State and Local Fiscal Problems

If we continue with the government-highways model at the state level while the federal government retrenches, a larger share of responsibility for highway funding will be placed on state and local governments. But these levels of government have serious fiscal problems of their own. On paper, all but 1 of the 50 states have balanced-budget requirements, either constitutional or legislated. But in practice those requirements are almost meaningless, since they are defined based on cash accounting, not on accrual accounting like what businesses use. That means that liabilities are not taken into account when doing the budget numbers, and this leads states to borrow money by issuing bonds to generate additional operating funds.

The respected financial experts Richard Ravitch and Paul Volcker headed a State Budget Crisis Task Force in 2012. Their report documented the major fiscal problems facing most states in coming decades.[7] Among the largest contributors are the expansion of Medicaid, whose costs are shared between federal and state governments, and enormous unfunded pension liabilities. They also pointed out the tendency of state governments to use various budget gimmicks to disguise the extent of their fiscal crises.

The largest problem facing most states is unfunded pension liabilities. Unlike most of the private sector, nearly all state and local governments still operate defined-benefit pension systems, rather than defined-contribution plans. In reporting on their fiscal soundness, most public employee pension funds assume an expected annual return on investment in the range of 7.5 to 8 percent, which is unrealistically high. They also fail to risk-adjust reported liability for unforeseen events such as major recessions.

Fewer than half of all US public employee pension plans made their full "annual required contribution" (ARC) in 2013, according to a paper by the public pensions expert Andrew Biggs.[8] The fraction of plans paying their full ARCs declined from 81 percent in 2001 to only 41 percent in 2015. The official ARC itself is a very low bar to meet, due to unrealistically high discount rates and long amortization periods. If these public-sector plans had to follow the rules that govern corporate plans, total employer ARC would more than quadruple, from 24 to 105 percent of payroll. The officially reported funded ratios for US public pension plans as a whole was 71 percent in 2013, with an aggregate unfunded liability of $922 billion. However, if those pension liabilities were calculated on a "fair-value" basis, using a corporate bond yield as private-sector pensions are required to do, and if market values were used instead of "actuarial/smoothed" assets, Biggs reports that the funded ratio would drop to 46 percent, and aggregate unfunded liability would increase to $2.6 trillion.

Another set of estimates comes from the Center for Retirement Research at Boston College. Its review of 4,000 state and local government pension plans in the United States found that even under the lenient accounting standards applied, they were on average only 72 percent funded by the end of 2015. Using a more realistic 4-percent discount rate, they were on average only 45 percent funded. On the latter basis, their overall unfunded liability totaled $4.1 trillion.[9]

Thus, state and local governments will have little scope for bailing out their own transportation budgets from general revenues. Between pension funds, Medicaid, and other demands, they will be in no position to seriously increase their transportation funding for several decades. This, too, makes a shift to self-funded highways more likely to be taken seriously.

Obsolescent Per-Gallon Fuel Taxes

Virtually the entire transportation research and policy community agrees that the per-gallon fuel tax is on its way out. Back in 2005 a special Transportation Research Board committee reached this conclusion, and urged research and planning for a transition to a more sustainable highway user charge.[10] Congress subsequently created an expert body, the National Surface Transportation Infrastructure Financing Commission, to review the situation. After assessing an array of alternatives, the commission unanimously recommended that mileage-based user fees were the best way forward.[11] Since then, state DOTs have taken the lead in carrying out research and pilot projects, with California, Iowa, Minnesota, and Oregon among the pioneering states.

As it hs done with the question of autonomous vehicles, the mass media have promulgated a caricature of how mileage-based user fees (MBUFs) would be implemented, and that vision has created considerable political and public opposition. Under this pipe dream, the federal government would lead the way with a federal "VMT tax" that would mandate a GPS box in every vehicle to keep track of the location and time of every mile driven. Many antihighway people seem to embrace this vision, seeing it as a way to tax automobile and truck users heavily for all the terrible things they do to the country. But to the average elected official and the average taxpayer-voter, that model invokes an intolerable Big Brother intrusion into their lives that is felt acutely in our post–NSA-snooping environment.

So let's look at what serious transportation people are actually proposing. First, any realistic MBUF effort will be led by state DOTs, not the federal government. Second, there is no support for mandating any single technical means of collecting MBUFs, such as GPS. Almost everyone supports offering motorists an array of choices, such as a flat annual ("all-you-can-drive") fee that requires no technology on the vehicle, an annual odometer reading linked to annual vehicle registration, or various kinds of in-vehicle technology, including a commercial GPS box that offers a package of services (such as pay-as-you-drive car insurance). Third, nearly all serious MBUF supporters propose the MBUF as a replacement for, not an addition to, gasoline taxes. And fourth, a number of experts reject the idea that the same system must be used for all different types of driving.

For example, in a Transportation Research Board paper, Chris Swenson and David Ungemah outlined the idea of a two-tier MBUF system.[12] A basic system, probably fairly low-tech or no-tech, would charge between one and two cents per mile to pay for most streets, roads, and minor highways. To use premium highways, such as urban expressways and long-distance Interstates, existing transponder technology that is now in widespread use on America's toll roads and express toll lanes would charge higher rates, consistent with the much higher cost to build and maintain these premium highways. We can already charge variable prices using transponders, as is done on express toll lanes; no other more costly or more intrusive technology is needed for that purpose.

Charging people per mile rather than per gallon has many benefits, as summarized in a Reason Foundation policy brief:[13]

- The per-mile charge is directly proportional to road use, like charges for electricity and water. You pay for what you use, period.
- The per-mile charge is far more transparent than fuel taxes, so people will see the direct link between paying and benefits.
- The per-mile charge is independent of propulsion source, so it would work just as well in 25 years if most or all vehicles are electric-powered.
- The charge can be different for different types of roads, such as Interstates versus local streets.
- Per-mile charges can be used to control congestion, which is mostly a problem on premium highways, such as urban freeways.

Those are all big improvements over the fading system of per-gallon fuel taxes.

Getting over the hurdle of objections to the caricature view of mileage-based user fees remains something of a challenge, but this is a debate we must have, given the declining viability of per-gallon taxes.

Drivers of the New Paradigm

Three positive factors will assist the new highway paradigm in gaining acceptance.

The Growing Global Track Record of Toll Concessions

Chapters 4 and 5 provided an overview of the toll concession model and its spread from Europe to Australia and to parts of Asia, Latin America, and more recently the United States. Many of the early adopters are far ahead of the United States in relying primarily on concessions for highway megaprojects. We have the long-standing model of France, where nearly the entire motorway network is built and operated by concession companies, with open entry for new firms when additions to the system, such as the monumental Millau Viaduct, are needed. We also have the examples of Santiago, Chile, and Sydney, Australia, whose tolled expressway systems were created and are operated by a set of highway companies with fully interoperable tolling systems.

In chapter 6 we saw that the toll concession system is much better at targeting highway investment to where it is most needed and to where it provides the most real benefits, as indicated by highway customers' willingness to pay. Making this model standard for large-scale projects will mean allocating investment on the basis of sound business cases rather than for political reasons, as is all too often the case under our current highway model. We also reviewed the rather dismal track record of transportation megaprojects done via conventional low-bid "design-bid-build" (DBB) government contracting: large cost overruns, late completion, traffic shortfalls, and design and construction that may need more maintenance than would be the case if the project were procured on the basis of its total life-cycle cost rather than its initial construction cost. The risks normally passed along to taxpayers can be mostly or entirely taken on by the investors in a toll-concession model.

We can also observe the benefits of financing long-lived highway infrastructure so that needed projects can get done now rather than decades in the future, as happens when they have to be paid for out of a DOT's annual cash flow. Shifting from cash funding to long-term financing will make it possible to reduce existing backlogs of worthwhile projects, while screening out boondoggles and white elephants that could not conceivably get financed by knowledgeable investors. Financing will also enable the timely reconstruction and replacement of the Interstate highways as they reach the end of their useful lives over the next several decades. There is no other prospect in sight for bringing about this needed modernization, and the consequences of simply letting the existing infrastructure decay are horrible to contemplate.

The highway field desperately needs innovation and fresh solutions to improve personal and freight mobility. In this book we have seen the introduction of express toll lanes by a toll concession company in California, the solution to filling in a missing link on the A86 ring road around Paris by a toll concession company, and the introduction of America's first elevated reversible express toll lanes by a toll expressway authority in Tampa that operates much like a commercial enterprise. It will likely be concession companies that finally introduce customer-friendly dedicated truck lanes on the most truck-intensive long-distance Interstates across the country.

Over several decades of transportation policy research, I have come to the conclusion that the toll-concession model is generalizable into a 21st-century highway corporation model for the entire US limited-access highway system, both rural and urban.

The Emergence of Global Infrastructure Investment Funds

Twenty years ago there was no such thing as a global infrastructure investment fund. Today, there are several hundred of them, and as of 2016 the largest 50 funds had raised $250 billion over the previous five years, according to the industry magazine *Infrastructure Investor*.[14] There is no complete tally of money raised by this new industry since its inception, but estimates of fund-raising during the decade ending in 2016 are in the vicinity of $300 billion.

This new category of investment fund came into existence in the 1980s due to the global trends toward privatizing (via sale or long-term lease) major government-owned infrastructure, such as airports, electric utilities, telephone systems, seaports, and government toll road operators. This was followed by the worldwide growth of long-term concessions as a better way to finance and develop new infrastructure that historically would have been funded directly by government. As the economic consultant David Haarmeyer pointed out in 2014, "For institutional investors, the [attractions] include stable, income-oriented returns, often inflation-linked, with low correlation with other asset classes. Because they have long economic lives and stable cash flows, infrastructure assets such as roads, bridges, and water supply facilities are well-suited to investors looking to match their long-term liabilities."[15]

Some of the earliest investment funds originated in Australia and Canada. In Australia, a 1992 requirement that all employees contribute a set percentage of their annual salary to their choice of retirement fund led to the creation of large pools of money that had to be invested in diversified long-term portfolios. Australia was then in the process of privatizing government enterprises, including all its major airports, and introducing toll concessions for new urban expressways, so the new funds directed portions of their portfolios to that sector. But since Australia is a small country, the funds soon needed to look beyond Australia. Macquarie Bank and then other institutions met this demand by creating some of the first global investment funds to invest in infrastructure. A similar process took place in Canada, led by public-employee pension funds such as the Ontario Municipal Employees Retirement System (OMERS). OMERS and others faced the same small-country problem as did Australia's funds, so they also branched out to invest in infrastructure in other countries.

The long-term leases of the Chicago Skyway and the Indiana Toll Road alerted US financial institutions to the potential of the US transportation market, and many of the leading names, such as Goldman Sachs and Morgan Stanley, created such funds, again with an international scope. As of 2016, according to *Infrastructure Investor*, of the 50 largest infrastructure investment funds (chosen on the basis of the amounts each had raised in the previous five-year period), 37 percent of the capital was raised by funds headquartered in the United States, 27 percent by Canadian funds, 18 percent by European funds, and 16 percent by Australian funds, with Asian and South American funds raising the balance.[16]

Most of these funds invest equity into infrastructure, whether existing facilities or ones to be developed. And since equity represents between 10 and 35 percent of the total cost of a project or facility, the rest is provided by others as debt—either bank debt or revenue bonds. Therefore, when an estimate of the total raised by equity funds is noted—such as the $300 billion cited above—that would represent about 25 percent of the value of projects that could be financed thanks to those equity investments. Factoring in the 75 percent provided by debt, the total amount of projects that could be financed by that equity is $1.2 trillion.

Much of the debate about infrastructure in America these days is about serious funding shortfalls, in the Highway Trust Fund and other federal infrastructure programs (ports, airports, seaports, etc.). Globally speaking, however, these funds are sitting on large pools of capital, looking for worthwhile projects to invest in—and the fund managers are eager to invest in the United States. The challenge for US transportation policymakers is to come up with enough worthwhile projects to take advantage of these treasure troves of money.

The surprise election of Donald Trump as US president in 2016 has increased the likelihood of increased private capital investment in US transportation infrastructure. Trump ran on a platform that included $1 trillion of investment to rebuild and modernize aging US. infrastructure, with a white paper proposing that this sum would be largely private investment in projects with user-fee revenue streams.[17] White House advisors such as Gary Cohn and D. J. Gribbin are strongly supportive of this approach, as is new DOT Secretary Elaine Chao. Interstate tolling has gained additional attention in the early months of 2017, in the context of private investment along the lines of Trump's proposal.

Pension Funds' Need for Infrastructure Investment Returns

Another important trend is that a growing number of US. public employee pension funds are beginning to allocate a larger portion of their portfolios to infrastructure. Historically, most US pension funds have included infrastructure in their portfolios, but this has been limited to traditional investor-owned utilities such as electricity, natural gas, pipelines, railroads, and water companies. Pension funds invest equity in various for-profit companies and hedge funds in hopes of making a larger return on their investment over time. So a larger market for pension funds to invest in US infrastructure depends on the extent to which airports, highways, bridges, and ports are being developed and operated by investor-owned companies, as is the case with toll-concession highway projects.

Because airports, highways, and seaports in the United States are nearly all government-owned, it is not possible for anyone to invest equity in them to buy a share of ownership. But the emergence of investor-owned airport, seaport, and toll road companies around the world offers pension funds a way to expand into these new categories of infrastructure. In 2013, for example, Australia's Future Fund purchased $2 billion worth of shareholdings in privatized airports in Australia and Europe from the infrastructure fund AIX. The UK pension fund called Universities Superannuation Scheme purchased an 8.65--percent stake in privatized London Heathrow Airport, and also acquired 21 percent of the UK air navigation service provider NATS. The Manchester Pension Fund, teaming with two commercial partners, committed $1.28 billion to the Manchester Airport City development project.

Two of the largest US public employee pension funds, CalPERS and CalSTRS, representing California's general public employees and its public school employees respectively, have been among the early US pension fund movers into infrastructure. Each pledged nearly $3 billion to the Clinton Global Initiative America for infrastructure investment, which in 2014 announced that total commitments from public employee pension funds had reached $10.2 billion.[18] Pension funds, like insurance companies, see a good match between long-lived infrastructure projects that generate steady and generally rising revenue streams and their own long-term liabilities. Thus, if federal and state transportation policies more fully embrace the transition to toll concessions, they will create more here-at-home opportunities for state pension funds to diversify their portfolios and earn stronger returns, thus helping them to whittle down their backlog of unfunded liabilities. The largest pension funds generally hire their own expert staff in order to make their own decisions about directly investing in infrastructure projects. Smaller pension funds, by contrast, typically place the infrastructure portion of their portfolio with one or more of the global infrastructure funds.

One of the most dramatic pension fund investments in the United States took place in 2015. After the original concession company for the Indiana Toll Road declared bankruptcy in 2014, the Indiana Finance Authority, acting on behalf of the creditors, put the remaining 66 years of the concession up for auction. The winning bid of $5.725 billion (compared with the original $3.8 billion winning bid in 2006) was made by Industry Funds Management, a global infrastructure investment fund owned by 30 Australian pension funds.[19] Joining in IFM's consortium for this bid were CalSTRS, the New York City Employees' Retirement System, the State Board of Administration of Florida, the Arizona State Retirement System, and the Illinois State Board of Investment, along with dozens of other U.S. public employee pension funds.

Summing Up

The six factors discussed above create the preconditions for the transition to the highway utility industry model advocated in this book. The primary highway funding source—per gallon fuel taxes—is on a declining trajectory toward becoming obsolete. Both federal and state governments will be under severe fiscal stress for the next 30 years or so as they struggle to cope with the retirement of the baby boom generation and deal with far larger liabilities than is prudent. They will be in no position to provide an alternative highway funding source out of their diminishing "general" (unallocated) revenues.

Our 20th-century highway model is failing to allocate its limited resources to the highest and best uses, as measured by benefit/cost ratios or return on capital invested. It is failing to reduce chronic highway congestion, and it seems unable to properly maintain the existing stock of highways and bridges. By contrast, we have growing US experience with a better model that has a long track record in other developed countries: toll concessions, in which companies have strong incentives to invest in highway projects that make good economic sense, to build them right, and to seek to please their customers.

To give further impetus to the need for a new model, America is faced with a hugely valuable and productive Interstate highway system that is wearing out and will need to be largely replaced and modernized over the next several decades. There is no current funding source for this $1 trillion endeavor, except long-term financing based on per-mile tolling. Since Interstate reconstruction will consist of a large number of highway megaprojects, and since we know how risky such projects are, the prudent way to carry them out is as toll concessions, where the largest risks can be shifted to investors instead of being borne by taxpayers.

It is ironic that at the very time that state DOTs and highway builders are bewailing the shortage of highway investment from the federal government, the global infrastructure investment funds, along with other institutional investors like pension funds and insurance companies, are eager to invest in transportation infrastructure. Their problem is the lack of a large "pipeline" of projects to invest in, not a lack of investment funds. Even public employee unions that were initially hostile to for-profit companies getting into airports, highways, and bridges are now increasingly supportive of their pension funds investing serious money into these very same concession companies. The security of their pensions depends on improving the performance of their pension funds' portfolios, and adding commercially viable airport, highway, and bridge investments will help to accomplish this.

In short, the old 20th-century paradigm of highways and bridges as the last major state-owned enterprise is failing. Examples of the new model demonstrate that highway companies paid directly by their customers perform better than state-owned-enterprises. Large-scale investment capital is waiting for the opportunity to invest in replacing and modernizing US highway infrastructure. It's time to begin the transition to this new and better model for 21st-century highways.

Acknowledgments

In researching and writing this book, I drew on the knowledge and experience of many people. It's not feasible to list them all, but I will attempt here to acknowledge those who have been particularly important.

In the 1970s, as a newcomer to California, I became friends with an engineer at Caltrans whom I met at a conference on economics and politics. Joe Gilly told me about the investor-owned toll roads in France, and this account was reinforced by what I learned about privately financed US and Canadian toll bridges in researching my 1980 book on competitive contracting, *Cutting Back City Hall* (Universe Books).

It was probably via the Transportation Research Board that I met the World Bank transport economist Gabriel Roth and discovered his pioneering research on road pricing in the United Kingdom in the 1960s. Gabriel produced some important policy studies for the Reason Foundation after his retirement from the World Bank, and his later books on private highways were very influential in my thinking.

During the George H. W. Bush administration, my writings on road pricing, tolling, and public-private partnerships (P3s) came to the attention of Steve Lockwood, who was the senior policy officer at the Federal Highway Administration. He conducted a series of workshops in which I took part and which led to supportive policy provisions in the 1991 ISTEA legislation. His subsequent speculations on future highway "trans-corps" were especially thought-provoking.

Two transportation journalists provided a cornucopia of information about tolling and P3s during the 1990s and 2000s. Peter Samuel developed *Toll Roads News* initially as a monthly print newsletter, and later as an amazing online resource of news and sometimes controversial commentary on worldwide developments in tolling. Bill Reinhardt continues to publish *Public Works Financing*, the newsletter of record for P3s in transportation and water utilities, and for the past two decades he has included a policy column by me in every issue.

A number of academics have taught me a great deal about transportation, though I've never taken a course from any of them. The largest concentration of them is in Southern California, where I lived for three decades, and it includes Martin Wachs and Brian Taylor at UCLA, Peter Gordon and James Moore at USC, and Dan Klein and Ken Small at UC Irvine. I benefited from networking with these and other academics and policymakers at many of UCLA's annual transportation and land-use conferences at Lake Arrowhead over the years. More recently, I have learned a great deal from Rick Geddes, a Cornell economist specializing in infrastructure. I have drawn on his book on highway P3s, *The Road to Renewal*, in chapter 6 in particular.

Many nonacademics who are very knowledgeable about transportation and land use have informed my thinking and become friends over the years. Again, at the risk of excluding many others, I want to single out Wendell Cox, Joel Kotkin, Randal O'Toole, and Alan Pisarski.

Over the years I have also learned a great deal from people in the transportation business, in both the private sector and the public sector. Many of them I've met via involvement with the P3 division of the American Road and Transportation Builders Association and the International Bridge, Tunnel, and Turnpike Association. They are far too numerous to list, but four longtime colleagues reviewed early drafts of several chapters, making many good suggestions: Ed Regan of the consulting firm CDM Smith, Steve Steckler of IMG Rebel, Jim Taylor of Mercator Advisors, and Geoff Yarema of the Nossaman law firm.

My transportation colleagues at the Reason Foundation have been a joy to work with over the years. They include former colleagues Sam Staley (now at Florida State University) and Geoff Segal (now at Macquarie), and my current colleagues Baruch Feigenbaum and Adrian Moore (whom I hired many years ago when I was Reason's CEO and who is now my boss, as vice president, policy).

My successor as Reason CEO, David Nott, has taken what I started and turned it into a powerhouse of a think tank over the past 15 years. He's been wonderfully supportive of my transportation policy work during these years.

I am also especially grateful to Kim Dennis of the Searle Freedom Trust, for that organization's many years of support for Reason's transportation program, in particular my position as Searle Freedom Trust Transportation Fellow at the Reason Foundation.

I am very grateful to Deirdre McCloskey, who made the initial connection for me with the University of Chicago Press. And I have enjoyed working with economics editor Jane Macdonald and senior manuscript editor Renaldo Migaldi to bring this book into existence.

Finally, my secret weapon is my wife of 34 years, Lou Villadsen. First, she has put up with my hectic schedule of travel to conferences across the country and sometimes overseas, occasionally coming along to destinations including Berlin, London, and Madrid. Second, she has provided emotional and moral support against the slings and arrows that come with putting forth ideas that challenge the status quo. Third, she has long served as a reviewer and editor of drafts of just about everything I write on transportation. She adds a lot of value as an intelligent non-transportation wonk, often catching things I write that presume knowledge many readers don't possess.

Notes

Chapter 1

1. *Summary of Travel Trends, 2009 National Household Travel Survey*, US DOT, Federal Highway Administration, FHWA-PL-11–022, June 2011.

2. *Commuting in America 2013*, trend brief 10, Commuting Mode Choice, figures 10–2 and 10–3, accessed at http://traveltrends.transportation.org.

3. *Freight Facts and Figures, 2013*, US DOT, Bureau of Transportation Statistics, 2014.

4. David Schrank, Bill Eisele, Tim Lomax, and Jim Bak, *2015 Urban Mobility Scorecard*, Texas A&M Transportation Institute, August 2015.

5. Jack Wells (chief economist, US Department of Transportation), "The Role of Transportation in the U.S. Economy," presentation to the National Surface Transportation Policy and Revenue Study Commission, June 26, 2006.

6. *2015 Status of the Nation's Highways, Bridges, and Transit: Conditions & Performance*, US Department of Transportation, chapter 8, December 2016.

7. Ibid., chapter 6.

8. "How Long Has It Been since Your State Raised Its Gas Tax?" Institute on Taxation and Economic Policy, February 10, 2015 (updated July 28, 2015).

9. One of the most cited studies is Theofanis P. Mamuneas and M. Ishaq Nadiri, "Production, Consumption and Rates of Return to Highway Infrastructure Capital," http://citeseerx.ist.psu.edu/viewdoc/download?doi-10.1.1.352.8782&rep1&type=pdf.

10. Robert W. Poole Jr. and Adrian T. Moore, *Restoring Trust in the Highway Trust Fund*, policy study no. 386, Reason Foundation, August 2010.

11. Jeff Davis, "History of the Gasoline Tax, Part 1," *Transportation Weekly*, April 20, 2010.

12. Bruce E. Seely, "The Beginning of State Highway Administration (1893–1921)," *TR News* 245, July-August 2006.

13. Jeff Davis, "The 100th Anniversary of Federal Aid for Highways," *Transportation Weekly*, July 25, 2012.

14. Federal Highway Administration, "Interstate Frequently Asked Questions," www.fhwa.dot.gov/interstate/faq.cfm#question6, accessed August 4, 2015.

15. Wendell Cox and Jean Love, "The Best Investment a Nation Ever Made," American Highway Users Alliance, June 3, 1996.

16. Robert W. Poole, Jr., "Yet Again, Do Roads Pay for Themselves?" *Surface Transportation Innovations* Reason Foundation, no. 89, March 2011.

17. "Federal Subsidies to Passenger Transportation," Bureau of Transportation Statistics, US Department of Transportation, December 2004, accessed at www.bts.gov/publications/federal_subsidies_to_passenger_transportation.

18. Federal fuel tax monies are distributed by Congress to the states, which use them to fund a large array of highways, including the Interstates, US-numbered highways, and many state-numbered rural and urban highways and arterials.

Chapter 2

1. Robert W. Poole Jr., "Fixing America's Freeways," *Reason*, March 2012.

2. David Schrank, Bill Eisele, Tim Lomax, and Jim Bak, *2015 Urban Mobility Scorecard*, Texas A&M Transportation Institute, August 2015.

3. Ted Balaker and Sam Staley, *The Road More Traveled: Why the Congestion Crisis Matters More than You Think, and What You Can Do About It* (Rowman & Littlefield, 2006)

4. Jack Wells (chief economist, US Department of Transportation), "The Role of Transportation in the U.S. Economy," presentation to the National Surface Transportation Policy and Revenue Study Commission, June 26, 2006.

5. *Commuting in America 2013*, trend brief 12, figure 2-1, January 2014, accessed at http://traveltrends.transportation.org.

6. Robert W. Poole, Jr., *Private Tollways: Resolving Gridlock in Southern California*, Reason Foundation policy study, May 1988.

7. AB 680 (Baker), enacted in June 1989.

8. Bill Reinhardt, "Trend-Setting SR 91 Express HOT Lanes Open on Dec. 27," *Public Works Financing*, December 1995.

9. Peter Samuel, "91X Doing OK," *Toll Roads Newsletter*, March/April 2001.

10. Gordon J. Fielding and Daniel B. Klein, *High Occupancy/Toll Lanes: Phasing in Congestion Pricing a Lane at a Time*, Reason Foundation policy study no. 170, November 1993.

11. Joy Dahlgren, "Are HOV Lanes Really Better?" *Access*, no. 6, Spring 1995.

12. Kenneth Orski, "The Growing Disenchantment with HOV Lanes," *Innovation Briefs*, September/October 1998.

13. See www.virginiadot.org/business/resources/ppta-overview.pdf.

14. Peter Samuel, "How Fluor-Lane Widened the I-495 Capital Beltway from 8 to 12 Lanes," Tollroadsnews.com, May 7, 2013.

15. Bill Reinhardt, "Financial Close Reached for I-95 Express HOT Lanes in Va.," *Public Works Financing*, July/August 2012.

16. Robert W. Poole Jr., "Texas Sets the Pace in Highway Finance," *Public Works Financing*, February 2004.

17. Bill Reinhardt, "LBJ Managed Lanes, The Ultimate Test," *Public Works Financing*, June 2010.

18. Bill Reinhardt, "Texas North Tarrant Road Financiers Take Traffic Risk," *Public Works Financing*, December 2009.

19. Stephen Lockwood, "The Private Provision of Mobility Services in the 21st Century: How it Happened," Center for Transportation Studies, University of Minnesota, December 5, 1995, accessed at http://hdl.handle.net/11299/165674.

20. Gabriel Roth, *Roads in a Market Economy* (Avebury Technical, 1996).

21. Gabriel Roth, ed., *Street Smart: Competition, Entrepreneurship, and the Future of Roads* (Transaction Publishers, 2006).

22. Randal J. Pozdena, "Where the Rubber Meets the Road: Reforming California's Roadway System," policy study no. 191, Reason Foundation, August 1995.

23. Matthieu Favas, "The Infrastructure Investor 50," *Infrastructure Investor*, November 2016.

Chapter 3

1. W. T. Jackman, *The Development of Transportation in Modern England* (Augustus M. Kelly Publishers, 1966).

2. Peter Samuel, "Churches in Toll Business on London Bridge," Tollroads news.com, March 10, 2003.

3. Bruce L. Benson, "The Rise and Fall of Non-Government Roads in the United Kingdom," in Gabriel Roth, ed., *Street Smart: Competition, Entrepreneurship, and the Future of Roads* (Transaction Publishers, 2006).

4. Samuel Smiles, *The Life of Thomas Telford, Civil Engineer* (John Murray Publishers, 1867).

5. A. W. Skempton, *A Biographical Dictionary of Civil Engineers in Great Britain and Ireland* (Thomas Telford Publishers, 2002).

6. Matthew Dresden, "Must a Bridge Be Beautiful, Too?" *Access*, no. 28, Spring 2006.

7. Daniel B. Klein, "Private Toll Roads in America: The First Time Around," *Public Works Financing*, September 1993.

8. Daniel B. Klein and Chi Yin, "Use, Esteem, and Profit in Voluntary Provision of Toll Roads in California, 1850–1902," *Economic Inquiry*, October 1996.

9. Jeff Davis, "The 100th Anniversary of Federal Aid for Highways," *Transportation Weekly*, July 25, 2012.

10. John Williamson, "Federal Aid to Roads and Highways since the 18th Century: A Legislative History," Congressional Research Service, Report 7–5700, R42140, January 6, 2012.

11. Burton Folsom, Jr., "Madison's Veto Sets a Precedent," *The Freeman*, January/February 2008.

12. Joseph S. Wood, "The Idea of a National Road," in Karl Raitz, ed., *The National Road* (Johns Hopkins University Press, 1996).

13. Billy Joe Peyton, "Surveying and Building the Road," in Karl Raitz, ed., *The National Road* (Johns Hopkins University Press, 1996).

14. Burton Folsom Jr., "Why Did the National Road Fail?" *The Freeman*, July/August 2004.

15. Estimated from the Federal Reserve Bank of Minneapolis Consumer Price Index estimation process for 1850; www.minneapolisfed.org/community/teaching-aids/cpi-calculator/consumer-price-index-1800, accessed August 11, 2015.

16. Folsom, "Why Did the National Road Fail?"

17. Ibid.

18. Robert G. Cullen, "The War Hero and the Rural Free Delivery He Made Possible," *TR News*, March-April 2008.

19. Bruce E. Seely, "The Beginning of State Highway Administrations," *TR News*, July-August 2006.

20. Ibid.

21. Jeremy L. Schroeder, "100 Years of the Lincoln Highway," presented at the 2013 Annual Meeting of the Transportation Research Board, January 2013.

22. Tammy Ingram, *Dixie Highway: Road Building and the Making of the Modern South, 1900–1930*, University of North Carolina Press, 2015.

23. Dan L. Smith, *The Bankhead Highway in Texas* (Bankhead Highway Publishing, 2013).

24. Davis, *The 100ᵗʰ Anniversary of Federal Aid for Highways*

25. Jeff Davis, "The History of the Gasoline Tax, Part 1," *Transportation Weekly*, April 20, 2010.

26. Ibid.

27. Ibid.

28. Philip W. Burch Jr., *Highway Revenue Policy and Expenditure in the United States* (Rutgers University Press, 1962).

29. Finla G. Crawford, *Motor Fuel Taxation in the United States* (Syracuse, NY: self-published, 1939).

30. Jeff Davis, "The History of the Gasoline Tax, Part II," *Transportation Weekly*, April 27, 2010.

31. Ibid.

32. Burch, *Highway Revenue Policy and Expenditure.*

33. Peter Samuel, "Willie Vanderbilt's Tollway," *Toll Roads Newsletter*, December 2001.

34. Robert A. Caro, *The Power Broker: Robert Moses and the Fall of New York* (Random House, 1974).

35. IBTTA, *75 Years of Driving Change*, International Bridge, Tunnel & Turnpike Association, 2007.

36. "History of the Ambassador Bridge," accessed at www.ambassadorbridge.com/Downloads/History.pdf.

37. Information in this and the following paragraph comes primarily from pages in the 1940 bond industry publication *Walker's Manual*, provided to the author in 1993 by Samuel H. Husbands of Dean Witter Reynolds in San Francisco.

38. Ibid.

39. Peter Samuel, personal communication, 2014.

40. IBTTA, "75 Years of Driving Change."

41. Huey P. Long, *Every Man a King* (Da Capo Press, 1996).

42. "American Icon: Incorporating Tension in the Brooklyn Bridge," http://xroads.virginia.edu/~ma03/pricola/bridge/corporate.html, accessed August 11, 2015.

43. Robert A. Caro, *The Power Broker* (Vintage Books, 1975), p. 616.

44. Dan Cupper, *The Pennsylvania Turnpike: A History* (Applied Arts Publishers, 1995).

45. Peter Samuel, "Putting Customers in the Driver's Seat: The Case for Tolls," policy study no. 274, Reason Foundation, November 2000.

46. Peter Samuel, "Roads without the State," *The Freeman*, January 1998.

47. Bruce E. Seely, "How the Interstate System Came to Be," *TR News*, May-June 2006.

48. Ibid.

49. Ibid.

50. Jonathan Gifford, "The Exceptional Interstate Highway System," *TR News*, May-June 2006.

51. Ibid.

52. James A. Dunn Jr., *Driving Forces: The Automobile, Its Enemies, and the Politics of Mobility* (Brookings Institution, 1998), p. 38.

53. Jeff Davis, "History of the Transportation Trust Funds, Part 2," *Transportation Weekly* 10, no. 36 (September 2, 2009).

54. Dunn, *Driving Forces*.

Chapter 4

1. The average 2014 US (federal plus state) gas tax for motorists was $0.41 per gallon. Germany's 2014 gas tax was $3.43 per gallon (8.4 times the US rate) and the UK rate was $3.55 per gallon (8.6 times the US rate). The European rates are derived from "The Life and Death of the Highway Trust Fund," Eno Center for Transportation, 2014.

2. Ibid.

3. "Autostrade of Italy," Wikipedia, http://en.wikipedia.org/wiki/Autostrade
_of_Italy, accessed March 10, 2014.

4. "Atlantia Profile, History," www.atlantia.it/en/profilo/storia.html, accessed
March 10, 2014.

5. Jose A. Gomez-Ibanez and John R. Meyer, *Going Private: The International
Experience with Transport Privatization* (Brookings Institution, 1993), chapter 8.

6. Ibid.

7. Jean-Yves Perrot and Gautier Chatelus, eds., *Financing of Major Infrastructure and Public Service Projects: Public Private Partnerships* (French Ministry of
Public Works, Transport, and Housing, 2000), p. 147.

8. Christian Gerondeau, *Transport in Europe* (Artech House, 1997), chapter 5.

9. Peter Samuel, "French Low Ceiling Tunnelways of Duplex A86 Comfortable
to Drive, 'Not Claustrophobic,'" Tollroadsnews.com, December 24, 2008.

10. Norman Foster and Thomas Leslie, *Millau Viaduct* (Prestel Publishing, 2012).

11. William Reinhardt, "All Eyes on French Toll Road Sale," *Public Works Financing*, September 2005.

12. Gomez-Ibanez and Meyer, *Going Private*.

13. Ibid.

14. Domingo Curcio, "Spanish Bravado Builds a Toll Road Empire," *Public
Works Financing*, Special Supplement, January 2002.

15. William Reinhardt, "Sacyr Now Spain's no. 2 Toll Operator," *Public Works
Financing*, June 2003.

16. Perrot and Chatelus, *Financing of Major Infrastructure and Public Service
Projects*, pp. 148–49.

17. "Opening Pandora's Box," *Infrastructure Investor*, February 2010.

18. William Reinhardt, "Portugal to Slash Availability Payments," *Public Works
Financing*, November 2012.

19. "Sydney Harbour Tunnel," Wikipedia, http://en.wikipedia.org/Wiki/Sydney
_Harbour_Tunnel, accessed March 19, 2014.

20. Bob Carr, "Good Roads Sooner: Public-Private Partnerships in New South
Wales," Reason Foundation, January 29, 2010; http://reason.org/news/show/good
-roads-sooner-public-priv, accessed August 12, 2015.

21. Peter Samuel, "Transurban Buys Doubly Broke Sydney Cross-City Tunnel," Tollroadsnews.com, November 11, 2013.

22. Emilia Tagaza, *Journey and Arrival: The Story of the Melbourne CityLink*
(Institution of Engineers, Australia, 2002).

23. John Gardiner and Ken Mathes, "Eastlink, Melbourne, Australia: A New
Paradigm in Public-Private Partnerships," presented at the 2007 Annual Meeting,
International Bridge, Tunnel & Turnpike Association, 2007.

24. William Reinhardt, "Melbourne Highway Deal Launched," *Public Works
Financing*, March 2009.

25. "Australia Project Faces Hurdle," *World Highways*, May 2015.

26. Michael West, "Buyer Found for CLEM 7," *Inspiratia Infrastructure*, October 2, 2013.

27. Peter Samuel, "BrisConnections Ceases Fighting Bankruptcy, Hands Over Toll Tunnelway in Brisbane to Administrators," Tollroadsnews.com, February 19, 2013.

28. Robert Bain, "Ethics and Advocacy in Forecasting Revisited: Consultants in the Dock," *LTT680*, September 4–17, 2015.

29. Robert Bain, *Toll Road Traffic & Revenue Forecasts: An Interpreter's Guide* (Publicaciones Digitales SA, 2009).

30. William Reinhardt, "Acciona Awarded Australian Toll Road," *Public Works Financing*, September 2010.

31. "Queensland Motorways Acquisition FC," *Inspiratia Infrastructure*, July 4, 2014.

32. Peter Samuel, "Japan's Tollster 'Privatization' Proceeds, but Gov. Falls Over Postal Divestiture," Tollroadsnews.com, August 10, 2005.

33. William Reinhardt, "China Road," *Public Works Financing*, November 2007.

34. Peter Samuel, "Central Government Struggling to Control Toll Roads in China," Tollroadsnews.com, February 28, 2008.

35. "Busan-Geoje Fixed Link," Wikipedia, http://en.wikipedia.org/Wiki/Busan_Geoje_Fixed_Link, accessed August 12, 2015.

36. Peter Reina, "Dual Purpose Tunnel Becomes a Very Smart Solution," *Engineering News-Record*, April 25, 2005.

37. William Reinhardt, "Mexico PPP Law," *Public Works Financing*, December 2009.

38. William Reinhardt, "Chile Concession Law Reforms Set," *Public Works Financing*, January 2008.

39. William Reinhardt, "Chile Fast-Tracks P3s," *Public Works Financing*, June 2014.

40. John Walker Hills, "The Road Fund: Road Expenditure and Motor Car Taxation," January 1923 (posted as "Document of the Week" by *Eno Transportation Weekly*, May 19, 2015).

41. John W. Smith, Alexander Jan, and Dan Phillips, "Providing and Funding Strategic Roads: An International Perspective with Lessons for the UK," ARUP and RAC Foundation, November 2011.

42. Sara Miller Llana, "In Precision-Driven Germany, Crumbling Bridges and Aging Roads," *Christian Science Monitor*, March 12, 2015.

43. Elizabeth Schulze, "Germany—Yes, Germany—Has an Infrastructure Problem," CNBC, September 14, 2016.

Chapter 5

1. Peter Samuel, "Private Extension," *Reason*, January 1990, p. 46.
2. "A Long Road to a Deal," *Infrastructure Finance*, Winter 1995, p. 24.

3. William G. Reinhardt, "First U.S. Private Startup Toll Road Is Financed and under Construction," *Public Works Financing*, January 1994, pp. 1–8.

4. HELP, Inc., "PrePass: About Us," www.prepass.com/Pages/AboutUs.aspx, accessed March 9, 2015.

5. Robert W. Poole Jr., "Private Tollways: Resolving Gridlock in Southern California," Reason Foundation, May 1988. http://reason.org/studies/show/private-tollways.

6. Robert W. Poole Jr, "In a Pinch, Turn Partly to Toll Roads and the Private Sector, *Los Angeles Times*, July 7, 1988.

7. Robert W. Poole Jr., handwritten notes on the first meeting of the Privatization Advisory Committee, Sacramento, California, August 2, 1989.

8. Poole, "Private Tollways."

9. William G. Reinhardt, "Infrastructure Entrepreneurs Pioneer Private Toll Roads," *Public Works Financing*, October 1990.

10. William G. Reinhardt, "SR 125 South Bay Expressway Opens," *Public Works Financing*, November 2007.

11. Poole, "In a Pinch."

12. Peter Samuel, "Camino Colombia in Creditor Hands, Fate Uncertain," *Toll Roads News*, January 15, 2004.

13. Peter Samuel, "PR's Other Concession: Teodoro Moscoso Bridge," TollRoadsNews.com, June 23, 2008.

14. William G. Reinhardt, "Arizona DOT Gets 10 Toll Road Conceptual Proposals," *Public Works Financing*, May 1992.

15. William G. Reinhardt, "Washington State Picks Six Developers to Help Solve Congestion in Puget Sound," *Public Works Financing*, September 1994.

16. William G. Reinhardt, "Minnesota DOT Gets Five Private Offers," *Public Works Financing*, November 1995.

17. Grant Holland, "Washington State Revisits Transport PPPs in New Law," *Public Works Financing*, July-August 2005.

18. Adrian Moore, ed., *Privatization 1998: 12th Annual Report on Privatization* (Reason Foundation, 1998), p. 55.

19. Public Private Transportation Act of 1995, www.virginiadot.org/business/resources/ppta-overview.pdf.

20. William G. Reinhardt, "Developer Fee $7.75 Million for Southern Connector Toll Road," *Public Works Financing*, February 1998.

21. Peter Samuel, "Greenville, SC Southern Connector Files for Bankruptcy," Tollroadsnews.com, June 25, 2010.

22. William G. Reinhardt, "White Knight Transurban Rescues Pocahontas Parkway in Virginia," *Public Works Financing*, April 2006.

23. Nicholas Krause, "Preferred Bidder for Virginia's Pocahontas Parkway Toll Road," *Inspiratia Infrastructure*, October 10, 2016.

24. Peter Samuel, "U.S. Tax: The 63–20 Not-for-Profit Contrivance," Tollroadsnews.com, December 8, 1997.

25. Hedlund is quoted in Samuel, "U.S. Tax."

26. Peter Samuel, "Dulles Greenway to Restructure with Bond Offering," *Toll Roads News*, December 1998.

27. Peter Samuel, "TxDOT Buys Broke Camino Colombia Pike from Hancock," TollRoadsNews.com, May 28, 2004.

28. Lynn Scarlett and David Haarmeyer, eds., *Privatization 1992: Sixth Annual Report on Privatization* (Reason Foundation, 1992), p. 24.

29. John O'Leary, ed., *Privatization 1994: Eighth Annual Report on Privatization* (Reason Foundation, 1994), p. 28.

30. John Kass, "Let It Be Said: Daley Brilliant in Skyway Deal," *Chicago Tribune*, October 20, 2004.

31. William G. Reinhardt, "Indiana Trumpets Its $3.85 Billion Toll Road Privatization," *Public Works Financing*, January 2006.

32. Steve Steckler, email to Robert Poole, May 30, 2014.

33. Robert W. Poole Jr., "Texas Sets the Pace in Highway Finance," *Public Works Financing*, February 2004.

34. William G. Reinhardt, "First Texas Toll Corridor Pact Signed with Cintra/Zachry," *Public Works Financing*, April 2005.

35. William G. Reinhardt, "Virginia's I-81 Awarded to Star Solutions," *Public Works Financing*, February 2005.

36. William G. Reinhardt, "Houston Toll Agency Eyes Privatization," *Public Works Financing*, November 2005.

37. Robert W. Poole Jr., "Sale or Lease of Existing Toll Roads," in Leonard Gilroy, ed., *Annual Privatization Report 2006* (Reason Foundation, 2006).

38. William G. Reinhardt, "Northwest Parkway Rescue Readied," *Public Works Financing*, May 2007.

39. William G. Reinhardt, "Pennsylvania Turnpike Privatization Rejected," *Public Works Financing*, September 2008.

40. William G. Reinhardt, "PR-22 Financial Close Sets the Market for Leases," *Public Works Financing*, September 2011.

41. Federal Highway Administration, "Tools & Programs. Debt Financing Tools, Private Activity Bonds (PABs)," January 2017; https://www.fhwa.dot.gov/ipd/finance/tools_programs/federal_debt_financing/private_activity_bonds, accessed April 27, 2017.

42. Report of the Legislative Study Committee on Private Participation in Toll Projects, Texas Legislature, Austin, TX, December 1, 2008.

43. William G. Reinhardt, "Dallas P3s Add Up to $7 Billion," *Public Works Financing*, September 2013.

44. Jeffrey A. Parker, "The Port of Miami Tunnel Breaks New Ground for Greenfield P3 Projects in the U.S.," *Public Works Financing*, November 2009.

45. William G. Reinhardt, "ACS Finances Florida I-595 Availability Pay Project," *Public Works Financing*, February 2009.

46. Robert Thomson, "Toll Lanes Lead Way to Major Expansion of Highway Capacity in Virginia and Maryland," *Washington Post*, December 25, 2014.

47. KRC Survey, online survey of 1,700 drivers in Washington, DC, metro area, May 2017.

48. Peter Samuel, "Virginia Supreme Court Makes Important Ruling for Tolls and P3s in Meeks Case," Tollroadsnews.com, October 31, 2013. The decision is online at www.courts.state.va.us/opinions/opnscvwp/1130954.pdf.

49. Peter Samuel, "Breaking Ground on Louisville, KY-IN Metro Area Toll Bridges," Tollroadsnews.com, August 29, 2012.

50. Ott Tammik, "Five Vying for Colorado's I-70," *Inspiratia Infrastructure*, June 25, 2015, www.inspiratia.com.

51. "Colorado Governor Vetoes P3 Reform Bill, Imposes Public Notification in Executive Order," National Council for Public-Private Partnerships, June 5, 2014.

52. Simon Santiago and Corey Boock, "North Carolina Achieves Financial Close on State's First Highway Public-Private Partnership," *Infra Insight*, Nossaman LLP, May 29, 2015.

53. William G. Reinhardt, "Rapid Bridges Commercial Close," *Public Works Financing*, January 2015.

54. Joseph Berger, "As New Tappan Zee Bridge Goes Up (Along with Tolls), Funding Questions Remain," *New York Times*, March 25, 2014.

55. Peter Samuel, "PANYNJ Moves Ahead with Goethals Replacement and Other Big Staten Island Toll Bridge Projects," Tollroadsnews.com, May 15, 2013.

56. "Arizona Ponders Using P3s to Meet Transportation Needs," National Council for Public-Private Partnerships, August 14, 2015.

57. Ariel Hart, "DOT Pulls Plug on $1 Billion I-75/I-575 Project," *Atlanta Journal-Constitution*, December 15, 2011.

58. Robert W. Poole Jr., *Orange County's 91 Express Lanes: A Transportation and Financial Success, Despite Political Problems*, policy brief No. 39, Reason Foundation, 2005.

59. Stephen Roberts, "California Supreme Court Allows Presidio Parkway to Proceed as P3," *Infra Insight*, Nossaman LLP, November 21, 2011.

60. William G. Reinhardt, "California Steps Back on P3s," *Public Works Financing*, April 2014.

Chapter 6

1. Author's telephone interview with Geoffrey Yarema, June 10, 2014.

2. Karen J. Hedlund, "Design-Build Critical to New Tollroad Financings," *Tollways*, Spring 2006.

3. Patrick Harder and Frank Liu, "FDOT Study Finds Significant Cost and Time Savings with Design-Build Project Delivery," *Infra Insight*, Nossaman LLP, February 2, 2015.

4. Robert W. Poole Jr. and Peter Samuel, *Transportation Mega-Projects and Risk*, policy brief 97, Reason Foundation, February 2011.

5. Ibid.

6. Alan Altshuler and David Luberoff, *Mega-Projects: The Changing Politics of Urban Public Investment*, (Brookings Institution Press, 2003), chapter 4.

7. Karen Trappenberg Frick, *Remaking the San Francisco–Oakland Bay Bridge: A Case of Shadow-Boxing with Nature* (Routledge, 2015).

8. Bent Flyvbjerg, Nils Bruzelius, and Werner Rothengatter, *Megaprojects and Risk* (Cambridge University Press, 2003).

9. Bent Flyvbjerg, Mette K. Holm, and Soren L. Buhl, "Underestimating Costs in Public Works Projects: Error or Lie?" *Journal of the American Planning Association* 68, no. 3 (Summer 2002), p. 279

10. Allen Consulting Group and University of Melbourne, "Performance of PPPs and Traditional Procurement in Australia," Infrastructure Partnerships Australia, 2008, http://infrastructureaustralia.org/research/pdf/InfrastructurePartnershipsAustralia_PPPReport_Final.pdf.

11. Macquarie Capital, *I-70 East Value for Money Report*, Colorado High Performance Transportation Enterprise, December 2013, https://codot.gov/programs/high-performance-transportation-enterprise-hpte/reports/i-70/vfm-report-december-2013-pk.pdf.

12. William G. Reinhardt, "Public Pension Fund Joins Private Team on Texas North Tarrant Toll Concession," *Public Works Financing*, January 2009.

13. Fidel Saenz de Ormijana and Nicolas Rubio, "Innovation Capture through the Alternative Technical Concept Process in PPPs in Texas: A Tool for Financial Viability," proceedings of the 2nd International Conference on Public-Private Partnerships, University of Texas, Austin, May 2015.

14. Chad Shirley and Clifford Winston, "Firm Inventory Behavior and the Return from Highway Infrastructure Investment," *Journal of Urban Economics* 55, no. 2 (March 2004).

15. Virginia DOT, "Gov. McAuliffe Announces Settlement to Recover Taxpayer Dollars from Route 460 Contract," July 2, 2015.

16. Patrick DeCorla-Souza, Douglass Lee, Darren Timothy, and Jennifer Mayer, "Comparing Public-Private Partnerships with Conventional Procurement," *Transportation Research Record No. 2346* (2013), pp. 32–39.

17. "Financial Analysis of Transportation-Related Public-Private Partnerships," CR-2011–147, DOT Office of the Inspector General, July 18, 2011.

18. "Using Public-Private Partnerships to Carry Out Highway Projects," Congressional Budget Office, January 2012, www.cbo.gov/doc.cfm?index=12647.

19. William G. Reinhardt, "Private Capital, Maintenance, Income Tax Payments

Total $13.4 Billion for Dallas Toll Concessions," *Public Works Financing*, September 2013.

20. Author's telephone interview with Geoffrey Yarema, June 10, 2014.

21. William G. Reinhardt, "Caltrans Settles Presidio Parkway Claims," *Public Works Financing*, September 2016, p. 1.

22. William G. Reinhardt, "$5bn Private Equity Invested in 25 Transportation DBFOM Deals," *Public Works Financing*, April 2017.

23. "Indiana DOT May Reconsider Availability Payments for Future P3s," National Council for Public-Private Partnerships, December 4, 2014, http://ncppp.org /indiana-dot-may-reconsider-availability-payments-for-future-p3s.

24. Daniel Schulman and James Ridgeway, "The Highwaymen," *Mother Jones*, January 2007.

25. R. Richard Geddes, *The Road to Renewal: Private Investment in U.S. Transportation Infrastructure* (AEI Press, 2011).

26. John H. Foote, "Analysis of the Public Policy Aspects of the Chicago Skyway Concession," Kennedy School of Government, Harvard University, 2006.

27. Richard Little, "Why the US Needs More Skyway Deals," *Infrastructure Investor*, March 2014.

28. Geddes, *Road to Renewal*, pp. 42–43.

29. The World Bank, *Bureaucrats in Business: The Economics and Politics of Government Ownership* (Oxford University Press, 1995).

30. Robert Caro, *The Power Broker: Robert Moses and the Fall of New York* (Random House, 1974).

31. Geddes, *Road to Renewal*, p. 51.

32. William Keisling, *Helping Hands: Illegal Political Patronage in Pennsylvania and at the Pennsylvania Turnpike* (Yardbird Books, 1995).

33. Robert W. Poole Jr., "A Tale of Two Texas Toll Roads," Reason.org, May 11, 2007, http://reason.org/news/show/a-tale-of-two-texas-toll-roads.

34. Peter Samuel, "NTTA Opens New Ramps on Sam Rayburn Tollway," Toll RoadsNews.com, December 7, 2010.

35. Mitchell Ross and Hugh O'Neill, "A Port Authority that Works," Rudin Center for Transportation Policy and Management, NYU, April 1, 2014.

36. Mark J. Magyar, "Embattled Port Authority Still Fighting Toll Hike Lawsuit," *NJ Spotlight*, January 6, 2014.

37. Shawn Boburg, "Port Authority Road Funds Probe Intensifies," NorthJersey.com, July 4, 2015.

38. Caro, *Power Broker*, pp. 1140–41.

39. Moody's Investors Service, "Triborough Bridge and Tunnel Authority & New Jersey Turnpike Authority," *Issues-in Depth*, September 14, 2016.

40. Robert W. Poole Jr., "Value-Added Tolling: A Better Deal for America's Highway Users," policy brief no. 116, Reason Foundation, March 2014.

41. *American Trucking v. New York State Thruway Auth.*, US District Court, South Dakota, August 10, 2016.

42. Susan Fleming, "Transparency and Oversight of Bi-State Tolling Authorities Could Be Enhanced," GAO-13–687, Government Accountability Office, September 13, 2013, www.gao.gov/products/GAO-13–687.

43. Maria Matesanz and Jim Hempstead, "Milking the Cash Cow," Moody's Investors Service, February 2012.

44. Poole and Samuel, "Transportation Mega-Projects and Risk," p. 5.

45. Robert A. Cerasoli, "A History of the Central Artery/Tunnel Project Finances," Massachusetts Office of the Inspector General, March 2001.

46. Peter Samuel, "Jorge Figueredo's 2008 Crits of NTTA Released," Tollroads news.com, July 18, 2012.

47. Peter Samuel, "Proper Accounting," *Public Works Financing*, November 1999.

48. Bob Covington, "Toll Transactional & Financial Accountability," presentation at IBTTA Summit on All-Electronic Tolling, Managed Lanes, and Interoperability, July 22, 2013.

49. Benjamin Colucci, "Dynamic Toll Lane: A Success Story as Part of the Public Private Partnership in the Commonwealth of Puerto Rico," proceedings of the 2nd International Conference on Public-Private Partnerships, University of Texas, Austin, May 2015.

50. Thomas Peele and Josh Richman, "Toll Scofflaws Get Free Ride with Confidential License Plates," InsideBayArea.com, December 12, 2010.

51. Peter Samuel, *Should States Sell Their Toll Roads?* policy study 334, Reason Foundation, May 2005.

52. Matt Flegenheimer, "Report Traces Port Authority's Flaws to a Crumbling Business Model," April 1, 2014.

53. Robert Wright, " 'Bridgegate' Opens Route for Reform of Public Assets," *Financial Times*, April 30, 2014.

54. Cherian George, et al., "U.S. Toll Road Privatizations: Seeking the Right Balance," Fitch Ratings, March 22, 2006.

55. William G. Reinhardt, "The Role of Performance-Based Infrastructure," *Public Works Financing*, November 2014.

Chapter 7

1. Terri Hall, "Why Public-Private Toll Roads Won't Work," *San Antonio Examiner*, April 18, 2012.

2. Bill Wilson (editorial director), "Taking a Licking," *Roads & Bridges*, July 2013.

3. Ginger Goodin, et al., "Expert Review Panel Final Report, I-405/SR 167 Corridor Tolling Study," Washington State Department of Transportation, December 2010, figure 5-2.

4. Office of Innovative Program Delivery, "TIFIA Report to Congress 2012," Federal Highway Administration, July 17, 2012.

5. William G. Reinhardt, SH 130 Refinancing Leaves TIFIA with $600m Equity Stake," *Public Works Financing*, July-August 2017.

6. Ariel Hart, "DOT Pulls Plug on $1 Billion I-75/I-575 Project, *Atlanta Journal-Constitution*, December 14, 2011.

7. *Report of the Legislative Study Committee on Private Participation in Toll Projects*, Texas Legislature, December 1, 2008, finds (on p 56): "Non-competition clauses are not unique to PPPs, and such clauses are often used in the public sector as well, such as SH 130, Sections 1–4."

8. See www.courts.state.va.us/opinions/opnscvwp/1130954.pdf.

9. Aman Batheja, "Road Tolls Proliferate as State Financing Falls Short," *New York Times*, November 29, 2012.

10. Ibid.

11. Aman Batheja, "As Perry Exits, Texas GOP Shifting Away from Toll Roads," *Texas Tribune*, July 4, 2014.

12. Henry Grabar, "Reinventing the American Highway: The Promise (and Pitfalls) of Learning to Love Tolls," *Salon*, July 20, 2014.

13. Robert W. Poole Jr., "Texas Toll Opponents Mostly Lose in Legislature," *Surface Transportation Innovations*, no. 140 (June 2015).

14. Robert W. Poole Jr., "How Texas Makes It Hard for Itself to Build Infrastructure," *Austin American-Statesman*, August 14, 2017.

15. Simon Santiago and Corey Book, "North Carolina Achieves Financial Close on State's First Highway Public-Private Partnership," *Infra Insight*, Nossaman LLP, May 29, 2015.

16. Rachel Alexander, "Toll Roads and Double Taxation: The Left and Libertarians Converge," Townhall.com, April 3, 2013.

17. Wes Benedict, untitled letter from the Libertarian Party national office, August 15, 2011.

18. Jonathan Last, "HOT and Bothered," *Weekly Standard*, April 14, 2014.

19. "SR 167 HOT Lanes Pilot Project, Second Annual Performance Summary," figure 12, Washington State Department of Transportation, 2010, www.wsdot.wa.gov/Tolling/SR167HotLanes/publications.htm; accessed Nov. 25, 2015.

20. Daniel Schulman and James Ridgeway, "The Highwaymen," *Mother Jones*, January/February 2007.

21. Zhibo Zhang, Qiang Bai, Samuel Labi, and Kumares C. Sinha, "General Framework for Evaluating Long-Term Leasing of Toll Roads: Case Study of Indiana I-90 Highway," *Transportation Research Record*, no. 2345 (Transportation Research Board, 2013).

22. William G. Reinhardt, "Australian Group Plunges Into U.S. Infrastructure," *Public Works Financing*, March 2015.

23. Phineas Baxandall et al., "Road Privatization: Explaining the Trend, Assessing the Facts, and Protecting the Public," Public Interest Research Group, September 6, 2007.

24. Phineas Baxandall, Kari Wohlschlegel, and Tony Dutzik, "Private Roads, Public Costs: The Facts About Toll Road Privatization and How to Protect the Public," US PIRG Education Fund, Spring 2009.

25. Ryan Holeywell, "Public-Private Partnerships Are Popular, but Are They Practical?" *Governing*, November 1, 2013.

26. Thomas P. Napoli, "Controlling Risk without Gimmicks: New York's Infrastructure Crisis and Public-Private Partnerships," Office of the State Comptroller, January 2011.

27. "Using Public-Private Partnerships to Carry Out Highway Projects," Congressional Budget Office, January 2012.

28. Mac Taylor, letter to Sen. Alan Rosenthal, California Legislative Analyst's Office, December 9, 2010.

29. Eric Jaffe, "The Uncertain Future of Public Roads," TheAtlanticCities .com, May 6, 2013.

30. Ellen Dannin, "Crumbling Infrastructure, Crumbling Democracy: Infrastructure Privatization Contracts and Their Effects on State and Local Governance," *Northwestern Journal of Law & Social Policy* 6, no. 1 (Winter 2011).

31. Elliott Sclar, "The Political Economy of Private Infrastructure Finance," prepared for the annual meeting of the Association of Collegiate Schools of Planning, October 1, 2009.

32. California Council of Land Trusts et al., "Principles for Public Private Partnerships," 2008.

33. James J. Regimbal, "An Examination of the Virginia Public-Private Transportation Act of 1995," Southern Environmental Law Center, November 2012.

34. Kate Holder, "TRN Snapshot of Organized Opposition to Tolling," Toll roadsnews.com, February 24, 2014.

35. Darwin Bond-Graham, "The New Privatization," *California Northern*, 2012.

36. Napoli, "Controlling Risk."

37. Taylor, letter to Rosenthal.

38. "The World's Biggest Capital Raisers," *Infrastructure Investor*, November 2016.

39. Robert W. Poole Jr., "Annual Privatization Report 2014: Infrastructure Finance," Reason Foundation, March 2014.

40. Robert W. Poole Jr., "Transportation Infrastructure Finance 2012," Reason Foundation, April 8, 2013.

41. Timothy J. Carson, "The Pennsylvania Turnpike: A Golden Goose in the Brave New P3 World," Pennsylvania Turnpike Commission, March 17, 2007.

42. Dennis J. Enright, "Then There Were Two . . . Indiana Toll Road vs. Chicago Skyway," NW Financial Group, LLC, November 1, 2006.

43. Peter Samuel and Geoffrey F. Segal, "Leasing the Pennsylvania Turnpike: A Response to Critics of Gov. Rendell's Plan," Reason Foundation, June 2007.

44. Dennis J. Enright, "Texas Hold 'Em: Will the State Go 'All-In' on Public Private Partnerships and Lose $2 Billion?" NW Financial Group, LLC, April 17, 2007.

45. Robert W. Poole Jr., "Tolling and Public-Private Partnerships in Texas: Separating Myth from Fact," Reason Foundation, May 2007.

46. See www.ooida.com/Legislative/state-issues.aspx, accessed August 15, 2015.

47. See www.tollfreeinterstates.com, accessed August 15, 2015.

48. Daryl S. Fleming et al., "Dispelling the Myths: Toll and Fuel Collection Costs in the 21st Century," Reason Foundation, November 2012.

49. Maria Matesanz and Jim Hempstead, "Milking the Cash Cow," Moody's Investors Service, February 12, 2012.

50. Robert W. Poole Jr., "Value-Added Tolling: A Better Deal for America's Highway Users," Reason Foundation, March 2014.

51. Robert W. Poole Jr., "AAA Opens Up to MBUFs and Value-Added Tolling," *Surface Transportation Innovations*, no. 153, July 2016.

Chapter 8

1. Gabriel Roth, *Paying for Roads: The Economics of Traffic Congestion* (Penguin Books, 1967).

2. Gabriel Roth, *Roads in a Market Economy* (Avebury Technical, 1996).

3. Stephen Lockwood, "The Private Provision of Mobility Services in the 21st Century: How It Happened," presentation given December 5, 1995, in *Getting from Here to There* (University of Minnesota Center for Transportation Studies, January 1996), http://hdl.handle.net/11299/165674.

4. "U.S. Electric Utility Industry Statistics," American Public Power Association 2015–2016 Annual Directory & Statistical Report, www.publicpower.org/files/PDFs/USElectricUtilityStatistics.pdf, accessed August 26, 2015.

5. David Levinson, *Enterprising Roads: Improving the Governance of America's Highways*, policy study no. 410, Reason Foundation, January 2013.

6. David Hensher, "The Transportation Sector in Australia: Economic Lessons and Challenges," *Transport Policy* 1, no. 1 (1993), pp. 49–67.

7. "Gadkari Wants to Take NHAI Public, Awaiting FinMin Nod," *Times of India*, September 19, 2017.

8. David Newbery and Georgina Santos, "Road Taxes, Road User Charges, and Earmarking," *Fiscal Studies* 20, no. 2 (1999), pp. 103–32.

9. America Thinks, "Envision Transportation Assets as Utilities," HNTB, November 21, 2011.

10. Washington State Department of Transportation, "Toll Division Operational Review," November 2013, p. 34.

11. Federal Highway Administration, "National Congestion Pricing Conference" (two-page conference summary), July 9–10, 2013.

12. Eric C. Peterson, "Transportation as Utility," Eno Center for Transportation, 2014, www.enotrans.org/eno-brief/transportation-as-utility.

13. Stephen Glaister, "Full Speed Ahead for the RAB Route," *Infrastructure Investor*, December/January 2012.

14. Note that this does not include tolls paid by those drivers who use any of the state's urban toll roads or Florida's Turnpike.

15. Committee on the Long-Term Viability of Fuel Taxes for Transportation Finance, *The Fuel Tax and Alternatives for Transportation Funding*, Special Report 285 (Transportation Research Board, 2006).

16. National Surface Transportation Infrastructure Financing Commission, *Paying Our Way: A New Framework for Transportation Finance*, February 2009.

17. Robert W. Poole Jr., *Ten Reasons Why Per-Mile Tolling Is a Better Highway User Fee Than Fuel Taxes*, policy brief 114, Reason Foundation, January 2014.

18. Randall J. Pozdena, *Where the Rubber Meets the Road: Reforming California's Highway Funding System*, policy study no. 191, Reason Foundation, August 1995.

19. Robert W. Poole Jr. and Adrian T. Moore, *Restoring Trust in the Highway Trust Fund*, policy study no. 386, Reason Foundation, August 2010.

20. Kenneth A. Small, Clifford Winston, and Carol A. Evans, *Road Work: A New Highway & Investment Policy* (Brookings Institution, 1989), p. 101.

21. Richard Geddes, "Public Policies within a Fully Priced Transportation Network: Lessons from Utility Regulation," Battelle, September 27, 2013, p. 16.

22. Ralph Erickson and R. Richard Geddes, "Public Policies within a Fully Priced Transportation Network: Lessons from Utility Regulation," Cornell Program in Infrastructure Policy working paper, September 2013.

23. This problem is known as the Averch-Johnson effect, after the two economists who first wrote about it. See H. A. Averch, "Averch-Johnson Effect," *The New Palgrave Dictionary of Economics*, Palgrave Macmillan, 2008

24. Gabriel Kolko, *Railroads and Regulation, 1877–1916* (Princeton University Press, 1965).

25. George Stigler, "The Theory of Economic Regulation," *Bell Journal of Economics and Management Science*, Spring 1971.

26. Derek Eckhart, "State and Local News: Dulles Greenway," *Piper Jaffray Transportation Market Update*, September 8, 2015.

27. Details on revenue-sharing provisions for the LBJ Express Lanes are found at http://ftp.dot.state.tx.us/pub/txdot-info/dal/lbj_635/cda/book1_exhibits/07_0909.pdf, accessed August 26, 2014.

28. Eduardo Engel, Ronald Fischer, and Alexander Galetovic, "A New Approach to Private Roads," *Regulation*, Fall 2002, pp. 18–22.

29. Eduardo Engel, Ronald Fisher, and Alexander Galetovic, *The Economics of Public-Private Partnerships: A Basic Guide* (Cambridge University Press, 2014).

30. Peter Samuel, "Thoughts on Taking Tolling into State DOTs: Editorial," Tollroadsnews.com, May 19, 2013.

31. Robert W. Poole Jr. and Daryl S. Fleming, *Should Florida Toll Agencies Be Consolidated?* policy study no. 401, Reason Foundation, February 2012.

32. Paul Goldsborough, "A History of Aeronautical Radio Inc. from 1929 to 1942," ARINC, July 2, 1951. Unpublished, accessed in ARINC archives, Annapolis, Maryland.

33. Duncan McCallum, "Ownership Rate Regulation, and Governance in Essential Service Monopolies," RBC Capital Markets, November 10, 2003.

34. David Ungemah and Chris Swenson, "Transportation Cooperatives," presented at the TRB Transportation Finance Conference, Irvine, California, July 11, 2014.

35. Gabriel Roth, "Using Road Pricing Revenues," online post at Congestion Pricing Forum, June 20, 1999.

36. R. Richard Geddes and Dimitar N. Nentchev, "Road Pricing and Asset Publicization," American Enterprise Institute, December 2013.

37. Productivity Commission, "Economic Regulation of Airport Services," March 2012, www.pc.gov.au/projects/inquiry/airport-regulation.

38. Australian Government Productivity Commission, *Public Infrastructure Draft Report* 1 (March 2014), p. 13.

39. Leon Corbett, Florida DOT project finance manager, email to author, August 6, 2014.

40. Department of State Treasurer, "Debt Affordability Study," State of North Carolina, February 1, 2014.

41. Jeff Campbell, "Toll vs. Nontoll: Toll Facilities Are Safer," *Tollways*, Winter 2008.

42. National Cooperative Highway Research Program Report 689, "Costs of Alternative Revenue Generating Systems," Transportation Research Board, March 2011.

43. Daryl S. Fleming et al., *Dispelling the Myths: Toll and Fuel Tax Collection Costs in the 21st Century*, policy study no. 409, Reason Foundation, November 2012.

44. Robert W. Poole Jr., *Truck-Friendly Tolls for 21st Century Interstates*, policy study no. 446, Reason Foundation, July 2015.

45. Robert W. Poole Jr., *Value-Added Tolling: A Better Deal for America's Highway Users*, policy brief no. 116, Reason Foundation, March 2014.

46. Maria Matesanz and Jim Hempstead, "Milking the Cash Cow," Moody's Investors Service, February 2012.

47. Jeffrey N. Buxbaum and Iris N. Ortiz, "Public-Sector Decision-Making for Public-Private Partnerships," NCHRP synthesis 391, Transportation Research Board, 2009.

48. Emilia Istrate and Robert Puentes, "Moving Forward on Public-Private Partnerships: U.S. and International Experience with PPP Units," Brookings Institution, December 2011.

49. Patrick DeCorla-Souza, Douglass Lee, Darren Timothy, and Jennifer Mayer, "Comparing Public-Private Partnerships with Conventional Procurement,"

transportation research record no. 2356, Transportation Research Board, 2013, pp. 32–39.

50. Office of Innovative Program Delivery, "Model Public-Private Partnerships Core Toll Concessions Contract Guide," (Federal Highway Administration, 2014, www.fhwa.dot.gov/ipd/p3/resources/p3_core_toll_concession_contract_guide.aspx.

Chapter 9

1. *How Federal Spending for Infrastructure and Other Public Investments Affects the Economy* (Congressional Budget Office, July 1991).

2. "Assessing the Relationship between Transportation Infrastructure and Productivity," *Searching for Solutions* 4, Federal Highway Administration, August 1992.

3. M. Ishaq Nadiri and Theofanis P. Mamuneas, "Contribution of Highway Capital to Industry and National Productivity Growth," Apogee Research, for the Federal Highway Administration, September 1996.

4. John G. Fernald, "Roads to Prosperity? Assessing the Link between Public Capital and Productivity," *American Economic Review* 89, no. 3 (June 1999).

5. Theofanis P. Mamuneas and M. Ishaq Nadiri, "Production, Consumption and Rates of Return to Highway Infrastructure Capital," August 2006, http://cite seerx.ist.psu.edu/viewdoc/download?doi-10.1.1.352.8782&rep1&type=pdf.

6. Jack Schenendorf and Elizabeth Bell, "Modernizing the U.S. Surface Transportation System," Association of Equipment Managers, 2011; Ed Regan and Steven Brown, "Building the Case for Tolling the Interstates," *Tollways* 8, no. 1 (Spring 2011); Jordi Graels, "Rebuilding Interstates: A Basic To-Do List for Project Delivery," *Tollways* 9, no. 1 (Summer 2011).

7. Randall J. Pozdena, *Where the Rubber Meets the Road: Reforming California's Roadway Funding System*, policy study no. 191, Reason Foundation, August 1995.

8. Chris R Swenson and David Ungemah, "Mileage Based User Fees: A Proposed Business Model Incorporating a System of Solutions," paper no. 13-4217 presented to the Transportation Research Board, January 2013.

9. Robert W. Poole Jr., *Interstate 2.0: Modernizing the Interstate Highway System via Toll Finance*, policy study No. 423, Reason Foundation, September 2013.

10. Federal Highway Administration, *Traffic Volume Trends*, February 2017.

11. Don Pickrell, David Price, Rachel West, and Garrett Hagerman, "Developing a Multi-Level Vehicle Miles of Travel Forecasting Model," Volpe National Transportation Systems Center, submitted to the Transportation Research Board, November 15, 2011.

12. "The Clockspeed Dilemma: What Does It Mean for Automotive Innovation?" KPMG, November 2015.

13. Lauren Isaac, "Driving toward Driverless: A Guide for Government Agencies," WSP Parsons Brinckerhoff, February 24, 2016.

14. Peter Samuel, Robert W. Poole Jr., and Joes Holguin-Veras, *Toll Truckways: A New Path toward Safer and More Efficient Freight Transportation*, policy study no. 294, Reason Foundation, June 2002.

15. Ibid., p. 6.

16. Robert W. Poole Jr., *Truck-Friendly Tolls for 21st Century Interstates*, policy study no. 446, July 2015.

17. Robert W. Poole Jr., *Rebuilding and Modernizing Wisconsin's Interstates with Toll Financing*, policy study no. 398, Reason Foundation and Wisconsin Policy Research Institute, September 2011.

18. In each of these gross revenue calculations, the gross traffic and revenue were reduced by taking into account a "diversion rate"—the fraction of cars and trucks that would opt not to use the Interstate if it was tolled. This is standard practice in toll traffic and revenue forecasting, with diversion rates proportional to the toll rate (i.e., the higher the toll rate, the greater the diversion). The study used diversion rates consistent with the relatively low per-mile toll rates used.

19. Daryl S. Fleming et al., *Dispelling the Myths: Toll and Fuel Tax Collection Costs in the 21st Century*, policy study no. 409, Reason Foundation, November 2012.

20. Robert W Poole Jr., "Modernizing the U.S. Interstate Highway System via Toll Finance," paper No. 14-0716, presented to the Transportation Research Board, January 2014.

21. See https://en.wikipedia.org/wiki/Interstate_Highways_in_Alaska, accessed October 6, 2016.

22. HNTB and Wilbur Smith Associates, "I-70 Dedicated Truck Lanes Feasibility Study, Phase 2," 2011.

23. Poole, "Truck-Friendly Tolls."

24. Robert W. Poole Jr., "Indiana Sets the Pace on Toll-Financed Interstate Reconstruction," *Surface Transportation Innovations*, Issue 166, August 2017.

25. Bluefield Research, *U.S. Private Water Market: Opportunities & Strategies*, July 2014.

26. Ed Regan, "The Toll Industry of the Future: Looking Ahead to 2030," presentation at IBTTA Annual Meeting, Austin, Texas, September 2014.

Chapter 10

1. Jeffrey R. Brown, Eric A. Morris, and Brian D. Taylor, "Planning for Cars in Cities: Planners, Engineers, and Freeways in the 20th Century," *Journal of the American Planning Association* 75, no. 2 (Spring 2009).

2. Dean Misczynski, "A Brief History of Regional Governance in California," *Metro Investment Report*, July 2001.

3. Auto Club of Southern California, "Traffic Study, Los Angeles Metropolitan Area," 1937.

4. Regional Planning Commission, *Freeways for the Region* (County of Los Angeles, 1943).

5. Richard Weingroff, "The Genie in the Bottle: The Interstate System and Urban Problems, 1939–1957," *Public Roads*, September/October 2000.

6. Sam Bass Warner Jr., *Streetcar Suburbs*, 2nd Edition (Harvard University Press, 1978).

7. Weingroff, "The Genie in the Bottle," p. 11.

8. Brown, Morris, and Taylor, "Planning for Cars in Cities," p. 170.

9. Brian D. Taylor, "When Finance Leads Planning: Urban Planning, Highway Planning, and Metropolitan Freeways in California," *Journal of Planning Education and Research* 20 (2000), pp. 196–214.

10. Ibid.

11. David M. Rubin, "How I-81 Came to Be and Why New York Owes Syracuse for a 60-Year-Old Mistake," *Syracuse Post-Standard*, January 12, 2014.

12. Charley Hannagan, "New York DOT Drops Tunnel Idea for I-81 through Syracuse," Syracuse.com, October 5, 2016.

13. Mike Savino, "I-84 Redesign Plans in Hartford Include Ground-Level and Underground Aspects," *Record-Journal*, August 10, 2017.

14. Mark Pazniokas, "ConnDOT Offers a Plan, and a Mea Culpa, for I-84 in Hartford," *CT Mirror*, September 8, 2016.

15. Mike Lindblom, "Bertha's Breakthrough Just 'Halftime' for Tunnel Project," *Seattle Times,* April 4, 2017.

16. Charles F. Otey, "DOT Deals Blow to Gowanus Tunnel Hopes," *Brooklyn Daily Eagle*, January 7, 2015.

17. Peter Harnick and Ben Welle, "Benefiting from a Cover-Up: Cities Reap Rewards for Decking Highways with Parks," *Governing*, January 2007.

18. Aileen Cho, "Making Moves on a Monumental Makeover," *Engineering News-Record*, August 24/31, 2015.

19. Tammy Vigil and David Mitchell, "CDOT Looking for Partners to Build $1 Billion I-70 East Project Through Denver," Fox 31 Denver, March 11, 2015.

20. Alistair Walsh, "Hamburg Deck Project in Germany Is Burying the A7 Autobahn to Make Parks and New Land," www.domain.com.au, accessed January 19, 2015.

21. Alana Semuels, "End of the Road for Some Urban Freeways," *Los Angeles Times*, September 18, 2014.

22. Angie Schmitt, "8 Monster Interchanges that Blight American Cities," Streetsblog USA, July 1, 2014.

23. Steve Polzin, "Commuting in America 2015," *Planetizen*, September 29, 2016.

24. Alan Pisarski and Steve Polzin, "Commuting Flow Patterns," Commuting in America 2013, brief 15, American Association of State Highway & Transportation Officials, January 2015; traveltrends.transportation.org/Documents/B15 _Commuting%20Flow%20Patterns_CA15-4_web.pdf.

25. Peter Gordon, Harry W. Richardson, and Myung-Jin Jun, "The Commuting Paradox: Evidence from the Top Twenty," *Journal of the American Planning Association*, no. 57 (1991); Alex Anas, "Why Are Urban Travel Times So Stable?" *Journal of Regional Science* 55, no. 2 (March 2015).

26. Brian D. Taylor, "Public Perceptions, Fiscal Realities, and Freeway Planning," *Journal of the American Planning Association* 61, no. 1 (Winter 1995), table 1.

27. Chen Feng Ng and Kenneth A. Small, "Tradeoffs among Free-Flow Speed, Capacity, Cost, and Environmental Factors in Highway Design," University of California, Irvine, www.economics.uci.edu /docs/2008–09/small-04.pdf, accessed August 28, 2008.

28. Kenneth A. Small and Chen Feng Ng, "When Do Slower Roads Provide Faster Travel?" *Access*, no. 41 (Fall 2012).

29. Kenneth A. Small and Chen Feng Ng, "Optimizing Road Capacity and Type," *Economics of Transportation*, no. 3 (2014).

30. Louis Neudorff et al., "Use of Narrow Lanes and Narrow Shoulders on Freeways: A Primer on Experiences, Current Practice, and Implementation Considerations," FHWA-HOP-16–060, Federal Highway Administration, July 2016.

31. Christian Gerondeau, *Transport in Europe* (Artech House, 1997), fig. 14, p. 340.

32. Chris Swenson et al., "Value Priced Queue Jump Study," CRSPE, Inc. with Cella & Associates, PBS&J, and Metro Transportation Group for Lee County, Florida, January 31, 2003.

33. Chris R. Swenson and Robert W. Poole Jr., *Reducing Congestion in Lee County, Florida*, policy study no. 374, Reason Foundation, February 2009.

34. Robert W. Poole Jr., Thomas A. Rubin, and Chris Swenson, *Increasing Mobility in Southeast Florida*, policy study no. 400, Reason Foundation, March 2012.

35. Robert W. Poole Jr. and Chris R. Swenson, "Managed Arterials: New Application of the Managed Lanes Concept," *Transportation Research Record*, no. 2297 (2012), pp. 66–72.

36. "Interstate 105 (California)," Wikipedia, https://en.wikipedia.org/wiki/Interstate 105 (California), accessed August 15, 2015.

37. Peter Samuel, *Innovative Roadway Design*, policy study no. 348, Reason Foundation, September 2006.

38. Peter Samuel, "Tampa EL Going Great: Underlines Case for All Electronic Toll Collection," Tollroadsnews.com, June 7, 2007.

39. Baruch Feigenbaum, *Increasing Mobility in Southern California: A New Approach*, policy study no. 447, Reason Foundation, November 2015.

40. Hal Eisner, "Could a 405 Expressway Tunnel Dramatically Improve Traffic?" www.myla.com, August 23, 2013.

41. Baruch Feigenbaum, *Increasing Mobility in Southern California*.

42. Stephen Young, "Dallas City Council Set to Finally Kill Trinity Toll Road," *Dallas Observer*, August 3, 2017.

43. Robert W. Poole Jr., *Reducing Congestion in Atlanta: A Bold New Approach to Increasing Mobility*, policy study no. 351, Reason Foundation, November 2006.

44. Samuel R. Staley, *Practical Strategies for Reducing Congestion and Increasing Mobility in Chicago*, policy study no. 404, Reason Foundation, July 2012.

45. Baruch Feigenbaum, *Reducing Congestion in Denver: A New Approach to Increasing Mobility*, policy study no. 442, Reason Foundation, January 2015.

46. Poole, Rubin, and Swenson, *Increasing Mobility in Southeast Florida.*

47. Feigenbaum, *Increasing Mobility in Southern California.*

48. Robert W. Poole Jr., "Rethinking the Politics of Freeway Congestion Pricing," paper #11-0166, presented at the annual meeting of the Transportation Research Board, January 2011.

49. Kenneth A. Small, Clifford Winston, and Jia Yan, "Differentiated Road Pricing, Express Lanes, and Carpools: Exploiting Heterogeneous Preferences in Policy Design," *Brookings-Wharton Papers in Urban Affairs* (2006), pp. 53–96.

50. George Carollo, Mike Garvin, Ray Levitt, Ashby Monk, and Andrew South, "Public-Private Partnerships for Infrastructure Delivery," Collaboratory for Research on Global Projects, Stanford University, 2012, Appendix B1.

51. Eduardo Engel, email to author, October 10, 2016.

52. William G. Reinhardt, "Chile Unveils P3 Infrastructure Plan," *Public Works Financing*, July-August 2015.

53. Salahdid Yacoubi, "Open Road Tolling: The Genesis of a Mutation," *Tollways*, Autumn 2005, pp. 31–43.

54. Bern Grush and Gabriel Roth, "Charging for Road Use When Road Systems Have Multiple Independent Road Owners," paper no. 13-1778, 2013 Transportation Research Board Annual Meeting, January 2013.

Chapter 11

1. Neil Howe and William Strauss, *Generations: The History of America's Future, 1584 to 2069* (William Morrow, 1991).

2. Tony Dutzik and Phineas Baxandall, "A New Direction: Our Changing Relationship with Driving and the Implications for America's Future," Public Interest Research Group, May 2013.

3. Alan Pisarski, "VMT and Its Causes," presentation at the Heritage Foundation, October 21, 2014/

4. Derek Thompson, "The Unluckiest Generation: What Will Become of Millennials?" *Atlantic*, May 2013.

5. David Pace and Don Pickrell, "Driven to Extremes: Has Growth in Automobile Use Ended?" Volpe National Transportation Systems Center, May 23, 2013.

6. Michael Manville, David King, and Michael Smart, "The Driving Turndown," *Journal of the American Planning Association* 83, no. 1 (Winter 2017).

7. Wendell Cox, "Dispersing Millennials," New Geography.com, July 9, 2014.

8. Leigh Gallagher, *The End of the Suburbs: Where the American Dream Is Moving* (Portfolio/Penguin, 2013).

9. Joel Kotkin and Wendell Cox, "Where Are the Boomers Headed? Not Back to the Cities," NewGeography.com, October 17, 2013.

10. Mary Umberger, "Millennials' Version of American Dream," *South Florida Sun-Sentinel*, December 22, 2014.

11. Cox, "Dispersing Millennials."

12. Jing Cao, "Gen. Y Zooming to Dealerships," *Bloomberg News*, April 28, 2015.

13. Craig A. Giffi et al., "The Changing Nature of Mobility," *Deloitte Review*, no. 15 (July 28, 2014).

14. Mark Mills, "We're a Long Way from 'Peak Car,'" *Wall Street Journal*, October 1, 2015.

15. Peter Gareffa, "Millennials Transform into Major Car Shoppers, Study Finds," Edmunds.com, April 6, 2016.

16. Diana T. Kurylko, "The Millennials Are Coming," *Automotive News*, February 27, 2017.

17. Kelcie Mechelle Ralph, "Stalled on the Road to Adulthood? Analyzing the Nature of Recent Travel Changes for Young Adults in America, 1995 to 2009," School of Urban Planning, UCLA, 2015, accessed at www.kelcieralph.org.

18. "The Search for the 'New Normal,'" *Public Works Financing*, June 2015.

19. Noreen McDonald, "Are Millennials Really the Go Nowhere Generation?" *Journal of the American Planning Association* 81, no. 2 (Spring 2015).

20. Evelyn Blumenberg, Brian D. Taylor, et al., "What's Youth Got to Do with It? Exploring the Travel Behavior of Teens and Young Adults," University of California Transportation Center, UCTC-FR-2012-4, September 2012.

21. Evelyn Blumenberg and Brian D. Taylor, "Understanding the Travel Trends of Teens and Young Adults," webinar hosted by the Eno Center for Transportation, March 23, 2017.

22. Joan Lowy and Emily Swanson, "Poll Shows Divide Over Transit Spending; Slight Majority Prefers Rural Living, Suburbs," Associated Press, June 26, 2015.

23. *Traffic Volume Trends*, Federal Highway Administration, February 2017 (accessed March 10, 2017).

24. David Schrank, Bill Eisele, Tim Lomax, and Jim Bak, *2015 Urban Mobility Scorecard*, Texas A&M Transportation Institute and INRIX, August 2015.

25. Samuel I. Schwartz, *Street Smart: The Rise of Cities and the Fall of Cars* (Public Affairs, 2015).

26. Bern Grush, et al., "Ontario Must Prepare for Vehicle Automation," Residential and Civil Construction Alliance of Ontario, October 2016, p. 6.

27. Robert W. Poole Jr., "Important New Thoughts on Autonomous Vehicles," *Surface Transportation Innovations*, no. 133 (November 2014).

28. Will Knight, "Proceed with Caution toward the Self-Driving Car," *MIT Technology Review*, April 16, 2013.

29. Gabrielle Coppola, Tom Metcalf, and Devon Pendleton, "Mobileye Offers Alternative Route to Google's Driverless Future," *Bloomberg Business*, July 14, 2015.

30. Steven E. Shladover, "The Truth about 'Self-Driving' Cars," *Scientific American*, June 2016.

31. Paul Hutton, "A Driverless Future?" *Thinking Highways (North America)* 9, no. 3, 2014.

32. M. L. Cummings and Jason Ryan, "Who Is in Charge? The Promises and Pitfalls of Driverless Cars," *TR News*, May-June 2014.

33. Chunka Mui, "MIT and Stanford Researchers Show Robotaxis Could Replace Private Cars and Public Transit," Forbes.com, April 17, 2014.

34. Eric Jaffe, "Imagine: A World Where Nobody Owns Their Own Car," *City-Lab*, February 13, 2014.

35. Bern Grush and John Niles, "Application Creep: Environmentally Sustainable Deployment for Autonomous Vehicles," Grush Niles Associates, 2015, http://endofdriving.org.

36. Bern Grush and Blair Schlecter, "Ownership Matters," *Thinking Highways*, Volume 12, August 2017.

37. Ricardo Daziano et al., "Are Consumers Willing to Let Cars Drive for Them? Analyzing Responses to Autonomous Vehicles," Resources for the Future, August 2016.

38. Johanna Zmud et al. "Revolutionizing Our Roadways: Consumer Acceptance and Travel Behavior Impacts of Autonomous Vehicles," Texas A&M Transportation Institute, April 2016.

39. "Shared Mobility on the Road of the Future," Morgan Stanley Research, June 15, 2016.

40. Baruch Feigenbaum, "Autonomous Vehicles Conference Deals with Policy and Regulation," *Surface Transportation Innovations*, no. 130 (August 2014).

41. KPMG, "The Clockspeed Dilemma: What Does It Mean for Automotive Innovation?" 2015.

42. Grush and Niles, "Application Creep."

43. Alan E. Pisarski and Richard Mudge, "Transportation in the Digital Age," presented at Aalto University Summer School on Transportation, Helsinki, Finland, August 2015.

44. Jeffrey J. LaMondia, et al., "Long-Distance Travel Mode Shifts Due to Automated Vehicles," paper for the 2016 annual meeting of the Transportation Research Board, January 2016

45. International Transport Forum, "Transition to Shared Mobility," Corporate Partnership Board Report, 2017.

46. Boston Consulting Group, "Self-Driving Vehicles, Car-Sharing, and the Urban Mobility Revolution," April 2017.

47. Lauren Isaac, "Driving towards Driverless: A Guide for Government Agencies," WSP/Parsons Brinckerhoff, February 24, 2016.

48. Steven E. Shladover, "Research and Policy Actions Needed to Support

(Shared) Automation Implementation," presentation at the 96th Annual Meeting of the Transportation Research Board, Washington, DC, January 10, 2017.

49. Bjorn Lomborg, *Cool It: The Skeptical Environmentalist's Guide to Global Warming* (Alfred A. Knopf, 2008); Ronald Bailey, *The End of Doom: Environmental Renewal in the Twenty-First Century* (St. Martin's, 2015).

50. Steven E. Polzin and Alan Pisarski, "Commuting Flow Patterns," *Commuting in America 2013*, brief 15, American Association of State Highway and Transportation Officials, January 2015.

51. "Places Apart: The World Is Becoming Ever More Suburban and the Better for It," *Economist*, December 6, 2014.

52. M. J. Bradley & Associates, "Comparison of Amtrak Trips to Motorcoach Trips," April 2013.

53. Union of Concerned Scientists, *Getting There Greener: The Guide to Your Lower-Cost Vacation*, UCS Publications, December 2008.

54. "Table 4-23, Average Fuel Efficiency of U.S. Light Duty Vehicles," Bureau of Transportation Statistics, 2011.

55. Wendell Cox, "Obama Fuel Economy Rules Trump Smart Growth," New Geography.com, September. 4, 2012.

56. Jeffrey B. Greenblatt and Samveg Saxena, "Autonomous Taxis Could Greatly Reduce Greenhouse-Gas Emissions of Light-Duty Vehicles," *Nature Climate Change*, July 6, 2015.

57. Robert Bruegmann, *Sprawl: A Compact History* (University of Chicago Press, 2005).

58. Randall G. Holcombe and Samuel R. Staley, *Smarter Growth: Market-Based Strategies for Land-Use Planning in the 21st Century* (Greenwood Press, 2001).

59. Randal O'Toole, *Gridlock: Why We're Stuck in Traffic and What to Do About It* (Cato Institute, 2009).

60. Wendell Cox, *War on the Dream: How Anti-Sprawl Policy Threatens the Quality of Life* (iUniverse, 2006).

61. Ted Balaker and Sam Staley, *The Road More Traveled* (Rowman & Littlefield, 2006), especially chapter 6.

62. Wendell Cox, "Middle-Income Housing Affordability: International Situation," Huffington Post, January 25, 2015.

63. Peter Gordon, Harry W. Richardson, and Myung-Jin Jun, "The Commuting Paradox: Evidence from the Top Twenty," *Journal of the American Planning Association* 57 (1991): 415–19.

64. Alex Anas, "Why Are Urban Travel Times So Stable?" *Journal of Regional Science* 55, no. 2 (March 2015).

65. Remy Prud'homme and Chang-Woon Lee, "Size, Sprawl, and the Efficiency of Cities," *Urban Studies* 36, no. 11 (October 1999).

66. Glen Weisbrod et al., "Economic Impacts of Congestion," NCHRP report 463, Transportation Research Board, 2001.

67. David T. Hartgen and M. Gregory Fields, *Gridlock and Growth: The Effect of Traffic Congestion on Regional Economic Performance*, policy study no. 371, Reason Foundation, August 2009.

68. Shlomo Angel and Alejandro Blei, "Commuting and the Productivity of American Cities," Marron Institute on Urban Management, New York University, January 2015.

69. Polzin and Pisarski, "Commuting Flow Patterns."

70. Adie Tomer, *Where the Jobs Are: Employer Access to Labor by Transit* (Brookings Institution, July 2012).

71. Andrew Owen and David Levinson, *Access across America: Transit 2014* (University of Minnesota Center for Transportation Studies, 2014).

72. David Levinson, *Access across America*, University of Minnesota Center for Transportation Studies, April 2013.

73. Elizabeth Kneebone, *Job Sprawl Stalls*, Brookings Institution, April 2013.

74. Elizabeth Kneebone and Natalie Holmes, *The Growing Distance between People and Jobs in Metropolitan America*, Brookings Institution, March 2015.

75. Robert W. Poole Jr., "'Job Sprawl' Still under Fire," *Surface Transportation Innovations*, no. 138 (April 2015).

76. Urban Land Institute, *Moving Cooler: An Analysis of Transportation Strategies for Reducing Greenhouse Gas Emissions*, 2009, accessed at http://www.movingcooler.info.

77. Transportation Research Board, *Driving and the Built Environment: the Effects of Compact Development on Motorized Travel, Energy Use, and CO_2 Emissions* (National Research Council, 2009).

78. Wendell Cox and Adrian T. Moore, *Reducing Greenhouse Gases from Personal Mobility: Opportunities and Possibilities*, policy study No. 388, Reason Foundation, November 2011.

79. Wendell Cox, *Urban Containment: The Social and Economic Consequences of Limiting Housing and Travel Options*, policy study no. 449, Reason Foundation, March 2016.

80. Sarah Siwek, *AASHTO Weekly Climate Change Brief*, January 6, 2011.

81. Thomas A. Rubin, *Does California Really Need Major Land Use and Transportation Changes to Meet Greenhouse Gas Emissions Targets?* policy brief, Reason Foundation, July 3, 2013.

Chapter 12

1. "Federal Debt Held by the Public," Federal Reserve Bank of Saint Louis, https://fred.stlouisfed.org/series/FYGFDPUN, accessed May 4, 2017.

2. "The Federal Government's Long-Term Fiscal Outlook, Spring 2012 Update," GAO-12-521SP, Government Accountability Office, 2012.

3. Leonard Gilroy, "GAO Warns on Federal Fiscal Outlook," Reason Foundation, April 30, 2015.

4. George C. Christy, *The National Debt: A Primer and a Plan*, BookLocker .com, 2011.

5. Jeff Davis, "General Fund Transfers to the Highway Trust Fund," Eno Center for Transportation, March 11, 2016.

6. National Commission on Fiscal Responsibility and Reform, *The Moment of Truth* (White House, December 2010), https://www.fiscalcommissiopn.gov/sites /fiscalcommission.gov/files/documents/TheMomentofTruth12_1_2010.pdf.

7. Richard Ravitch and Paul Volcker, Report of the State Budget Crisis Task Force Report, July 2012, www.statebudgetcrisis.org.

8. Andrew G. Biggs, "The State of Public Pension Funding: Are Government Employee Pension Plans Back on Track?" AEI Economic Perspectives, American Enterprise Institute, September 2015.

9. "Pensions: Fade to Grey," *Economist*, September 24, 2016.

10. Transportation Research Board, *The Fuel Tax and Alternatives for Transportation Funding: Special Report 285* (National Academy of Sciences, 2006).

11. National Surface Transportation Infrastructure Financing Commission, *Paying Our Way: A New Framework for Transportation Finance*, 2009.

12. Chris R. Swenson and David Ungemah, "Mileage Based User Fees: A Proposed Business Model Incorporating a System of Solutions," paper #13-4217, presented at annual meeting of the Transportation Research Board, January 2013.

13. Robert W. Poole Jr., *Ten Reasons Why Per-Mile Tolling Is a Better Highway User Fee Than Fuel Taxes*, policy brief 114, Reason Foundation, January 2014.

14. Matthieu Favas, "The Infrastructure Investor 50," *Infrastructure Investor*, November 2016.

15. David Haarmeyer, "The Real Infrastructure Stimulus: Long-Term Investor Capital," *Regulation*, Winter 2013–14.

16. Favas, "The Infrastructure Investor 50."

17. Wilbur Ross and Peter Navarro, "Trump versus Clinton on Infrastructure," October 27, 2016, peternavarro.com/sitebuildercontent/sitebuilderfiles/infrastructure report.pdf.

18. Robert W. Poole Jr., "Transportation Finance," in Leonard Gilroy, ed., *Annual Privatization Report 2015* (Reason Foundation, May 2015).

19. Robert W. Poole Jr., "'Bankrupt' Toll Road Worth $5.7 Billion," *Surface Transportation Innovations*, no. 138 (April 2015).

Index